麦田里的守望者

［美国］ J. D. 塞林格 著

孙仲旭 译

译林出版社

献 给

我 的 母 亲

01

你要是真的想听我聊,首先想知道的,大概就是我在哪儿出生,我糟糕的童年是怎么过来的,我爸妈在我出生前是干吗的,还有什么大卫·科波菲尔故事式的屁话,可是说实话,那些我都不想说。首先我嫌烦,其次,如果我提到我爸妈什么很私人的事,他们准会气得吐血。他们对这种事总是很敏感,特别是我爸。他们人都**挺好**[1]的——这个先不提——可又都敏感得要命;再说,我他妈又不打算口述整个一部自传还是怎么样。我只跟你说说去年圣诞节前后我经历的几件荒唐事吧,在那之后,我整个人就垮掉了,不得不到这儿放松一下。我是说我也是这么告诉D.B.的,他是我**哥**,在好莱坞,离这个破地方不太远,他几乎每个周末都来看我。我可能下个月回家,他还会开车送我。他刚买了一辆捷豹牌汽车,是那种能开到时速三百公里左右的英国产小汽车,花了他将近四千块。他现在有的是钱,**以前**可不是。他在家那阵子,还不过是个一般的作家呢。如果你从来没听说过他,我可以告诉你他写过一本特棒的短篇小说集——《秘密金鱼》。书里最好的一篇就是《秘密金鱼》,写的是有个小孩儿养金鱼,谁也不给看,因为是他自个儿花钱买的。这篇让我喜欢得要命。他现在去了好莱坞,这个D.B.,当了婊子。要说有什么让我讨厌,那就得数电影了,你根本别跟我提。

我还是从离开潘西中学那天说起吧。潘西中学在宾夕法尼亚州的埃

---

[1] 本书中的黑体加点字均对应着原作中作者着重强调的字眼,特此说明。——编者注

吉斯镇，你很可能听说过，不管怎么样，你很可能看到过它的广告。他们在上千种杂志上做广告，上面总有个棒小伙子在骑马跨越障碍物。好像在潘西除了打马球，别的什么都不干似的，可是我在那儿附近从来一匹马也没见过。骑马小伙的下方总是印着一行字："一八八八年以来，我们一直致力于把男孩培育成出类拔萃、善于思考的年轻人。"纯属蒙人，跟别的学校比起来，他们在潘西做的培育工作他妈的强不到哪儿去。我在那儿根本没见识过一个出类拔萃、善于思考的家伙，可能有两个吧，就那么多，不过很可能在他们来潘西之前，就已经是那样了。

总之，那天是星期六，是跟萨克森豪尔中学橄榄球比赛的日子。在潘西，跟萨克森豪尔的比赛被当成天大的事。这是年末的最后一场比赛，潘西赢不了的话，大家就该自杀什么的。我记得当时是下午三点钟左右，我他妈正高高地站在汤姆逊小山顶上，就在革命战争还是什么时候留下的一门破大炮旁边。从那儿看得到两支球队在四下里死掐。看台那边看不太清楚，不过能听见潘西这边看台上一片大呼小叫，喧声震天，因为今天除了我，几乎全校人都在那儿。但是萨克森豪尔那边看台上人数寥寥、不成气候，因为随客队来的人几乎一向没多少。

橄榄球比赛从来没几个女孩儿到场，只有毕业班的学生才可以带女孩儿去看。这所学校怎么看怎么糟糕透顶。我想待的地方，就是至少在那儿偶尔能看到几个女孩儿，即便她们只是一个劲儿搔手臂或者擤鼻子，甚至只会傻笑还是怎么样。塞尔玛·瑟默这妞儿——她是校长的闺女——倒是经常去球场上露露脸，但是说起来她算不上那种能让你想入非非的女孩儿，不过她还算挺不错。有次在从埃吉斯镇开出的大巴上，我跟她坐一起，我们多少聊了几句。我喜欢她。她鼻子长得不小，手指甲全是啃短的，好像还在流血。她戴着那种垫高了的破胸罩，绷得鼓鼓的，你会有点儿同情她。我喜欢她，因为她没多说她爹如何如何了不起之类的屁话，大概她也知道她爹是个卑鄙虚伪的货色。

我之所以高高地站在汤姆逊小山顶上，而不是在下边看比赛，是因为我刚刚跟击剑队一块儿从纽约回来。我是击剑队的破领队，够牛吧。那天上午我们去纽约跟麦克伯尼中学比赛，只不过没赛成，我把剑还有别的装备什么的全给忘在破地铁上了。也不能全怪我，我老是得起身看地图，好知道在哪儿下车。所以我们两点半就回到了潘西，而不是在晚饭时候。坐火车回来的一路上，整队人都不理我，这件事说起来挺滑稽的。

我没在下边看比赛还有另外一个原因：我要去跟斯潘塞老先生告别，他是我的历史老师，得了流感，我琢磨圣诞节放假前很可能见不到他。他给我留了张纸条，说在我回家前想见见我，他知道我不会再回潘西了。

忘了跟你说，我被开除了。放完圣诞节假，我也不用再回来了，因为我有四门课不及格，而且根本没用功。他们一再警告我得开始用功——特别在期中时，我爸妈来校时跟老瑟默校长见了面——可我还是没有。所以我被开除了。潘西经常开除人，它的教学水平排名很靠前，确实不假。

当时已经是十二月，天气冷得邪门，特别在那个破山顶上。我只穿了一件两面穿的外套，没戴手套什么的。一个星期前，有人进我房间偷了我的驼毛大衣。我的毛里子手套就放在大衣口袋里，也给偷走了。潘西到处有小偷，这儿颇有些家里很有钱的家伙，但照样到处有小偷。越是收费高的学校，里面的小偷就越多——我不是开玩笑。总之，我就一直站在那门破炮旁边看下边的比赛，屁股都快给冻掉了。只是我没有很投入地看比赛，那么闲待着，实际上是想感受一下离别的滋味。我是说，以前我也离开过一些学校还有地方，当时根本没感觉正在离开那儿，我不喜欢那样。不管那种离别是伤感的还是糟糕的，但是在离开一个地方时，我希望我**明白**我正在离开它。如果不明白，我甚至会更加难受。

我还算幸运——突然，我想起一件事，让我知道我他妈是要滚蛋了。我突然想起来有一次，还是在十月份吧，我、罗伯特·蒂奇纳还有保罗·坎贝尔在教学楼前扔橄榄球玩。这两个家伙都不错，特别是蒂奇纳。那是在晚饭前，天色越来越黑，我们还是把球扔来扔去玩。天色越来越黑，球都几乎看不到了，可我们还是不想停下来。到最后我们不得不停下来，教我们生物的老师——赞贝西先生——从教学楼上探出头，叫我们回宿舍准备吃晚饭。能想起那种事，我就能在需要时找到离别的感觉——至少大多数时候都能。一找到这种感觉，我马上转过身，顺着另一边山坡朝斯潘塞老先生家的方向跑下小山。他不住在校园，而是住在安东尼·韦恩街上。

我一直跑到大门口，然后歇了一阵子来喘口气。说实话，我的气很短，首先是因为我烟抽得很凶——可那是以前的事，他们让我戒了烟；另外，我去年长高了十六厘米多。这样一来我差点儿得了肺结核，所以要来这儿做这些该死的检查什么的，不过我还算挺健康。

一缓上气，我就跑过二零四道。地面全他妈结了冰，差点儿让我他妈的摔了一跤。我根本不知道干吗要跑——我想我只是喜欢那样吧。穿过马路后，我感觉自己有点儿像是要消失了。那天下午很不对劲儿，冷得要命，又没出太阳。每次过马路，我都感觉自己像是要消失。

乖乖，我一到斯潘塞先生家就按门铃，我真的冻僵了，耳朵疼，手指也几乎动弹不得。"快点儿，快点儿，"我几乎马上就喊起来，"快开门。"终于，斯潘塞老太太开了门。他们没雇仆人什么的，总是自己来开门。他们不是很有钱。

"霍尔顿！"斯潘塞老太太说，"见到你真好！亲爱的，快进来！冻得不轻吧？"我想她是高兴见到我的，她喜欢我，至少我想她是。

乖乖，我进门的动作可真够快的。"您好，斯潘塞太太！"我说，"斯潘塞先生怎么样？"

"把外套给我，亲爱的。"她说。她没听到我问斯潘塞先生怎么样，她有点儿耳背。

她把我的外套挂进门厅的壁橱。我用手往后拨拉了一下头发，我一般都是理锅盖寸头，所以根本不用怎么梳。"您好吗，斯潘塞太太？"我又问了一遍，只不过声音大了点，好让她听到。

"我很好，霍尔顿，"她关上壁橱，"**你怎么样?**"从她问我的语气，我马上知道斯潘塞老先生告诉过她我被开除了。

"还好。"我说，"斯潘塞先生怎么样？感冒好了吗？"

"好了！霍尔顿，他现在看样子一点儿事也没有——我不知道**怎么**……他在自个儿的房间，亲爱的，快进去吧。"

02

他们分房住,岁数都在七十岁上下,要么还要老一点。他们过得自得其乐,不过当然是以傻里傻气的方式。我知道这样说可能有点儿损,可我不是有意说损话,只是说以前我老琢磨斯潘塞老先生,你要是对他琢磨得太多,就会纳闷他那样活着还有什么破劲儿。我是说,他的背已经全驼,体态很难看。上课时,他在黑板上写字时,每次一弄掉粉笔,前排哪个学生就得起身捡起来递到他手上。在我看来,这真是目不忍睹。可是你如果对他琢磨得刚好够多,但又不太过分,就会觉得他那样活着对他自个儿还不算太赖。比如有个星期天,我和几个同学去他家喝热巧克力时,他让我们看一条纳瓦霍人织的毛毯,破破烂烂的,是他和斯潘塞太太在黄石公园从一个印第安人手里买的。看得出,斯潘塞老先生从买这样东西中享受到了极大的乐趣。我就是这个意思,拿像斯潘塞老先生一样老得不中用的人来说,他们能从买毛毯这种事中享受到极大的乐趣。

他的房门开着,礼貌起见,我还是敲了敲。我看到他就在那儿,坐在一把大皮椅上,全身裹着我刚才提到的毛毯。我敲门时,他抬头看到了我。"是谁?"他嚷着问,"考尔菲尔德吗?进来吧,孩子。"课堂之外,他老是嚷着说话,有时候招人烦。

我一进门,就有点儿后悔不该来。他正在读《大西洋月刊》,房间里到处是药丸、药水,什么东西都有股维克斯滴鼻水味,很让人沮丧。我不太想见到病人,可是还有更让人沮丧的呢:斯潘塞先生穿了件破旧不堪的浴袍,大概他生下来穿的就是这件吧。我不是很想看老头儿穿睡衣加浴袍的样子,老是露出坑坑洼洼的胸膛。还有腿,在沙滩上还有别的地方见到,老头儿的腿上总是白白的,不长汗毛。"您好,先生,"我说,"您的纸条我收到了,非常感谢。"他给我留过一张纸条,要我放假前来他这儿坐一下,告个别,因为我不会再回来了。"您没必要留纸条,反正我肯定会来跟您道别的。"

"坐下吧,孩子。"斯潘塞老先生说,他是说让我坐床上。

我坐了下来。"先生,您的感冒怎么样了?"

"孩子,我要是感觉再好点儿,就又该看医生了。"斯潘塞老先生说。这句话让他得意得不行,疯子似的笑了起来。最后他总算平静下来,问我:"你怎么不去看比赛?我还以为今天是大赛的日子呢。"

"是今天,刚才我还在看。只不过我刚刚跟击剑队一块儿从纽约回来。"我说。乖乖,他的床硬得像石头。

接着他就变得严肃得要命,我知道他会。"这么说你要走了,是吗?"他问。

"是的,先生,我想是吧。"

他开始了点头那老一套,你这辈子也不会见过有谁像他那样爱点头。你永远搞不清楚他这样特别爱点头是在想事儿呢,还是仅仅因为他是个不错的老头儿而已,一个连东南西北都分不清楚的老头。

"瑟默博士怎么跟你说的,孩子?我知道你们谈了一阵子。"

"对,我们谈过了,确实。我在他的办公室待了有两小时吧,我猜的。"

"他是怎么跟你说的?"

"噢……关于人生是场比赛什么的,还有人人都应当遵守比赛规则。他挺和气,我是说他没有大发脾气还是怎么样,只是一再说人生是场比赛什么的,您也知道。"

"人生的确是场比赛,孩子。人生的确是场比赛,你得遵守比赛规则。"

"是的,先生。我知道的确是,我知道。"

比赛,屁话。好一场比赛。如果你参加的那方全是些厉害的角色,就是场比赛,没错——我承认。可如果你参加的是另一方,里面一个厉害角色也没有,还谈何比赛?什么也不是,比什么赛。"瑟默博士给你父母写信了吗?"斯潘塞老先生问我。

"他说星期一会写。"

"你跟他们联系了吗?"

"没有,先生,我还没有跟他们联系,因为大概星期三晚上就能回家见到他们了。"

"你觉得他们知道这个消息后会有什么反应?"

"嗯……他们会很生气,"我说,"真的会,这已经差不多是我上的第四所学校了。"我摇了摇头,我挺爱摇头。"乖乖!"我说。我也挺爱说"乖乖!",一方面是因为我的词汇量很糟糕;另一方面,有时候我表现得比我的实际年龄小。我那时十六岁,现在十七岁了,不过有时候我还像十三岁左右的样子。这实在有点儿讽刺,因为我身高一米八九,有白头发,真的,我右侧的头发一片花白,从小就那样。可我有时候的举止还像十二岁左右,谁都这么说,特别是我爸。这话有点儿谱,但也不是完全对,人们总以为有些事完全对,我他妈无所谓,不过当别人要我有点儿长大的样子,我有时候会觉得烦。有时候我表现得比我的年龄大很多,真的,可别人从来对此视而不见,他们总是视而不见。

斯潘塞老先生又点起头,还抠起了鼻孔。他装作好像只是捏捏鼻子,其实他那根大拇指早伸进去了。我想他是觉得那样做无所谓,因为屋里除了他,只有我。我不介意他那样做,就是觉得看别人抠鼻孔太恶心了一点。

接着他又说:"我有幸跟你父母见过面,那是他们来跟瑟默博士小坐的时候。他们人都极好。"

"对,他们是这样,很不错。"

极好,这词儿我最烦。真虚伪,每次听到这个词我就想吐。

突然,斯潘塞老先生像是有什么特别精彩、一针见血的话要说给我听。他在椅子上坐直了一些,扭了扭身子。不过那是个假警报,他只是把《大西洋月刊》从大腿上拿起来,想把它扔到床上,扔到我旁边,却没扔到。虽然只隔了五厘米,他还是没扔到。我起身把它捡起来放到床上。突然,我他妈想赶快离开这儿,我觉得有一套高明得不得了的教导就要出来了。我对听教导倒不是很反感,可不想就这么一边被教导,一边闻着维克斯滴鼻水的味道,还看着斯潘塞老先生穿着睡衣加浴袍的样子,真的不想。

开始了,随便吧。"孩子,你是怎么回事?"斯潘塞老先生问我。他这样问,也显得很严厉。"你这学期学了几门课?"

"五门,先生。"

"五门。几门不及格?"

"四门。"我在床上挪了挪屁股,我从来没坐过那么硬的床。"我语文过了,"我说,"因为《贝奥武甫》和'兰德尔,我的儿子'什么的,我在伍顿中学全学过,我是说我学语文不需要太用功,除了时不时要写篇作文。"

我说话他根本没听,你说什么时,他几乎从来不听。

"我给你的历史打了不及格,因为你绝对是一无所知。"

"我知道,先生。乖乖,我知道,您也没办法。"

"绝对是一无所知。"他又说了一遍。这种事真让我来气:他第一遍说,你都已经**承认**了,偏偏他还要重复一遍,接着他又说了**第三遍**。"绝对是一无所知,我很怀疑你一学期下来,课本一次都没翻过。有没有?跟我说实话,孩子。"

"嗯,我可以说浏览过两三遍吧。"我告诉他。我不想伤他的感情,他对历史可是迷恋之至。

"你浏览过两三遍,呃?"他说——挖苦味十足,"啊,你的考卷就在衣柜上边,最上边那张,麻烦你拿过来。"

这真是个下作十足的伎俩,可我还是过去取下来拿给他——我也别无选择。我又坐到他那张硬如水泥板的床上。乖乖,你想象不到我心里有多后悔来跟他道别。

他把试卷递给我,那动作就好像它是堆臭大粪什么的。"我们是从十一月四日到十二月二日上关于埃及人的课的,"他说,"你在可选问答题中**选择**写他们,想不想听听你写了什么?"

"不,先生,不太想。"我说。

可他还是照念不误。当老师的想做一件事时,你拦都拦不住,他们就是**照做**不误。

> 埃及人就是居住在北非某地区的古代高加索人种,如我们所知,非洲是东半球最大的大陆。

我只得坐着**听**那些屁话,真是个下作的伎俩。

> 我们现在对埃及人很感兴趣,原因有多方面。现代科学仍无法揭示埃及人把死人包裹起来,让他们的脸部经过无数个世纪不腐烂所采用的药物配方。这个有趣的谜对二十世纪的科学而言,仍然相当难解。

他放下我的试卷不念了,我开始有点儿恨他。"你的**答案**,怎么说呢,到此为止。"他还是用那种很挖苦人的口气说。你根本想不到一个老头儿说话会这么带刺儿。"不过,你倒是在这页试卷上给我写了一小段话。"他说。

"我知道我写了。"我说。我话接得很快,因为想在他开始大声念**那**

段话之前让他打住,不过那是不可能让他打住的,他那时兴奋得像是个马上要炸响的炮仗。

> 亲爱的斯潘塞先生(他大声念道):我所知道的关于埃及人的事就这么多了。尽管您的课讲得很有意思,可我好像还是对他们提不起太大兴趣。您不给我及格也没关系,因为我反正除了语文,别的全都会不及格。
>
> 敬重您的,霍尔顿·考尔菲尔德

他念完后,放下我那张破试卷看着我,就好像刚刚跟我打了一局乒乓球还是怎么样,把我他妈收拾得片甲不留似的。他那样大声念出那段废话,我想我这辈子都无法原谅他。如果反过来是他写的那段话,我就不会念给他听——真的不会。首先,我之所以写下那段破话,只是不想让他因为没给我及格而觉得太难受。

"孩子,我没给你及格,你是不是为这埋怨我?"他说。

"不,先生!我当然不会。"我说。我他妈真希望他别老是叫我"孩子"了。

试卷这档事完了后,他想把它扔到床上,只不过不出意外又没扔到地方,我又得起身捡起,把它放到那本《大西洋月刊》上面。每隔两分钟就得这么做一次,够**烦人**的。

"换了你是我,你会怎么办?"他说,"跟我说实话,孩子。"

唉,看得出,他为没让我及格真的感觉很糟糕,所以我不得不胡扯一通,说我是个真正的笨蛋,等等。换了是我,我会跟他做得一模一样,还有大多数人不理解当老师的苦衷。就是那种话,老生常谈而已。

不过有趣的是,我正胡扯呢,脑子里可以说琢磨起了另外一件事。我家在纽约,我在琢磨中央公园靠南边那个湖,我琢磨等到家时,它会不会全结了冰,结了冰的话,那些鸭子又会去哪儿。我想知道鸭子在冰冻结实之后去了哪儿，会不会让人用卡车送去动物园或者别的什么地方，要么它们只是飞走了事。

我还算幸运，我是说我能一边跟斯潘塞老先生扯些不痛不痒的套话，一边还能想着那些鸭子。有趣哦，跟老师说话时不用太动脑子。突然，他在我瞎扯时打断我的话，他老是这样。

"你对这一切感觉怎么样，孩子？我很想知道，很想。"

"您是说我考试不及格被潘西开除？"我问他。我有点儿想让他遮住那个坑坑洼洼的胸膛，没什么可观之处嘛。

"如果没弄错，我相信你以前在伍顿还有埃克顿岗中学也有点儿不顺。"他这么说话，不只带刺儿，还有点儿让人恶心。

"在埃克顿岗不算很不顺，"我告诉他，"我在那儿倒不是因为不及格被开除，算是退学吧。"

"能不能说说为什么？"

"为什么？咳，先生，说来话长，我是说够复杂的。"我不太想跟他从头说起，反正他也理解不了，根本不是他那路人所能理解的。我之所以离开埃克顿岗中学，最主要的，是因为我在那儿被装模作样的家伙所包围，如此而已。那儿装模作样的家伙他妈的车载斗量。就说校长哈斯先生吧，他是我这辈子所见过的最虚伪的杂种，比这儿的老瑟默还要坏上十倍。例如每逢星期天，他四处去和每一个开车来看孩子的家长握手，一副真他妈魅力无穷的样子，但对几位有点儿上了年纪、模样又滑稽的学生家长则不是这样。你该见识一下他怎样对待我室友的父母。我是说如果哪位学生的妈妈有点儿胖、俗气什么的，或者谁的爸爸穿了那种肩很宽的套装，还脚蹬俗里俗气的黑白两色皮鞋，老哈斯就会只是和他们握握手，送上一副虚伪的笑容，然后就去和另外两位家长聊上可能有半小时。我受不了那一套，能让我发疯。我一开始觉得很没劲儿，后来就气得发疯，我恨那所破埃克顿岗中学。

斯潘塞老先生问了我什么话，我没听到，在想着老哈斯。"什么，先生？"我问。

"你对离开潘西有没有感到特别**难受**？"

"噢，我是有点儿难受，是的，当然……还不算很难受吧，反正还没到那个程度，我想我还没有真正感觉到这件事的打击吧。有些事情要过一阵子，才能感受到它的打击。我现在想的就是星期三回家。我是个笨蛋。"

"孩子，你一点儿也不操心你的将来吗？"

"噢，我操心的，没错。当然，当然，我操心的。"我想了有一分钟，"但可能想得不太多，不太多，我想是这样吧。"

"你**会**的，"斯潘塞老先生说，"你会的，孩子，等到为时已晚，你会的。"

我不乐意听他那么说，听着好像我死掉了还是怎么样，让人很泄气。"我想我会的。"我说。

"我想教给你一些道理，孩子。我在尽力**帮助**你，我在尽力帮助你，尽我所能。"

他确实在帮我，这看得出，只是我们之间有十万八千里的差距，如此而已。"我知道您在帮助我，先生。"我说，"太感谢您了，我不是开玩笑。我感激您，真的。"我从床上站起身。乖乖，就算再坐十分钟就能救我的命，我也做不到。"不过问题是这会儿我得走了，我有不少器材放在健身房，得带回家，必须去取，真的。"他抬头看看我，又点起了头，一脸特别严肃的样子。突然，我他妈对他万分同情。可是想想我们之间十万八千里的差距，他往床上扔什么都往地上掉的样子，他那露着胸膛的寒碜的旧浴袍，还有让人想到感冒的满屋子维克斯滴鼻水气味，我一分钟也没法多待。"这么着吧，先生，别为我担心。"我说，"真的，我不会有事的。我正在经历一个阶段，谁都会经过某些阶段，不是吗？"

"我说不上来，孩子，我说不上来。"

我讨厌听别人这么答话。"当然,当然,谁都会。"我说,"我是说真的,先生。请别为我担心。"我把手轻搭在他肩上。"好不好?"我说。

"喝点热巧克力再走好吗?斯潘塞太太会——"

"我也想,真的,不过问题是这会儿我得走了,得直接去健身房。还是谢谢了,十分感谢,先生。"

我们握了握手,说了通废话,只不过让我感觉真他妈难受。

"我会给您写信的,先生。小心您的感冒,就这样了。"

"再见,孩子。"

我给他关上门然后往客厅走时,他对我喊了句什么,我没听清楚。我很肯定他向我喊的是"祝你好运!"我希望不是,我真他妈希望不是这句。我从来不会对别人喊"祝你好运!"想想就会觉得,那样喊听起来很恐怖。

03

你这辈子也不会见到像我这么厉害的假话精。不得了。甚至比如说我要去店里买本杂志,如果有谁问我去哪儿,我可能告诉他我正赶着去看歌剧呢,真是没治了。所以我跟斯潘塞老先生说要去健身房拿器材什么的,完全是瞎说的,我根本不把我的破器材往健身房放。

在潘西,我住在奥森伯格纪念侧楼的新宿舍,那儿只住三、四年级的学生。我上三年级,跟我同屋的上四年级。这幢楼以一个名叫奥森伯格的家伙的名字命名,他在潘西上过学,从潘西毕业后,靠殡葬生意赚了不少钞票。一开始,他在全国各地设立营业点,你只用每回花上五块钱左右,就能把你的家人埋掉。你该见识一下奥森伯格这家伙。他很可能只是把人塞进袋子扔到河里完事。总之,他给了潘西一堆钞票,所以这幢楼以他的名字命名。年度首场橄榄球赛时,他开他妈一辆大凯迪拉克来学校,我们还非得都在大看台上起身给他来一个"火车头"——那是种欢呼方式。第二天上午,他在礼拜堂讲了话,大概讲了十个钟头。他一开始讲了有五十个听烂了的笑话,以此显示他这个人多么平易近人。真了不起。然后他说他每次遇到挫折什么的,总是马上跪下向上帝祈祷,从来不觉得难为情。他说我们应该时时向上帝祈祷——跟上帝说话什么的——不管身在何处。他还说我们要把耶稣当成自己的好朋友,等等。他说他经常跟耶稣说话,甚至在开车时,他真的让我乐死了。我完全能想象出这个虚伪到家的杂种开着车一边换上一挡,一边请耶稣再送他几具尸体。他讲话里唯一好玩的,是他讲到半截,正在说他如何如何了不起、有头有脸时,突然,就坐在我前排的一个家伙——埃德加·毛尔绍洛——放了个头号响屁。在礼拜堂之类的地方放屁很失礼,但是很好玩,毛尔绍洛这货,差点儿没他妈把房顶给崩掉。大家都憋着没大笑,奥森伯格装作根本没听到。可是校长老瑟默就挨着他坐在讲台上,看得出他听到了。乖乖,他真是恼透了。他当时什么话也没说,但第二天晚上让我们去教学楼上的必修课大教室集合,他上去训了一通话,说前一天在礼拜堂捣乱的那个学生不配在潘西上学。我们想让毛尔绍洛这货在老瑟默啰唆时再放一个,可他当时没心情。总之在潘西,我就住那儿——奥森伯格纪念侧楼的新宿舍。

离开斯潘塞老先生家回到宿舍房间倒是很不错,因为大家都去看比赛了,房间里开着暖气,我正好透口气。这里感觉有点儿温馨。我脱了外套,取下领带,解开衬衫领子,然后戴上那天上午在纽约买的帽子。那是顶红色的猎帽,帽檐很长,是那天上午出地铁后我在一家体育用品商店的橱窗里看到的,也就是刚刚想起来把破剑忘在地铁上之后。这顶帽子只花了我一块钱。我戴的时候,是把帽檐转到后边——很俗气,我承认的确是,可我就喜欢那样戴,挺好看。我拿起一本那阵子在看的书坐到椅子上。每个房间里都有两把椅子,我一把,我的同屋沃德·斯特拉雷德一把。椅子扶手全都破破烂烂的,因为大家老是坐到扶手上,不过椅子坐着还算舒服。

我正在看的那本书是从图书馆误借的,他们给我拿错了书,我回到宿舍才发现。他们给我的是《走出非洲》,作者是伊萨克·迪内森。一开始我以为这本书很差劲,然而并非如此,实际上很不错。我识字很少,但是读的书挺多。我最喜欢的作家是我哥 D. B.,其次是林·拉德纳。我哥送了我一本林·拉德纳的书做生日礼物,就在我去潘西上学之前。里面有几个很有趣、很精彩的剧本,不过书中又有这么一个短篇,说的是一个交通警察爱上了一个很可爱、但是很喜欢开飞车的女孩儿。只是那个警察已经结婚,没法娶她。后来那个女孩儿死掉了,就是因为经常开飞车。这一篇让我喜欢得要命。我最喜欢的书，就是起码时不时能让人感到好玩的书。我也看过很多古典名著，如《还乡》之类，挺喜欢。我还看过不少关于战争的书，还有些侦探小说，但是都不能让我喜欢到骨子里。真正让我喜欢到骨子里的书，是那种你读了后，希望它的作者是你最好的朋友，随便你什么时候想，都可以给他打个电话，但这种情况不多。我倒想给伊萨克·迪内森打个电话。还有林·拉德纳，不过据 D. B. 所言，这位作家已经死了。就拿萨默塞特·毛姆的《人性的枷锁》来说，这本书我去年夏天读过，确实是本很好的书，但是我不会想给毛姆打个电话。我说不上来，只不过他不是我想给他打电话的那种人，如此而已。我倒宁愿给托马斯·哈代打个电话，我喜欢他书里那位尤斯塔西娅·维尔。

总之，我就那样，戴着新帽子坐下来开始读《走出非洲》。我已经看过一遍，不过有几个地方还想再看一遍。可是刚看了三页左右，就听见有人掀浴室帘子进来，根本不用抬头，我就知道是谁。罗伯特·阿克利，住我隔壁的家伙。我们这幢侧楼里，每两个房间之间有个淋浴房，阿克利一天要往我这儿钻上八九十次。整幢宿舍楼里，他可能是除了我，唯一一个没去看比赛的，他几乎哪儿都不去。这家伙很古怪，是四年级学生，在潘西的整整四年里，除了"阿克利"，大家从来没叫过他别的名字。连他的室友赫布·盖尔也没叫过他"鲍勃"或者"阿克"。他哪一天结了婚，他老婆很可能也叫他"阿克利"。他是那种个头很高很高、肩膀浑圆的家伙，大约有一米九二，长了一口难看的牙齿。自从他住在隔壁以来，我从来没见过他刷牙。他的牙齿看上去总好像长了苔藓，恐怖至极。如果你在食堂里看到他满嘴土豆泥再加上青豆之类，简直他妈的让你恶心得要吐。另外，他还长了很多粉刺，不像一般人那样只是前额或者下巴上有，他长得满脸都是。不单这个，他为人也很差劲，可以说是个招人厌的家伙。说实话，我不太喜欢他。

我能感觉到他正站在我椅子后面的淋浴台上，在张望斯特拉雷德在不在。他对斯特拉雷德恨之入骨，只要他在，就从不过来。他他妈的几乎对**每个人**都恨之入骨。

他从淋浴台上下来进到我的房间。"嗨。"他说。他一开口经常那样，好像心烦到极点或者累到极点似的。他不想让别人觉得是他来**串门**还是什么的，而是想让你觉得他是走错路到了这儿，真是岂有此理。

"嗨。"我应了一声，却仍然埋头看书。对阿克利这种人，你从书本上一抬头就完蛋。不过有他在，你**早晚**都会完蛋，但是只要不马上抬头，至少完蛋得没那么快。

他在房间里踱起了步，很慢，一贯如此，从桌子上和壁橱里抄起私人物品看。乖乖，他有时候真让人着急。"击剑击得怎么样？"他问。他只是不想让我读书、不让我自得其乐罢了，他对击剑是他妈毫不关心。"我们赢了，是吧？"他又问。

"**谁也没赢**。"我头也没抬地说。

"什么？"他又问。他老是让你什么话都说两遍。

"**谁也没赢**。"我说着瞟了他一眼，看他在我的壁橱里翻什么。那会儿，他拿起以前我在纽约时经常一块儿玩的女孩萨莉·海斯的照片。自从我把那张破照片放那儿以来，他最少拿起来看过五千回，看完后，还老是不放回原处。看得出他是故意的，没错。

"谁也没赢？"他说，"怎么搞的？"

"我把他妈的剑什么的全忘地铁上了。"我还是没有抬头看他。

"**地铁**上？我的天！你是说给你**搞丢了**？"

"我们坐错了地铁，我得不停起身看车厢上的破地图。"

他走过来，刚好挡住光。"嗨，"我说，"你进来后我这一句看了有二十遍了。"

换了谁都听得出他妈的话音，就阿克利不能。"会让你赔吗？"他问。

"不知道，管他妈的。要不你坐**下来**还是怎么着，阿克利小孩儿？

你他妈正好挡住光。"叫他"阿克利小孩儿",他不乐意。他经常说我是个小屁孩儿,因为我十六,他十八,我叫他"阿克利小孩儿",让他气得要命。

他还是站在那儿,他**绝对**是那种你叫他闪开,他偏偏就是不挪窝的家伙。他最后还是会的,可是你**让他挪**,他反而会磨蹭得更厉害。"你他妈在读什么?"他问。

"破书。"

他用手掀起书本看书名。"好看吗?"他问。

"我正在读的这一句特棒。"情绪对头时,我说话很能带刺儿,可他还是没听出来。他又在房间里踱开了步,把我的还有斯特拉雷德的个人物品拿来拣去。最后,我把书扔在地上,有阿克利这么一个家伙在旁边晃悠,没法看书,不可能。

我他妈窝在椅子上,看阿克利这小子把这儿全当成是自个儿的地方。这趟从纽约回来,我感觉有点儿累了,打起哈欠,接着就稍微逗起乐来。有时候我只是不想让自己烦着,就会很起劲儿地逗乐。我所做的,是把猎帽的帽檐转过来拉下盖住眼睛,那样就他妈什么也看不见了。"我觉得我眼睛快瞎了。"我用很嘶哑的声音说,"亲爱的妈妈,这儿一切变得这么**暗**。"

"我向上帝发誓,你疯了。"阿克利说。

"亲爱的妈妈,伸**手**过来,你怎么不伸**手**过来?"

"岂有此理,别小孩子气了。"

我开始像个瞎子似的拿手在面前摸索,也没站起来还是怎么样。我一直在说:"亲爱的妈妈,你怎么不伸**手**过来?"当然只是逗乐而已,有时候干这种事让我觉得其乐无穷,我也知道能把阿克利这货气得要命。他老是能激发出我虐待狂的一面,我经常这样折磨他。不过最后我还是打住了,把帽檐拨拉到脑后,歇一歇。

"谁的?"阿克利问我,手里拿着我同屋的护膝给我看。阿克利这家伙**什么**都要抄起来看,就连打球用的下体护具之类,也会抄起来看。我说那是斯特拉雷德的,他就把它扔到他的床上。他是从**壁橱**里拿出来的,所以要往**床**上扔。

他走过来坐在斯特拉雷德那把椅子的扶手上,他从来不坐到**椅子上**,老是坐扶手。"你他妈哪儿搞的帽子?"他问。

"纽约。"

"多少钱?"

"一块。"

"上当了你。"他开始用火柴头剔指甲,他老是在剔指甲,这多少有点儿滑稽。他的牙齿看上去总好像长了苔藓,耳朵也总他妈脏得要命,倒是经常剔指甲,我想是他觉得那样做,就会让自己变成一个很**干净**的人。他剔着剔着,又看了一眼我的帽子。"我老家的人猎鹿时就戴那种帽子,岂有此理。"他说,"那是顶猎鹿帽嘛。"

"要是才他妈怪呢。"我取下帽子打量着。我眯上一只眼睛,好像正在瞄准它。"这是顶杀人帽,"我说,"我戴这顶帽子杀人。"

"你家里人知不知道你被开除了?"

"不知道。"

"哎,斯特拉雷德去他妈哪儿了?"

"看比赛,约了女朋友。"我打了个哈欠。我那会儿哈欠连天,首先是因为房间里太他妈热了,让人昏昏欲睡。在潘西,要么把人冻死,要么把人热死。

"了不起的斯特拉雷德。"阿克利说,"嗨,你的剪刀借我用一下好不好?好拿吗?"

"不好拿,已经装起来了,在壁橱最上面。"

"拿来用一下,好不好?"阿克利说,"我想把这个指甲刺剪掉。"

他才不管你装起来了没有,而且已经放在壁橱最上面什么的,所以我还是给他拿了。拿的时候,我差点儿丢了老命。一打开壁橱门,斯特拉雷德装在木盒子里的网球拍正好砸到我的脑门上,哪的一大声,疼得要命。阿克利这货差点儿没他妈笑死,他用那种尖得不得了的假嗓子大笑特笑。从我开始把手提箱拿下来到从里边取出剪刀,他一直在那儿大笑。这种事,比如说别人给石头砸了脑袋还是怎么样,能让阿克利笑断肠子。"你他妈幽默感真强,阿克利小孩儿。"我告诉他,"你知道吗?"我把剪刀递给他,"我给你当经纪人,我他妈让你上电台。"我又坐到椅子上,他剪起他那牛角状的大个儿指甲。"剪到桌子什么的上面好不好?"我说,"剪到桌子上好吗?我可不想晚上光着脚踩到你的破指甲。"可他照样继续把指甲剪到地板上。真没教养,没错。

"斯特拉雷德跟谁约会?"他问。他老是特别关心斯特拉雷德跟谁约会,尽管他对斯特拉雷德恨之入骨。

"不知道,怎么了?"

"没什么,乖乖,我受不了那个狗娘养的,那个狗娘养的真让我受不了。"

"他对**你**可是迷得不得了呢,他跟我说起过你他妈是个大好人。"我说。我在逗乐时经常说"大好人"这个词,以此解闷。

"他老是一副高人一等的**样子**,"阿克利说,"我就是受不了那个狗娘养的,你会觉得他——"

"嗨,指甲剪到**桌子**上好不好?"我说,"我跟你说了有五十——"

"他老是他妈的一副高人一等的样子,"阿克利说,"可我根本不觉得这个狗娘养的脑子好使,他觉着他是,他**觉着**他可能是最——"

"**阿克利!**岂有此理,**请**你把破指甲剪到桌子上好不好?我跟你说了有五十遍了。"

他总算开始把指甲剪到桌子上去,想让他干什么事,只能吼他才行。

我看了他一会儿,然后说:"你之所以讨厌斯特拉雷德,是因为他说过你偶尔也该刷刷牙这种话。他不是存心侮辱你,岂有此理。他**说话**

方式不对,不过倒也不是存心侮辱你还是怎么样,只是说如果你稍微刷刷牙,会看起来帅一点,自个儿感觉也好。"

"我刷的,少来这一套。"

"不,你没有。我见识过了,你不刷牙。"我说,可我不是存心说难听话,我还有点儿同情他呢,我是说如果别人说你从来不刷牙,这算什么事儿。"斯特拉雷德还行,坏不到哪儿去。"我说,"你不了解他,问题就在这儿。"

"我还是要说他是个狗娘养的,他是个自高自大的狗娘养的。"

"他是自高自大,可在有些方面又很大方,他真的是。"我说,"打个比方吧,假如你他妈很喜欢斯特拉雷德打的领带或者别的什么东西——打个比方而已,你知道他会怎么做?他很可能取下来就送给你了,他真的会。要么——你知道他会怎么做?他会把它放到你的床上还是怎么样。他他妈真的会把领带送给你,多数人很可能只是——"

"扯淡,"阿克利说,"我要是有他那么多钞票,我也会。"

"不,你不会。"我摇摇头,"不,你不会,阿克利小孩儿。你要是有他那么多钞票,你会是天下第一号——"

"别叫我'阿克利小孩儿',他妈的,我岁数大得能当你见鬼的爹了。"

"不,你甭想。"乖乖,他有时候真让人来气,他从来不漏过机会告诉你他十八你十六。"头一条,我他妈才不要跟你一家呢。"我说。

"好,那就别叫我——"

突然门开了,斯特拉雷德这家伙急匆匆地闯了进来。他向来急匆匆的,总是一副煞有介事的样子。他走到我面前,很他妈开玩笑地拍了拍我的两边脸颊——有时候我觉得那样很烦人。"听着,"他说,"你今天晚上有事出去吗?"

"说不上来,可能会吧。外面他妈的怎么回事——在下雪?"他的大衣上落了一层雪。

"对。喂,你今天晚上要是不去哪儿,能不能把你那件千鸟格夹克借给我穿?"

"比赛谁赢了?"我问他。

"才赛了一半。我们要出去。"斯特拉雷德说,"不开玩笑,你今天晚上穿不穿那件千鸟格夹克?我那件灰色法兰绒的上面溅上了些东西,到处都是。"

"我不穿,但是也不想它让你的破肩膀给撑大了。"我说。我们几乎一样高,不过他的体重是我的两倍左右,他的肩膀很宽。

"撑不大的。"他急匆匆地走到壁橱前。"阿克利老兄,你好吗?"他对阿克利说。斯特拉雷德这个人至少还算挺友好,尽管他的友好有点儿虚伪,但至少总跟阿克利打招呼。

阿克利在他说"老兄,你好吗"时,只是咕哝了一两声。他不会跟斯特拉雷德**搭话**,**可是**不敢连咕哝也不咕哝。接着他对我说:"我该走了,回头见。"

"好吧。"我说。他能回自己的房间,我才真的是求之不得呢。

斯特拉雷德这家伙开始脱下大衣,还把领带什么的全解开脱下。"我不如快点儿刮一下脸。"他说。他的胡须长得很旺盛,真的是。

"跟你约会的人呢?"我问他。

"在附楼那边等。"他拿着他的盥洗家什,胳膊下边夹着毛巾离开了房间,没穿衬衫什么的。他老是光着身子走来走去,因为他自以为体形还他妈不错,不过他体形确实不错,我得承认。

04

我没什么事,就也去了厕所那边,在他刮胡子时跟他扯扯闲话。厕所里只有我们俩,别人都还在看比赛。那儿真他妈热,窗户上全凝结了一层水汽。里面有十个洗手盆,都紧贴着墙,斯特拉雷德用的是中间那个。我坐在他旁边的洗手盆上,把出冷水的水龙头开了又关——这是我紧张时的习惯动作。斯特拉雷德边刮胡子边吹口哨,吹的是《印度之歌》。他的口哨声音很尖,几乎每次都跑调。他老是挑《印度之歌》或者《第十大道大屠杀》之类难的曲子吹,连口哨行家也难吹好。他真的能把一首曲子糟蹋得不成样子。

你记不记得我刚才说过,在个人习惯上,阿克利可以说是个邋遢货?斯特拉雷德也是,但他是以另外一种方式,更应该说,他是那种没有多少人了解的邋遢货。他看上去总是挺不错,可是你该见识一下比如说他的剃须刀吧,总是锈得一塌糊涂,沾满泡沫、胡楂和别的脏东西,他从来不清洗。把自己收拾完之后,他看上去还挺像模像样的。总之,他是个没有多少人了解的邋遢货,如果你像我这样了解他,就会知道。他把自己外表收拾得很好,是因为他自恋到了疯狂的程度,自以为是西半球最帅的家伙。他确实够帅,我承认,但顶多就是那种照片贴到班级年册上,让你的父母一看就会问"这孩子是谁?"的帅气家伙。我是说,他顶多就是那种在年册照片上看着够帅的家伙。我在潘西认识很多人,我觉得都比斯特拉雷德帅得多,可是他们的照片贴在年册上就不会让人觉得帅。从照片上看,他们要么鼻头太大,要么长了对招风耳。这种事我见得多了。

不管怎么样,我当时就坐在斯特拉雷德旁边的洗手盆上,斯特拉雷德在刮胡子,我把水龙头开了又关。我还戴着我的红色猎帽,帽檐朝后。对这顶帽子,我真的是爱不释手。

"嗨,"斯特拉雷德说,"想不想帮我个大忙?"

"什么?"我问,并不是很热心。他总在请人帮他个大忙。拿这种超级靓仔或者自我感觉是个厉害角色的家伙来说吧,他们经常请你帮个大忙,只因为他们有种疯狂的自恋劲儿,觉得你也对他们神魂颠倒,巴不得帮他们一个忙。说起来,这也有点儿滑稽。

"你今天晚上出去吗?"他问我。

"可能,也可能不,说不准,怎么了?"

"我为星期一的历史课还得读一百页左右的书,"他说,"给我写篇语文课作文好不好?要是星期一交不出这篇破玩意儿,我就死定了,所以得请你帮忙,好不好?"

真是够讽刺的,没错。

"我被这个鬼地方开除了,你还叫我写什么破作文呢。"我说。

"唉,我知道,可问题是交不上作文我就死定了。帮哥们儿一回忙,哥们儿,好不好?"

我没有马上搭理他。对斯特拉雷德这种杂种,就得拖他一下。

"写什么?"我问他。

"什么都行,只要是描述性的。一个房间或者一座房子,或者你住过的地方什么的——你也知道,只要他妈的有描述性就行。"他说着打了个大大的哈欠,碰到这种事儿,真他妈让我烦得要命,我是说如果碰到别人一边要你帮他妈的一个大忙,一边还在那儿打哈欠。"只是别写得太好就行。"他说,"那个狗娘养的哈策尔觉得你语文很厉害,他知道我跟你同住。我是说你别把逗号什么的全用对了。"

这又是一件让我烦得要命的事,我是说既然你写作文不错,却还是会有人来跟你说起逗号的事。斯特拉雷德老是这样,他想让你觉得他作文写得糟糕的唯一原因,是他把逗号全标错了地方,在这方面,他有点儿像阿克利。有次我跟阿克利一起看篮球赛,我们这边球队里有个很厉害的家伙,名叫豪伊·科伊尔,他从中场就能投中,连篮板都不碰。阿克利在他妈整场比赛里,一直说科伊尔**身体条件**极佳,是块打球的料。天哪,我真烦听那种破话。

过了一会儿,我在洗手盆上坐烦了,就后退几步跳起了踢踏舞,只是他妈的找点乐子。我其实并不怎么会跳踢踏舞,但厕所地板是石头的,倒是个练踢踏舞的好地方。我模仿起电影里的家伙,就是哪部**歌舞片**里的。尽管我对电影像对毒药一样避之则吉,模仿起来可是其乐无穷。斯特拉雷德这货一边刮胡子,一边从镜子里看着我。要的就是有人看,我是个人来疯。"我是破州长的儿子。"我说。我极其陶醉,跳来跳去。"他不想让我当踢踏舞演员,想让我念牛津,可是在我他妈的血液里,流的就是踢踏舞。"斯特拉雷德笑起来,他的幽默感还不算太糟糕。"现在是《齐格飞歌舞团》首演之夜,"我有点儿接不上来气,我的气太短了,"主演上不了场。他醉得像一摊烂泥,他们找谁来救场?我,正是我,老破州长的小儿子。"

"帽子哪儿来的?"斯特拉雷德问我。他指的是我的红色猎帽,这还是他头一次注意到。

我反正接不上来气,就不再逗乐了。我取下帽子,大约第九十遍打量它。"今天上午在纽约买的,一块钱,喜欢吗?"

斯特拉雷德点点头。"挺好。"他说。他只是在说好听话,因为他马上就说:"喂,你到底帮不帮我写作文?我得知道。"

"有时间就帮,没时间就不。"我说着又过去坐在他旁边的洗手盆上。"你跟谁约会?"我问他,"菲茨杰拉德?"

"见鬼,不是!跟你说过,我跟那母猪完了。"

"是吗?老兄,让给我吧。不开玩笑,她对我脾气。"

"拿去吧……对你来说她岁数太大了。"

突然——也不为什么,真的,只是我可以说刚好在兴头上,想取取乐而已——我想跳下洗手盆,给斯特拉雷德来个单臂扣颈。那是种摔跤动作——你要是不知道的话——把对方脖子箍住,如果你想,能把他憋死。我就那么干了,像他妈一头豹子似的扑到斯特拉雷德身上。

"住手,霍尔顿,岂有此理!"斯特拉雷德说,他不太想逗乐,因为他正在刮胡子。"你想让我怎么着——把我他妈的头给割掉?"

可是我没有松开,我这个单臂扣颈动作做得很到位。"我这样箍着你,挣开就行。"我告诉他。

"<u>太过分了</u>。"他放下剃须刀,手臂往上猛地一发力,就挣脱了我。他是个力气特大的家伙,我则不堪一击。"喂,别胡闹了。"他说完又开始刮第二遍。他总是刮两遍,好看上去光彩照人,用的就是那个破剃须刀。

"跟你约会的不是菲茨杰拉德,那是谁?"我问他,又坐到他旁边的洗手盆上,"是菲莉斯·史密斯那小妞儿吗?"

"不是,本来跟她,可是计划全乱套了。我现在跟巴德·陶女朋友的室友约会……嗨,差点忘了,她认识你。"

"谁认识我?"

"我约会的那位。"

"是吗?"我说,"她叫什么?"我挺感兴趣。

"我在想呢……呃,叫琼·加拉格尔。"

乖乖,听到他说那个名字,我差点儿伸腿<u>完蛋</u>。

"是简·加拉格尔。"听到他说那个名字,我甚至从洗手盆上站起身,差点儿他妈的伸腿完蛋。"你他妈说得没错,我认识她。她事实上正好跟我做过邻居,前年暑假的事。她养了他妈一条大个儿杜宾犬,我就是那么认识她的。她的狗经常到我们这边——"

"你刚好挡住亮了,霍尔顿,岂有此理。"斯特拉雷德说,"你非得站那儿?"

乖乖,我很激动,真的。

"她在哪儿?"我问他,"我得下去跟她打个招呼什么的。她在哪儿?附楼那儿吗?"

"对。"

"她怎么会提到我?她在B. M.中学上学吗?她说过可能去那儿,也可能去西普利中学。我猜她去了西普利中学。她怎么会提到我?"我很激动,真的。

"我不知道,岂有此理。起来好不好?你坐到我毛巾上了。"斯特拉雷德说。我坐在他的破毛巾上。

"简·加拉格尔,"我说,还是缓不过劲儿,"我的天哪!"

斯特拉雷德正在把护发油往头上抹,我的护发油。

"她会跳舞,"我说,"芭蕾舞什么的。她当时经常每天跳两小时,天气最热那会儿也是。她担心会让她的腿长得难看——很粗还是怎么样。我那会儿一天到晚跟她下国际跳棋。"

"你经常一天到晚跟她下什么?"

"国际跳棋。"

"跳棋,我的天!"

"对。她那些王棋一个也不动,任何一个子变成王棋后,她就不再动了,只是把王棋放在后排,一溜摆开,然后从来不用。她只是喜欢把它们全放在后排时的样子。"

斯特拉雷德没说什么,多数人对这种事都不会感兴趣。

"她妈跟我们在同一家高尔夫俱乐部,"我说,"我那时偶尔去当球童赚点钞票花。有两次我给她妈当球童,她九个洞要打一百七十杆左右。"

斯特拉雷德几乎没听我说,而是在梳理他漂亮的头发。

"我至少该下去跟她打个招呼。"我说。

"你干吗不去？"

"我会的，等会儿就去。"

他又开始重新把头发往两边梳，他梳头得花个把小时。

"她爸妈离婚了，她妈又嫁了一个酒鬼。"我说，"那人长得精瘦，腿上毛烘烘的，我还记得他一天到晚穿短裤。简说他按说是个编剧还是什么破玩意儿，可是我见到的他一天到晚都在喝酒。还有，只要收音机里播，他就一个不漏地听那些破神秘故事，还光着身子绕房子跑圈儿，简在场他也那样。"

"是吗？"斯特拉雷德说。这真让他来劲了，就是那个酒鬼光着身子绕房子跑圈儿，简也在场的事。斯特拉雷德是个急色色的杂种。

"她的童年过得很糟糕，我不是开玩笑。"

这句倒没让他来劲儿，只有特别黄色的东西才能。

"简·加拉格尔，我的天。"她在我脑子里可是挥之不去，真的。"我至少该下去跟她打个招呼。"

"你他妈干吗光说不去？"斯特拉雷德说。

我走到窗前，可是往外什么也看不到，因为厕所里温度高，窗户上凝结了很多水汽。"我这会儿没心情。"我说。我真的没，那种事得有心情才会去干。"我以为她去了西普利上学，本来还以为她绝对去了那儿。"我在厕所里又来回走了一会儿，我也没有别的什么事情可做。"她喜欢看比赛吗？"我问。

"我想是吧，不知道。"

"她有没有跟你说过我们以前经常玩跳棋？要么说了别的？"

"不知道。岂有此理，我也是刚认识她。"斯特拉雷德说。他终于把他漂亮的破头发梳停当，正在收拾他那堆破盥洗家什。

"喂，代我向她问好，好吗？"

"好吧。"斯特拉雷德答应了，可是我知道他大概不会，永远别指望他这种家伙会代人问好。

他回房间了，我在厕所多待了一会儿，想着简这妞儿，然后我也回了房间。

我回到房间后，斯特拉雷德正站在镜子前打领带，他这辈子把他妈一半时间都花在照镜子上了。我坐在椅子上瞄了他一阵子。

"嗨，"我说，"别跟她说我给开除了，好吗？"

"好。"

这也是斯特拉雷德的好处之一，不像阿克利那样，你不用每一件屁大的事儿都跟他解释。之所以如此，我想很可能是因为他并不是很关心，这才是真正的原因。阿克利不一样，他是个特别爱打听的杂种。

他穿上了我那件千鸟格夹克。

"老天，听着，你别把哪儿都撑大了。"我说。那件衣服我大概只穿过两次。

"不会。我的烟他妈的哪儿去了？"

"书桌上，"他总是不知道自己把东西放哪儿了，"你的围巾下面。"他把烟装进外套口袋——**我的**外套口袋。

我猛地把帽檐转到前面，变变样。一下子，我有点儿紧张起来，我这人常紧张。"哎，你准备跟她去哪儿约会？"我问，"还没想好？"

"不知道，有时间就去纽约。她外出只签到九点半，岂有此理。"

我不喜欢他说话的口气，就说："她这样做，很可能只是不知道你这杂种英俊潇洒、魅力无穷。她早知道的话，很可能会签到明天上午九点半。"

"你他妈说对了。"斯特拉雷德说，惹他生气倒不是很容易，他太自负了。"不开玩笑，给我写那篇作文噢。"他说着穿好外套准备走了，"别写得太好，只要他妈的是描述性的就行，好吗？"

我没理他，不想理他，只说了句："你问问她下跳棋时，是不是还把王棋全放在后排。"

"好的。"斯特拉雷德说，可是我知道他不会问。"喂，悠着点儿。"

他就他妈嗵嗵嗵跑出了房间。

他走后，我又坐了半小时之久，我是说，我只是坐在椅子上，无所事事。我一直想着简，想着斯特拉雷德跟她约会的事。这让我不安得快疯掉了。我前面说过，斯特拉雷德是个急色色的杂种。

突然，阿克利又照例从他妈浴室帘子外蹿了进来。我别别扭扭地过了一辈子，这回总算打心底里高兴见到他，他让我把心思拉了回来。

他赖着不走，一直待到差不多晚饭时间，跟我聊在潘西所有他恨之入骨的人，还挤着下巴上的大粉刺，根本不用手帕。说实话，我甚至觉得这杂种根本就**没有**手帕，反正从来没见他用过。

05

在潘西,我们每星期六晚上都吃同样的饭菜,按说这是件了不起的事,就因为有牛排。可是我敢赌一千块,他们之所以这样安排,是因为有一大帮家伙的父母星期天会来学校,老瑟默很可能算计每个当妈的都会问她们的宝贝儿子昨天晚上吃了什么,儿子就会告诉她:"牛排。"骗人骗到了家。你该见识一下那些牛排,又硬又干的小块块,想切开都难。晚饭时跟牛排一起来的,是里面有很多小块块的土豆泥,甜点是谁都不吃的苹果布丁,不过初中部那些小孩儿可能会吃,他们根本不开窍——还有像阿克利那种家伙会吃,他们**什么**都吃。

不过从食堂出来还算不错。外面已经下了有七八厘米厚的雪,而且还在没头没脑地下,看上去真他妈漂亮。我们就四下里玩起来了,扔雪球,逗乐子,很小孩子气,不过大家都挺开心的。

我没有约会什么的,就跟一个叫马尔·布罗萨德的朋友——他是摔跤队的——商量好坐巴士去埃吉斯镇吃汉堡包,也许再看场破电影。我们都不想整晚傻坐着。我问马尔介不介意叫上阿克利一块儿去。我这样问他,是因为阿克利星期六晚上除了待在房间里挤粉刺,向来**无事可做**。马尔说他不**介意**,但对这主意也不是很感冒——他不太喜欢阿克利。这么着,我们就回到房间准备出发。穿胶套鞋什么的时候,我吆喝着问阿克利想不想去看电影。他隔着浴室帘子听得一清二楚,可是没有马上搭腔,他这种家伙,老是不愿意马上搭腔。最后他还是从破帘子那边过来了,站在淋浴台上问还有谁去——他总是要问问都有谁去。我敢发誓，要是这家伙去哪儿坐船失事，在你救他上他妈的小艇之前，他还要问问是谁划桨的呢。我说还有马尔·布罗萨德，他说："**那个杂种……好吧，等会儿。**"你会觉得他赏了你一个大面子。

他这一去准备了有五个小时才好。等他时，我走到窗户前并把它打开，赤手捏了个雪球。雪很好捏，不过我没有往哪儿扔。**一开始**想往路对面一辆汽车上扔，但看到那辆汽车白乎乎的挺好看，就没扔。后来又想往消防栓上扔，也白乎乎的，挺好看，就也没扔。到最后我哪儿也没扔，只是关上窗户，手拿雪球在房间里踱来踱去，把它捏得越来越瓷实。过了一阵子，我和布罗萨德、阿克利一块儿上巴士时，手里还捏着雪球。巴士司机把车门打开，要我扔掉它。我告诉他我不会砸谁，可是他不相信。人们从来不相信你的话。

布罗萨德和阿克利都看过正在放的电影，我们只是买了几个汉堡包吃，还玩了一会儿弹球机，然后就坐巴士回潘西。没看成电影我根本无所谓。电影应该是部喜剧片，加里·格兰特主演，全是那种垃圾。再说，我以前也跟布罗萨德和阿克利一块儿看过电影，他们俩看到根本不可笑的地方，就会笑得跟野狗似的，我根本不喜欢跟他们坐在一起看电影。

回到宿舍后才九点差一刻。布罗萨德这家伙是个桥牌瘾君子，开始到处找人凑局。阿克利这小子又黏到我的房间里，算是换个地方待。只是他没有坐在斯特拉雷德那把椅子的扶手上，而是趴在我床上，脸就搁在我的枕头上。他开始一边声音很单调地说话，一边挤粉刺。我跟他暗示了上千遍想让他走，他就是赖着不走，只是声音很单调地聊着去年夏天一个据说跟他干了那事的小妞儿。他跟我说了上百遍，每遍说的都不一样。一会儿说是在他表哥的别克汽车里干的，一会儿又说是在哪儿的海滩木板路下面，自然全是一派胡言。要让我说有谁是处男，那就得数他了，我怀疑他碰都没碰过女人。最后我不得不跟他明说我得给斯特拉雷德写一篇作文，他得滚蛋，好让我能集中思想。最后他还是走了，但照例拖了半天才走。他走后，我穿上睡衣和浴袍，戴上猎帽，开始写作文。

但问题是，我想不起来有什么房间或房屋，让我可以像斯特拉雷德要求的那样来描述，反正我对描述房间或者房屋也不是很感兴趣。后来我写的是我弟弟艾里的棒球手套，很值得一写，真的。我弟弟艾里有个左撇子用的外场接球手套——他是个左撇子。但这个棒球手套值得描述的原因，是他在上面写满了诗歌，手指、手掌那儿全是，用的是绿色墨水。他在上面写字，是因为他想当他站在外场，但没人击球时可以读一下。他死了，得的是白血病，死于一九四六年七月十八日，当时我们在缅因州住。你也会喜欢上他的。他比我小两岁，但比我聪明五十倍，聪明绝顶。他的老师老是写信给我妈，说班上有艾里这样的学生真令人欣慰。这可不是瞎吹捧，他们说的是真心话。他不单是我们家最聪明的，而且从许多方面来说，也最讨人喜欢。他从来不跟别人发火，按说长着红头发的人极易动怒，但艾里从来不，而且他的头发颜色很红。我跟你说他的头发红到什么程度吧：我从十岁起就开始学打高尔夫球，记得有一次，我十二岁那年的夏天，正准备开球，我觉得我要是突然转身，就会看到艾里。我那么做了，一点儿没错，他就在围栏那边，坐在自行车上——就是高尔夫球场的围栏，他坐在那儿，在我后面有一百五十码远看我开球。他的头发就是红成了那样。天哪，他可真是个好孩子。他经常在饭桌上想起什么事，笑得几乎从椅子上出溜下来。我十三岁时，家里人要把我送去做心理分析什么的，因为我把车库的车窗全砸碎了。我不怪他们，真的。他死的那天晚上，我睡在车库里，用拳头把他妈的窗户全砸碎了，只是为了他妈的发泄而已。我甚至还想把我们那年夏天用的旅行车的车窗全砸了，只是当时我的手已经全破了，没法砸。我得承认这件事干得很蠢，可当时我几乎不知道自己在那样做。可惜你是不认识艾里啊。到现在每逢下雨还是怎么样，我的手还时不时感到疼，也没办法攥紧拳头——攥不瓷实——但除此之外我不太担心，我是说，**反正**

我也不会去当个破外科医生还是小提琴手什么的。

这么着，我给斯特拉雷德写的作文就是关于这个，艾里的棒球手套。刚好它也在我手边，就在我的手提箱里，我就取出来抄了几首诗。我只是把艾里的名字换了，这样别人就不会知道写的是我弟弟的，而不是斯特拉雷德的。我也不是特别想写它，只是想不到别的什么可以描述，而且我好像还有点儿喜欢写它。这花了我一个小时左右，因为我不得不使用斯特拉雷德的破打字机，它老是卡住。我没用我的打字机，因为我把它借给了楼下的一个家伙。

写完时，我估计有十点半了，可我还是不困，就往窗外看了一会儿。外面雪已经停了，不时还能听到哪儿的汽车发动不起来的声音，也能听到阿克利这货在打呼噜，从浴室的破帘子那边传过来，清晰可闻。他的鼻窦有毛病，睡觉时呼吸不是很顺畅。这家伙毛病几乎占全了：鼻窦炎，粉刺，脏牙，口臭，脏指甲。这种狗娘养的家伙，你肯定多少会有点同情他。

06

有些事情不容易回想起来,这会儿,我脑子里在想斯特拉雷德那天晚上跟简约会后几点才回来。我是说我记不清走廊上传来他他妈的脚步声时,我正在干吗。大概正在往窗外看,但我发誓我实在记不清了。我他妈担心得很,原因正在于此。我要是真的为什么事担起心来,不仅会坐立不宁,甚至想上厕所,只是我不会去,因为太担心而去不了,也不想因上厕所而中断担心。你了解斯特拉雷德的话,你也会担心。我有两回跟这杂种一块儿约会过女孩,我可不是瞎说,他是个肆无忌惮的家伙,真的是。

我们宿舍的走廊上铺的全是地板革,能听到他他妈的脚步声自远而近。我甚至不记得他进房间时,我是在哪儿坐着——在窗户边呢,还是坐在我的或者他的椅子上,实在想不起来。

他进了房间,一边抱怨着外头有多冷,接着问:"人都他妈的到底去哪儿了?这儿像他妈的太平间。"我懒得搭理他,要是他他妈笨得想不到这是星期六晚上,人们要不是出去就是睡了,要么回家过周末,我才懒得告诉他呢。他开始脱衣服,他妈的一个字儿也不提简,一个字儿也不提。我也不提,只是看着他。他只是谢谢我借给他千鸟格夹克,他用衣架把它撑好放进壁橱。

接着,他在解领带时,问我有没有帮他写那篇破作文。我说就放在他的破床上。他走过去,边解衬衫扣边看作文。他站在那儿看作文,手还在他的光胸脯和肚子上摸来摸去,脸上的表情极蠢。他经常抚摸自己的肚子或胸脯,自恋得要命。

突然他说:"**岂有此理**,霍尔顿,这写的是一只破**棒球**手套。"

"那又怎么了?"我说,口气冷淡得要命。

"什么叫**怎么了**?我跟你说过,必须是写他妈一个**房间**或者房子什么的。"

"你说过必须是描述性的,写棒球手套有他妈什么不一样?"

"他妈的,"他真的是恼透了,也气极了,"你老是什么都反着来,"他看着我,"怪不得你他妈的被开除了。"他说,"你他妈干**任何一件事**,都不按照别人交代的干,我就这个意思,他妈的任何一件事。"

"那好,你还给我吧。"我说着走过去,从他手里扯过来撕碎了。

"你他妈**干吗撕了**?"他问我。

我根本没理他,只是把碎纸扔进了垃圾篓,然后躺在床上。很久,我们都一句话也不说。他脱得只剩下短裤,我躺在床上点了根烟。学校禁止在宿舍抽烟,除非在半夜三更大家全睡着了或者不在时,没人能闻到烟味就好。另外,我抽烟只是为了惹火斯特拉雷德,干任何一件违纪事情都能把他气得够呛。他从来不在宿舍抽烟,只有我抽。

他还是一个字儿也没提简,最后我说:"要是她外出只签到九点半,你回来可他妈够晚的。你有没有让她签到晚了?"

我问他时,他正坐在床边剪他的破脚指甲。"晚了几分钟,"他说,"谁他妈周末出去会签到九点半?"**天哪**,我真恨他。

"你们去纽约了吗?"我问。

"你疯了?她才签到九点半,他妈的怎么去?"

"够呛。"

他抬头看着我。"喂,"他说,"你想在房间里抽烟,去厕所抽怎么样?你可能是他妈要滚蛋了,我还得在这儿一直待到毕业呢。"

我拿他的话当耳旁风,真的。我继续大抽特抽,只是稍稍换成侧躺,看他剪他的破脚指甲。什么学校啊,老是能看到别人剪破脚指甲或者挤粉刺什么的。

"你有没有代我向她问好？"我问他。

"问了。"

问个屁，就凭这杂种。

"她怎么说？"我问，"你有没有问她是不是还把王棋全放在后排？"

"没有，我没问她。岂有此理，你他妈以为我们一晚上干吗了，下跳棋？"

我根本没理他。天哪，我真恨他。

"你没有跟她去纽约，那又是去哪儿了？"过了一会儿我问他。我几乎控制不住让自己的声音别颤得厉害。乖乖，我真是越来越紧张。我就是有种感觉，什么不对劲儿的事情已经发生了。

他剪完他的破脚指甲，从床上起来，只穿着破短裤，就他妈的捣起乱来。他走到我的床前俯身向着我，玩笑味十足地拿拳头捣我的肩膀。"别闹了。"我说，"你没有跟她去纽约，那是去哪儿了？"

"哪儿也没去，我们就坐在破汽车里。"他开玩笑地又轻轻捣了我肩膀一拳。

"别闹了！"我说，"谁的车？"

"埃德·班基的车。"

埃德·班基是潘西的篮球队教练，斯特拉雷德这小子是他跟前的红人，因为他是队里的灵魂人物，只要他想用，埃德·班基总会把车借给他。学校规定不准学生向教职工借车，可是那些搞体育的杂种全都抱成团。我上过的每所学校里，搞体育的杂种全都抱成团。

斯特拉雷德老是在我肩膀上比画。他手里本来拿着牙刷，那会儿噙在嘴里。"你干吗了？"我问他，"在埃德·班基的破车里就跟她干上了？"我的声音颤得很厉害。

"说什么呢？是不是想让我拿肥皂洗你的嘴巴？"

"你有没有？"

"哥们儿，这可是职业秘密哟。"

接下来的事我记得不太清楚，只知道我从床上起身，像是要去厕所还是哪儿，然后我用尽全力打了他一拳，正对着他的牙刷打，好戳穿他的破喉咙，只是我打偏了，没打中，只打到他的头部一侧，大概让他有点儿疼，可是也没达到我希望的那种程度。本来很可能让他疼得要命，但我是用右手打的，那只手攥不紧拳头，都是因为受过的伤，我跟你说过。

不管怎么样，之后我记得的，就是他他妈倒在地板上，他跪在我的胸口上，满脸通红。他用他的破膝盖顶住我胸口，而他有一吨重。他也抓住了我的手腕，所以我没办法再打他。我那一拳打死他就好了。

"你他妈怎么回事？"他一直在问，那张蠢脸越来越红。

"把你的破膝盖从我胸口上挪开，"我对他说，我几乎在吼，真的，"快点，别压着我，你这个臭杂种。"

可他还是不起来，一直抓着我的手腕，而我一直骂他是狗娘养的，等等，这样过了有十个钟头。我几乎想不起来我都对他说了什么。我说他自以为想跟谁干就能跟谁干，根本不关心那个女孩儿是不是把王棋全放在后排，他之所以不关心，是因为他是他妈的大蠢蛋。叫他蠢蛋他很不乐意，凡是蠢蛋都不乐意别人叫他们蠢蛋。

"给我闭嘴，霍尔顿，"他满脸通红地说，"你马上给我闭嘴。"

"你根本不知道她叫简还是琼，你他妈是个蠢蛋！"

"马上给我闭嘴，霍尔顿，真他妈的——我警告你，"他说——我真把他气坏了，"再不闭嘴，我就揍你了。"

"把你这蠢蛋的破膝盖给我挪开。"

"我放开你，你闭不闭嘴？"

我根本没理他。

他又说了一遍："霍尔顿，我让你起来，你闭不闭嘴？"

"好吧。"

他放开我，我也站了起来。我的胸口被他的破膝盖顶得真他妈疼。"你是个又下流又傻、狗娘养的蠢蛋。"我告诉他。

他可**真的**是火冒三丈，把他那大破手指伸到我脸前晃着，嘴里还说："霍尔顿，他妈的，我现在警告你，最后一次，再不闭上你的鸟嘴，我要——"

"我干吗要？"我说——几乎在大叫，"你们这些蠢蛋全这德行，从来不想讨论什么事，从这点就能看出来谁是蠢蛋，蠢蛋从来不聊些聪明——"

他就真的给我来了一下，我所记得的，就是我他妈又倒在地板上，不记得他有没有把我揍晕过去，不过我想不会，把人揍晕过去还真不容易，除非在那些破电影里，我倒是鼻血流得一塌糊涂。抬头时，看到斯特拉雷德这小子几乎就站在我跟前，胳膊下面夹着破盥洗家什。"我叫你闭嘴，你他妈干吗不闭嘴？"他说，听上去他很紧张。他大概害怕我摔到地板上时，把头还是哪儿摔坏了，很可惜，没有。"是你自找的，真该死。"他说。乖乖，看样子他可真担心。

我根本不想费力站起来，只是在那儿躺了一阵子，然后又不停地叫他蠢蛋加狗娘养的。我气极了，几乎在咆哮。

"听着，去洗洗脸，"斯特拉雷德说，"听到没？"

我叫他去洗洗他自己的破脸——这话很孩子气，但我当时气急败坏。我叫他在去厕所的路上顺便把施密特太太也干了。施密特太太是看门人的老婆，六十五岁左右。

我一直坐在地板上，直到斯特拉雷德关上门，顺走廊去了厕所后，我才站起身来。我的破猎帽到处找不到，最后还是找到了，就在床下面。我戴上帽子，帽檐朝后，像我喜欢的那样。然后去照镜子看自己的尊容。你这辈子也不会看到那么多血。我满嘴、满下巴全是血，连睡衣和浴袍上也有。看到成了那样，我一半是害怕，一半又很入迷，血呀什么的，让我看起来有点儿横。我这辈子就打过两次架，全打输了。我并非特横，说实话，我更喜欢息事宁人。

我觉得这番闹腾阿克利这小子很可能全听到了，而且当时还没睡，就掀起浴室帘子进了他那边，只是去看看他他妈的在干吗。我几乎从来没进过他的房间，那儿老是有股怪味，全是因为他那要命的个人习惯。

07

这儿只有一点点光亮,全是从我们房间透过浴室帘子照过来的。我能看到阿克利正躺在床上,我他妈太清楚了,他肯定是万分清醒。"阿克利?"我叫他,"你醒着吧?"

"对。"

里面很黑,我踩到地板上不知道是谁的鞋上,差点儿他妈的摔了个跟头。阿克利在床上坐起来,撑着胳膊。他脸上抹了很多白乎乎的东西,治粉刺的,黑暗里有几分可怕。"你他妈在干吗?"我问他。

"什么他妈的我在干吗?我正想**睡觉**呢,你们这两个家伙搞出那么大动静。他妈的到底为什么打架?"

"灯呢?"我找不到开关,手在墙上摸来摸去。

"干吗开灯?……就在你手边。"

我终于找到开关把灯打开,阿克利这家伙抬手遮光,免得刺眼。

"**天哪!**"他叫了一声,"你他妈到底怎么了?"他是说我流了那么多血。

"跟他妈斯特拉雷德比画了两下。"我说着坐到了地板上。他们的房间里从来没有椅子,也不知道把他妈的椅子都弄哪儿去了。"喂,"我说,"我们玩会儿扑克怎么样?"他可是个扑克迷。

"你还在**流血**呢,岂有此理。你最好上点儿东西。"

"会止住的。喂,你到底想不想玩会儿扑克?"

"**扑克**,岂有此理,你脑子里有没有一点儿谱,这会儿几点了?"

"不晚，才十一点左右，十一点半吧。"

"**才**！"阿克利说，"喂，我明天上午还要去做**弥撒**，岂有此理。已经他妈的半夜了，你们又吵又打——到底他妈的为什么？"

"说来话长，阿克利，我也不想烦你，是为你好。"我告诉他。我从来不跟他说我自己的事，第一个原因就是他比斯特拉雷德还蠢，跟阿克利比起来，斯特拉雷德可以说是他妈的天才了。"嗨，"我说，"我今天晚上睡埃利的床行不行？他明天晚上才回来，对不对？"我他妈知道得一清二楚，埃利几乎他妈的每个周末都回家。

"**我**不知道他他妈到底什么时候回来。"阿克利说。

乖乖，那可真让我来气。"你他妈什么意思，不知道他什么时候回来？他从来不到星期日**晚上**不回来，不是吗？"

"对，可是岂有此理，我也不能就这么跟别人说，想睡就可以睡到他的破**床上**。"

他这样把我气死了。我坐在地板上伸手拍拍他的破肩膀。"你是个大好人，阿克利小孩儿，"我说，"你知道吗？"

"不，我是说实话——我不能跟别人说他可以睡到——"

"你是个真正的大好人，是个绅士，还是个文化人呢，小孩儿。"我说。他真的是。"你有没有烟？你要说没有，我可要立马断气了。"

"我没有，这是实话。喂，到底他妈的为什么打架？"

我没理他，只是起身走过去往窗外看。突然，我感到很孤独，几乎希望自己死掉算了。

"到底他妈的为什么打架？"阿克利问。他已经问了有五十遍，纠缠这个真让人腻烦。

"跟你有关。"我说。

"岂有此理，跟**我**有关？"

"对，我是为了保护你的破名誉。斯特拉雷德说你为人很差，说这话我可跟他没完。"

这句话让他精神了。"他真的说过？不是开玩笑吧？他真的说过？"

我告诉他我只是开玩笑，然后走过去躺倒在埃利的床上。乖乖，我感觉真是糟透了，感到他妈的孤独至极。

"这个房间里有臭味，"我说，"我从这儿就能闻到你的臭袜子，你从来不洗吗？"

"不乐意的话，你知道自己可以怎么办。"阿克利说，他可真会说话啊，"把他妈灯关掉好不好？"

可我没有马上把灯关掉，只是躺在埃利的床上，脑子里想着简，还有别的事。想起她和斯特拉雷德在肥屁股埃德·班基的车里待着，能把我逼得彻底疯掉。每次一想起这件事，我就想从窗口跳下去。首先，你不了解斯特拉雷德，我可是了解他。在潘西，多数人只是一天到晚嘴里念叨跟女孩儿性交——就像阿克利那样——可斯特拉雷德是动真格的，我自己就跟至少两个和他干过的女孩儿熟，这是事实。

"给我说说你精彩纷呈的这辈子里有什么故事吧，阿克利小孩儿。"我说。

"把他妈灯关了好不好？明天上午我还得去做弥撒呢。"

我起身把灯关了，只要能让他开心，然后又躺到埃利的床上。

"你准备怎么着——睡埃利的床？"阿克利问我。乖乖，他可真会招待人。

"可能，也可能不，别担心。"

"我不是担心，只是很他妈的不想看到埃利突然回来，让他看到别人——"

"放心吧，我不睡这儿，我不会辜负你他妈的盛情款待。"

几分钟后，他就呼噜打得震天响了。总之，我继续躺在那儿，就在黑暗中，努力不去想简这妞儿和斯特拉雷德待在混蛋埃德·班基的汽车里，但几乎不可能。问题是，我知道斯特拉雷德的招数，这可真是添乱。我们一块跟女孩儿约会过，就在埃德·班基的汽车里，他和女朋友坐后排,我们坐前排。这家伙真有两招。他一开始是很低声地、用**一本正经**的腔调跟他女朋友说话——就好像他不仅是个靓仔,还是个讨人喜欢、**一本正经**的家伙。我听他说话差点儿没他妈吐出来。他的女朋友一直在说:"别——**请你别这样**。请别。**请你别这样**。"可是斯特拉雷德这小子还是用林肯总统般一本正经的腔调跟她说话。到后来,车后座那儿静得出奇,真是太让人难堪了。我想他那天晚上没能跟那个女孩儿干成事儿,不过也他妈差不离,**他妈的差不离**。

我正躺在那儿努力什么也不想时,听到斯特拉雷德从厕所回到我们的房间里。我能听到他放下他的破盥洗用具什么的,还打开了窗户,他是个新鲜空气狂。后来很快他就关灯了,根本没找一下我去了哪儿。

就连外面的街道也让人沮丧,根本再也听不到什么汽车声。我感觉很孤独,很糟糕,甚至想把阿克利叫醒。

"嗨,阿克利。"我叫他,有点儿压着嗓子,免得让斯特拉雷德隔着浴室帘子听见。

可是阿克利没听到。

"嗨,**阿克利**!"

他还是没听到,睡得像块石头。

"嗨,阿克利!"

好,这下他听见了。

"你他妈的怎么回事?"他说,"我睡着了,岂有此理。"

"喂,进修道院得办什么手续?"我问他,我多少在琢磨这个念头,"是不是非得是天主教徒什么的才可以?"

"**当然**非得是天主教徒。你这个杂种,把我弄醒就为问这个蠢问题——"

"啊,你继续睡觉吧,反正我也不打算进。我这人倒霉就倒霉在很可能会进了一间修道院,里面的教士却跟我不是同一类人,全是些蠢杂种,要么只是杂种。"

我说完后，阿克利这货他妈的直挺挺地坐了起来。"听着，"他说，"你说**我**什么我都无所谓，可是他妈敢拿我的**信仰**开玩笑，岂有此理——"

"放心，"我说，"没人拿你他妈的信仰开玩笑。"我从埃利的床上下来往门口走去，我不想在这个破环境里再待下去了。我停了一下抓起阿克利的手，跟他假惺惺地大握特握。他把我的手甩开。"什么意思？"他问。

"没什么意思，看到你他妈真是个大好人，只是想谢谢你，如此而已。"我说，用的是一本正经的口气。"你出类拔萃，阿克利小孩儿，"我说，"知道吗？"

"小聪明，总有一天有人会把你揍——"

我根本懒得听他说完，关上破门就到了走廊上。

人们要么全睡了，要么出去了，要么回家度周末，走廊上很静很静，令人沮丧。莱希和霍夫曼的房门外，有个考利诺斯牌的牙膏盒，向楼梯走去时，我用脚上的羊皮边的拖鞋一路踢着它。我在想该干吗，想到也许可以下去看看马尔·布罗萨德那家伙在干吗。我突然改了主意，一下子，我又想好了真的该干吗，我他妈要离开潘西——就在当天夜里，我是说我不等到星期三还是怎么样，我只是不想再逗留了，这儿让我感觉难过万分，寂寞万分。我决定去纽约的旅馆租个房间——很廉价的那种——然后优哉游哉地过到星期三。到了星期三，我便会休息充分、容光焕发地回家。我估计我爸妈在星期二或星期三之前，很可能不会收到老瑟默的信，那封信会告诉他们我被开除了。我不想在他们得知这个消息并将其充分消化前到家，我不想在他们一得知这一消息时，就在他们跟前出现。我妈会变得歇斯底里，但是当她充分消化了一件事后，就不会太糟糕。更何况，我也多少需要小小地休个假，我的精神太紧张了，真的。

总之，那就是我决定要做的事。我回到房间打开灯，开始收拾行李，我已经打点好不少东西。斯特拉雷德这小子根本没醒。我点了一根烟，穿好衣服，然后把两只格拉斯顿牌手提箱收拾好，总共只花了两分钟左右。在收拾东西方面，我算是个快手。

但在收拾东西时，有件事让我有点沮丧：我得把我妈事实上就在没几天前寄给我的新滑冰鞋装进去，那让我感到沮丧。我想象得出我妈走进斯伯丁商店，向售货员问了无数个傻乎乎的问题——可现在我又被学校开除了，这让我挺难受的。她给我买的型号不对——我想要速滑比赛用的，她却给我买了玩冰球的那种——但同样让我难受。几乎每次别人送我礼物，到头来都让我觉得难受。

收拾完以后，我随便点了一下我有多少钞票，不记得确切是多少，可也不算少。大约一星期前，我奶奶刚给过我一沓钱。我这个奶奶在钞票上很大方。她的记性全没了——她老得要命——每年总要给我寄四次左右的钱，算是生日礼物。虽然我的钞票不少，但我觉得多点儿钱总会用得着，谁也说不准。我就走下楼，叫醒了弗雷德里克·伍德拉夫，我的打字机就是借给了这个家伙。我问他愿意出多少钱买我的打字机。他是个有钱佬，可他说不知道，不太想买。最后他还是买了。这台打字机我买时花了约九十块钱，卖给他只卖了二十块。因为被我叫醒，他还不高兴呢。

收拾完东西准备走时，我在楼梯口站了一会儿，最后看了一眼这条破走廊。我有点儿流眼泪了，也不知道为什么。我戴上我的红色猎帽，就像我喜欢的那样，把帽檐拉到后面，然后用他妈最大的嗓门喊了一声："**好好睡吧，你们这帮蠢蛋！**"我敢说，这层楼上的混蛋全让我吵醒了，然后我他妈就走了。不知道哪个笨蛋往楼梯上扔了些花生壳，差点儿没他妈让我摔断我的破脖子。

08

那时已经太晚,打不到的士什么的,我就一路走到了火车站。路不算太远,不过他妈的冷得要命,积雪让我难以行走,两只手提箱也他妈不断碰撞我的腿。可我有点儿喜欢这空气,问题只是冷空气让我的鼻子疼,疼的还有我的上嘴唇里面,斯特拉雷德这小子在那儿来了一下,正好嘴唇垫到牙齿,疼得很。我耳朵倒是暖暖和和的,我买的帽子有护耳,就把它拉了下来——我他妈才不在乎我什么模样呢。反正附近看不到什么人,人们都在被窝里呢。

在火车站我的运气还算好,等十分钟左右火车就来了。等车时,我用手抓些雪洗了洗脸,我脸上还有不少血。

一般说来,我喜欢坐火车,特别是夜里。车灯全亮着,窗外很暗,有人在过道上走来走去卖咖啡、三明治,还有杂志。我一般是买个火腿三明治和四本左右杂志。如果坐的是夜班火车,一般说来,我甚至能忍住不吐,读上一篇杂志里那种弱智的短篇小说。你也知道,就是那种短篇,里头有很多性格虚伪、下巴瘦削的名叫大卫的家伙,还有同样虚伪、名叫琳达或是马西娅的女孩,她们老是给那些混蛋大卫们点烟斗。通常,我坐夜班火车时甚至能读一篇这种恶心人的短篇小说,但这次不一样,我不想看,坐在那里什么也不干,只是把猎帽取下放进口袋。

突然,一位女士在特伦顿上车并坐到我旁边。因为已经很晚,整节车厢几乎是空的,可她就是过来坐到我旁边,而不去坐空位子,原因是她带了个大包,而我正好坐在第一排座位上。她把包放在过道正中,那样放,无论是售票员还是别人,都会被绊个跟头。她戴了几朵蝴蝶兰,好像她刚参加完一个大型派对。我想她大概四十到四十五岁,模样倒挺好。女人真让我着迷,真的。我不是说我特别好色还是怎么样——虽然我的确很好色,但我是说我仅仅喜欢她们而已。她们老是把自己的破包放到过道中间。

不管怎么样,我们就在那儿坐着。突然她对我说:"对不起,请问那不是潘西中学的条签吗?"她抬头看我放在行李架上的手提箱问我。

"对,是的。"我说。她说对了,我的一只格拉斯顿牌手提箱上的确贴着潘西的条签,我承认那很俗气。

"噢,你在潘西上学吗?"她问我。她说话声音很好听,几乎是你在电话里会听到的那种好听的声音,她该随身带他妈一部电话。

"是的,我在那儿上学。"我说。

"噢,太好了!那么也许你认识我的儿子欧内斯特·莫罗?他也在潘西上学。"

"对,我认识,他跟我一个班。"

她的儿子无疑是潘西有史以来最混蛋的学生,他老是在洗澡后,拎一条吸了水的毛巾沿走廊一路走一路抽别人的屁股,一点没错,就是那种货色。

"噢,太好了!"这位女士说,但并不显得俗气,只是很和气的样子。"我们这次见面我一定要告诉欧内斯特。"她说,"亲爱的,可以告诉我你叫什么吗?"

"鲁道夫·施密特。"我告诉她。我可不想把自己这辈子的事全向她抖出来,鲁道夫·施密特是宿舍的看门人。

"你喜欢潘西吗?"她问我。

"潘西?还不算太糟糕吧。这儿称不上**天堂**什么的,可是也跟别的大多数学校一样好,有些教职工挺敬业。"

"欧内斯特很喜欢。"

"我知道他是这样,"我说着开始有点儿胡诌起来,"他的适应能力很强,真的,我是说他真的知道怎样调整自己。"

"你是这么认为的?"她问我,听上去她极感兴趣。

"欧内斯特?当然。"我说,然后看着她脱掉手套。乖乖,她戴了一手珠宝。

"我刚才下的士时弄断了一片指甲。"她说着抬头看我,面带一丝微笑。她的笑容亲切得要命,真的。多数人几乎不怎么微笑,要么笑得很难看。"欧内斯特他爸和我有时候担心他,"她说,"我们有时候觉得他不是很擅长交往。"

"您是说——?"

"唉,他是个很敏感的孩子,真的,他从来不是很擅长跟别的孩子交往,可能是他处理事情有点太认真吧,跟他的年龄不相称。"

敏感,这个词把我乐死了。说莫罗这家伙敏感,就跟说他妈马桶座敏感差不多。

我好好看了她一眼,她看上去一点儿也不傻,好像他妈的一清二楚她儿子是个什么样的混蛋,但这种事情向来说不准——我是说不管拿谁的妈来说,都有点轻度神经不正常。但我还是喜欢莫罗的妈,她不错。"抽根烟好吗?"我问她。

她往四周看了看。"我看这儿不是可以抽烟的车厢,鲁道夫。"她说。鲁道夫,把我乐死了。

"没关系,我们可以抽到他们来吵为止。"我说。她从我这儿拿了根烟,我给她点着。

她抽烟的模样优雅,嘴里抽进烟,但并不猛咽,她这个年纪的女人多数会那样。她魅力非凡,你要是真的想知道,她也很性感。

她有点儿怪怪地看着我。"可能是我弄错了,不过我看你的鼻子在流血,亲爱的。"她突然说。

我点点头，拿出了手帕。"挨了雪球，"我说，"里头裹了很多冰的那种。"我也许该原原本本告诉她是怎么回事，但是太费时间。我还是喜欢她的，开始有点儿后悔告诉她我的名字是鲁道夫·施密特。"厄尼这家伙，"我说，"他在潘西可是属于最受欢迎的，您知道吗？"

"不知道。"

我点点头说："确实，大家要经过相当长一段时间才能了解他。他有意思，很多方面都**怪怪的**——您明白我的意思吗？就说我头一次见到他的时候吧。头一次见他时，我觉得他是那种很势利的人，我原来就是那样想的。可他不是，他只是个性很突出而已，人们要过一段时间才能了解他。"

莫罗太太一句话也没说。乖乖，你真该看看她那副样子，我把她固定到座位上了。当妈的想听别人说的，全是她们的儿子如何如何卓尔不群那种话。

后来我就**真的**扯得天花乱坠起来。"您有没有听说过竞选的事？"我说，"班上的竞选？"

她摇摇头。我已经把她哄得迷迷糊糊的了，真的。

"是这样的，班上我们有几个人想选厄尼这家伙当班长，我是说没别人了，这份工作只有他才能干好。"我说——乖乖，我心里乐得不行，"可当选的是另一个，哈里·芬瑟，他**之所以**当选，原因既简单又明显，是因为厄尼不让我们提他的名。他不仅太腼腆，而且谦虚得要命，他**拒绝了**……乖乖，他可**真够**腼腆的，您该让他努力克服这一点。"我看着她，"他没跟你们说过吗？"

"没有，他没有。"

我点点头。"这就是厄尼，他不会说。这就是他的缺点之一——太腼腆、太谦虚了。您真的该教教他，有时候不要那么拘谨。"

就在那时，售票员来查莫罗太太的车票，借此机会我的胡诌告一段落，但我也为胡诌了半天而感到开心。像莫罗这种老是拿毛巾抽别人屁股的家伙——他是真的想抽疼别人——他们不只小时候混蛋，而且一辈子都这样。但是我可以跟你打赌,在我那番胡诌之后,莫罗太太会一直认为他是个很腼腆、很谦虚的人,不让我们提名他当班长。她可能会,这说不准,在这种事情上,当妈的都没那么精明。

"您想不想喝杯鸡尾酒?"我问她,我觉得自己想来一杯,"我们可以去餐车,好不好?"

"亲爱的,你能要酒喝了吗?"她问我,口气倒不算难听。她太迷人了,所以这样说也不显得难听。

"唉,不,严格说来还不能,可是凭我的个子,一般都能买到。"我说,"而且我的白头发也不少。"我侧过身子给她看我的白头发,让她乐得要命。"来吧,一块儿去,干吗不呢?"我说。我喜欢跟她在一起。

"我真的还是觉得我不喝为妙。太谢谢你了,亲爱的。"她说,"不过,餐车很可能关门了。现在已经很晚了,你也知道。"她说得没错,我完全忘了当时已经几点钟了。

然后她看着我,问起我害怕她会问的问题。"欧内斯特写信说他星期三到家,圣诞节假期从<u>星期三</u>开始,"她说,"我希望你不是因为家里人有病,被突然叫回去的。"她看样子真的有点儿担忧,看得出,她并非仅仅出于爱管闲事。

"没有,家里人都挺好,"我说,"是我有事,我要动个手术。"

"噢,<u>我太难过了</u>。"她说,她真的是。我马上就后悔那样说,可是太晚了。

"不算太严重。我脑子上有个小肿瘤。"

"噢,<u>不是吧</u>?"她用手捂住了嘴巴。

"噢,根本没事!刚好长在靠外边的地方,而且很小,他们两分钟左右就能把它取出来。"

然后我就开始读从口袋里掏出来的时刻表,只是为了不再胡诌下去。一旦开了头,我只要喜欢,能胡诌上几小时。不骗你,<u>几小时</u>。

在那之后,我们就没谈多少话,她开始读她带的一本《服饰与美容》杂志,我往车窗外看了一会儿。她在纽瓦克下车,关于我要做的手术,她说了很多祝我好运的话,一直叫我鲁道夫,还邀请我夏天去马萨诸塞州格洛斯特找厄尼玩,说她家房子就在海滩边,还有个网球场,但我只是向她表示了谢意,说我到时要和奶奶一起去南美洲,纯粹是骗她而已,因为我奶奶几乎从来足不出户,除非可能去看破午后场电影什么的。就算给我金山银山,我也不会找那个混蛋莫罗,就算走投无路我也不会。

09

在潘恩火车站下车后,我所做的第一件事就是钻进电话间,想着给谁打个电话。我把两只手提箱放在电话间外面,好看得见,可是一进里面,又不知道该打给谁。我哥 D. B. 在好莱坞,小妹妹菲比一般九点钟就上床睡觉——不能打给她。打了她也不会介意,但问题是她不会接,而会是我爸或我妈接,就算了。接着我想给简·加拉格尔的妈妈打个电话,问问简什么时候开始放假,但我不太想,再说那时打也未免太晚了。后来我想到以前经常在一起玩的女孩儿萨莉·海斯,因为我知道她已经放假——她给我写过一封虚情假意的长信,邀请我圣诞夜去帮她修剪圣诞树什么的——可我担心会是她妈接电话。她妈认识我妈,我能想象她会急得要命地要打个电话给我妈,说我在纽约。再者,我可不是很想跟海斯太太通电话。她有次跟萨莉这妞儿说我没规矩。她说我没规矩,而且缺少生活目标。后来我又想到伍顿中学的一个校友卡尔·卢斯,可是我不太喜欢他。结果我一个电话也没打,只是在电话间里待了有二十分钟,然后出来拎着手提箱走到有的士的隧道那儿,打了一辆车。

我太他妈心不在焉了,给了司机我家的地址,习惯而已,我是说我完全忘了要找间旅馆待两天,直到假期开始后再回家。穿过公园一半时,我才想起这茬事儿,就跟司机说:"嗨,能掉头时掉个头好不好?我给你的地址错了,我想再回市中心去。"

这个司机算是个聪明的家伙。"这儿不行,老弟,是条单行道,我得一直开到第九十街才能掉头。"

我不想跟他争执。"好吧。"我说着忽然想起什么事,"嗨,听我说,"我说,"你知不知道中央公园靠南边那个湖里的鸭子?就是那个小湖?也许你知道那些鸭子在湖水结冰后去哪儿了?你也许知道?"我也意识到,他知道的机会可能只有百万分之一。

他扭头看着我,好像我是个疯子。"伙计,你搞什么名堂?"他问,"跟我开玩笑?"

"不是——我只是想知道而已。"

他没再说什么,我也没有。直到我们开出公园,到了第九十街时他问我:"好吧,伙计,去哪儿?"

"唉,是这样,我不想住东区的旅馆,怕碰到熟人,我在隐姓埋名旅行。"我说。我实在不想说什么"隐姓埋名旅行"之类的陈词滥调,可是跟这种俗套的人说话,我也总是显得俗套。"你也许知道现在在'塔夫脱'或者'纽约客'这两个地方演出的乐队是谁带的?"

"不知道,老弟。"

"嗯——那就把我送到埃德蒙特旅馆吧。"我说,"你想不想半路停一下我们去喝杯鸡尾酒?我请客,我兜里有钱。"

"我不行,老弟,对不起。"跟他在一起真不错,性格特好嘛。

到埃德蒙特旅馆后,我登记入住。还在车上时,我就戴上了猎帽,纯粹是他妈觉得好玩而已,但在登记前,我取下了帽子,不想让人看着像个傻蛋还是怎么样。这有点儿讽刺,因为我当时还不知道,这家旅馆里尽是些变态佬和蠢蛋,怪人到处都有。

他们给我的房间很差劲,窗外除了旅馆另一边,别的什么也看不到。我倒无所谓,当时也实在沮丧,根本无所谓风景好不好。带我去房间的服务员是个很老的家伙,六十五岁上下,跟这个房间比起来,他的样子更让人沮丧。他是那种秃了顶,却还要把全部头发从边上梳上去遮住秃顶的家伙,我宁愿秃顶也不愿意那样。不管怎么样,这种工作对六十五岁上下的人来说还真不赖,帮人拎箱,等着拿小费。我觉得他脑子不是太灵光,不管怎么样,这真是要命。

他走后,我往窗外看了一会儿,外套也没脱下来,我无事可做。我要是跟你说说旅馆那边能看到什么,你准会吃惊,他们竟然懒得拉上窗帘。我看到一个灰头发、看上去很是一表人才的家伙身上只穿一条短裤,正在干什么我说了你也不会相信。他先把手提箱放在床上,拿出来的全是女人衣服,然后就往身上穿。真的是女人衣服——丝袜、高跟鞋、胸罩,还有件耷拉着两根带子的紧身内衣什么的。接着,他穿上一件很紧的晚礼服。向上帝发誓,真的是这样。后来,他开始在房间里走来走去,小碎步,像女人那样。他还抽着烟,照镜子。他也是一个人,除非还有人在浴室里——我看不到那么多。后来,几乎就在这间房的正上方,我从窗户看到一男一女在用嘴巴互相喷水,很可能是高杯酒,不是水,可我看不到他们的杯子里盛的是什么。反正是男的先喝一口,然后全吐到**女**的身上,她也对**男的**如法炮制——**一轮一下**,真离谱。你该看看他们的样子,他们一直歇斯底里的,好像那是自古以来最好玩的。我不是开玩笑,那家旅馆里尽住着这种变态佬。我很可能是整个这儿唯一正常的混蛋——这话说得不算过分。我他妈差点儿要去给斯特拉雷德这小子发个电报,要他马上坐火车来纽约,他在这家旅馆能拿第一呢。

问题是,这种破事看上去也有几分引人入胜,尽管你根本没指望会这样。比如说那个被喷得满脸是水的女孩儿吧,她长得很漂亮。我是说这就是我的大毛病,就我**内心**而言,你可能从来没见过我这样的色情狂。有时候,我能想到些只要有机会就能毫不犹豫去干的**很**下流的事。我甚至想象如果两个人都喝得有几分醉,用嘴往女的脸上喷水那种事也许很好玩,只是有几分下流。问题是我不**喜**欢这样,琢磨一下就会觉得这主意很馊。我觉得如果你并非真的喜欢一个女孩儿,就不该跟她瞎胡闹。**真的喜**欢她,就应该喜欢她的脸。如果你喜欢她的脸,就不该对她的脸做出这种下流事,比方说往她脸上喷水。有时候下流事做过头会很好玩,这可真是太糟糕了。当你不想太下流,不想破坏什么美好的东西时,女孩儿可帮不上你的忙。两年前我认识一个女孩儿,比我还下流,乖乖,她可真够下流的!我们在一起玩得很开心,虽然有阵子玩得有点儿下流。对于性,我永远不太清楚,从来不知道自己他妈的到了哪一阶段。我老是在性这方面给自己定些条条框框,可是一回头全打破了。去年我曾给自己约法三章,不再跟我很看不上的女孩儿胡闹,但是在同一个星期,我就又破戒了——其实就在同一天**晚上**,我从头到尾都在跟一个极其虚伪、名叫安妮·路易丝·舍曼的女孩儿搂脖子亲热。我对性这件事就是不明白,向上帝发誓,我真的不明白。

我一直站着,在琢磨是不是给简这妞儿打个电话——我是说往她上的B.M.中学打个长途电话,而不是打电话给她妈问她什么时候到家。按说这么晚不该打电话找学生,可是我想好不管是谁接的电话,我都会告诉对方我是简的舅舅,说她舅妈刚刚因为车祸死了,我必须马上跟简通话,这样应该行得通。我没打电话的唯一原因,是我没心情,没心情的话,这种事情也做不像。

过了一会儿,我坐在椅子上抽了两根烟,我得承认我很是情欲亢奋。突然,我想到一个主意。我拿出钱包,找到一张写有地址的纸条,是一个在普林斯顿上学的家伙写给我的,去年夏天我跟他在一个派对上认识。后来我还是找到了地址,尽管在钱包里放得有点儿变色,但是还能看出。在那个地址住的女孩儿准确点说,不算是妓女什么的,不过偶尔也愿意客串一下,上普林斯顿的那个家伙告诉我的。他有次带她去了在普林斯顿举办的一场舞会,差点为此被学校开除。她当过杂耍剧团的脱衣舞演员什么的。不管怎么样,我拿过电话机给她打了个电话。她的名字叫费丝·卡文迪什,住在第六十五街和百老汇大街交叉口的斯坦福·阿姆斯旅馆——没说的,是个藏污纳垢的地方。

一开始,我以为她没在家还是怎么样,没人接电话。最后终于有人接了电话。

"喂?"我说。我把声音装得低沉,好不让她怀疑我的岁数。我总算还有副低沉的嗓音。

"喂?"是个女的声音,语气根本不是很友好。

"费丝·卡文迪什小姐吗?"

"**你**是谁?"她说,"谁他妈这么晚打电话给我?"

这句话可以说让我有点儿吃惊。"唉,我知道这会儿够晚的了,"我说,用的是很成熟的声音,"希望你能原谅我,我只是迫切想跟你联系上。"我把话说得很他妈亲切动人,真的。

"你**是**谁?"她问我。

"噢,你不认识我,我是埃迪·伯赛尔的朋友。他建议我要是来纽约,可以跟你聚一聚喝杯酒还是怎么样。"

"**谁**?你是**谁**的朋友?"乖乖,她在电话里真像只母老虎,几乎他妈的跟我嚷着说话。

"埃德蒙·伯赛尔,也叫埃迪·伯赛尔。"我说。我也不记得他的名字叫埃德蒙还是埃德华。我跟他只有一面之交,就是在那次破派对上。

"我不认识谁叫那个名字,老兄。要是你觉得我喜欢半夜三更被吵醒——"

"埃迪·**伯赛尔**,上普林斯顿的,记得吗?"我说。

可以想象,她正在脑子里检索这个名字。

"伯赛尔,伯赛尔……上普林斯顿的……普林斯顿大学?"

"没错。"我说。

"你是普林斯顿大学的吗?"

"嗯,差不多吧。"

"噢……埃迪**怎么样**?"她说,"不过你这会儿给人打电话也真是的,天哪。"

"他还好,他让我向你问好。"

"嗯,谢谢。也请你代我向**他**问好,"她说,"他这人极好,现在在干吗?"突然,她显得很他妈友好。

"噢,你知道,老样子。"我说。我他妈怎么知道他在干吗?我跟他不过是点头之交,根本不知道他当时还在不在普林斯顿。"这么说吧,"我说,"你愿不愿意跟我去哪儿喝杯鸡尾酒?"

"你究竟知不知道这会儿几点了?"她说,"对了,你叫什么?可以告诉我吗?"她突然带上了一点儿英国口音,"听着好像你岁数不大嘛。"

我笑了。"谢谢,这话我爱听。"我说——口气很他妈亲切,"我叫霍尔顿·考尔菲尔德。"我应该给她报个假名,但当时没想到。

"好,你瞧,考弗尔先生,我不习惯半夜三更跟人定约会。我是个上班族呢。"

"明天是星期天。"我告诉她。

"嗯,反正呢,我得睡个美容觉,你也明白这个理。"

"我想我们也许可以只喝一杯吧,现在又不算太晚。"

"嗯,你很可爱哦。"她说,"你从哪儿打的电话?现在到底在哪儿?"

"我?我在电话间。"

"噢,"她说,接着有半天没说话,"嗯,我也特想什么时候跟你见见面,考弗尔先生。你的声音听着很有魅力,听着你也是个很有魅力的人,可是现在的确太晚了。"

"我可以去你那儿。"

"嗯,要在平时呢,我会说这样极好。我是说我会很希望你能过来喝一杯,可是我室友刚好病了,她整晚躺在那儿一刻没睡,我是说她这会儿刚睡着。"

"噢,真不巧。"

"你住哪儿?也许明天我们可以一块儿喝两杯。"

"明天不行,"我说,"只有今天晚上才行。"我真蠢,不该那样说的。

"噢,这样啊,那我可就太抱歉了。"

"我会替你向埃迪问好。"

"真的吗?我希望你在纽约过得愉快,这地方极好。"

"我知道,谢谢,晚安。"我说完挂了电话。

乖乖,我**真的**把事情全搞砸了,至少应该能跟她喝一两杯什么的。

10

当时还挺早,说不准几点钟,但也不会太晚。我不喜欢根本不困就躺到床上,于是打开手提箱取出一件干净的衬衫,进浴室洗了一下后换上。我该干吗呢?我想到可以下楼去看看"薰衣草厅"里有他妈什么好玩的。这家旅馆里有间夜总会,名叫"薰衣草厅"。

换衬衫时,我他妈差点要给我的小妹妹菲比打个电话。我真想跟她通电话,跟她这么一个懂事的人。可我不能冒这个险,因为她还只是个小孩子,根本不会起床接电话,更别说到电话机旁边了。我想我可以在听到是我爸或我妈接电话时就挂断,不过那也不行,他们会知道是我打的。我妈不管怎么样都会知道是我打的,她能未卜先知。不过没说的,我真想跟菲比这丫头聊聊天。

你应该见见她,你这辈子都不会见到哪个小孩儿像她这样,又漂亮又聪明。她真的很聪明,我是说上学以来,她得的全是 A。事实上,我在我们家最笨。我哥 D. B. 是个作家,我弟弟艾里——就是死去的那个,我跟你说过——是个奇才。比较起来,我是唯一一个实打实的笨蛋。你真该见见菲比这丫头。她的头发颜色偏红,有点像艾里的,夏天时剪得很短,那时候她会把头发拢在耳后。她的耳朵长得小巧玲珑。不过到了冬天,她就把头发留得很长。我妈有时给她扎辫子,有时不扎,那样也很好看。她才十岁,长得很瘦,像我一样,可是她瘦得好看,是溜冰女孩的那种瘦。有次我隔着窗户看她穿过第五大道去公园,她就那副样子,像溜冰女孩那样苗条。你会喜欢她的,我是说如果你跟菲比丫头说什么事,她总是能准确理解你的意思。我是说你甚至可以带她去任何地方。比如说,如果你带她去看的是一部糟糕的电影,她能看出它糟糕。如果你带她去看的电影很好,她也会知道电影很不错。D. B. 和我带她去看过一部法国电影——《面包师的妻子》,雷米主演,她喜欢得要命。可她最喜欢的,还是《三十九级台阶》,罗伯特·多纳特主演。她把这部破电影记得滚瓜烂熟,因为我带她去看过十遍左右。比如说,当多纳特从警察那儿逃脱,进入一间苏格兰农舍后,菲比会大声跟着电影说话,就是里面那个苏格兰人说"你能把鲱鱼吃完吗?"时。她记住了电影里的每一句对白。当里面的教授——实际上是个德国间谍——向多纳特举起他那根中间关节少了一块的小指时,菲比已经比他抢先伸出手指——她在黑暗中向我举起她的小指,就在我面前。她很不错,你也会喜欢她的。不过她唯一的毛病,是偶尔过分热情,对一个小孩儿来说,感情太丰富了,真的。她还会做别的事,一有空就写书,只是都没写完,全是关于一个名叫黑兹尔·韦瑟菲尔德的小孩儿,菲比却拼写成哈兹·韦瑟菲尔德。此人是个女侦探,按说是个孤儿,不过她爸经常出现,总是"一位高大英俊的绅士,二十岁上下",让我乐死了。菲比这丫头,我向上帝发誓,你会喜欢她的。她甚至一丁点儿大时,就已经很聪明了。我和艾里以前经常带她去公园玩,特别是在星期天。艾里有艘帆船模型,经常星期天带到公园玩,我们就经常也带菲比丫头去。她戴着白手套,走在我们俩中间,大小姐似的。我和艾里随便聊起什么时,菲比这丫头一直在听。有时我们会感觉不到她在旁边,因为她太小了,但是她会让你知道她在旁边。她老是打断我们的话,把我或是艾里推一下问:"谁?谁说的?是鲍比还是那个小姐?"我们就会告诉她是谁说的,她会"噢"一声,然后继续听我们聊天。艾里让她给迷死了,我是说艾里也很喜欢她。她现在十岁了,不再是个丁点儿小孩儿。可她还是让谁都喜欢得要命——反正有点脑子的都会。

总之,她是那种你总想跟她在电话里聊天的人,可我很担心是我爸或者我妈接的电话,那样他们就会发现我在纽约,而且被潘西开除了,等等。所以我只是穿上衬衫,收拾好后就坐电梯下到大堂看看。

除了几个皮条客模样的家伙和婊子样的金发姑娘,大堂里几乎别无他人,但是听得到"薰衣草厅"里有乐队在奏乐,我就进去了。里面人不是很多,但他们还是给我找了个糟糕的位子——在最后边。我应该拿一块钱在领位侍者的鼻子下面晃晃。在纽约,乖乖,钱真能通神——这可不是开玩笑。

乐队很垃圾,是巴迪·辛格的乐队,铜管乐非常喧闹,但不是好的喧闹——是过时的那种。里面很少有我这样岁数的人,事实上我这样的一个也没有,主要是那些带着女朋友、一副人前炫耀模样的老头儿,只有邻桌那里坐着三个三十岁上下的女人。她们都长得很丑,戴的帽子让人一看就知道她们不是真正的纽约人,其中一个倒不算太差,金发的那个。她有点儿可爱的样子,就是金发那个,我就暗暗用眼神撩她。但就在那时,侍者过来问我点什么。我点了苏格兰威士忌和苏打水,并跟他说别混起来。我说得很利索,因为如果你哼哼唧唧地点,他会觉得你不满二十一岁,不卖给你可以晕乎一下的烈酒。可我在他那儿还是遇到了一点小麻烦。"对不起,先生,"他说,"您有没有能证明年龄的证件?也许您带了驾驶执照?"

我冷冷地瞪着他,就好像他他妈的对我造成了极大的侮辱。我问他:"我看着像不到二十一岁吗?"

"对不起,先生,但是我们有我们的——"

"好了,好了,"我说,我琢磨那就他妈的算了,"给我拿杯可乐吧。"他转身要走,我又把他叫回来。"你就不能往里面少掺点儿朗姆酒什么的?"我问他,语气很亲切,"我不能坐在这种俗气地方不让自己晕乎一下,你就不能往里面掺点儿朗姆酒什么的?"

"很抱歉,先生……"他说着撂下我走掉了,我没跟他争执。他要是被抓到卖酒给不到年龄的年轻人,就会丢饭碗,而我他妈就是这样的年轻人。

我又开始跟邻桌三个巫婆样的女人递眼神,就是长着金色头发的那个,对另外两个那样,完全是饥不择食的缘故。但我表现得还不算很下流,只是冷冷地瞟她们三个人而已。她们怎么样呢?我那样看她们时,她们只是蠢蛋似的咯咯傻笑,大概觉得我太小了,不该跟人瞄来瞄去,我真他妈气坏了——本来别人还会觉得我想娶她们还是怎么样呢。她们那样取笑过我之后,按说我应该摆出一副冷冰冰的样子,可麻烦的是当时我想跳舞。有时候我很想跳舞,那会儿就是。这么着,我突然侧过去一点说:"你们哪位想跳舞吗?"我说得并不粗鲁,事实上彬彬有礼的,可是真他妈的,她们觉得我**那样说**是紧张过度,咯咯笑得更厉害了。我不是开玩笑,她们真的是三个蠢蛋。"来吧,"我说,"我跟你们一个一个跳,好吗?怎么样?来吧!"我当时真的想跳舞。

最后,还是那位金发女郎站起来跟我跳舞,因为都看得出我其实只是邀请她。于是我们两人就走到舞池那儿,另外两个丑八怪简直要笑出毛病。当时我肯定对她们冷冰冰的,才懒得搭理她们呢。

不过还算值得,那位金发女郎算是个跳舞好手。在跟我跳过舞的女孩儿里头,她算是跳得最棒的之一。我不是开玩笑,有些蠢不可及的女孩儿跳起舞来真能让你目瞪口呆。要是跟一个聪明的女孩儿跳舞,有一半的可能,她会领着**你**在舞池里跳来跳去,要么跳得很糟糕,那最好还是跟她坐着一起喝醉算了。

"你跳得真好,"我告诉这位金发女郎,"你应该专门干这行,我不是开玩笑。我有次跟职业跳舞的一起跳,她跳得只有你一半好。你有没有听说过马尔科和米兰达?"

"什么?"她问我。她根本没听我说话,眼睛只是扫来扫去。

"我问你有没有听说过马尔科和米兰达?"

"我说不上来,没有,我说不上来。"

"唔,他们是跳舞的。就说那个女的吧,她不太红。虽然她**该会跳**

的全会,可还是不怎么红。你知不知道什么样的女孩儿是真正的跳舞高手?"

"你说什么?"她问我。她根本没听我说话,不知道她的心思正在这间舞厅的哪儿转悠呢。

"我问你知不知道什么样的女孩儿是跳舞高手?"

"嗯——嗯。"

"哎,就像我这样,把手放在她背上,如果我感觉不到手下面有屁股、腿、脚,什么也没有的话——那她就是个跳舞高手。"

可她没听,我也半天没跟她说话,我们只是跳舞。天哪,这个糊涂蛋女孩舞跳得可真好。巴迪·辛格跟他的烂乐队在演奏《就是那种事》,这首曲子尽管让他们糟蹋得不轻,可是毕竟还剩了点儿味道,这是首很棒的曲子。跳舞时,我没玩什么花样——我最讨厌那种在舞池里卖弄万般花样的人——可我带着她跳舞移动的范围也不小,她一步都没落下。好笑的是,我以为她也喜欢,直到她突然蹦出一句:"我跟朋友昨天晚上看见彼得·洛尔了。"她说:"就是那个电影演员,他本人。他当时在买报纸,挺可爱的。"

"你们运气不错,"我告诉她,"你们真的是,知道吗?"她真是个蠢蛋,可是舞也跳得真好。我实在忍不住,就在她的笨脑袋顶上轻轻亲了一下——你也知道——就在主管愚蠢的那块上,可是那样做让她生气了。

"嗨!你什么意思?"

"没什么,没什么意思。你舞跳得真好。"我说,"我有个小妹妹,上他妈的四年级。你跳得跟她不相上下,她可以说是古往今来跳得最好的。"

"说话注意点儿,好不好?"

乖乖,遇到淑女了。天哪,她是个女王。

"你们从哪儿来的?"我问她。

可她没答话,我想她正忙着用眼睛扫来扫去,看彼得·洛尔老兄来了没有。

"你们从哪儿来的?"我又问她。

"什么?"她说。

"你们从哪儿来的?不想说算了,我也不想让你紧张。"

"华盛顿州西雅图。"她说。她能告诉我,算是给了我很大一个面子。

"你真够健谈的,"我告诉她,"你知道吗?"

"什么?"

我就此打住,反正她也理解不了。"他们来支快曲子的话,我们跳点儿吉特巴好不好?不是那种过时的,不用蹦起来还是怎么样——而是优雅轻松的。如果是快曲子,那些老头儿和胖子都会坐下,够地方,好不好?"

"我无所谓,"她说,"嗨,你究竟多大了?"

不知道为什么,这让我来气了。"天哪,你就别扫兴了。"我说,"我十二岁,岂有此理,我长得老成点儿。"

"**听着**,我跟你说过,我不喜欢你这样说话。"她说,"你再这样跟我说话,我就去跟我的朋友们坐一块儿,你也知道。"

我一道歉就道个没完,因为那时乐队奏起一支快曲子。她跟我跳起了吉特巴——不过特别优雅轻松,不显得俗气。她真的很棒,只需要搭着她就行了。转圈时,她小巧的屁股扭来扭去,好看至极。说真的,她完全迷住了我。到我们坐下时,我快爱上她了。女孩儿就这样,每次她们做出什么漂亮事,虽然她们长得未必很顺眼,要么甚至有点儿蠢,可你还是几乎要爱上她们,从来是他妈**找不着北**的感觉。女孩,天哪,她们能让你疯掉,真的。

她们没邀请我坐到她们那张桌去——主要是因为她们太无知了——不过我还是去她们那边坐下了。跟我共舞的金发女郎叫伯尼斯什么的——姓克莱布斯或是克雷布斯,另外两个样子丑的名叫马蒂和拉弗内。我告诉她们我叫吉姆·斯蒂尔,只是他妈的觉得好玩。后来我就试着跟她们进行稍微有点儿层次的聊天,但实际上不可能,除非强迫她们。我简直分不出她们三个里头谁最蠢。她们三个人的眼睛都在这间破厅里扫来扫去，好像在盼着随时会进来一大帮破**电影明星**。她们很可能以为那些电影明星到纽约后，只在"薰衣草厅"晃悠，而不是去斯托克夜总会或者"摩洛哥"那种地方。不管怎么样，我花了半个小时左右，才打听清楚她们在西雅图是干吗的。她们都在同一家保险公司工作。我问她们是不是喜欢自己的工作，可是你又能指望这三个糊涂蛋能有什么像样的回答？我以为丑的两个——马蒂和拉弗内是姐妹，可是我问起时，她们觉得很受侮辱。看得出，她们谁也不乐意长得像对方，也不能怪她们，这事儿反正很好玩。

我跟她们都跳了舞——所有三个——轮流跳。那个长相难看的拉弗内跳得还不算太差，但是另一个，马蒂，差得简直令人忍无可忍，跟她跳，就好像拽着自由女神像跳舞。跟她拽来拽去跳舞，想得到一点儿乐趣，就只能找点儿乐子。我告诉她我刚才看见电影明星加里·库珀了，就在舞池那边。

"**哪儿**？"她问我——激动得要命，"**哪儿**？"

"噢，你刚好错过了，他刚出去。我说的时候你干吗不看？"

她几乎停下来不跳了，目光开始越过众人的头顶到处看来看去，想找到他。"噢，真糟糕！"她说。我几乎伤透了她的心——真的。我因为跟她开这种玩笑，真他妈后悔得不得了，跟有些人开不得玩笑，即便是他们活该。

可是还有很滑稽的事儿呢。我们回到座位上后，马蒂这妞儿跟另外两位说加里·库珀刚走出去。乖乖，拉弗内和伯尼斯这俩妞儿听了几乎要自杀。她们全都兴奋起来，问马蒂有没有看到他。马蒂这妞儿说她只是瞥到了一眼，她让我乐死了。

酒吧那天夜里就要打烊了，我赶在打烊前，给她们每人买了两份酒，自己也又要了两份可乐。那张破桌子上放满了玻璃杯，一片狼藉。那个丑样的拉弗内一直跟我开玩笑，因为我只喝可乐，而她还挺有幽默感。她和马蒂喝的是汤姆柯林斯鸡尾酒——在十二月中旬，真是岂有此理，她们根本不懂。金发女郎伯尼斯要的是波本威士忌兑水，还真的干掉了。她们三个一直在用眼睛搜索电影明星，很少说话——彼此间也是。马蒂这妞儿说的话比另两位要多，但她总说着俗里俗气、令人生厌的话，就像称呼厕所为"小姑娘的房间"那种话，还觉得巴迪·辛格的乐队里那个又老又不中用的单簧管手很棒，在他站起来不冷不热地来段独奏时。她称他的单簧管为"甘草棍"，真够俗气的。另一位长相难看的拉弗内自以为说话很风趣，一直催着让我给我爸打电话，看他那天晚上在干吗。她还一直追问我爸有没有女朋友，问了四遍之多——没错，够风趣的。伯尼斯这妞儿，就是金发那个，几乎从不说话，每次问她什么话，她总要来一句："什么？"这样过上一阵子，就会让人来气。

她们喝完酒后，突然三个人一起在我面前站起来，说是该睡觉了，第二天要一大早去看无线广播城综艺剧场的首场演出。我劝她们多待一会儿，可是她们不肯，我只好跟她们说再见。我说如果去西雅图，我会找时间去看她们，但我怀疑不会，我是说去看望她们。

包括香烟什么的，账单上的数额大概是十三块。我觉得她们至少应该表示一下嘛，要为我和她们坐到一起前她们喝的酒付账——当然我也不会让她们出，可是她们至少应该提一下。我无所谓，只是她们太无知，戴的帽子又那么难看，花里胡哨，还有什么要起早去无线广播城综艺剧场看首场演出的事，让我觉得没劲。如果有谁，比如说哪个女孩子戴着难看的帽子，一路来到纽约——天哪，是从华盛顿州西雅图来的——就为起早去看无线广播城综艺剧场的首场演出，这种事没劲儿得让我受不了。要是她们没告诉我那个，给她们三个买一百份酒我也愿意。

她们走后不久，我也离开了"薰衣草厅"，反正快打烊了，乐队已经收场好久。首先呢，这种地方差劲得要命，让人待不下去，除非跟一个舞跳得特别好的人在一起，要么侍者让你点真正喝的，而不是可乐而已。除非能买点烈酒来喝醉，或者跟一个让你神魂颠倒的女孩儿在一起，否则世界上没有一家夜总会能让人久待。

11

去大堂的半路上,我突然又想起了简·加拉格尔这妞儿,想起来就放不下。我坐在大堂里那把让人看一眼就会呕吐的椅子上,想着她和斯特拉雷德坐在混蛋埃德·班基的汽车里的情形。虽然我他妈很肯定斯特拉雷德没跟她干——我太了解简这妞儿了——心里却还是放不下。我太了解她了,真的。我是说包括跳棋,凡是运动她都挺感兴趣。我认识她之后的那年整个夏天,我们几乎每天上午都打网球,下午打高尔夫球。我真的特别了解她,我指的不是**身体**方面什么的——不是那方面——可我们见面特别频繁。了解一个女孩儿,并不一定自己得很好色。

我怎么会认识她呢?是这样的,她家养的杜宾犬经常跑到我们家草地上排泄,我妈很恼火,打电话给简的妈妈大吵了一通——我妈碰到这种事情会大吵大闹。之后过了两天,我看到简趴在俱乐部的游泳池边,就跟她打招呼。我知道她和我们是邻居,但之前我们从来没说过话还是怎么样。我跟她打招呼时,她冷冰冰的。我费了他妈的大半天劲儿才让她相信,我他妈才根本不在乎她的狗在哪儿拉屎撒尿呢,叫我说,它就是拉到我家客厅里也行。不管怎么样,反正后来我和简成了朋友。当天下午,我们就在一起打了高尔夫球。她打丢了八个球,我还记得,八个啊。我花了很多时间教她至少在挥棒击球时别闭眼。在我的帮助下,她的球技总算有了长足的进步。我打高尔夫球特在行,如果我告诉你我多少杆就能打完一场,你大概不会相信。我有次差点儿上了一部电影短片,但最后关头改了主意。我琢磨像我这么一个对电影深恶痛绝的人,如果让他们拍进电影短片,那我就是个虚伪的人。

简这妞儿,是个有趣的女孩儿。我并不想把她形容得很漂亮,可是我完全被她迷住了。她有点儿饶舌,我是说在说到一件让她激动的什么事时,她的嘴巴会上下翻飞,包括嘴唇什么的都是,逗死我了。她的嘴巴从来没有合严实过,总是张开一点点,特别是在她打高尔夫做击球动作时,另外在看书时也是那样。她总是在看书,而且看的是很好的书,还看很多诗。除了我的家里人,我只给她看过艾里的手套,就是上面写满诗的那只。她从来没见过艾里,因为那是她在缅因州过的第一个夏天——之前那个夏天,她去的是科德角——我跟她说过很多关于艾里的事,她喜欢听。

我妈不是很喜欢她,我是说在简和她妈没跟她打招呼时,我妈老觉得那是怠慢她。我妈经常在村子里遇到她们,因为简经常和她妈开她家那辆拉萨雷尔牌敞篷汽车去市场。我妈根本不觉得简漂亮,可是我觉得她漂亮,我就是喜欢她的样子,这就够了。

我记得有天下午,那是我和简这妞儿接近搂脖子亲热的唯一一次。那天是星期六,外面下着瓢泼大雨,我在她们家的走廊上——她家有条用玻璃跟外面隔开的宽走廊。我们在玩跳棋。我喜欢时不时跟她开个玩笑,因为她把王棋全放在后排不动。可是我没有跟她过分开玩笑,谁也不会跟简这样的小女孩儿过分开玩笑。我觉得只要有机会,我很喜欢跟女孩儿开玩笑,把她们搞得狼狈不堪,好玩。我最喜欢的女孩儿,是那种我从来不太想跟她们开玩笑的女孩儿,有时候我觉得她们也**喜欢**你跟她们开开玩笑——实际上,我**知道**她们喜欢——但是如果你已经认识她们相当长一段时间,而且从来没跟她们开过玩笑,这个头就难开。好了,我还是跟你说说我那天下午是怎样跟简接近搂脖子亲热的吧。当时雨下得特别大,我和她待在她家的走廊上,她妈嫁的那个醉鬼突然走到走廊这边问简家里有没有烟。我跟他不熟,但他看上去是那种除非为了从你这儿得到什么,否则就不会跟你多说话的人,他的为人很差。在他问知不知道家里哪儿有烟时，简这妞儿没搭理他。他又问了一遍，简还是没理，根本没抬头。最后那个家伙又进屋了。他走了后，我问简到底他妈的是怎么回事，她连**我**也不搭理。她装作好像在专心思考下步棋该怎么走。突然，一滴眼泪啪的一下砸到棋盘上，就在红色那格里——乖乖，现在我好像还能看到。她只是用手指把那滴眼泪抹得渗进了棋盘。我不知道为什么，可是心里不安得要命。我怎么做的呢？我过去让她在沙发椅上挪挪好让我坐下——我几乎坐到了她的**大腿**上。后来她就**真的**哭了起来。接下来我所记得的，是到处亲她——**哪儿都亲**——眼睛、**鼻子**、前额、眉毛……还有**耳朵**——除了嘴巴以外的整张脸，她好像不让我亲到她的嘴。总之，那就是我们最接近搂脖子亲热的一次了。过了一会儿，她起身进屋换了一件红白色羊毛衫，我觉得漂亮极了。我们就去看了场破电影。在路上，我问她卡达希先生——是那个酒鬼的名字——有没有对她不轨。她年龄很小，可是身材极好，换了我，根本就不会走过卡达希那个杂种的面前让他看见。可她说没有，我从来没弄清楚究竟他妈的是怎么回事。对有些女孩儿，你简直永远他妈的搞不清楚是怎么回事。

  我不想就因为她从来不跟我搂脖子亲热或者胡闹，而给你一种印象她是那种冷冰冰的人还是怎么样，不是的。比如说，我经常跟她手拉手，我也知道那听起来算不上什么，可是跟她拉手的感觉真的是美妙无比。大多数女孩儿你要是拉住她们的手，她们的手在你手里就他妈像死掉了一样，要么她们觉得手非得不停地**动来动去**，好像害怕让你感到厌烦还是怎么样。简跟她们不一样。我们会在开始看一场破电影或者干吗时，很快就拉起手，直到电影放完，一直没动，也不大做文章。跟简在一起，根本不用担心我的手出不出汗，知道的就是自己快乐，真的。

  我刚好还想起另外一件事。有次在看电影时，简做了件让我激动不已的事。当时正在放新闻片什么的，我突然感觉脖根处搁了一只手，是简的手。这件事很有意思，我是说简还很小，你如果看到一个女的把手放在别人的脖子上或背上，她们会有二十五到三十岁左右，而且通常是对她们的丈夫或者小孩子那样——我偶尔跟我妹妹菲比这样。可是如果这个女孩儿的岁数很小还是怎么样，她这么做，就太舒服了，让你几乎开心得要命。

总之，这就是我坐在那把样子让人恶心欲吐的椅子上想起来的事。这个简啊，每次想到她跟斯特拉雷德一起坐在混蛋埃德·班基的汽车里，就几乎能让我发狂。我知道她根本不会让斯特拉雷德占到什么便宜，却还是能让我发狂。说实话，我根本不想谈这个。

大堂里几乎没人，连那几个婊子样的金发女郎也看不到了。我突然想他妈离开这个破地方，这儿太让人沮丧了。我也不犯困还是怎么样，就回房间穿上了我的外套。我还往窗外看了一眼，看那些变态佬是不是还在行动，可那边灯全关了。我又坐电梯下去，打了辆的士，跟司机说我要去厄尼夜总会。厄尼夜总会是位于格林威治村的一家夜总会，我哥D.B.没去好莱坞卖身前，去那儿去得挺勤，偶尔还带我一块儿去。厄尼是个弹钢琴的黑人大胖子，极其势利。除非你要么是个厉害角色，要么是个名流什么的，否则他根本不会搭理你，不过他的钢琴弹得确实好，事实上好得甚至有点儿俗气。我也说不好我这话具体指的是什么，可是我还是要这么说。我当然喜欢听他弹琴，可有时候真想上去掀了他的钢琴。我觉得原因是他弹琴时，有时*听上去*好像他就是那种人，除非你是个厉害角色，否则就不会搭理你。

12

我搭的这辆的士可真够旧的,有股气味,好像有人刚刚吐在里面。很晚时,不管去哪儿,我打到的的士上总会有这种恶心人的气味。更糟糕的是外面很静、很荒凉,就连星期六夜里也是这样。街上几乎看不到什么人,只是偶尔能看到一男一女在过马路,互相搂着腰还是怎么样。要么有一群流氓模样的家伙跟他们的女朋友在一起,为了根本不算有趣的事,全都笑得跟野狼似的。半夜还有人在大街上大笑,这纽约也太恐怖了。几英里外都听得见,让人感觉很孤单,很沮丧。我一直想着能回家跟菲比丫头吹会儿牛多好。后来,在车上坐了一会儿后,我跟的士司机聊上了。他叫霍维茨,比上一个的士司机要好得多。不管怎么样,我想他也许知道那些鸭子的事。

"嗨,霍维茨,"我说,"你有没有路过中央公园的湖那儿?中央公园最南边?"

"什么地方?"

"湖。就是那个小湖,那儿有些鸭子,你知道。"

"对,怎么了?"

"那你是知道在那儿游来游去的鸭子了?春天还有别的时候会有的?也许你知道它们冬天去哪儿了?"

"谁去哪儿了?"

"鸭子。也许你知道?我是说会不会有人用卡车什么的把它们运走了?要么它们自己飞走了——去南方或者别的地方?"

霍维茨老兄把身子完全扭过来看着我,他是那种很没耐心的人,又不算坏人。"我他妈怎么知道?"他说,"我他妈怎么会知道这种破事儿?"

"哎,别来气嘛。"我说。他是有点儿来气了。

"谁来气了?谁也没有来气。"

我不跟他说话了,谁叫他他妈的这么敏感。可是他自己又先开口,再次完全扭过来说:"鱼哪儿也不去,就留在老地方,那些鱼,就待在破湖里边。"

"鱼——那不一样。鱼另当别论,我说的是鸭子。"我说。

"有什么不一样?没什么不一样。"霍维茨说。不管说什么,他的口气听上去都像是为什么事来气。"跟鸭子比起来,对鱼来说冬天是更难过点儿。岂有此理,你动动脑子吧,岂有此理。"

我沉默了有一分钟,然后说:"好吧,可是当湖里全结了冰,人们能在上面滑冰时,那些鱼呀什么的怎么过?"

霍维茨老兄再次转过身子。"他妈的什么叫怎么过?"他对我嚷着,"原来在哪儿还在哪儿,岂有此理。"

"它们不能对冰只是视而不见,不能只是视而不见啊。"

"谁视而不见了?谁也没有视而不见!"霍维茨说。他变得很他妈激动,我担心他会把车一家伙撞上路灯柱什么的。"它们就活在他妈的冰里面,那是天性,天哪。它们整个冬天就冻在一个地方。"

"是吗?那它们吃什么?我是说如果它们冻得硬邦邦的,没办法游来游去找吃的还是怎么样。"

"它们的身体呀,岂有此理——你是怎么回事?它们的身体会吸收进营养什么的,就是直接从他妈海草什么的玩意儿那里。它们身上的孔一直开着,这就是天性,岂有此理。你明白我的意思吗?"他再次他妈的完全扭过来看着我。

"噢。"我说。我不再多说,担心他会把这辆破的士报销还是怎么样。再说，他这人敏感成这样，跟他讨论什么事情绝对不愉快。"你有没有兴趣停下来跟我去哪儿喝一杯？"我说。

可是他没搭理我。我想他还在琢磨，就又问了他一遍。他是个挺不错的家伙，挺让人开心。

"我没时间喝酒，伙计。"他说，"你他妈才多大岁数？干吗不回家睡觉？"

"我不困。"

我在厄尼夜总会门口下车并付过车费后，霍维茨老兄又提起了鱼，他肯定也是念念不忘。"听着，"他说，"如果你是一条鱼，大自然母亲当然会照顾你，对不对？你不会以为那些鱼到冬天就死掉吧？"

"不会，可是——"

"你他妈说对了，死不了。"霍维茨说完就开着车一溜烟跑掉了。他可能是我遇到的最敏感的家伙，不管说什么，都让他来气。

尽管已经很晚，厄尼夜总会这地方还是人挤人。多数是上中学和大学的蠢材。世界上几乎每所破学校都比我上的那所学校圣诞节放假早。人很多，几乎没法寄存外套。不过那儿挺安静，因为厄尼正在弹钢琴。他坐在那张琴凳上时，好像那按说是件神圣的事，天啊，他弹起琴来无人可比。另外还有大约三对人跟我一样在等位子，都一直又推又挤、踮着脚尖，只为看一眼老厄尼弹琴时的样子。有他妈一面大镜子放在钢琴前，还有大聚光灯对着他，好让大家看得见他弹琴时的脸。看不到他弹琴的手指，只能看到一张又大又老的脸。真是不得了。我不太清楚我进去时他弹的是什么，但不管是什么，他算是彻底糟蹋了这首曲子。高音地方，他总是要加上一些愚蠢的、卖弄性的颤音，另外还加上许多花里胡哨的玩意儿，让我很厌恶。你该听听那群人在他弹完一曲后的反应，让人想吐。他们为之疯狂，跟那种看电影时看到并不怎么好玩的地方就笑得跟野狼似的蠢蛋没什么两样。我向上帝发誓，如果我是个弹钢琴的或者演员什么的，而那些笨蛋认为我很厉害，我是不会喜欢的。我根本不希望他们为我鼓掌。人们老是为不该鼓掌的鼓掌。我要是个弹钢琴的，会躲在他妈的柜子里弹。不管怎么样，他一曲弹完，每个人都拍烂了巴掌。老厄尼在凳子上扭过身子，鞠了个很虚伪、很谦卑的躬，好像他除了是个厉害的钢琴家，还是个很他妈谦卑的家伙，很虚伪——我是说对他这样一个很势利的人来说。虽然说起来有点儿可笑，可是他弹完后，我还真的有点儿为他感到可惜，甚至认为他已经不知道自己有没有弹对。这也不能全怪他，我认为部分责任应该归于那些拍烂巴掌的笨蛋——只要给他们机会，谁都能让他们毁掉。反正那些事又让我感到沮丧而且恶心，我他妈差点儿取回我的外套回旅馆，可那时还是太早了，我不太想自个儿待着。

后来，他们终于带我到一张很差劲的桌子那儿，背靠着墙，前面有根破柱子挡着，坐在那儿什么也看不到。那张桌子很小，要是邻桌不肯起身让路——他们从来不肯，那些混蛋——你简直得爬到你的椅子那边。我要了苏格兰威士忌和苏打水，那是除了冰冻代基里酒之外，我最喜欢喝的。你只要有六岁左右，就能在厄尼夜总会里要到烈酒。这儿灯光很暗，况且没人管你几岁。你甚至可以是个吸毒的瘾君子，没人管你。

我被一群蠢材所包围，不是开玩笑。挨着我左侧的另外一张小桌那儿——几乎就在我头顶上——坐着一个长相滑稽的家伙和一个长得同样滑稽的女孩。他们跟我岁数差不多，也可能大上一点儿。真好笑。看得出，他们小心翼翼，不敢把一丁点儿酒很快喝完。因为我也没别的事情可做，就听了一会儿他们的谈话。那个男的在跟女的说那天下午他看的一场职业橄榄球赛，把整场比赛说得巨细无遗——我不是开玩笑，我从来没听过谁说话像他那样无聊。听得出，他的女伴对这场破比赛根本没兴趣，可是她长得比他还滑稽呢，所以我估计她还非听不可。长相实在难看的女孩儿日子不好过啊，有时候我很同情她们。有时候我根本没法瞧她们一眼，特别在她们跟那些笨蛋在一起时，还得听他喋喋不休地谈论一场破橄榄球赛。我右边人们的谈话更差劲。我右边这位长得很像那些上耶鲁大学的家伙,穿了套灰色法兰绒西装,还有件有点儿同性恋味道的塔特萨尔花格呢背心,在名牌大学上学的混蛋全那副模样。我爸想让我上耶鲁或是普林斯顿什么的,可是我发誓就算我要**死了**,那种名牌大学我还是一所都不会去上,要命。那个耶鲁生模样的家伙跟一个特别漂亮的女孩儿在一起。乖乖,她长得真好看,可是你该听听他们聊的是什么。首先呢,他们都有点儿醉意。男的在干吗呢?他一边在桌子下面对她摸摸索索,一边说他们宿舍有个家伙吞了一整瓶阿司匹林,差点儿自杀的事。他的女友一直在说:"太**可怕了**……别,亲爱的,请别那样,别在这儿。"想想看吧,一边对人家摸摸索索,一边又跟她说谁谁自杀的事!这两位,把我乐死了。

我一个人坐在那儿,不用说感到百无聊赖,除了抽烟、喝酒,没有别的事情可干。不过我让那个侍者问老厄尼愿不愿意过来跟我喝一杯,我让他告诉厄尼我是 D. B. 的弟弟,可是我想他根本没帮我带话,那种混蛋,从来不会帮你带话。

突然,有个女孩儿走过来说:"霍尔顿·考尔菲尔德!"她叫莉莲·西蒙斯,我哥有阵子跟她来往过,她有对大奶子。

"嗨。"我说。我当然得试着站起来,可是在我坐的地方,起身不大容易。她跟一个海军军官在一起,腰杆笔直,好像脊梁上别了根拨火棒似的。

"见到你太棒了!"莉莲·西蒙斯那妞儿说,虚伪到了十分,"你哥怎么样?"她真正想知道的只是这个。

"他很好,在好莱坞。"

"在**好莱坞**?**太棒了**!他在**干吗**?"

"不知道,写东西吧。"我说。我不想多谈这件事,看得出,她觉得他去了好莱坞很了不起,几乎每个人都会这样想,可是大多数人从来没看过他的小说,想到这里真让我生气。

"太让人高兴了。"莉莲那妞儿说,然后就给我介绍那个当海军的家伙，叫布洛普中校什么的。那种家伙自以为跟人握手时，劲要大得能把别人的手指根根捏碎，才能避免被当成同性恋。天哪，我真烦那一套。"你自个儿吗，小家伙？"莉莲那妞儿问我。她他妈几乎把过道上来来去去的人全挡住了，看得出她还挺喜欢那样。有个侍者在等她让开道，可是她根本没注意到，真有趣。看得出侍者不太喜欢她，就连那个海军军官也不太喜欢她，尽管他是在跟她约会。我不太喜欢她，没人会。让人不由得有点儿同情她。"小家伙，你没个女孩儿陪吗？"她问我。我一直站着，她根本没让我坐下来。她是那种能让人一站就是几个小时的人。"他够帅吧？"她对那个海军军官说，"霍尔顿，你真是每时每刻都在越长越帅。"海军军官让她让开路，说她把过道挡严实了。"霍尔顿，跟我们一块儿坐吧，"莉莲那妞儿说，"带上你的酒。"

"我正要走呢，"我告诉她，"我得跟别人见个面。"看得出，她只是想笼络我，好让我向 D. B. 提起她。

"好吧，你这个小东西，随便你。见到你哥跟他说我讨厌他。"

然后她就走了，那个当海军的跟我互相说了句"很高兴见到你"之类的话。这种事总让我特别恼火，我老是跟我一点儿也不高兴见到的人说什么"很高兴见到你"。可是如果你想混下去，这种话还非说不可。

在跟她说我要和别人见面后，除了开路，我他妈别无选择。我甚至没法多待一会儿听老厄尼弹些不高不雅的东西，但我当然绝对不想跟莉莲·西蒙斯这妞儿还有那个海军待一块儿，会把自己给烦死。所以我走了，但是在取外套时，这件事让我心里很窝火。总是有人来扫你的兴啊。

13

我一路走回旅馆，整整四十一个街区。这样做不是因为想走路还是怎么样，更大程度上，是我不想再钻进钻出另外一辆的士了。就像有时厌倦了坐电梯，你会突然决定步行，不管多远或者多高。我还是个小孩子时，经常走楼梯上我们家的公寓，在十二楼。

不知道的话，根本看不出外面下过雪，人行道上几乎一点也没有，就是冷得要命。我从口袋里取出红猎帽戴上——我他妈才不管我模样如何呢，我连帽耳朵也拉了下来。我真想知道在潘西，是谁偷了我的手套，因为我的手很冷。倒不是说我知道是谁干的，就会如何如何，我是那种胆子很小的人，尽量不表现出来，可我真的胆小。比方说，要是在潘西发现是谁偷了我的手套，我很可能会走进那个小偷的房间说："好吧，把手套交出来怎么样？"小偷很可能会用很无辜的语气说："什么手套？"我会怎么做呢？我很可能会走到他的壁橱那儿，从比如说他的破胶套鞋里还是哪儿找到藏着的手套，会把手套拿到他面前问："这他妈是你的？"小偷很可能会装出一副很虚伪、很无辜的样子说："我这辈子从来没见过这双手套，是你的你就拿去好了，我才不想要这种破玩意儿呢。"然后我很可能只是在那儿站五分钟左右，戴好我的破手套。可我想做的，是照他下巴上来一拳还是怎么样——把他的鬼下巴打碎，问题是我没胆量那样做。我会只是站在那儿，装出一副凶样子。我可能怎么做呢？我可能说些很尖锐、很难听的话来惹火他——而不是照他下巴上来一拳。不管怎么样，要是我说了什么尖刻难听的话，他很可能站起来走到我跟前说:"喂,考尔菲尔德,你是不是说我是小偷?"**然后**呢,像"你他妈说对了,你是个偷东西的无耻杂种!"那种话我说不出来,我很可能会说:"反正我他妈知道我的手套到了你的破套鞋里。"这个家伙马上就拿准了我不会揍他,很可能会说:"听着,讲清楚,你是不是说我是小偷?"我很可能会说:"谁也没说谁是小偷,我知道的,就是我的手套到了你的破套鞋里。"这样一来一往,可能搞上<u>几小时</u>。可是到最后,我会离开他的房间,根本没给他来一拳。我很可能会去厕所里偷偷吸根烟,看镜子里的自己变得越来越凶。总之,这就是我一路走回旅馆时脑子里想的事。当个胆小的人不好玩,也可能我并非**完全**没胆量,说不上来。我觉得部分原因可能是我胆子小,部分是因为我是那种丢了手套根本不会太上心的人。我有个毛病,就是对丢东西这种事从来不是很上心——我还是小孩子时,这一点经常把我妈气得要命。有些家伙能花**几天**时间找丢了的东西,但好像从来没什么东西能让我觉得丢了会很在意。这可能就是我所说的,只有部分原因是胆小吧,可这不是什么理由,真的。做人应该无所畏惧,如果你觉得该给别人下巴上来一拳,而且你也可以说想那么干,那就应该干,我只是不善于此。我宁愿把他推下窗口,或者拿斧头把他的脑袋剁下来,也不愿意在他下巴上来一拳。我讨厌比拳头。我倒不是很介意挨打——虽说我当然也根本不想那样——可是比拳头时,我最害怕的是对方的脸。看着别人的脸让我受不了,这是我遇到的麻烦,如果两个人都蒙着眼还是怎么样倒不算太坏。琢磨一下的话,你会觉得这是种好笑的胆小,可毕竟是胆小,好吧,我不拿自己开玩笑。

我越想我的手套和我的胆小,就越是沮丧。走着走着,我决定在哪儿停一下喝点儿酒。在厄尼夜总会那边,我只要了三份酒,最后一份甚至没喝完。我有个特点就是酒量特大,情绪对头时,能喝上一整夜,还一点都显不出。有次在伍顿中学,一个星期六晚上,我和另外一个同学雷蒙德·戈德法布一起买了一品脱苏格兰威士忌,并在礼拜堂里没人时干掉了。他喝得浑身酒臭，而我根本没显出喝了酒，头脑很清醒，不晕。睡觉前我吐了，不是非吐不可——是我强迫自己吐的。

没到旅馆前，我正要走进一家样子邋遢的酒吧，两个喝得烂醉的家伙刚好出来，跟我打听怎么搭地铁。其中一个长得很像古巴人，给他们指路时，他一直往我脸上喷酒气。结果，我根本没进那家破酒吧，只是回到了旅馆。

整个大堂里空无一人，那里有股好像几百万个熄掉的雪茄烟头的气味，真的。我不困，但感觉有点儿糟糕，很沮丧，我几乎希望自己死掉算了。

后来，我一下子就惹上了大麻烦。

我走进电梯，开电梯的家伙上来就问我："伙计，想不想开心一下？要么你觉得太晚了？"

"什么意思？"我问他，不明白他指的是什么。

"想不想那个一下？"

"我？"我问道。那样回答很蠢，可是被别人当面问这种话真叫人难堪。

"你几岁了，老大？"这个电梯工问我。

"怎么了？"我说，"二十二。"

"嗯，好吧，要不这么着，你有没有兴趣？五块一回，十五块一晚。"他看了看手表，"一直到中午。五块一回，十五块一直到中午。"

"好吧。"我说。这有违我的原则，但是我心里太沮丧了，根本没考虑。麻烦全在这儿，感觉很沮丧时，根本没办法思考。

"什么好吧？来一回还是一直到中午？你得告诉我。"

"来一回吧。"

"好吧，你住哪间房？"

我看我的钥匙上带着的红色东西，上面有我的房间号。"一二二〇。"我说。我已经开始后悔让这一切开了头，但是已经晚了。

"好吧，我一刻钟内叫个女孩儿上去。"他打开电梯门，我出来了。

"嗨，她长得好不好？"我问他，"我可不想要个老太婆。"

"根本不会。放心吧，老大。"

"钱给谁？"

"给她。"他说，"去吧，老大。"他几乎贴着我的鼻子关上了电梯门。

我回到房间，往头发上抹了些水，我这种短头发没法梳得好。然后我试了试嘴里臭不臭，因为抽了不少烟，还有在厄尼夜总会喝了威士忌和苏打水。我只用把手放嘴前面往上面呼气，鼻子就能闻得到，好像还不算臭。可我还是刷了牙，又换上一件干净衬衫。我知道不必为一个妓女什么的打扮得光光鲜鲜还是怎么样，不过那样也算有事可做。我有点儿紧张，欲望越来越强，但还是有点儿紧张。说实话，我还是个处男呢，真的。我以前倒真的颇有几次机会破身，可总是没过那道坎，总会遇到点什么事。比方说，如果是在那个女孩儿的家里，她父母经常回来得不是时候——要么是担心他们会回来。或者在别人的汽车后座上，前排总坐有别人的相好——我是说某个女孩儿——她老是想知道整辆破车里**都在**发生什么事，我是说前排那个女孩儿老是扭过头，看后面座位上有他妈什么好事。反正总会有什么事情。倒是有一两次我差点干上了，我记得特别有那么一次，可还是出了点岔子——我根本记不清是什么。问题是多数情况下，我几乎跟一个女孩儿干上时——我是说不是妓女什么的——她老是叫你停下来，我的毛病是我真的停下来，多数人才不会呢，可是我没法不停。我永远搞不明白她们是真**想让**你停呢，还是她们只是吓得要死，要么是她们尽管嘴上一直叫你停，目的却是等你**真的**干完后就归罪于**你**，而不是她们。总之，我每次都停下来。麻烦还在于，我会可怜起她们，我是说多数女孩儿总是又蠢又傻，在跟她们搂脖子亲热半天后，你能**看着**她们变得越来越没脑子。拿一个变得热情洋溢的女孩儿来说，真的会一点儿脑子都没了。我说不上来。她们叫我停我就停，老是在送她们回家后，我才后悔当初**不停**就好了，可还是每次都停下来。

不管怎么样,我在换上一件干净衬衫时,可以说想到某种意义上说,这会是我的大好机会。我想到既然她是个妓女,我可以在她身上先练练,以便结婚还是什么时候能用上。我有时会为那种事担心。在伍顿中学时,我读过一本书,里面有个很有深度、文雅而且好色的家伙,我还记得他叫布兰查德先生。那是本很糟糕的书,可是这位叫布兰查德的家伙很有能耐。他在欧洲的里维埃拉那儿有座大城堡,一有空就去搞女人。他是个真正的浪荡公子,倒是让女人迷恋不已。书里有一段,他说女人的身体就像小提琴什么的,只有很高明的音乐家才能拉好。那本书很俗气——我当时就感觉到了——可我还是对小提琴这个比喻念念不忘,说起来,这也算是我有点儿想练练的原因,以备某天结婚之需。《考尔菲尔德和他的魔琴》,乖乖,俗了,我意识到了,但是还不算太俗。我倒不介意在这方面棒一些。你真想知道,我就说句实话吧,有一半时间,我跟女孩儿瞎闹时,为找到想找的地方真他妈困难重重,太离谱了,你该明白我指的是什么。就说我那次差点儿跟她办成事的女孩儿吧,我跟你说过的。我花了几乎有一个小时,才把她的破胸罩扒下来,等到终于扒掉时,她就差往我脸上吐口水了。

就那么着,等妓女上门时,我在房间里走来走去。我一直希望她长得漂亮,可我也不是很在乎,有点儿只想干过了算。终于有人敲门,我去开门时,刚好被放在走道上的手提箱绊了一跤,差点让我他妈摔破了膝盖。我摔跤的时机总是绝佳,不是绊上手提箱就是绊上别的什么东西。

打开门后,那个妓女就站在那儿。她穿了件驼绒大衣,没戴帽子。她可以说是个金发女郎,不过看得出她染过头发,倒是根本不老也不丑。"你好。"我说。乖乖,口气文雅得要命。

"你就是莫里斯说的人?"她说。语气好像他妈的不太友好。

"那个开电梯的?"

"对。"她说。

"对,没错。进来好吗?"我说。我有点儿变得越来越没那么冲动了,真的。

她进房间后,马上把外套脱掉,可以说是扔到了床上。她里面穿了条绿连衣裙。接着她在房间里跟桌子配套的椅子上侧着身子坐下来,开始上下晃动她的脚。她跷起二郎腿,一只脚开始上下晃动。作为一个妓女,她很紧张,真的。我想是因为她的岁数太他妈小了,跟我差不多。我坐在她旁边的一把大椅子上,请她抽烟。"我不抽。"她说。她声音很细,几乎听不见她在说什么。请她抽烟还是怎么样时,她一次也没说谢谢,根本不懂事。

"自我介绍一下吧,我叫吉姆·斯蒂尔。"我说。

"你有手表吗?"她说。她他妈才根本不关心我叫什么呢,这不用说。"嗨,你几岁了?"

"我?二十二。"

"有才怪呢。"

这话说得很有趣,好像她真的是个小孩儿。一般能想象妓女什么的会说"瞎说"或者"少来",而不是"有才怪呢"。

"**你**多大了?"我问她。

"大得不会跟人说这个。"她说。真是会说话啊。"你有手表吗?"她又问了我一遍,然后站起身把裙子全拉过头顶脱下。

她那样做时,我自然感觉怪怪的,我是说她**突然**那样做的。我也知道,如果有人在你面前站起身往上拉掉裙子,你的反应按说是很冲动,可是我没有。性冲动在我当时的感觉中,差不多**最**不明显,我那时心里的沮丧感远远超过了性冲动。

"嗨,你有手表吗?"

"没,没,我没有。"我说。**乖乖**,我感觉可真不自然。"你叫什么?"我问她。她现在身上就剩一条粉色衬裙,让人感觉很窘,真的。

"桑妮。"她说,"嗨,开始吧。"

"你不想聊会儿吗?"我问她。这话问得很孩子气,可是我当时感觉太他妈不自然了。"你很着急赶时间吗?"

她看着我,好像我是个神经病。"你他妈想聊什么?"她说。

"我说不上来,随便吧,我只是觉得你也许想聊会儿。"

她又坐到桌边那把椅子上,看得出她不太愿意。她又开始把脚晃来晃去——乖乖,她是个情绪紧张的女孩儿。

"抽根烟好吗?"我问她,忘了她不抽烟。

"我不抽烟。听着,你想聊就聊,我还有事呢。"

可我想不到聊什么,想问问她是怎么做了妓女,等等,却不敢问,反正大概她也不会讲。

"你不是纽约人,对吧?"我最后说,想到的就这一句。

"好莱坞。"她说着起身走到她放裙子的床那边,"你有没有衣架?我不想把裙子全搞皱了,崭新的呢。"

"当然有。"我马上说,正巴不得起身干点什么呢,就把她的连衣裙拿到衣橱那儿帮她挂好。说来有趣,帮她挂裙子时,我心里有种不舒服的感觉。我想到她走进一家店里买它时,那儿谁也不知道她是个妓女什么的。买连衣裙时,售货员很可能以为她只是个普通女孩儿而已。太让我难过了——究竟为什么,我也说不清。

我又坐下来,想继续聊天,跟她聊天真是没劲儿。"你每天晚上都工作吗?"我问她——问了后才觉得这样问有点儿蠢。

"对。"她在房间里走来走去,从桌子上拿起菜单看。

"你白天干吗?"

她微微耸了耸肩膀,她长得很瘦。"睡觉,看电影。"她放下菜单看着我,"嗨,开始吧,我没多少——"

"你看,"我说,"我今天晚上感觉不太好,说实话,我今天晚上很难受。我会给你钱的,你不介意我们不干那个吧?你很介意吗?"问题是，我真的不想干了。说实话，我心里的沮丧感超过了性冲动。她让我沮丧，她那身绿裙子也是。再说，我想我永远也不会跟一个整天看破电影的人干那个，真的觉得不能。

她走到我面前，脸上表情诡异，像是不相信我的话。"你怎么了？"她问我。

"也没什么。"乖乖，我越来越紧张，"是这样，我没几天前刚做了个手术。"

"是吗？在哪儿？"

"在叫'勺骨'的什么地方。"

"是吗？那是他妈哪儿？"

"勺骨？"我说，"对了，其实是在脊椎管里，我是说在脊椎管里很深的地方。"

"是吗？"她说，"那可够呛。"说着就坐到我他妈的大腿上。"你很可爱啊。"

她让我很紧张，我继续扯谎扯得没边没沿。"我还在恢复期。"我告诉她。

"你长得像电影里的一个家伙，你知道是谁，你知道我说的是谁，叫他妈什么来着？"

"我不知道。"我说。她就是不肯从我他妈的大腿上下来。

"你肯定知道。那个跟梅尔文·道格拉斯在一块儿，演投球手的？梅尔文·道格拉斯的小弟弟？从小船上摔下来的那个？你知道我说的是谁。"

"不，我不知道，电影我能不看就不看。"

接着她就开始逗弄我，很下流。

"请你别弄了好不好？"我说，"我没心情，跟你说了，我刚动过手术。"

她还是没从我的大腿上下来，而是狠狠瞪了我一眼。"听着，"

她说,"那个疯子莫里斯叫醒我的时候,我还在**睡觉**呢,你要是以为我——"

"我说过既然你来一趟,我会给你钱,真的会,我有不少钱,只是实际上,我正处于大手术的恢复期——"

"那你他妈干吗跟那个疯子莫里斯说你想找个**女孩**?要是你他妈刚刚在他妈哪儿动了手术,干吗还叫我来?嗯?"

"我本来以为感觉会好很多,估计得有点儿太乐观了。不开玩笑,对不起,你要是肯起来一会儿,我去把钱包拿过来,真的。"

她恼火得要命,可还是从我他妈的大腿上站了起来,好让我从抽屉里拿钱包。我抽出一张五块的递给她。"太谢谢你了,"我告诉她,"感激不尽。"

"这是张五块的,你得掏十块。"

看得出,她耍起花样了。我害怕的就是遇到这种事——真的怕。

"莫里斯说是五块,"我告诉她,"他说十五块一直到中午,一回只要五块。"

"十块一回。"

"他说是五块,对不起——真的——我只能出这么多。"

跟刚才一样,她稍微耸了耸肩,然后冷冰冰地说:"把我的裙子拿过来好不好?要么太麻烦您了?"她真是个很可怕的小孩子,她的声音尽管才一点点大,还是能让你多少有点儿心惊胆战。如果她是个岁数大的妓女,脸上再化一副浓妆,给人的感觉就根本没这么可怕了。

我过去给她取出连衣裙,她穿上后把床上的驼绒大衣捡了起来。"再见,废物。"她说。

"再见。"我说。没说谢谢什么的,没说挺好。

14

桑妮这妞儿走后,我在椅子上坐了一会儿,抽了两根烟。外面天色越来越亮。乖乖,我感觉太糟糕了,你想象不到我有多沮丧。我开始说话,好像是在大声说出来,说给艾里听,我很沮丧时,往往就会那么做。我一再说让他回家骑上自行车,然后在博比·法伦家门口跟我会合。在缅因州时,博比·法伦跟我家住得很近——那是几年前的事了,经过是这样:有一天,我和博比要骑自行车去西得比高湖,带着午饭什么的,还带了气枪——我们都还是小孩子,想着可以打什么东西玩。不管怎么样,艾里听到我们商量,也想去。我不让他去,说他还是个小孩儿。就这样,现在我偶尔感觉很沮丧时,会一再说给他听:"好吧,你回家骑上自行车,然后在博比家门口跟我会合。快点儿。"倒不是我以前去哪儿都不带他,我带的,只是那天没有。他没有不高兴——他从来不会为什么事不高兴——可是在我变得很沮丧时,仍会不停想着这件事。

不过最后我还是脱衣服睡觉了。躺上床后,我觉得应该做个祈祷什么的,可是没法做,我想做时常常没法做。首先呢,我算是个无神论者。我喜欢耶稣,但不是很喜欢《圣经》里别的绝大部分。就说十二门徒吧,说实话,我对他们烦得要命。耶稣死后他们还不错,可是耶稣在世时,他们对他不仅没用,反而碍事,所作所为总是让他失望。除了十二门徒,我几乎喜欢《圣经》里的所有人。说实话,除了耶稣,《圣经》里我最喜欢的是那个疯子,就是住在坟墓里,老是用石块割伤自己的家伙。我喜欢他甚于喜欢十二门徒十倍,那个可怜的家伙。在伍顿中学上学时,我经常就此事跟别人争论,那是住在走廊尽头的一个家伙,名叫阿瑟·蔡尔兹。蔡尔兹这小子是个贵格派教友,老是在读《圣经》。他这个人很不错,我喜欢他,但是对《圣经》里的许多东西,我们就是意见不同,特别对于十二门徒。他总是说,如果我不喜欢十二门徒,就只能说明我根本不喜欢耶稣。他说因为十二门徒是耶稣**挑选**的,所以应该喜欢他们。我说我知道的确是耶稣挑选了他们,可他只是**随意**挑选了他们,他没时间到处去仔细鉴别每个人。我说我不是说错在耶稣还是怎么样,他没时间那样做并不怪他。我记得我问过蔡尔兹这小子他认为犹大——就是出卖耶稣那位——自杀后会不会下地狱。蔡尔兹说理所当然,我刚好在这点上跟他看法不一致。我说我可以跟他赌一千块,犹大从来没被耶稣打下地狱。如果我现在有一千块,这个赌我也照打不误。我想某位**门徒**可能这么干——而且是马上——可耶稣没这么干,我赌多少钱都行。蔡尔兹说我的毛病就是不上教堂什么的。说起来,这句话说得没错,我的确不去。首先呢,我爸妈的信仰不同,我们家到我这一代全是无神论者。说实话,我根本受不了那些牧师。我上过的几所学校里,牧师开始布道时,全是一副慷慨激昂的架势。天哪,我真讨厌那样子。我就是不明白他们干吗不他妈自自然然地说话,他们开口时,听起来很虚伪。

总之,我躺在床上时,根本他妈的没法祷告。每次一开始,我就想起桑妮叫我废物时的情形。后来,我干脆在床上坐起来,又抽了根烟,味道很差。离开潘西后,我肯定抽了有两包。

突然,就在我在床上抽烟时,有人敲门。我一个劲儿希望敲的不是**我的**房门,但是我他妈知道得太清楚是我的。我说不好我**怎么**知道,可我就是知道,还知道是**谁**敲的呢,我能未卜先知。

"谁?"我问。我很害怕,碰到这种事我很胆小。

没人说话,只是又敲起来,声音大了一点。

最后我只穿着睡衣下床去开门。我根本不用开灯,因为天已经亮了。站在那儿的,是桑妮和拉皮条的电梯工莫里斯。

"怎么了?你们想干吗?"我问他们。乖乖,我的声音颤抖得要命。

"没什么,"莫里斯这家伙说,"只是要五块钱。"只有他说话,桑妮那妞儿只是站在他旁边,张着嘴巴。

"我给过她钱了,给了五块,问她吧。"我说。乖乖,我的声音颤抖得真厉害。

"老大,该是十块,我跟你说过的。十块一回,十五块一直到中午,我跟你说过的。"

"你可不是这么说的,你说一回是五块,十五块一直到中午,对吧?我清清楚楚听到你——"

"把门开大点,老大。"

"干吗?"我说。乖乖,我的心脏几乎他妈的要跳出嗓子眼。我真希望至少我是穿好了衣服,碰到这种事,只穿着睡衣太不像样了。

"快点儿,老大。"莫里斯这家伙说着用他的脏手猛推了我一下,我他妈差点儿一屁股坐到地上——他是个五大三粗、狗娘养的家伙。后来我所记得的,就是他和桑妮都进了房间,看那架势,好像这个破地方是他们自己的。桑妮那妞儿坐到窗台上,莫里斯这家伙坐在那把大椅子上,解开领子——他身穿电梯工的制服。乖乖,我真紧张。

"好了,老大,拿来吧,我还要回去干活呢。"

"我跟你说过有十遍了,我一分钱也不欠你们的。我已经给了她五——"

"少废话,拿来吧。"

"凭什么我得再给她五块?"我说,我的声音颤抖得厉害,"你们想敲诈我。"

莫里斯这家伙把制服上的扣子全解开了。他里面只穿了个衬衫假领,根本没穿衬衫什么的。他的肚子又大又肥,毛烘烘的。"谁也没有敲诈谁。"他说,"拿来吧,老大。"

"我不给。"

我说了后,他从椅子上起身向我走来,看上去就好像他很累很累,要么很烦很烦。天哪,我真的吓坏了。我记得我大概是抱着胳膊,我觉得如果我他妈不是只穿着**睡衣**,情况还没那么糟糕。

"拿来吧,老大。"他一直走到我跟前,我在那儿站着。他只会说这一句:"拿来吧,老大。"真是个蠢蛋。

"我不给。"

"老大,这可是你让我不得不对你动点儿粗了,我也不想,不过看来非得这么着。"他说,"你欠我们五块。"

"我不欠你们五块,"我说,"你敢动粗,我就会大叫,把旅馆里的每个人都吵醒,还有警察什么的。"我的声音颤抖得一塌糊涂。

"叫吧,把他妈嗓子叫破都行,没问题。"莫里斯这家伙说,"你想让你爸妈知道你跟个婊子过了一晚上吗?就你这种大家公子?"他说话可真厉害,很难听,真的是。

"别烦我了。如果你**当初说的**是十块,那另当别论,可是你分明——"

"到底给不给?"他把我顶在那扇破门上,居高临下地对着我,他那毛烘烘的烂肚子就挡在那儿。

"别烦我了,快滚出去。"我说。我的胳膊还在抱着,天哪,我可真是个笨蛋。

这时桑妮头一次开了口。"嗨,莫里斯,想不想让我去拿他的钱包?"她说,"就放在那个什么的里面。"

"好吧,去拿。"

"别动我的钱包!"

"拿到了。"桑妮说,手里对我晃着五块钱,"看见了吗?我拿的只是你欠我的钱,我可不是小偷。"

突然,我哭了起来。我后悔得不得了,干吗要哭呢,可我真的哭了。"对,你不是个小偷,"我说,"你只是偷了五——"

"闭嘴。"莫里斯说着推了我一下。

"嗨,甭理他了。"桑妮说,"快点儿,嗨,他欠我们的已经拿到了,走吧。嗨,快点儿。"

"我就来。"莫里斯答应着,但是没动地方。

"我是说真的,莫里斯,甭理他了。"

"是谁出口伤人?"他说,一副他妈的清白无辜的样子,接着用手指狠弹了一下我的睡衣。我不告诉你他弹了哪儿,可是让我疼得要命,我说他是个混账下流的蠢蛋。"说什么?"他说着把手放在耳朵背后,好像是个聋子,"说什么?我是什么?"

我可以说还在哭着,我他妈简直气疯了,而且很紧张。"你是个下流的蠢蛋,"我说,"你是个敲诈人的蠢蛋,再过两年,你就会变成那种在街上向人讨一毛钱,好去喝口咖啡的穷光蛋。你那身脏外套上沾的全是鼻涕,你还会——"

这时他揍了我一拳,我根本没有试着躲开,感到的只是肚子上挨了要命的一下。

可我也没被打昏还是怎么样,因为我还记得我倒在地板上,抬头看他们走出去,还把门给带上了。后来我在地板上躺了很久,跟那次和斯特拉雷德打完架后一样,只是这次我觉得我快死了,真的。我有种要被淹死还是怎么样的感觉,问题是我几乎无法呼吸。最后,我起来去厕所时,只能弯着腰,手捂着肚子。

我疯了,向上帝发誓,我真的是。去厕所走到半路时,我开始有点儿装作我的肚子上挨了颗子弹,莫里斯这家伙打的。我这是正要去厕所喝一大杯波本威士忌什么的稳稳情绪,准备好真正开始行动。我想象自己从他妈厕所出来,穿着整齐,口袋里揣了把自动手枪,脚步有点儿趔趄。然后我会走楼梯,不坐电梯。我会紧紧扶着栏杆,嘴边不时淌下一点儿血。我会怎么样呢？我会走下几层楼——捂着肚子，血流得到处都是——然后按电梯铃，莫里斯这家伙一开门，就会看到我手里握了一把手枪。他会大叫，声音很尖，是吓破胆的声音。他向我求饶，可我不管，照样拿枪打他，把六颗子弹全打进他毛烘烘的肚子里。然后，我会把手枪扔进电梯门——在我抹掉上面的指纹后。之后我会一路爬回房间，给简打个电话，叫她过来给我包扎肚子。我还想象在我流血时，她点了根烟拿着让我抽。

全是他妈的破电影，能毁了你，我不是开玩笑。

我在厕所里待了有一个钟头，洗个澡而已。然后我又回到床上，过了很久才睡着——我根本不困——后来真的睡着了。可我真正想干的是自杀，我觉得我想从窗户跳下去。要是能先搞清楚在我落地后，肯定有人马上盖住我，我大概真的会。我可不想让一群蠢货伸长脖子，看我那副血淋淋的样子。

15

我没睡太久,因为醒来时,我想才十点钟左右。抽完一根烟后,我马上觉得肚子很饿。之前最后一次吃东西,还是跟布罗萨德和阿克利去埃吉斯镇看电影时吃的那两个汉堡包,已经是很久以前的事了,感觉好像已经过了半个世纪。电话机就在我旁边,我开始拨电话下去,叫他们给我送早餐,可又有点儿担心是由莫里斯这家伙送上来。你要是以为我很想再次见到莫里斯,那你可是疯掉了。所以我只是在床上躺了一会儿,又抽了一根烟。我想到可以给简这妞儿打个电话,看她有没有到家,可是我没心情。

我所做的,是给萨莉·海斯这妞儿打了个电话。她上的是玛丽·A.伍德拉夫中学,我知道她已经到家,因为几星期前她给我写过一封信。我不是很迷她,不过说来认识她也有好几年了。我这样的蠢人一直觉得她很聪明,之所以如此,是因为她知道很多戏剧以及文学之类的玩意儿。如果有谁知道很多这类东西,要想发现这人是不是真蠢,就需要过上相当长一段时间才可以。以萨莉这妞儿为例,我是过了**好几年**才发现这点的。我觉得要不是我们老是他妈的黏在一起,我可能很早就会发现这一点。可我有个大毛病,就是不管是谁,只要跟我一起黏糊糊过,我都会觉得她是个脑瓜很聪明的人。这两者之间是他妈毫无联系,可我仍然老是这样认为。

不管怎么样,我给她打了个电话。先是她们家女佣接的电话,然后是她爸爸,最后才是她来听电话。"萨莉吗?"我问。

"我是——你是谁呀?"她问。她可真是有点儿虚伪,我已经跟她爸爸说过我是谁了。

"霍尔顿·考尔菲尔德。你好吗?"

"霍尔顿!我很好!你呢?"

"非常好。喂,你怎么样?我是说学校里怎么样?"

"还可以,"她说,"我是说——你也知道的了。"

"太好了。听我说,不知道你今天忙不忙。虽然今天是星期天,可星期天总会有一两场日场戏,也就是慈善演出什么的。想不想去看?"

"我很想去,极好啊。"

极好,要说有哪个词儿最让我讨厌,就得数它了,真虚伪。我脑子里一闪念,想告诉她忘了什么日场戏的事,可我们还是闲聊了半天,应该说是她闲聊了半天,我没法插话。一开始,她说的是某个哈佛大学生的事——很可能是个大一的,她当然没说——他对她穷追不舍,**白天黑夜**都给她打电话,白天黑夜——逗死我了。接着她又说还有一个家伙,是西点军校在校生,为了她也是要死去活来。真是不得了。我让她两点钟在贝尔特摩饭店的大钟下等我,别去晚,因为演出大概两点半开始,而她一贯爱迟到。然后我就挂掉了电话。她真叫我头疼,不过长得倒挺好。

跟萨莉这妞儿约好后,我起床穿好衣服,收拾好行李。离开房间前,我又往窗外看了一眼,想看看那些变态佬在干吗,可是他们的窗帘全拉上了。一到第二天早晨,这些家伙全都变成本分十足的人。我于是乘电梯下楼结账,没看到莫里斯那家伙,不过我当然也懒得找他,那个杂种。

我在旅馆外打了辆的士,可是对于去哪儿没他妈一点儿概念。我无处可去,那天才是星期天,我要到星期三才能回家——要么**最早**也只能在星期二,当然我也不想再去另外一家旅馆被狠揍一顿。我就让司机送我去中央大火车站,就在贝尔特摩饭店附近,迟一点我会跟萨莉在那儿见面。我合计了一下该怎么办。我要先把手提箱寄存到那里的保管箱，他们给了我钥匙后我去吃早餐，我有点儿饿了。还在的士上时，我把钱包掏出来随便数了数钱。我记不清到底剩多少，可是根本没多少了。过去两周左右，我花钱如流水，真的。从本质上说，我是他妈大手大脚的人，花不完就会丢掉。两次会有一次，我可以说甚至会在餐馆或夜总会之类的地方忘了拿找回的钱。我爸妈为此气得要命，也不能怪他们。不过我爸很有钱，我不知道他挣多少——这种事他从来不跟我说——我想会是很多。他是个公司的律师，干那种活真的能大把搂钱。还有一点让我知道他有钱，他一再投资百老汇演出，却老是亏本。他这样投资，把我妈气得发疯。我弟弟艾里死后，她一直感觉身体很差，精神很紧张。也是因为这个缘故，我特别不想让她知道我又被开除了。

把手提箱放进火车站的一个保管箱后，我就走进一家小小的三明治吧吃早餐。我那顿早餐吃得很多，是对我来说——橙汁、火腿、炒蛋、烤面包片和咖啡。一般情况下，我只喝点橙汁。我的饭量很小，真的，所以我他妈才瘦成了皮包骨头。照我这样子，应该多吃点含淀粉之类的垃圾，好长些分量，我却从来没那样吃过。在外面吃饭，我通常只吃一个瑞士奶酪三明治喝一杯麦乳精。虽说吃得不多，可是麦乳精里有很多维生素。H. V. 考尔菲尔德，我的名字是霍尔顿·维生素·考尔菲德。

我正在吃鸡蛋时，两个修女拎着手提箱还有别的东西走进来，就在餐台边挨着我坐下。我想她们是去另外一间修道院之类的地方，在等火车。看来她们不知道究竟该怎样放手提箱，我就帮了她们一把。她们的手提箱是看上去很不值钱的货色——不是真皮之类。这没什么，我也知道，但是我讨厌看到别人用这种便宜货。这听起来很不像话，但是如果别人拎着这种便宜的手提箱，仅仅*看*到箱子，我甚至就会讨厌起这个人来。这种事我遇到过一次。在埃克顿岗中学时，有段时间我跟一个叫迪克·斯莱格尔的住一起。他的手提箱是那种很便宜的货色，他经常把它放到床下边，而不是搁到架子上，那样就不会有人看到他的和我的放在一起。这件事让我觉得真他妈没劲儿,老是想把我的扔掉算了,甚至跟他**换**也行。我的手提箱是马克·克罗斯牌的,是真正牛皮之类的玩意儿,估计值不少钱。可是说来好笑,后来就发生了这么一件事:我最后**把我的**手提箱放到**我的**床下边,而不是搁到架子上,这样一来,斯莱格尔这家伙就不会有他妈的自卑情结了。可是他怎么做呢?就在我把手提箱在床下放了一天后,他又拖出来搁到架子上。他干吗要那样做,我是过了一阵子才琢磨出来。原来,他想让别人以为我的手提箱是他的,他真的是这个目的,在这点上,他是个很可笑的家伙。他经常就我的东西说些很难听的话,比如说我的手提箱吧,他经常说太新了,太有中产阶级味了,这是他他妈最喜欢说的话。他要么在哪儿读到过,要么在哪儿听说过。我的东西全他妈有中产阶级味,连我的钢笔也是,尽管他经常向我借用,可是仍然有中产阶级味。我们在一起才住了两个月,后来我们俩都申请换房间。好玩的是,和他分开后,我还有点儿想念他呢,因为他他妈的还挺有幽默感,我们在一起有时很开心。如果说他也想念我,我才不会觉得奇怪呢。一开始,他说我的东西有中产阶级味时,只是跟我开玩笑,我他妈也不当回事——事实上,这**的**确好玩。然后过上一阵子就看得出,他不再是开玩笑了。问题是,如果你的手提箱比他们的好很多,你们就很难做室友——如果你的是真正的**好**货色,而他们的并不是。你觉得他们要是有脑子,而且很有幽默感,就不会把谁的手提箱更好当回事,但是他们在乎,他们的确在乎。这就是我跟像斯特拉雷德那样的笨杂种一起住的原因,至少他的手提箱跟我的一样好。

扯远了,当时那两个修女就坐在我旁边,我们算是聊了起来。挨着我坐的那个修女拎着一个麦秆编的篮子,就是在圣诞节你可以看到修女以及救世军小女孩提着向人募捐的那种篮子。她们站在街角,特别在第五大道上,就是在大百货公司之类地方的门口那儿。我旁边那个修女的篮子掉在地上,我伸手帮她捡起来。我问她是不是出来搞慈善募捐的,她说不是。她说装箱时没法把篮子装进去,所以只好拎在手上。她看着我时笑得很甜。她鼻子挺大,戴着不是很好看的铁边眼镜,不过那张脸长得真漂亮。"我还以为你们是募捐的呢。"我说,"我可以少捐点儿,你们可以先保管,一直到募捐的时候。"

"噢,你真是太好了。"她说。另一个修女,也就是她的朋友,也扭头看我。那位在边喝咖啡边看一本小黑书。好像是《圣经》,不过太薄了,只是本跟《圣经》有关的书。她们要的早餐都是烤面包片和咖啡,让我感到沮丧。要是我吃的是火腿和鸡蛋什么的,而别人只是要了烤面包片和咖啡,我就会很不开心。

她们接受了我捐的十块钱,还一直追问我确不确定能捐那么多。我说我身上还有不少钱呢,她们却好像不怎么相信我的话,最后她们还是收下了,一个劲儿向我表示感谢,以至于让我感到难堪。我跟她们换了个话题,谈些一般的事,问她们是去哪儿。她们说自己是老师,从芝加哥来,要去不知位于第一百六十八还是第一百八十六街,要么是在住宅区那边更远地方的一间修道院教书。那个坐在我旁边、戴着铁边眼镜的说她教语文,她的朋友教历史和有关美国政府的课。然后我他妈的一个劲儿琢磨起坐在我旁边教语文的那位作为一个修女,在读到有些书时会怎么想。那些书倒不一定很黄,而是有些爱来爱去的内容,比如说托马斯·哈代的小说《还乡》里面的尤斯塔西娅·维尔吧,这个人物不是很淫荡,但尽管这样,我还是忍不住好奇对一个修女来说,在读到有关尤斯塔西娅这妞儿的地方时,心里会怎么想。我当然什么也没说,只是说语文是我学得最好的一门课。

"噢,是吗?噢,我真高兴!"那个戴眼镜教语文的说,"你今年读了什么?我很想知道。"她真的很和气。

"这个嘛,我们学的主要是盎格鲁-撒克逊文学。《贝奥武甫》,格伦德尔,还有'兰德尔,我的儿子',全是那种。可我们有时还得另外读些书,好多拿些学分。我读过托马斯·哈代的《还乡》,还有《罗密欧与朱丽叶》《恺撒——"

"噢,《罗密欧与朱丽叶》!太好了!你难道不觉得它特别好吗?"她的口气不怎么像是个修女。

"对,我喜欢,我很喜欢。有几个地方我不喜欢,但总的说来很感人。"

"哪些地方不喜欢?还记得吗?"

说实话,跟她讨论《罗密欧与朱丽叶》有点儿让人尴尬。我是说在这出戏里,有些地方男女之情写得挺多,而她是个修女。但既然她问起来,我就跟她讨论了一会儿。"嗯,我不是很喜欢罗密欧和朱丽叶,"我说,"我是说我还算喜欢他们,可是——我说不好。他们有时候挺招人烦的,我是说茂丘西奥老兄死的时候,我感觉比看到罗密欧和朱丽叶死还要难过。问题是茂丘西奥被捅死后,我一直不太喜欢罗密欧。捅死人的是朱丽叶的堂哥,叫什么来着?"

"提尔伯特。"

"没错,是提尔伯特,"我说——我老是忘了那个家伙叫什么,"那得怨罗密欧,我是说整部戏里我最喜欢的就是茂丘西奥老兄。我说不好。蒙太古还有凯普莱特家族的人都还行——特别是朱丽叶——可是茂丘西奥,他有点儿——不容易说清楚,他很聪明,而且很会逗乐。问题是我看到有人被杀,就会气得发疯——特别是一个很聪明、很会逗乐的人——该怨别人。罗密欧和朱丽叶,至少怨他们自己。"

"你在哪儿上学?"她问我,大概是不想再谈罗密欧和朱丽叶的事。

我告诉她是潘西。她说她听说过,还说那是所很好的学校,我没有反驳她。然后另外一个修女,就是那个教历史和有关美国政府的,开口说她们该走了。我把她们的账单拿过来,可是她们不让我付钱,那个戴眼镜的非要我把账单给她。

"你已经够慷慨的了,"她说,"你是个很可爱的孩子。"她很和气,一点儿没错。她让我有点儿想起了欧内斯特·莫罗这货的妈妈,就是在火车上遇到的那位,特别在她微笑时,简直一个样。"我们跟你聊得真愉快。"她说。

我说跟她们聊，我也觉得很愉快，这是真话。我心想，如果不是因为跟她们聊天时，我从头到尾都在担心她们会突然想了解我是不是信天主教，我还可以聊得更愉快些。天主教徒总是想知道你是不是天主教徒，这种事我遇到过很多次。我知道部分原因是我的姓是爱尔兰姓，而且爱尔兰人后裔一般都信天主教。事实上，我爸曾经是个天主教徒，但和我妈结婚后，他就放弃了天主教信仰。不过天主教徒总想弄清楚你是不是天主教徒，甚至在他们还不知道你姓什么时也是这样。在伍顿中学时，我认识一个信天主教的同学，路易斯·山尼，他是我在那儿认识的第一个同学。那是开学的第一天，我和他坐在学校的破医务室外面的头两把椅子上等待体检，我们聊起了网球。他对网球特别感兴趣，我也是。他说他每年夏天都去福里斯特希尔看全国比赛，我说我也是。我们就聊起了几位网球好手，聊了大半天。他知道很多网球的事，特别是就他那样一个小孩子而言。然后过了一会儿，就在他妈聊着天时，他问了我一句："你也许知道镇上哪儿有天主教堂？"问题是，从他问我的样子看得出，他是想了解我是不是天主教徒，他真的是这个目的。倒不是他有偏见还是怎么样，只是想知道而已。我们聊网球让他觉得挺开心，但如果知道我是个天主教徒，看得出他将会更开心。这种把戏总让我特别来气，我不是说它让我们没法继续聊下去了还是怎么样——并非如此——可肯定对聊天没他妈什么好处，这就是我对那两个修女没问我是不是天主教徒感到高兴的原因。就算她们问了，也不会让聊天没法继续下去，但很可能感觉不一样。并不是说我对天主教徒有什么不满，没有。我要是个天主教徒，很可能也会那样。说起来，这就跟我说过的手提箱的事情一样。我是说如果你想愉快地聊天，问这个绝无任何好处，我只是这个意思。

两个修女起身准备离开时，我干了件很愚蠢、很让人难堪的事。我当时正在抽烟，起身跟她们说再会时，不小心把烟喷到了她们脸上。我不是故意的，可的确那样干了。我像个疯子似的一个劲儿道歉，她们很有礼貌，并不在意，可这总是件很让人难堪的事。

她们离开后，我开始为只给她们十块钱而感到后悔，但问题是我跟萨莉·海斯这妞儿约好要看演出，得留点钞票买戏票什么的，可我还是有点儿后悔。钱这个王八蛋，到头来总他妈让人伤心不已。

16

吃完早餐才中午十二点左右,跟萨莉那妞儿见面要等到两点,我就开始走路,走了很远。我在想着那两个修女,没办法不想。我老是想着她们提的又旧又破的草篮,教书之余,她们会提着那种篮子到处募捐。我一个劲儿想象我妈或者别人——要么是我姑妈,要么是萨莉·海斯那位疯疯癫癫的妈妈——提着个又旧又破的篮子,站在一家百货商场外头为穷人募捐。难以想象啊。想象我妈那样做还不算难,难的是对另外两个。我姑妈挺乐善好施的——她为红十字会做过很多事——可她很讲究穿着,凡是做跟慈善有关的事,她总是很讲究穿着,还抹上口红之类的破玩意儿。我想象不出来,如果她做慈善工作时只能穿黑衣服,也不能抹口红,那她还会去搞什么慈善活动。萨莉·海斯这妞儿的妈妈更离谱,要让她提个篮子到处募捐,就只有一个办法,那就是每个人捐款的同时也拍拍她的马屁。如果他们只是把钞票扔进篮子便走人,不跟她说一句话,对她视而不见,那她干一小时左右就会撂挑子。她会觉得厌烦,会把篮子交给别人,然后去哪个豪华地方吃午餐。这就是我喜欢那两个修女的原因,首先你看得出,她们从来不会去什么豪华地方吃午餐。我一想到这儿,就感到他妈的特别难受,就是她们从来不会去什么豪华地方吃午餐还是怎么样。我知道这不是很重要,可还是为此感到难受。

我开始往百老汇的方向走,只是他妈的觉得想那样,因为我好几年没去过那儿了。另外,我想找一家星期天开门的唱片店,想给菲比买张名叫《小小的雪莉·比恩斯》的唱片。这张唱片很难找,是关于一个小孩儿因为掉了两颗门牙嫌丢人,不肯出门的故事,我在潘西时听过。一个不跟我住同一层楼的同学有这张唱片,我想让他卖给我,因为知道菲比准会喜欢得不得了,可是他不肯。这是张很老也很棒的唱片,是个名叫埃丝特尔·弗莱彻的黑人女歌手大约二十年前录的。她唱得很有南方爵士乐和妓院的风格,可是一点儿也不腻人。换个白人女歌手来唱,准会把这首歌唱得很他妈**可爱**。可是埃丝特尔·弗莱彻这妞儿太他妈会唱了,这是我听过的最棒的唱片之一。我琢磨能在一家星期天开门的唱片店里买到这张唱片,然后把它带去公园。菲比星期天经常在公园里溜冰,我也知道她主要在哪儿玩。

那天不像前一天那么冷,可还是没出太阳,所以走路不是很舒服,不过眼前就有很好看的一幕。一家人正好在我前面走,看得出,他们刚从教堂出来——两个大人和一个六岁左右的小孩儿。他们看起来有点儿像是穷人。当爹的头上戴了顶珍珠灰色的帽子,穷人想穿得像模像样时,特别喜欢戴那种帽子。他和他老婆只管边走边聊,完全不管他们的小孩儿。那个小孩儿太可爱了,他不在人行道上,而是在紧挨马路牙子的马路上走。他装作在一条笔直的线条上走路,像小孩子会做的那样,还一直在哼唱。我走得离他近了些,好听到他在唱什么。他在唱一首歌:"如果有人抓到别人在穿越麦田。"他的声音很小,看得出,唱歌只是他妈的自得其乐而已。街上汽车呼啸而过,尖厉的刹车声到处响个不停。他爹妈对他不管不问,他还是靠着马路牙子走,唱着"如果有人抓到别人在穿越麦田"。那让我感觉好了点,不是很沮丧了。

百老汇那儿人头攒动,混乱不堪。那天是星期天,而且才中午十二点左右,却依然是人头攒动。人人都赶着去看电影——就在派拉蒙或是阿斯特、滨河、首都之类的破影院。更糟糕的是,因为是星期天,所以每个人都打扮得整整齐齐。而最差劲的是,看得出他们都**想**看电影。看着他们,真让我受不了。我对那些没别的事情可做,所以只好去看电影的人尚能理解,但是那些确实**想**看电影,而且脚步飞快,好早点赶到的人，他们让我觉得他妈的没劲儿透顶。特别当我看到成千上万人在那儿排着长长的队，一直沿着街区排下去，万分耐心地等候进场时。乖乖，我真恨不得飞着离开百老汇这破地方。我运气不错，找的第一家唱片店里，就有《小小的雪莉·比恩斯》这张唱片。他们要价五块，因为这张唱片很难买到，我无所谓。乖乖，这张唱片让我一下子心花怒放，真想一步跨到公园，去看菲比这丫头在不在，好给她唱片。

从唱片店出来后，经过一家杂货店我就进去了。我琢磨也许可以给简的家里打个电话，看她放假回来了没有，就进了电话间，给她打了个电话，可唯一的麻烦是她妈妈接的电话，就只好挂掉，我可不想跟她没完没了地聊，反正我根本不想跟哪个女孩的妈妈在电话上聊。不过我至少应该问一下简回来了没有，这对我没什么，可我不是很想问她，做这种事，得有心情才行。

我还得买他妈的戏票，就去买了份报纸看有什么戏。因为是星期天，所以演出只有三场左右。我去买了两张前排的票，剧名叫《我了解我的爱》，是场慈善演出什么的。我不太想看，但我了解萨莉这妞儿，她可是虚伪至极。只要跟她说我已经买了那出戏的票，她就会两眼发直，兴奋得不得了，就因为是伦特夫妇演的。她喜欢那种故作深奥且枯燥的戏，且由伦特夫妇演出。我不喜欢看，而且说句实话，我对任何戏剧都不太喜欢。戏剧不像电影那样糟糕，可是当然也根本不值得着迷。首先是因为我讨厌演员，他们从来演得不像真实的人，还自以为演得像。有些好演员演得还稍微沾点儿边，可是也不好看。如果有哪个演员确实不错，却总是能让人看得出，他们也这样自我认为，这就坏了事。就拿劳伦斯·奥利维尔来说吧，我看过他在《哈姆雷特》里的演出，去年 D. B. 带我和菲比看的。去看之前，他请我们吃了顿午餐。他已经看过这出戏，午餐时把它讲得让我其他妈想看，但是到看的时候，我却不太喜欢，我就是看不出劳伦斯·奥利维尔爵士有何精彩绝伦之处，真的。他说话声音很好听，长得也帅极了，看他在舞台上走动或决斗什么的倒不赖，但是跟D. B.向我描述的哈姆雷特对不上号。他他妈太像个将军了，而不是个性格忧郁、总把事情办砸了的家伙。整出戏里，最好的一幕是当奥费利娅这妞儿的哥哥——就是最后跟哈姆雷特决斗的那位——动身时，他爹给了他诸多建议。就在他爹给他诸多建议时，奥费利娅这妞儿跟她哥有点儿胡闹起来，把他的匕首从鞘里抽出来，对他挤眉弄眼，他还得装作很有兴趣听他爹在那儿大扯特扯。这一幕不错，让我喜欢得不得了，不过这种地方难得得到多少。唯一让菲比这丫头喜欢的，是哈姆雷特用手拍狗头，她觉得既滑稽又好看，的确如此。我得去看剧本才行，麻烦的是看这种东西时，我总是只能自个儿去看。如果哪个演员把它表演出来，我几乎不怎么听，而是一直担心他会不会表演得虚伪。

买了伦特夫妇演出的戏票后，我就打了辆的士去公园。我本来可以坐地铁什么的，因为口袋里的钞票有点儿见少了，可我只是想尽快离开百老汇那个破地方。公园里不怎么样。天气不太冷，太阳还是没露面。公园里除了狗屎、老头儿吐的痰和扔的烟头，以及好像坐上去就会知道全会是湿的长椅，似乎就没有别的。这幅景象真叫人泄气。不仅如此，时不时还会没来由地走着走着，就起一身鸡皮疙瘩。这儿完全没有快到圣诞的气氛，好像什么节也不会来到，可我还是往叫"林荫道"的那边走去，因为那是菲比在公园里常去的地方，她喜欢在靠近乐队演奏台的地方溜冰。说来好玩，我还是个小孩子时，也常爱去那儿溜冰。

可我到了那地方后，附近看不到她。倒是有几个小孩儿在溜冰，还有两个男孩在拿一个棒球玩游戏，但就是没见菲比。我看到一个跟她岁数差不多的小女孩一个人坐在长椅上拧紧溜冰鞋，想着她可能认识菲比，能告诉我她去哪儿了，就走过去挨着她坐下后问她："请问你认识菲比·考尔菲尔德吗？"

"谁？"她说。她下身穿了条牛仔裤，上身穿了一二十件羊毛衫，看得出都是她妈妈手织的，因为鼓鼓囊囊的，难看至极。

"菲比·考尔菲尔德，她住在第七十一街，上四年级，在——"

"你认识菲比?"

"对,我是她哥。你知道她去哪儿了?"

"她在卡隆小姐的班上,对不对?"这个小不点儿问我。

"我不知道。对了,我想是吧。"

"她很可能在博物馆,我们上星期六去过了。"小不点儿说。

"哪座博物馆?"我问她。

她微微耸了耸肩膀。"不知道,"她说,"反正是博物馆。"

"我知道,可是是有画的那个呢,还是有印第安人的?"

"有印第安人的。"

"非常感谢。"我说着起身要走,但又忽然想到这天是星期天。"今天是星期天。"我告诉小不点儿。

她抬头看着我说:"那她不会在那儿。"

她拧紧溜冰鞋时拧得很吃力,没戴手套什么的,两手冻得通红,我就帮了她一把。乖乖,我有好多年没摸过溜冰鞋钥匙了,感觉却一点儿也不陌生。你可以再过五十年,在某个天色漆黑的时候拿一把溜冰鞋钥匙放到我手里,我还能说出是什么。帮她拧紧时,她对我说了声谢谢。她是个很可爱而且有礼貌的小孩儿。天哪,我给一个小孩儿拧紧溜冰鞋什么的,而他们显得可爱而且有礼貌时,我真是太高兴了。小孩儿多数都那样,真的是。我问她愿不愿意跟我去喝杯热巧克力什么的,可她说不行,谢谢了。她说她得跟她的朋友见面。小孩儿老是要去跟朋友见面,让我乐死了。

尽管是星期天,菲比不会跟她班上的同学一起去参观,尽管天气很潮湿,感觉很糟糕,我还是一路走着,穿过公园去自然历史博物馆。我知道那个用溜冰鞋钥匙的小不点儿指的就是那座,我可以说对它了如指掌。菲比上的学校跟我以前上的是同一所,以前我们也经常去那儿。我们有位老师,艾格尔汀格小姐,几乎他妈的每星期六都带我们去。有时看动物,有时看印第安人在古代做的东西,如陶器、草篮之类。想起那些，我心里很高兴，甚至现在也是。我记得我们看完印第安人的东西后，会到大礼堂看一部名叫《哥伦布》的电影。他们老是放哥伦布发现美洲的电影。一开始，是哥伦布费尽老劲儿游说费迪南德国王和伊莎贝拉女王借钱给他买船，然后是水手们造哥伦布的反什么的。谁都他妈的不关心哥伦布怎么着，只是大家都带了很多糖块和口香糖什么的，所以礼堂里有股很好闻的气味，让人老是觉得外面在下雨——没下也这样觉得——而礼堂里是世界上最后一块干燥而且温暖的好地方。我真喜欢这座破博物馆。我记得去礼堂要穿过一间印第安人的屋子，那间屋子很长、很长，在里面只许小声说话。老师在前面走，一班人跟在后面，分成两排，每人有个伙伴，通常我都是跟一个名叫格特鲁德·莱文的小女孩儿一起。她老是想拉着我的手，可她的手不是黏糊糊，就是汗津津的。地面全是石头铺的，要是手里拿了些玻璃球掉到地上，它们就会跳来跳去跳个没完，响作一团。老师就会让全班停步，然后走回来看究竟是怎么回事，可是艾格尔汀格小姐从来不发火。后来我们会经过一个印第安人打仗用的长长的独木舟，约有他妈的三辆凯迪拉克汽车接起来那么长，里面坐着二十个印第安人，有人划桨，有人只是站着，样子很凶，脸上都涂了颜色。独木舟后部坐了个很瘆人的家伙，戴了张面具。他是巫医，尽管让我毛骨悚然，可我还是喜欢他。还有，如果在经过时你碰了桨或者别的什么，警卫中的某一个就会说："孩子们，什么也别碰。"不过他的语气总是很温和，不像个破警察什么的。之后会经过一个大玻璃箱，里面有个印第安人用两根木棍一起搓着取火，还有个印第安女人在织一条毛毯。她弯着身子，所以能看到她的胸脯什么的。我们经常会偷偷瞟一眼，连女孩儿也是，因为她们也只是小孩子，胸部不比我们的大到哪儿去。然后，就在要进礼堂前，我们会经过门边那个爱斯基摩人。他坐在冰湖上的洞口边，正在从洞里钓鱼，洞旁边有一两条他已经钓上来的鱼。乖乖，那座博物馆里到处是玻璃箱，楼上还有更多，里面有从水洞里饮水的鹿，还有冬天飞往南方的小鸟，能看出离你最近的鸟全是标本,用铁丝吊着。远处的只是画上去的,但看样子都好像真的在往南飞。要是低下头差不多仰视,会觉得它们好像更是急着往南方飞。不过那座博物馆最好的一点是里面无论什么,都会保持原样不变,什么都不会改变地方。你可以去那儿去上十万次,那个爱斯基摩人钓到的还是那两条鱼,小鸟还在飞向南方,鹿还在从水洞里饮水,它的角还那么漂亮,腿还那么漂亮精瘦,那个露胸脯的印第安女人还在织同样的毯子。什么都不会改变,改变的只有你,倒不是说你长大了很多还是怎么样,准确点说并非如此,你只是变样了,如此而已。你这次穿了件大衣,要么上次在队里跟你做伴的那个小孩儿得了猩红热,这样你就有了个新伙伴;要么是代课老师带队,而不是艾格尔汀格小姐;要么你听到你父母在浴室里大吵一架;要么经过街上的一个水坑,上面有层汽油闪着彩虹般的光亮。我是说你会在某种程度上不一样了,我说不清楚我究竟什么意思。就算能够,我也说不准不想解释呢。

走路时,我从口袋里取出猎帽戴上。我知道不会碰到认识我的人,而且外面太潮了。我走啊走啊,脑子里老是想着菲比丫头跟我一样,星期六去那座博物馆的事,而且每次去,她都会有点儿不同。想这种事不会让我沮丧,可是也不会让我特别开心。有些东西该保持现状,应该把它们粘在大玻璃箱子里就别动了。我知道不可能,反正我认为不这样就太糟糕了。总之,我走路时一直想着的就是那些事。

我经过一个游乐场,就停下来看两个很小的小孩儿玩跷跷板。其中一个有点儿胖,我就把手放到了那个精瘦的小孩儿这头,好平衡一下重量。可是我看得出他们不喜欢我在旁边,就让他们自己玩了。

后来就发生了一件有意思的事。到博物馆门口后,我突然觉得就算给我一百万,我也不想进去了——我就是不感兴趣——而我可是穿过整座破公园,一路盼望着来到这儿的呀。菲比在里面的话,我大概会进去,可是她不在,我就打了辆的士去贝尔特摩饭店。我不太想去,可是我他妈已经跟萨莉约好了。

17

到了后还很早,我就坐在大钟旁边大堂里的一张皮沙发上看女孩儿。很多学校早就放假了,所以附近有数不清的女孩儿要么站着,要么坐着,在等她们约的人出现。她们有的腿交叉着,有的腿没交叉,有的腿很漂亮,有的腿很难看。有的女孩儿看上去很不错,有的看上去让人觉得如果了解她,就知道她是个贱货。那样真不错,看风景,你该明白我的意思。但是说起来,那样也有点儿让人沮丧,因为我一直在琢磨她们以后到底会他妈遇到什么事,我是说在她们高中或大学毕业后。我琢磨她们很可能会跟那些蠢货结婚,那些家伙老是吹嘘自己的破车一加仑汽油能跑多少多少英里,要么会因为输了高尔夫球闷闷不乐,孩子气十足,连玩乒乓球这种破比赛时也是。还有那种很下作的家伙,从来不读书的家伙,惹人烦的家伙——不过我得小心点,我是说得小心别说有些家伙是惹人烦,我老是吃不透他们,真的。在埃克顿岗中学时,我跟一个名叫哈里斯·麦克林的同学一块儿住了两个月左右。他很聪明,可也是我遇到过的人中最烦人的一个。他说话粗声粗气,嘴巴几乎从来没合上过,一直在说话,从不住口,而且最让人难以忍受也是最关键的,是他说的从来不是你想听的。可是他有一样很在行,我从来没见过有谁吹口哨比这个混蛋吹得还好,在铺床或者往壁橱里挂东西时——他老是在往壁橱里挂东西,真让我着急——如果不用他那副粗嗓门说话,就会一边干一边吹口哨。他竟然还会吹一点古典音乐,但通常只是爵士乐。他能把一些像《铁皮屋顶布鲁斯》那样爵士味十足的曲子吹得既好听又毫不费劲——就在他往壁橱里挂东西时——真的好听至极。当然，我从来没**告诉**他我觉得他口哨吹得很棒，我是说，谁也不会走到别人面前对他说："你口哨吹得很棒。"尽管他快把我烦得疯掉了，我还是跟他同住了差不多整整两个月，就因为他口哨吹得特棒，是我听过的吹得最好的。所以说，我对惹人烦的人不了解。也许不应该因为哪个好女孩嫁给他们就很不开心，他们中的大多数不会伤害别人，也许不为人知的是他们的口哨都吹得很棒什么的，谁他妈知道？反正我不知道。

终于，萨莉这妞儿开始走上台阶，我往下走去接她。她的样子特别漂亮，真的。她穿了件黑色的大衣，还戴了一顶好像是黑色的贝雷帽。她几乎从来不戴帽子，但那顶贝雷帽看着不错。有趣的是，第一眼看到她时，我觉得我想跟她结婚呢。我疯了，我甚至不怎么**喜欢**她，可是一下子觉得我爱上了她，想跟她结婚。向上帝发誓，我疯了，我承认。

"霍尔顿！"她说，"见到你真是太棒了！**我们好久**没见面了。"跟她在哪儿见面时，她说话嗓门很大，叫人难堪。别人倒不会介意这一点，因为她他妈太漂亮了，可她那样总是让我很反感。

"见到**你**真好，"我说，这也是真心实意的话，"**你**怎么样？"

"绝对太棒了，我来晚了吗？"

我说没有，事实上她晚了十分钟左右，我他妈无所谓。《星期六晚邮报》什么的上面会登些破漫画，画的是男的在街角等，恼火得要命的样子，就因为约好的女友来晚了——全是胡画的。如果一个女孩儿见到你时很漂亮，谁他妈还会在乎她来晚了？谁也不会。"我们最好快点儿，"我说，"戏两点四十开演。"我们开始走下台阶去打的。

"看什么戏？"她问。

"不知道，有伦特夫妇演出，我只能买到这场戏的票。"

"伦特夫妇！噢，太棒了！"

我跟你说过，她听到是伦特夫妇演的就会疯掉。

打的去剧院时，我们在车上多少胡闹了一会儿。一开始她不肯，因为她抹了口红什么的,可是我对她引诱个没完,她也没办法。有两次,这辆破的士开着开着来了个急刹车,我他妈差点儿从座位上掉下去。这些混账司机从来不看往哪儿开,我肯定他们是这样的。我再跟你说件事,让你看我疯到何等程度:我们搂了半天后终于分开时,我跟她说我爱她。这当然是谎话,但事实上,我那样说的时候,是真心真意的。我疯了,向上帝发誓,我疯了。

"噢,亲爱的,我也爱你。"她说。接着,这口气还他妈没出完呢,她又说:"你答应我,留长头发吧,寸头开始过时了,再说你的头发很好看。"

好看个屁。

那出戏不像以前看过的有些那样差劲,可是也有点废话连篇,是关于一对老两口生活中没完没了的一段。开头时,他们都很年轻,女孩儿的父母不想让她嫁给那个男的,可她还是嫁了,后来就是他们一年年变老。当丈夫的去打仗了,当妻子的有个酒鬼弟弟。我对这种玩意儿没法很感兴趣,我是说我不太关心那家人有谁死了还是怎么样,无非全是一帮演员而已。那对夫妻倒是不错的老两口——说话很风趣——可我就是没办法对他们很感兴趣。首先呢,他们在整出戏里从头到尾要么喝茶,要么喝别的什么破玩意儿。每次看到他们,就有位管家在他们面前倒茶,要么那个妻子在给别人倒茶。他们每个人都一直上上下下舞台——老是看他们坐下去站起来,看得人头晕眼花。阿尔弗雷德·伦特和林恩·方丹演那对老两口,他们很不错,可是我不怎么喜欢,只能说他们与众不同吧。他们演得不像生活中的人,也不像演员,这很难解释清楚。他们演起来更像他们自知身为名流什么的,我是说他们还不错,可是过于不错了。他们其中一位说了一通后,另一位会紧接着说。按说演得应该像人们说话、互相插话那样,但问题是,他们演得过于像人们说话、互相插话了。他们表演得有点儿像老厄尼那样,就是在格林威治村弹钢琴的那位。一件事如果你做得太棒了,然后一来二去,不注意的话,你就会开始有点儿炫技,这样一来,你就没那么棒了。但不管怎说，他们还是演出里绝无仅有的——我是说伦特夫妇——只有他们看样子还像真的有脑子，我得承认。

第一幕结束后，我们跟那么多蠢材一起出去抽根烟。真是不得了，你这辈子也不会看到那么多装模作样的家伙凑到一起。每个人都大抽特抽，还在谈论那出戏，好让别人都听到，并了解他这个人有多聪明。有个傻乎乎的电影演员在我们旁边抽烟，我不知道他叫什么，他总在战争片里演一个要攻上高地时临阵退缩的家伙。他跟一个极其漂亮的金发女郎在一起，两人都尽量装出一副不胜厌烦的表情，好像他根本不知道别人正在看他，谦逊得要命，我觉得真是好玩。除了对伦特夫妇赞不绝口，萨莉这妞儿说话不多，因为她在忙着伸长脖子东张西望，扮出一副迷人的样子。突然，她看到大堂那边有个她**认识**的蠢材。身穿深灰色法兰绒西装和带格子纹的背心，绝对是那种名牌学校的学生，真是不得了。他靠近墙壁站着，在猛抽香烟，显出一副烦躁透顶的样子。萨莉这妞儿一个劲儿说："我**认识**那个在哪儿上学的男生。"无论带她去哪儿，总有她**认识**的人，要么是她自以为认识。她一个劲儿说着，直到我烦得要命，就对她说："你认识他，干吗不过去跟他好好亲亲嘴？他会高兴的。"我这么一说，她就生气了。最后，还是那个蠢材看到她，过来跟她打招呼。你真该看看他们打招呼的样子，活像两人有二十年没见过面了，你会觉得他们小时候在同一个浴缸里洗过澡还是怎么样，老朋友长、老朋友短，叫人想吐。好玩的是，他们很可能才见过**一次**面而已，就在装模作样的家伙们参加的一次派对上。最后，他们肉麻半天后，萨莉这妞儿为我们做了介绍。他名叫乔治，姓什么忘了——根本想不起来——在安多弗中学上学。不得了，真是不得了。你该见识一下萨莉这妞儿问他对这出戏的观感时他那副尊容。他是那种装模作样的家伙，为了回答别人的问题，得给自己腾点**地方**才行。他后退一步，刚好踩到身后一位女士的脚上，很可能把她的脚趾全踩碎了。他说这出戏**本身**算不上大手笔，可伦特夫妇当然绝对是天使。天使，岂有此理，**天使**，逗死我了。然后，他和萨莉这妞儿开始谈起许多他们都认识的人，我这辈子从来没听过那么虚伪的谈话。他们各逞所能，尽快想起各个地方，然后想到有什么人住在那儿，并提起他们的名字。到该回到座位上时，我真的快吐了，真的是。然后，第二幕演完后，他们**接着**聊，真他妈烦人。他们继续想起更多地方、更多住在那里的人。更要命的是，那个**蠢材**一副虚伪十足的名校学生腔调，就是那种很是懒洋洋的、自以为是的腔调，听着活像个女人，当起电灯泡来倒毫不**客气**，这杂种。戏结束后，我甚至有一阵子以为他他妈的会跟我们一起打车，因为他跟着我们走了有两个街区，可是他说还要跟一帮装模作样的家伙去喝鸡尾酒。我能想象到他们全坐在某间酒吧，一帮人都穿着花格子纹马甲，用他们那种懒洋洋、自以为是的腔调品评戏剧、书本和女人。那种家伙，让我恶心得要命。

在听那个上安多弗中学的装模作样的杂种扯了足足有十个小时后，等到我们坐上一辆的士时，我有点恨起萨莉这妞儿来。我已经打定主意送她回家——我真的准备好了——可是她说："我有个棒主意！"她老是有棒主意。"哎，"她说，"你什么时候回家吃饭？我是说你不是特别急着赶回家吧？你是不是必须在几点前赶回家？"

"我？不，没定什么时间。"我说。乖乖，我这辈子还没说过比这更真实的话呢，"怎么了？"

"我们去无线广播城滑冰吧！"

她有的总是这类主意。

"去无线广播城滑冰？你是说现在？"

"只玩个把小时。你不想去吗？你要是**不想去**——"

"我没说我不想去，"我说，"没问题，要是你想去的话。"

"真的吗？不想去就别这么**说**，我是说我**无所谓**，去不去都行。"

她真无所谓才怪呢。

"可以去租一套可爱的小滑雪裙，"萨莉这妞儿说，"珍妮特·卡尔茨上星期穿过的那种。"

这就是她那么热衷去的原因,她想穿那种刚好遮住屁股的小裙子。

我们就去了那儿。他们给了我们冰鞋后,又给了萨莉一件兜着屁股的蓝色小裙子。我得承认,她穿上后真他妈好看,我想她自己也不会不知道。她老是走在我前面,好让我看到她的小屁股有多好看。确实很好看,我得承认。

但好笑的是,我们是整个破滑冰场上滑得最差劲的,我是说的确**最差**,那儿有些高手。萨莉这妞儿的脚脖子总是左弯右弯,直到最后几乎弯到冰上为止。不只难看得要命,大概也疼得够呛。我知道我的脚腕是那样,疼得要命。在别人眼里,我们俩肯定是一景。更糟糕的是那儿至少有两百个看客,根本没别的事情可干,只是站在那儿看别人摔来摔去。

"你想不想进去找张台子坐,喝杯饮料什么的?"最后我跟她说。

"这可是你今天想到的最棒的主意了。"她说。她在**自戕**,残忍哪,我真的同情起她来。

我们脱下破冰鞋进了酒吧,可以在那儿喝杯饮料,看那些滑冰的重蹈你的覆辙。我们一坐下,萨莉这妞儿就取下手套,我给了她一根烟,看样子她不是很开心。侍者走过来,我帮她点了可乐——她没喝——我点了威士忌和苏打水,可是那个狗娘养的不肯给我拿,所以我也点了可乐。后来我划起火柴来,我处于某种心情时,经常那样做。我让火柴棒一直燃烧,直到没法拿住才丢进烟灰缸。这是种精神紧张时的习惯。

忽然,萨莉这妞儿很突然地问我:"喂,我得搞清楚,你圣诞节来不来我家帮我修剪圣诞树?我得搞清楚。"她因为滑冰时扭了脚踝,仍然有点儿恼火。

"我写信说过我会,你问了我有二十遍了,我当然会帮你。"

"我是说我得搞清楚。"她说着开始在这间破屋子里左看右看。

我突然不划火柴了,隔着桌子靠近了她,我脑子里颇有一些话题。

"嗨，萨莉。"我说。

"什么？"她说。她正在看室内那头的一个女孩儿。

"你有没有觉得受够了？"我说，"我是说你有没有害怕过除非去做点什么，否则无论什么都会糟透了？我是说你喜欢学校还有跟它有关的一切吗？"

"学校烦得要命。"

"我是问你讨不讨厌它？我知道学校烦得要命，可我问的是你讨厌它吗？"

"嗯，我不是真的讨厌它。你总得——"

"那我是讨厌它。乖乖，我真讨厌。"我说，"可是还不止如此呢，我讨厌一切，讨厌纽约的生活，等等。的士，还有麦迪逊大道上的巴士，那些司机什么的，老是嚷着叫人从后门下车，还有被介绍给称伦特夫妇是天使的虚伪的家伙，还有当你只是想出去一下时，却非得坐电梯上上下下，还有布鲁克斯兄弟服装店里的伙计，一天到晚给人量裤子，还有人们老是——"

"请你别嚷嚷。"萨莉这妞儿说。这话真好笑，因为我根本没有嚷嚷。

"就拿小汽车来说吧，"我说，我的声音很平静，"多数人对小汽车可真是迷得要命，连车上划一道痕都害怕。他们老是说自己的车一加仑汽油能跑多少英里。他们如果已经有了辆崭新的汽车，就开始想换辆更新的车。我根本不喜欢汽车这玩意儿，我是说我根本没兴趣。我宁愿骑他妈一匹马，天哪，马至少还通点儿人性。有匹马还至少——"

"我根本听不懂你在说什么，"萨莉这妞儿说，"你从一个话题跳——"

"你知道吗？"我说，"你很可能是我这会儿待在纽约还是哪儿的唯一原因。要不是有你，我很可能会去他妈很远很远的地方，到森林里或者别的什么破地方。实际上，我在这儿只是因为你。"

"你真可爱。"她说。但是看得出,她想让我他妈换个话题。

"你应该什么时候去男校见识一下,找个时候吧。"我说,"里面全是些装模作样的家伙。能做的就只有学习,这样可以学得脑子灵光,好到时候买辆破凯迪拉克汽车。你还非得装着他妈的在乎橄榄球队赢不赢球,整天聊天除了谈女孩儿、烈酒和性就没有别的。每个人都聚成他妈的一小拨一小拨,篮球队的一拨,信天主教的一拨,爱他妈学习的一拨,打桥牌的一拨,连每月一书俱乐部的也聚成一拨。如果你想来点聪明——"

"喂,**听着**,"萨莉这妞儿说,"很多男生在学校里学到的可不止**那些**。"

"我同意!我同意的确是这样,但只是有些人而已!可是**我**学到的就这些。你明白吗?这就是我要说的,这正是我他妈要说的,"我说,"我几乎什么也没学到,我毁了,**全**毁了。"

"你当然是。"

这时,我突然有了个主意。

"你看,"我说,"我想这样。你想不想他妈的远远离开这儿?我想这样:我在格林威治村认识一个家伙,我们可以借他的车用两星期。他跟我上过同一所学校,还欠我十块钱。明天早上,我们可以开车去马萨诸塞州和佛蒙特州,就是那带地方,明白吗?那里他妈的漂亮得很,真的。"我越想越激动得要命。我伸手抓住萨莉这妞儿的破手,我他妈真是个**傻瓜**。"我不开玩笑,"我说,"我在银行里还存有大约一百八十块,可以等明天上午银行开门后取出来,然后去借那个家伙的车,我不是开玩笑。我们先待在木屋营地之类的地方,钱花完了,我可以去哪儿找个工作。我们就住在有小溪什么的地方。再往后,我们可以结婚还是怎么样,冬天烧柴都是我自己砍的。天哪,我们能过得美满无比!你说呢?快点儿!你说呢?你会不会跟我那样过?求你了!"

"你没法那样做。"萨莉这妞儿说,听起来她恼火得够呛。

"为什么没法？他妈的为什么没法？"

"别跟我大叫，求你了。"她说。真是瞎说，因为我根本没有大叫。

"因为你没办法，如此而已。第一，我们实际上都还是**小孩子**。你有没有想过，要是你的钱花完了，却**找不到**工作该怎么办？我们会**饿**死的。整个想法太**异想天开**了，根本——"

"这不是异想天开。我能找到工作的，这点你别担心，你根本不用担心。有什么关系呢？怎么回事？你难道不想跟我走吗？不想就**直说嘛**。"

"问题不在**这儿**，**根本**不在这儿。"萨莉这妞儿说。我多少讨厌起她来。"我们会有很多很多时间去做那些事的——所有那些，我是说你上了大学，另外要是我们结了婚，就会有很多很棒的地方可以去。你只是——"

"不，不会有的，根本不会有很多地方可以去，那会完全不一样。"我说着又变得泄气至极。

"什么？"她说，"我没听清。你一会儿跟我大叫，一会儿又——"

"我说不会，我们上了大学后，不会有什么好地方可去。你好好听着，那会完全不一样的。我们会不得不乘电梯下楼，拎着手提箱什么的。我们会给每个人打电话说再见，还从旅馆里给他们寄明信片，等等。我会在一家公司工作，挣很多钞票，坐的士或者麦迪逊大道上的巴士上班，整天看报纸、打桥牌，还去电影院看很多烂短片、流行新片和新闻纪录片。新闻纪录片，真离谱，里边老是报道一场无聊的赛马，哪位女士在船头砸了瓶酒，还有一只穿裤子的大猩猩骑破自行车的事儿。根本不会跟现在一样了，你根本不明白我的意思。"

"也许是我不明白！也许你也不明白。"萨莉这妞儿说。到那会儿，我们互相讨厌极了。看得出，再想努力来点有点儿头脑的交谈是毫无可能的，全是由我引起的，我后悔得要命。

"好了，我们走吧。"我说，"跟你说实话，你让我觉得可恶至极。"

乖乖，那句话真的让她气翻了。我知道我不该那样说，通常情况下，我很可能也不会那样说，可是她真的让我感到沮丧至极。一般情况下，我从来不会对女孩儿说那种粗鲁话。乖乖，她可真的气翻了天。我道歉道个没完，可是她不接受我的道歉，甚至哭了起来。这可让我有点儿害怕了，因为我有点儿害怕她会回家告诉她爸爸，说我称她可恶。她爸是那种块头大、不怎么说话的混蛋，不是很喜欢我，有次他跟萨莉这妞儿说我他妈话太多。

"不开玩笑，真的对不起。"我一直跟她说。

"对不起，对不起，真好笑。"她说。她还是有点儿在哭。突然，我真的为我说了那句话而感到有点儿对不起她。

"好了，我送你回家吧，不是开玩笑。"

"我自己能回去，谢谢你。你要是以为我会让你送我回家，那你就是脑子有毛病了。我还从来没听到哪个男的敢那样对我说。"

想一想，整件事情多少有点儿滑稽。突然，我做了件根本不该做的事，我笑了起来，是那种声音很大、很愚蠢的笑声。我是说如果在看电影什么的时候，我坐在自己的后面，我会探过身叫我自己闭嘴。这样一来，萨莉这妞儿更是气疯了。

我还是在她旁边黏糊了一会儿，一个劲儿道歉，想让她原谅我，可是她不肯。她一直说让我走，别烦她，最后我真的把她丢那儿了。我进去取了我的鞋还有别的东西后，就自个儿走掉了。我不该那样，可当时我真他妈受够了。

说实话，我根本不知道我怎么会开口跟她聊起那么多事儿，我是说到别的地方，去马萨诸塞州以及佛蒙特州之类的话。就算她想跟我走，我很可能也不会带她，我想一起走的怎么也不会是她。然而最要命的是，在叫她跟我走时，我是真心实意的。这最要命，向上帝发誓，我是个疯子。

18

离开滑冰场后,我感觉有点儿饿,就走进一家店里买了块瑞士奶酪三明治和一杯麦乳精。然后我钻进一间电话亭,想着可以给简这妞儿再打个电话,看她到家没有。我是说我整晚上都没事,想给她打个电话,她在家呢,我就带她找地方跳跳舞或者去别的地方玩。认识她那么久,我从来没跟她跳过舞还是怎么样,不过有一次看过她跳舞,像是个跳舞好手。那是在一家夜总会的国庆舞会上,当时我跟她还不是很熟,觉得不应该插一脚,从跟她约会的男孩那儿把她拉过来。她在跟一个名叫艾尔·派克的很差劲的家伙约会,这人在乔特中学上学,我跟他不太熟。他老是在游泳池那儿晃悠,穿一条白色拉斯泰克斯牌游泳裤,老是玩高台跳水。他整天玩的不过是转体半周之类老掉牙的一套。他只会这一种动作,却自以为很了不起。四肢发达,头脑简单。不管怎么样,简那天晚上就是跟他约会。我没法理解,我发誓我真的没法理解。后来我们开始交往后,我问她怎么会跟艾尔·派克这种爱招摇的混蛋约会。简说他不是爱招摇的人,还说他有自卑情结。简看样子好像可怜他还是怎么着,她还不仅看样子是,而且是当真的。女孩儿的这点真是有趣,每次你说起一个不折不扣的混蛋时——很卑鄙或者自负等——你跟一个女孩儿提起这点时,她会告诉你他有自卑情结。他也许真的**有**,但是在我看来,这也不能说明他们不混蛋。女孩儿啊,你永远不知道她们在想什么。有次我安排一个叫罗伯塔·沃尔什的女孩的室友跟我的一个朋友约会,他叫鲍勃·鲁宾逊,**他真的**有自卑情结。很明显,他为自己的父母感到没面子，因为他们说话很土，也不是很有钱。可他不是个混蛋什么的，而是个很不错的家伙。可是罗伯塔·沃尔什的这位室友根本不喜欢他，跟罗伯塔说他太自负了——而她觉得他自负的理由，是他碰巧提到自己是辩论队的队长。就这么一点儿小事，她居然认为他自负！女孩儿的毛病就在于要是她们喜欢上一个男生，无论此人混蛋到何种程度，她们还会说他有自卑情结；要是她们不喜欢哪个男生，不管这人有多好，或者他有多么严重的自卑情结，她们一样会说他自负，就连聪明的女孩儿也是这样。

不管怎么样，我又给简这妞儿打了个电话，可是没人接，只好挂掉了。我就开始在通讯簿里找，看看他妈的到底能找谁晚上跟我聚一聚。可麻烦的是，我的通讯簿上只记了三个人：简，安托利尼先生——他是我在埃克顿岗中学上学时的老师，另外还有我爸爸的办公室电话。我老是忘了把别人的名字写上去，所以最后我给卡尔·卢斯这小子打了个电话，他在我离开伍顿中学后从那儿毕业，比我大三岁。说起来我并不是很喜欢他，可他是那种聪明绝顶的家伙——他曾是伍顿中学的学生中智商最高的——我想他也许愿意跟我去哪儿吃晚饭，然后来点儿稍微有水平的谈话，他有时还是很能让人开窍的，我就给他打了个电话。他现在在哥伦比亚大学上学，住在六十五街，我知道他会在家。跟他通上电话后，他说没法跟我一起吃晚饭，不过可以十点钟到五十四街的威克酒吧跟我喝一杯。我想他接到我的电话很吃惊，因为我有次骂他是个肥屁股的装模作样的家伙。

当时离十点钟还挺早，可以消磨一下时间，我所做的，是去无线广播城看电影。我可能从来没有干过这么差劲的事，可是这地方很近，我也想不到还可以干吗。

我进场时那场破演出正在演，"小火箭"舞蹈队踢腿正踢得起劲儿，就是站成一排，胳膊搂着旁边人的腰踢腿。观众疯了似的鼓掌，我后面有个家伙老是跟他老婆说："你知道那叫什么？精确。"逗死我了。然后,"小火箭"舞蹈队下场后,一个身穿礼服、脚踩溜冰鞋的家伙上场了,开始从几张小桌子下面钻过,一边钻,还一边讲笑话。他溜得很好,我却喜欢不起来,因为我老是想象他为了能登台表演而**练习**溜冰时的样子。这样想似乎很蠢,我想只是我心情不好的原因吧。他表演完之后,每年圣诞节无线广播城都会有的演出就开始了。有许多天使从包厢里,还有每个角角落落的地方露头,另外还有些扛着十字架之类的家伙到处乱串。然后他们一伙——有几千个吧——疯了似的唱《来吧,信徒们!》。真是不得了。我知道它本应该是宗教性很强,而且很好看的,可是天哪,我就是看不出一伙演员在舞台上扛着十字架到处乱串,有何宗教意义或者悦目之处。他们搞完后又走出包厢时,看得出他们为了去抽根烟还是干吗简直急不可待。我前一年跟萨莉这妞儿一块儿看过,她老是说那些戏装什么的太漂亮了,等等。我说如果耶稣他老人家看到这些——还有稀奇古怪的戏装什么的——他没准会吐的。萨莉说我是个亵渎宗教的无神论者。大概是吧。耶稣真的有可能喜欢的,会是乐队里那个打定音鼓的家伙。我从大约八岁起,就开始看他打鼓了。我和弟弟艾里要是跟我爸妈一块儿来看,经常会离开座位到最前面去,好去看他打鼓。他是我所看过的鼓手中最棒的。整首乐曲中,他只有一次机会打几下鼓,可他没打时,也从来没显得不耐烦过。他打鼓时,总是打得很悦耳动听,脸上有种紧张的神色。有次我们跟我爸一块儿去华盛顿,艾里给他寄了张明信片,可我敢打赌他从来没收到,当时我们不太清楚地址该怎样写。

那套圣诞节的把戏结束后,破电影就开始了。烂得要命,我倒是看得一眼不漏。是关于一个英国佬的,此人名叫亚历克,姓什么不清楚。他先是在打仗,后来又在医院里失去记忆什么的。他出院后拄了根拐杖,在伦敦到处一拐一拐地走,不知道自己到底他妈的是谁。他实际上是个公爵,但是他他妈的不知道。后来在巴士上,他遇到一个温柔可亲、真挚友好的女孩。她的破帽子被风吹跑,让他抓住了。他们就上巴士顶层坐下,聊起了查尔斯·狄更斯,那是他们都喜欢的作家。他带了本《雾都孤儿》,她也带了一本。我当时差点儿吐了。总之,他们马上相爱了,就因为他们都对查尔斯·狄更斯迷得要命。他帮她做出版生意。那个女孩儿是个出书的,生意却做得不怎么样,因为她哥是个酒鬼,把钞票全花光了。她哥也算命苦,因为打仗时,他是个医生,现在神经被震坏了而没法给人做手术,所以整天酗酒,不过他还算是个说话很风趣的人。总之,后来亚历克这小子写了一本书,那个女孩把它出版了,结果他们狠赚一笔。正当他们准备结婚时,另外一个女孩——马西娅这妞儿——出现了。马西娅是亚历克失去记忆前的未婚妻。他在书店签名售书时,她认出了他。她跟他说他的真实身份是个公爵,可他不相信,也不愿意跟她去看望他的母亲,他的母亲瞎得一点儿也看不见。但是另外一个女孩,就是那个温柔可亲的女孩非要他去——她很高尚——结果他就去了。可他还是回忆不起来,甚至当他那条大丹犬扑过来跟他亲热,他母亲用手在他脸上到处摸索,还拿来他小时候经常到处拿着玩的玩具熊时,他还是回忆不起来。但是后来有一天,几个小孩在草地上打板球,他的头被一个板球狠砸了一下。马上,他全他妈想起来了,跑去在他母亲的额头上亲个没完。他又当起了公爵,却把搞出版的温柔可亲的女孩忘个一干二净。我可以跟你讲讲后面的故事,但是讲的话,我有可能会吐,我不是想**倒你胃口**还是怎么样。天哪,这玩意儿让人哪有什么**胃口**看。总之,电影结尾是亚历克跟那个温柔可亲的女孩结了婚,那个当哥的酒鬼的神经毛病治好了,还给亚历克的母亲动手术,让她又能看见了,后来那个当哥的酒鬼跟马西娅这妞儿配成了一对。最后一幕是大家都坐在长餐桌前,肚皮都快要笑破了,因为那条大丹犬领着一窝小狗进了屋。我想那是因为大家都以为那条狗是公的,要不还能为什么。我想说的是,你如果不想吐得一塌糊涂,就别去看。

让我受不了的是我旁边的一个女人。看这场破电影时,她一直在哭,越是到了虚伪得厉害的地方,越是哭得起劲。你会以为她是个心肠好得不得了的人，所以才那样，可是因为我就挨着她坐，知道她并不是。她带来的那个小孩儿根本他妈的不看电影，想上厕所，可她就是不带他去，还老是说要他老老实实坐着。她的心肠好得跟他妈的一匹狼差不多。就拿那种看电影时看到虚伪的地方就哭得一塌糊涂的人来说，十个里头有九个都是内心卑鄙的混蛋，我不是开玩笑。

看完电影后，我就开始往威克酒吧的方向走去，我要跟卡尔·卢斯这小子在那里见面。走路时，我一直在想打仗的事，看那种关于打仗的电影，总让我想到很多打仗的事。我心想，让我去打仗，我肯定受不了，真的。把我单独挑出来枪毙倒不算太糟糕，可是我得在部队里待他妈很长一段时间，问题全在这儿。我哥D.B.在部队里待了他妈四年，也打过仗——参加了诺曼底登陆等——可我真的认为他宁愿打仗，也不愿意在部队里待。我当时几乎还是个小孩儿，不过还记得他经常休假时回家。他几乎一直只是躺在床上，甚至几乎不进客厅。后来他出国参战，可他没有负伤还是怎么样，也没机会开枪打人，只是整天开一辆指挥车，拉着一位愣头愣脑的将军到处去。有次他告诉我和艾里，如果非让他开枪打人，他根本不知道该往哪个方向开。他说过部队里的混蛋简直跟纳粹部队里的混蛋一样多。我记得艾里有次问他能参战是不是件好事，因为他是个作家，让他有很多写作素材。他就让艾里把他的棒球手套拿过来，问艾里谁是最好的战争诗人，是鲁珀特·布鲁克还是艾米莉·狄金森。艾里说是艾米莉·狄金森。我对此不太清楚，因为我诗读得不多。可是有一件事我的确清楚：要是让我进了部队，一天到晚跟一帮像阿克利、斯特拉雷德及莫里斯那样的家伙一起出操什么的，我肯定会疯掉。我参加过童子军，大约有一星期时间，我就连盯住前面那个家伙的脖后梗都受不了，可他们还老是叫我们盯住前面那人的脖后梗。我发誓，再来场战争的话，最好他们挑我出来让行刑队把我毙掉算了，那我也不会反对。我对D.B.也不了解。他对战争恨之入骨，去年夏天却让我读一本《永别了，武器》。他说这本书特棒，这让我无法理解。书里有个叫亨利的少尉，按说是个不错的人。我不明白 D. B. 怎么一方面那么憎恨战争，一方面又喜欢那样一个装模作样的家伙。我是说，比如他一方面喜欢林·拉德纳的书，或是另外一本他喜欢得不得了的书——《了不起的盖茨比》——另一方面又会喜欢像《永别了，武器》这样一本虚伪的书。我这样说了后，D. B. 不高兴，说我太小了，不懂欣赏，可是我不这么看。我告诉他我喜欢林·拉德纳和《了不起的盖茨比》，而且的确如此。我万分喜欢《了不起的盖茨比》，这个盖茨比，真是个堂堂正正的人物，这本书让我喜欢得要命。不管怎么样，我对发明了原子弹这件事有点儿开心。再来场战争的话，我他妈会端坐到原子弹的弹头上。我自愿报名，向上帝发誓，我会的。

19

你如果不住在纽约,我可以告诉你威克酒吧是在一家有点儿时髦的旅馆——西顿旅馆里。以前我去那儿去得很勤,不过现在不去了,我是慢慢戒掉的。它是那种按说很有档次的地方,里面挤满了装模作样的家伙。那儿有过两个法国妞儿,蒂娜和雅尼纳,每天晚上大约出场三次弹琴唱歌,一个弹钢琴——弹得糟糕透顶,一个唱歌,多数歌曲要么是下流的,要么用法语唱。雅尼纳唱歌之前,总要对着破麦克风轻声细语地说上几句,比如她会用很蹩脚的英语说:"现在我们想为你们献上一首《你要法国妞儿吗?》,唱的是一个法国小姑娘去了大城市,正像纽约这样,然后跟一个布鲁克林的小伙子好上了。希望你们喜欢。"在这么轻声细语、装得万分可爱地说完后,她就开始唱一首烂歌,一半用法语,一半用英语,满场装模作样的家伙高兴得疯了似的。你要是在那儿待得够久,听着那帮装模作样的家伙拍巴掌还是怎么样,你会讨厌世界上所有的人,保证你会。吧台侍者也是个下流货,一个大号的势利鬼。如果你不是个厉害角色或者名流什么的,他就几乎根本不跟你说话。如果你**的确**是个厉害角色或者名流什么的,那他甚至更让人恶心,会堆着一脸媚笑凑到你面前,好像你认识他就会知道,他也是个很他妈了不起的角色。"哟!康涅狄格那边怎么样?"要么"佛罗里达那边怎么样?"那地方真要命,我不是开玩笑。我去那儿去得越来越少,最后根本不去了。

我到了后时间还挺早。我坐在吧台那边,酒吧里人很多。趁卢斯这货还没到,我要了两份加苏打水的威士忌。我是站着点的,好让他们看到我有多高，别以为我他妈没成年。然后我看了一会儿那帮装模作样的家伙。我旁边有个家伙正跟他带来的一个小妞儿大侃特侃，一直说她那双手很有贵族气质，让我乐死了。吧台那头坐的全是些搞同性恋的家伙，不过外表上看不太像，我是说他们没把头发留得太长还是怎么样——可是不管怎么样，还是能看出他们是同性恋。最后，卢斯这家伙总算露面了。

卢斯这小子，真是个宝贝。我在伍顿上学时，他是我的学生辅导员，可他对我的辅导仅仅是聊性，是在一帮人深夜聚集到他的宿舍时。他对性知道得真不少，特别是关于性变态什么的。他老是给我们讲很多邪门之人的事，有人到处找绵羊干，还有些家伙把女人衬裤缝在帽子里头当衬里，净是这种事。还有男女同性恋的事。卢斯这货知道全国都有谁是同性恋，你只用提个人名——**不管是谁**——卢斯这货就会告诉你此人是不是同性恋。有时候难以置信，特别是当他说有些电影演员什么的是同性恋时。他说是同性恋的有几个竟然已经结了婚，真是岂有此理。有人会追着他问："你说乔·布洛是个同性恋？乔·**布洛**？那个长得高大威猛、老是演匪徒还有牛仔的？"卢斯这货会说："那肯定。"他老是说"那肯定"，说这种事跟结没结婚无关，还说世界上有一半结了婚的男人都是同性恋，连他们自己也不知道。他说你要是具备了作为同性恋的所有特性什么的，就会几乎一夜之间变成同性恋，经常把我们吓得够呛。我一直想着有一天我会变成同性恋。我曾经觉得，说起来卢斯这小子的可笑之处，是他自己就有点儿同性恋。他经常在你经过走廊时对你说"试试这个大小如何"，然后猛捣你的敏感部位。他每次上厕所时，老是他妈的不关那格厕所门，在你刷牙或者干别的什么时跟你说话。这种事有点儿同性恋意思，没错。我认识好几个真正搞同性恋的，都是在学校里，他们老是搞这种玩意儿，所以我总怀疑卢斯这小子说不准也是。不过他是个脑子很灵的家伙，真的。

他跟别人见面时，从来不说"你好"什么的。坐下后，他一上来就说他只能待几分钟，说还有约会，然后要了份低糖的马提尼酒。他叫酒保拿糖度很低的，不放橄榄。

"嗨，我给你找了个搞同性恋的，"我告诉他，"就在吧台那头。现在别看，我特意留给你的。"

"很风趣啊，"他说，"还是老样子的考尔菲尔德，什么时候开始长大？"

他让我搞得很烦，没错，可是他让我开心，他是那种能让我特别开心的人。

"你的性生活如何？"我问他。他就烦别人问他这种事。

"悠着点儿，"他说，"老天，你往后靠，悠着点儿。"

"我够悠着点儿了，"我说，"哥伦比亚大学怎么样？你喜欢吗？"

"那肯定，否则我也不会去那儿上学了。"他说。他自己有时候也挺惹人烦的。

"你学什么专业？"我问他，"性变态学？"只是跟他开玩笑而已。

"你这是怎么着——说话风趣吗？"

"不是，开玩笑而已。"我说，"嗨，听我说，卢斯，你是个聪明人，我需要你的建议。我正处于很糟糕——"

他对我大声哼了一声。"听着，考尔菲尔德，你要是想坐下来**安安静静**地喝一杯，安安静静地聊——"

"好了，好了，"我说，"别激动。"看得出，他不想跟我讨论什么严肃的话题。这种脑袋瓜聪明的家伙就这毛病，他们从来不想讨论什么正经事，除非他们想。因此我所做的，是跟他讨论起一般的话题来。"说真的，你的性生活如何？"我问他，"还跟在伍顿时的那个小妞儿来往吗？那个特别——"

"我的天，不是那个了。"他说。

"怎么回事？她怎么了？"

"**我一点儿**也不知道。既然你问起来，据我所知，她现在很可能是新罕布什尔州的头号婊子了。"

"这话可不好听，既然她一直赏脸让你跟她干，你至少不应该这么说她。"

"噢，我的天！"卢斯这小子说，"这就是典型的考尔菲尔德式聊天吗？你马上告诉我。"

"不是，"我说，"反正这样不好，如果她赏脸让你——"

"我们非得顺着这个讨厌至极的思路往下说吗？"

我什么也没说，有点儿担心我不闭嘴的话，他会一走了之，把我一个人撂这儿。所以我只是又要了份酒，想喝个一醉方休。

"你现在跟谁来往？"我问他，"可以告诉我吗？"

"你不认识。"

"是吗，那是谁？没准儿我认识。"

"住在格林威治村的一个女孩，是个雕刻家，你要是非想知道的话。"

"是吗？不是开玩笑？她多大？"

"岂有此理，我又没问过她。"

"噢，那大约呢？"

"我想可能三十多，快四十吧。"卢斯这小子说。

"快四十？是吗？你喜欢这样吗？"我问他，"你喜欢那么老的？"我之所以这样问，是因为他的确在性那方面懂得很多，我认识的人中像他这样的少有。他才十四岁时，就不是个处男了，是在楠塔基特岛时，真的。

"我喜欢成熟的女人，那肯定，如果你问的是这个。"

"真的？为什么？我不是开玩笑，就因为她们在性那方面更棒？"

"喂，咱们先把这件事情说清楚，我今天晚上对这种考尔菲尔德式的问题拒绝回答。你他妈到底什么时候才开始长大？"

我有一阵子什么话也没说，让这聊天晾一会儿。接着卢斯这小子又要了份马提尼，并跟酒保说要糖度低得多的。

"喂，你跟她交往多久了，那个搞雕塑的妞儿？"我问他，我真的很感兴趣，"你在伍顿时认不认识她？"

"不怎么认识，她才刚来美国几个月。"

"是吗？她是哪儿人？"

"她刚好是从上海来的。"

"别开玩笑！我的天，是个中国人？"

"显而易见。"

"别开玩笑！你喜欢这样吗？喜欢她是个中国人？"

"显而易见。"

"为什么？我想知道——真的。"

"既然你问起来，我只是刚好发现东方哲学比西方哲学更让人满意。"

"你是这么认为的？你说的'哲学'是什么意思？你是说在性还有别的方面吗？你是说在中国，这方面学问更好？你是不是这个意思？"

"不一定非得在中国，岂有此理，我说的是东方。我们非得这样没头没脑地聊下去吗？"

"哎，我可是认真问你的。"我说，"别开玩笑，为什么东方哲学比较好？"

"老天，这可说来话长。"卢斯这小子说，"他们只是刚好把性看作既是肉体的又是精神的体验。你要是觉得我——"

"我也这么认为的呀！我也认为性是你刚才怎么说的——既是肉体的又是精神的体验，我真的这么认为，但是又取决于我他妈跟谁干。我要是跟谁干这事，我甚至不——"

"考尔菲尔德，别这么大声，岂有此理。你要是没法压低声音，干脆我们什么也别——"

"好吧，可是你听我说。"我说。我激动了，所以声音的确有点儿高，有时候我激动的时候，说话声音的确会有点儿高。"可我的意思是这样，"我说，"我知道性既是肉体的又是精神的，而且是艺术的。可我是说你不会跟**每个人**都干吧——每个搂脖子亲过的人——不能让它都往这个方向发展。对吧?"

"**别说这个了**,"卢斯这家伙说,"你介意吗?"

"好吧,可是你听我说,就拿你跟那个中国妞儿来说吧,你们在一起哪些方面不错?"

"别说这个了,我说过。"

我问得有点儿太隐私了,我也意识到了。但这就是卢斯叫人烦的地方,我们在伍顿中学时,他会让你跟他描述一下**你**所经历过的最隐私的事,可是你一问**他自己**的事情,他就不乐意。这些脑袋瓜聪明的人根本不愿意跟你进行有水平的交谈,除非让他们全盘决定该谈什么。**他们**闭嘴时,老想让你也闭嘴,他们回到他们的房间时,你也得回自己的。我们在伍顿中学时,有件事让卢斯这小子很不高兴——真的能看出他不喜欢——他在自己的房间里向我们一帮人在性的方面发表一番高论后,我们再黏一会儿,自己再侃上一阵子。我是说除了卢斯之外的其他人,包括我,就在别人的房间里侃。卢斯这小子就不高兴,他总希望在他出完风头后,大家都闭上嘴巴,各回各的房间。他害怕有人会比**他**说得更精彩。他真让我开心。

"我可能会去中国,我的性生活没法提。"

"那当然,你的头脑还不成熟。"

"不错,真的是,我知道。"我说,"你知道我的毛病在哪里?如果跟一个我不是很喜欢的女孩儿在一起,我从来没法变得很冲动,我是说**很**冲动。我是说我必须很**喜欢**她才行,如果不是,我可以说就对她没他妈什么兴趣了。乖乖,这真的把我的性生活搞得不像样,我的性生活太差劲了。"

"天哪,这是理所当然的。我上次见你时跟你说过该怎么办。"

"你是说去看精神分析专家?"我问他。他跟我说过,我该怎么办就是指那个,他爸爸是个精神分析专家。

"去不去随你的便,岂有此理,你怎么过日子又他妈不关我的事。"

有一阵子我没开口,在思考。

"假如说我去找你爸爸,让他给我做精神分析,"我说,"他会拿我怎么样?我是说他会拿我怎么样?"

"他根本不会拿你他妈怎么样,岂有此理,他只是跟你谈话,你也跟他谈话而已。首先,他会帮助你认识你的思维模式。"

"什么来着?"

"你的思维模式。你的思维运行是按照——听着,我不想跟你上一节精神分析入门课。你要是有兴趣,给我爸打电话约个时间。没兴趣就别打。说实话,你打不打,我根本无所谓。"

我把手搭到他肩膀上。乖乖,他可真逗。"你真是个待人友好的混蛋,"我告诉他,"你知道吗?"

他看看手表。"我得撤了,"他说着站起身,"挺高兴见到你。"他叫酒保把他的账单拿过来。

"嗨,"就在他要走之前,我说,"你爸爸有没有给你精神分析过?"

"我?问这干吗?"

"不干吗,他有没有?做过吗?"

"不能真正算是。说起来,他帮助过我调整自己,全面分析倒从来没必要。你干吗问?"

"不干吗,只是好奇而已。"

"好了,悠着点。"他说着放下小费什么的就要走了。

"再喝一杯吧。"我叫他,"求你了,我孤独得要命,不是开玩笑。"

可是他说没办法,说他那时已经晚了,说完就走了。

卢斯这小子,绝对是个讨厌的家伙,不过他的词汇量的确很大,我在伍顿中学时,他的词汇量在那里的全体学生中是最大的,学校里测过一次。

20

我继续坐在那儿越喝越醉,等着蒂娜和雅尼纳两个妞儿出场表演,可是她们没出来。有个样子像是同性恋、留着波浪式卷发的家伙出来弹钢琴,然后是个以前没见过的,叫瓦伦西亚的小妞儿出来唱歌。她也好不到哪儿去,但是比蒂娜和雅尼纳强点儿,至少她唱的都是好歌。钢琴紧挨着我坐的吧台,瓦伦西亚这妞儿几乎就站在我旁边。我多少给她递了几次那种眼色,可她装作根本没看到。换个时候我很可能也不会那样干,可是当时我喝得醉醺醺的。她唱完后离开大厅时走得很快,我根本没机会请她跟我喝一杯,就把领班侍者叫过来,让他去问瓦伦西亚小妞儿愿不愿意跟我喝一杯。他说他去问,可是他很可能根本不会给我带话。人们向来不会给人带话。

乖乖,我就坐在那间破酒吧里,一直待到一点钟左右,醉得一塌糊涂。我几乎看不清东西,不过有一样我是做到了,我他妈小心得要命,不让自己发酒疯什么的。我不想让任何人注意到我还是怎么样,或者问我多大。可是乖乖,我几乎看不清东西。喝得很醉时,我就会玩肚子上挨了枪子的无聊把戏。这间酒吧里就我一个人肚子上挨了枪子,我一直拿手捂在夹克下面,就在肚子那儿,不让血滴得到处都是。我不想让人知道我竟然负了伤,在**掩饰**这样一个事实,即我是个负伤的混蛋。最后我终于想做一件事,就是给简这妞儿打个电话,看她到家没有。我就结了账,然后离开吧台到了电话那里。我一直把手放在夹克下面,免得让血滴下来。乖乖,我可真够醉的。

可是进了电话间后,我又不太有心情给简这妞儿打电话了,我想我当时太醉了。后来怎么样呢,我给萨莉·海斯这妞儿打了个电话。

我拨了有二十个号码才拨对她家的电话。乖乖,我真的是什么也看不见。

"喂?"听到有人来接他妈的电话时,我就说,有点儿像是在嚷,我太醉了。

"谁啊?"一个很是冷冰冰的女人声音问道。

"是我,霍尔顿·考尔菲尔德,请让我跟萨莉说话。"

"萨莉睡了,我是萨莉的奶奶。霍尔顿,你怎么这时候打电话?知不知道几点了?"

"知道,我想跟萨莉说话。很重要的事,叫她来听。"

"萨莉睡了,小伙子。明天打电话给她吧,晚安。"

"叫醒她!叫醒她,嗨,快去吧。"

接着电话那边换了声音。"霍尔顿,我在听呢,"是萨莉这妞儿,"你又有什么棒主意?"

"萨莉?是你吗?"

"是——别大叫了。你喝醉了吗?"

"对,你听我说,听我说,嗨。我圣诞夜去你家,好不好?我给你修剪那棵破树,好不好?好不好,嗨,萨莉?"

"好吧,你喝醉了,现在去睡觉吧。你在哪儿?跟谁在一起?"

"萨莉?我会去给你修剪树的,好不好?好不好,啊?"

"好吧,现在你去睡觉吧。你在哪儿?跟谁在一起?"

"没别人,只有我,在下,鄙人。"乖乖,我喝得太醉了!竟然还捂着肚子呢。"他们揍了我,洛基山的土匪揍了我。你知道吗?萨莉,你知道吗?"

"我听不清你说什么。你现在就去睡觉,我得挂了。明天给我打电话吧。"

"嗨，萨莉！你想不想让我给你修剪树？你想让我去，对不对？"

"对。晚安，回家睡觉吧。"

没等我说完，她就挂断了电话。

"晚安，晚安，萨莉宝贝，小甜心爱人萨莉。"我说。你能不能想象我醉成了什么样？后来我也挂了电话。我琢磨她很可能刚跟人约会回来，我想象她跟伦特夫妇到某个地方去了，还有那个上安多弗中学的蠢材。他们一堆人坐成一圈，一边喝茶，一边一块儿聊些高深的东西，个个讨人喜欢、装模作样的样子。我打心底里后悔给她打电话，我喝醉时，就是个疯子。

我在那个破电话间里待了很久，差不多一直抓着电话听筒，好不让自己晕倒。说实话，我当时感觉不是很好。最后我还是出来了，像个蠢蛋似的摇摇晃晃地走进男厕所。我往一个洗手盆里接满冷水，然后把头浸进去，一直浸到耳朵。我根本懒得把脑袋弄干还是怎么样，只是让他妈往下滴水。接着我走到窗户边的暖气片那儿坐了上去，暖暖和和的。之所以让我感觉不错，只是因为我在哆嗦个没完。好玩的是，我一喝醉老是他妈的猛哆嗦。

我无事可做，就一直坐在暖气片上数地板上的小白格子。我身上快湿透了，差不多有一加仑水正顺着我脖子往下滴，领子、领带全湿透了，可是我他妈才无所谓。我太醉了，所以没法在乎。后来没多久，给瓦伦西亚弹钢琴的那个家伙进来梳他的金发卷儿。他的头发很卷，他长得像个同性恋。他梳头时，我们聊了几句，只是他他妈的态度不够友好。

"嗨，你回酒吧会不会见到那个小妞儿瓦伦西亚？"我问他。

"大概会吧。"他说。这个会说话的混蛋，我碰到的尽是会说话的混蛋。

"喂，代我向她致意。问问她那个混账侍者有没有帮我带话，好不好？"

"你干吗不回家，老弟？你到底几岁了？"

"八十六。喂，代我向她问好，好吗？"

"你干吗不回家，老弟？"

"别说我了。乖乖，你钢琴弹得真他妈好。"我告诉他，只是恭维他而已，事实上，他弹得很臭。"你应该上电台演出。"我说，"就凭你这样的靓仔，还长了一头破金发卷儿。你需不需要经纪人？"

"回家吧，老弟，当个好人。回家睡觉吧。"

"我无家可归，不开玩笑——你需要经纪人吗？"

他没理我，只是出去了。他已经梳好头并拍打停当，所以就走人了，跟斯特拉雷德一样。这种靓仔全一个样，只要把他妈的头发梳理停当，就撇下你走掉了。

最后，我从暖气片上下来，出去走到衣帽间时，我哭了起来。我不知道为什么，但的确在哭，我想是因为感到太他妈沮丧而且孤独吧。后来，我出去到了衣帽间时，却找不到那张破卡片了。可那个管存衣帽的女孩儿很好，还是给了我外套，还有我那张《小小的雪莉·比恩斯》——我还带着它呢。我给她一块钱，因为她太好了，她不肯要，并一直叫我回家睡觉。我多少试了试跟她约会，就在她下班后，可她不同意，说她岁数大得能当我妈。我让她看我的破白头发，还告诉她我四十二岁了——当然是胡扯而已，可她还是挺不错的。我给她看我的破红猎帽，她也喜欢，她让我出门前戴上，因为我的头发还很湿，她说得没错。

到外面后，我感觉醉得不是太厉害了，可是又变得很冷，我的牙齿他妈的上下磕碰个没完，没办法止住。我向麦迪逊大道走去，然后开始等巴士。我几乎没剩下多少钱，要开始省着用，不能再坐的士什么的。我也不想坐什么破巴士，况且根本不知道该去哪儿。后来怎么样呢，我开始往公园的方向走。我琢磨可以经过那个小湖，看看那些鸭子在他妈干吗，还在不在，我不知道它们是不是还在那儿。因为离公园不远，我也没别的地方可去——甚至不知道该去哪儿睡觉——所以就去了。我也不困还是怎么样，只是心情低落得要命。

后来，就在我要走进公园时，发生了一件很要命的事。我把买给菲比丫头的唱片掉到地上，摔成了有五十片。唱片装在一个大信封里，可还是摔碎了。我他妈差点儿哭起来，那让我感觉太难受了。我所做的，只是从信封里倒出碎片放进我的外套口袋。碎片根本没什么用，但我不想扔掉了事。后来我就进了公园，乖乖，里边可真暗。

我这辈子都住在纽约，对中央公园就像对手心手背那样熟悉，因为我小时候一天到晚都在那儿溜冰、骑自行车。可是那天夜里为找到那个湖，我真是费了老劲。我知道它的准确位置——就在靠近中央公园的南边那儿——可还是找不到。我一定比我以为的还要醉。我一直走啊走啊，那儿越来越黑，越来越瘆人。我在公园里一直一个人也没碰到，这还好，万一碰到人，我很可能会被吓得跳起八丈高。最后我终于找到了，它有一半结冰，一半没有，可是附近一只鸭子也看不到。我绕着这个破湖的边上走——事实上，我他妈有次差点儿掉进去——可还是一只鸭子也看不到。我想它们也许的确在附近哪儿，可能就在水边，靠近长草的地方，睡着了还是怎么样。那就是我几乎掉下去的原因，可是我一只也找不到。

最后，我在一条长椅上坐下来，那儿没他妈那么暗。乖乖，我还是哆嗦得一塌糊涂。就算戴着猎帽，我后脑勺的头发仍然好像全结成了一小坨一小坨的冰，我因此担心起来，觉得我很可能得肺炎死掉。我开始想象有成千上万个蠢材来参加我的葬礼。住在底特律的我的爷爷——跟他一起坐破巴士时，他会一条街一条街地叫着街名，还有我的姑妈、婶母、舅母等——我有大约五十个，还有讨厌的表亲、堂亲等。真是浩浩荡荡啊。艾里死后，他们全来了，整整他妈的一大帮蠢人。有个我叫姑妈的，她又蠢又有口臭的毛病，一直在说艾里躺在那儿有多安详之类的话。D.B.告诉我的，我当时不在场，还在医院——我把手弄伤后，就不得不去医院治疗。总之,我当时一直担心的就是头发上结的一小坨一小坨的冰会让我得肺炎,然后我会死掉。我为我爸妈他们真是感到万分难过。特别是我妈,直到现在,她还是没能从失去我弟弟艾里的打击中恢复过来。我一直在想象她不知道该怎样处理我的衣服和体育器材什么的。唯一让我觉得不错的,是我知道她不会让菲比丫头参加我的破葬礼,因为她还只是个小孩,单单这一件事不错。然后我想到这一大群蠢人把我塞到一块破墓地里去,墓碑上写着我的名字,周围全是死人。乖乖,你死了,他们可真的给你安排得妥当啊。我有个很强烈的愿望,就是如果我<u>真的</u>死了,希望有人会有点儿脑子,把我扔到河里之类的地方得了,可就是别把我塞到哪个破墓地里去。人们星期天会带来一些花放你胸口上,全是胡闹。谁死了还想要花?没有人。

　　天好时,我爸妈会颇为经常地去往艾里的墓上放一束花。我跟他们去过几趟,后来就不去了。第一个原因是,不用说,我不喜欢看到他待在那个破墓地,周围全是死人和墓碑什么的。出太阳时还不算太糟糕,可是有两次——<u>两次</u>——我们在那儿时下起雨来,真是糟透了。雨水淋到他的破墓碑上,淋到他肚子之上的草上,淋得到处都是。来上坟的人都拼命跑向他们的汽车,差点儿把我气疯。来上坟的人全都钻进他们的小汽车并打开收音机,然后去找个不错的地方吃饭——除艾里之外的每个人,我受不了这样。我知道墓里面只有他的肉体,他的灵魂在天堂之类的屁话,可我还是受不了,我只希望他没有被埋在那儿。你是不认识他啊,可是如果你认识他,你就能明白我的意思。有太阳还不算太糟糕,可太阳也是想出就出,想不出就不出。

　　过了一会儿,只是为了不去想肺炎,我拿出我的钱,想在路灯那不济的亮光下数数还有多少。我只有三个一块、五个两角五和一个一角的硬币——乖乖,离开潘西后,我可是花了笔巨款啊。后来我所做的,是往下走到湖边,把两角五和一角的硬币往没结冰的地方打了水漂。我也不知道我干吗要那样做,但的确那样做了。我想也许当时以为那样做,能让我不想肺炎和死亡之类的事情，但是这个效果也没有达到。

我开始想我要是得了肺炎死掉，菲比的感受会是怎样。那样想有点孩子气，可是我忍不住不想。如果发生这种事，她会感觉很难受，因为她很喜欢我，我是说她很迷恋我，她真的是。不管怎么样，我就是放不下这些想法，所以后来我合计了一下该怎么办。我琢磨我最好还是偷偷溜回家看她，以防万一我死掉。我有家里的钥匙，打算偷偷溜回家，悄悄地，然后跟她聊上一阵。唯一担心的是我家的前门吱吱响得很厉害。那是幢很老的公寓楼，管理员是个懒骨头的混蛋，不管什么都是吱吱嘎嘎响。我担心我爸妈可能听到我溜进家，可是我打定主意，不管怎样都要试试。

我就他妈的离开公园回家了，一路走回去的。路不太远，我不累，竟然也不醉了，只是很冷，附近一个人也看不到。

21

到家时,我发现通常值夜班开电梯的皮特不在,这么多年,都没有那次运气好。开电梯的家伙我从来没有见过,所以我琢磨只要不碰见我爸妈,就能跟菲比丫头打个招呼便走,根本谁都不会知道我回来过。这次运气真是太好了。更好办的是,这个新来的电梯工好像不是个聪明人。我用很随便的口气叫他把电梯开到迪克斯坦先生家那层,迪克斯坦家是住在我们那层的另外一家住户。我已经取下猎帽,免得招人猜疑还是怎么样。我一副好像特别着急的样子进了电梯。

他关好电梯门正要载我上去,却又转过身说:"他们不在家,在参加十四楼办的派对。"

"没关系,"我说,"说好我等他们回来,我是他们的侄子。"

他用有点儿愚蠢和怀疑的眼光看了我一眼。"伙计,你最好还是在大堂等。"他说。

"我也想啊——真的,"我说,"可是我的腿有点儿毛病,只能把它固定在一个位置,我想我最好还是坐在他们家门外的椅子上等。"

他根本不明白我他妈到底在说什么,所以只是"噢"了一声就把我载上去了。乖乖,还不错,有意思。你只用说些谁也听不懂的话,就几乎想让他们干什么,他们就会干什么。

我在我们家那层走出电梯——腿跛得很厉害——开始走向迪克斯坦家。然后,听到电梯门关上后,我扭头朝我们家走去。我做得天衣无缝,竟然丝毫没有醉意。我掏出钥匙开了门,声音极小,然后非常、非常小心地进了屋,把门关上。我真该去当小偷。

门厅那里不用说真他妈暗,不用说我也不能开灯,一盏也不行。我必须小心别碰到任何东西,以免搞出噼里啪啦的声音。不过我当然知道已经到家了。我们家的门厅里,有种跟其他任何地方都不一样的气味。我也不知道到底是他妈什么味,不是花椰菜,也不是香水,我也不知道是他妈什么味,可我总会知道自己到了家。我开始脱下外套想把它挂进门厅处的衣橱,里面却已经挂满了衣架,打开橱门时响成一片,我就穿着外套,没往里面挂。然后我开始走向菲比丫头的房间,很慢很慢。我知道女佣听不见我的脚步声,因为她只有一个耳鼓好。小时候,她的一个哥哥拿麦秆捅进了她的耳朵,她跟我说过一次。她耳朵背得很。可是我**爸妈**,特别是我妈的耳朵灵得像猎犬,所以经过他们的房间时,我是很轻很轻地走过,竟然屏住了呼吸,真离谱。拿我爸来说,你就是拎把椅子砸到他脑袋上,他也不会醒,可是我妈呢,你在西伯利亚那么远的地方只用咳嗽一嗓子,她就能听到。她精神紧张得要命,有一半时间,她会整夜睡不着觉,抽烟。

走了个把小时,我终于到了菲比丫头的房间,可她不在。我是忘了,忘了D. B.去好莱坞或者别的地方时,她老是睡他的房间。她喜欢在那儿睡,因为那是家里最大的房间,还因为里面有D. B.从费城一个酗酒女人那里买下的一张书桌,大得要命,另外还有张大床,约有十英里长,十英里阔。我不知道他从哪儿买的那张床,反正菲比这丫头就喜欢趁D. B.不在家时睡他的房间,他也让她睡。你该见识一下她在那张破书桌上做家庭作业之类时的样子。那张书桌几乎跟那张床一样大,她在上边做家庭作业时,几乎看不到她,可她喜欢的就是这类东西。她不喜欢自己的房间,因为据她讲太小了。她说她喜欢伸展开,把我逗得要死。菲比这丫头有什么可伸展的?什么也没有嘛。

总之,我他妈蹑手蹑脚走进D. B.的房间,然后拧亮书桌上的灯。菲比这丫头根本没醒。拧亮灯后,我看了她一会儿。她躺在那儿睡着了，脸差不多到了枕头边，嘴巴大张着，看着真有趣。拿大人来说，他们睡着时，嘴巴张开的样子很难看，但小孩儿就不，小孩儿那样还行，即便他们的口水流了一枕头，却还是挺好看。

我蹑手蹑脚在房间里走了一圈，看了一会儿里面的东西。我变得感觉好极了，完全没想着要得肺炎什么的，只剩下好的感觉。菲比丫头的衣服放在挨着床边的一把椅子上。对一个小孩儿而言，她很整洁，我是说她不像有些小孩儿那样，只是乱放东西，她绝不懒散。她把一件夹克和一件棕色套装——那是我妈在加拿大给她买的——挂在椅子靠背上，她的衬衫还有别的衣服放在座位上。鞋袜并排放在椅子正下方，我从来没见过那双鞋，是双新鞋，那种深褐色软帮鞋，有点儿像我穿的那双，跟我妈在加拿大给她买的套装搭配得好极了。我妈把她打扮得很好看，真的。我妈在有些方面的品位不得了。她买滑冰鞋什么的根本不在行，可是买起衣服来，她的选择无可挑剔。我是说菲比总有几件衣服穿起来好看得不得了。拿多数别的小孩儿而言，尽管父母有钱，可他们仍然经常穿得特别难看。我真希望你能看到菲比丫头穿我妈在加拿大给她买的衣服时的样子，我不是开玩笑。

我坐在D. B.老兄的书桌上，看上面放的东西，多数是菲比的学习用品，等等，主要是书本。最上面那本是《算术很好玩！》。我拿起来翻看第一页，菲比丫头在上面题了这样的字：

菲比·韦瑟菲尔德·考尔菲尔德

4B-1班

这让我乐死了。岂有此理，她的中间名是约瑟芬，而不是韦瑟菲尔德，可她不喜欢约瑟芬这个名字，每次我见到她，她老是给自己改一个新的中间名。

那本算术书下面是本地理书，地理书下面是本拼写簿。她的拼写很好，她每门课都很好，但最好的是拼写。拼写簿下面是一堆笔记本，她的笔记本有五千本左右，你从来没见过哪个小孩儿有这么多。我打开最上面的看第一页，上面写着：

> 伯尼丝，休息时跟我碰头，我有非常、非常重要的事情要跟你说。

第一页上就写了这些字，第二页上写着：

> 为什么阿拉斯加东南部有那么多罐头厂？
> 因为那里有很多三文鱼
> 为什么那里有宝贵的森林？
> 因为那里气候适宜
> 我们的政府为提高阿拉斯加州爱斯基摩人的生活水平做了哪些事？
> 　明天要查一查！！！
> 　菲比·韦瑟菲尔德·考尔菲尔德
> 　菲比·韦瑟菲尔德·考尔菲尔德
> 　菲比·韦瑟菲尔德·考尔菲尔德
> 　菲比·韦·考尔菲尔德
> 　菲比·韦瑟菲尔德·考尔菲尔德先生
> 　请传给雪莉！！！
> 　雪莉，你说你是射手座
> 　可你来我家时
> 　你那仅有的金牛座带来了你的冰鞋

我坐在D. B.的书桌上翻完了那本笔记本，没用多久。我可以整日整夜读这种玩意儿,也就是哪个小孩儿的笔记——菲比或者别人的。小孩儿的笔记逗得要命。然后,我又点了一根烟——那是我的最后一根烟,我那天肯定抽了有三盒左右。后来,我把她叫醒了。我是说我也不能下半辈子就那样坐在书桌上,况且我害怕我爸妈会突然闯进来看到我。至少在这发生前,我要跟菲比打个招呼,就把她叫醒了。

她很容易醒,我是说你不用向她嚷还是怎么样,几乎只用坐在床边说:"醒醒,菲比。"瞧,她就醒了。

"**霍尔顿!**"她马上说。她搂着我的脖子,很亲昵,我是说对一个小孩儿而言是这样,她有时甚至过于亲昵了。我亲了她一下,接着她问:"你什么时候<u>回来</u>的?"看得出,她看到我开心得要命。

"别这么大声,就是刚才。你怎么样?"

"我很好。你有没有收到我的信?我给你写了五页——"

"收到了——别这么大声,谢谢了。"

她给我写过这么一封信,可是我没机会回。信里全是说她在学校参演的戏剧,她叫我星期五不要跟别人约会还是怎么样,好赶回来看这出戏。

"演戏的事怎么样了?"我问她,"叫什么来着?"

"《美国人的圣诞庆典》,这出戏很臭,可我演的是本内迪克特·阿诺德,我的角色几乎最重要。"她说。乖乖,她可真是精神抖擞,说起这些玩意儿时,她会变得很兴奋。"一开始我快死了,一个鬼魂在圣诞夜来问我感不感到羞耻,你也知道,就是因为背叛了国家,等等。你去不去看?"她在床上坐得笔直。"我在信里就写了这些事,你去不去?"

"我当然会去,理所当然会去。"

"爸爸没办法去,他要飞到加利福尼亚。"她说。乖乖,她可真是精神抖擞,只要等两秒钟,就会变得精神抖擞。她坐在床上——也有点儿在跪着——坐得笔直,还抓着我的破手。"咦,妈妈说你**星期三**回来,"她说,"她说是**星期三**。"

"我提前回来了。别这么大声,你会把别人都吵醒的。"

"几点了？他们很晚才会回来，妈妈说的。他们去康涅狄格州诺沃克参加一个派对。"菲比丫头说，"你猜我下午干吗了？我看了什么电影？你猜！"

"我不知道——听我说，他们有没有说几点——"

"《医生》，"菲比丫头说，"是利斯特基金会的特别放映，只放一天——就今天一天。电影全是关于肯塔基州的一个医生，他拿毛毯捂到了一个小孩儿的脸上，这个小孩儿是个残疾人，不会走路，后来他被关进了监狱。电影很棒。"

"听我说一句，他们有没有说几点——"

"他可怜那个小孩儿，我是说医生，所以拿条毯子捂到她脸上，想捂死她，后来他被判了终身监禁。可那个被他往头上捂毯子的小孩儿经常来看望医生，还感谢他为她所做的事。这位医生是个好心的杀人犯，只是他知道自己坐牢罪有应得，因为医生不应该从上帝那儿拿任何东西。是我们班上一个女生的妈妈带我们去看的，这个女生是艾丽斯·霍尔姆堡，是我最好的朋友，她是唯一在整个——"

"等一下，好不好？"我说，"我在问你，他们有没有说什么时候回来？"

"没说，不过会是很晚。爸爸开车去的，免得担心坐不上火车。我们家的车上现在有收音机了！不过妈妈说开车时，谁也不能听。"

我有点儿放心了，我是说我终于不再担心他们会在家里逮住我。我心想，管他的，要逮就让他们逮吧。

你该看看菲比丫头的样子。她穿了件蓝色的睡衣，领子上印有红色的大象，她酷爱大象。

"这么说是部好电影了，对吗？"我说。

"棒极了，就是艾丽斯感冒了，她妈妈老是问她感觉是不是得了流感，就在放电影的时候，老是在一些关键地方，她妈妈老是歪着身子隔着我问艾丽斯感觉是不是流感，让我着急。"

接着，我告诉她那张唱片的事。"哎，我给你买了张唱片，"我告诉她，"可是在回家的路上摔碎了。"我从外套口袋里掏出碎片给她看。"我那会儿醉了。"我说。

"碎片给我，"她说，"我要保存。"她从我手里把碎片全拿过去放进床头柜的抽屉，她可爱得要命。

"D. B. 圣诞节回来吗？"我问她。

"可能回也可能不回，妈妈说的，全得看情况。他可能不得不待在好莱坞，要写一部关于安纳波利斯的电影剧本。"

"安纳波利斯，我的天！"

"是个爱情故事什么的。你猜谁会在里面演出？哪个明星？你猜！"

"我不感兴趣。**安纳波利斯**，我的天，D. B. 又了解什么**安纳波利斯**？我的天。那跟他写的短篇小说又有什么联系？"我说。乖乖，这种事真能气疯我，混账的好莱坞。"你胳膊怎么了？"我问她。我看到她肘部贴了很大一块橡皮膏，之所以能看到，是因为她穿的睡衣是无袖的。

"那个男孩，柯蒂斯·温特劳布，我们班上的。我在公园里正下台阶时，他推了我一下。"她说，"想不想看看？"她开始揭胳膊上那张破橡皮膏。

"别撕。他干吗把你推下台阶？"

"不知道，我想他是讨厌我吧。"菲比丫头说，"我跟另外一个女生，塞尔玛·阿特伯里，把墨水什么的给他的风衣上弄得全是。"

"那样可不好，岂有此理，你像什么样——三岁小孩儿吗？"

"不是，不过每次在公园，我到哪儿他就跟到哪儿。他老是跟着我，让我着急。"

"他大概是喜欢你，你没理由把墨水什么的——"

"我不要他喜欢。"她说完开始表情古怪地看着我。"霍尔顿，"她说，"你干吗不是**星期三**回来？"

"什么？"

乖乖，你得时刻留神她，你要是以为她不聪明，那你就是疯了。

"你干吗不是**星期三**回来？"她问我，"你不是又被开除了吧？对不对？"

"我跟你说过，学校让我们提前走了，学校让整个——"

"你真的被开除了！真的！"菲比丫头说着就拿拳头打我的腿，她只要想，就很爱动拳头。"你**真的**被开除了！噢，**霍尔顿**！"她用手捂着嘴。她变得很激动，我向上帝发誓，她真的是。

"谁说我被开除了？谁也没说——"

"你**真的**被开除了，**真的**。"她说着又拿拳头打我，你要是以为不疼，那你就是疯了。"爸爸会**干掉**你的！"她说完"嗵"一声趴到床上，还用一个破枕头捂住头。她经常那样，有时候她可真是个疯子。

"好了，别这样。"我说，"谁也不会干掉我。谁也不会，就连——**好了**，菲比，把那个破玩意儿拿开。谁也不会干掉我。"

可她不肯，她不想就没法强迫她。她只是说了又说："爸爸会干掉你的。"她用那个破枕头捂住头时，几乎根本没法听清楚她说什么。

"谁也不会干掉我，理智点吧。首先，我会离开这儿。我可能怎么做呢？我可能会到农场之类的地方找个活干一段时间。我认识有个人的爷爷在科罗拉多州有个农场，我可能去那儿找个活干。"我说，"我走的话，什么时候走，我会跟你保持联系。好了，别捂住头了。好了，嗨，菲比。求你了，求你了，好不好？"

她还是不肯拿开枕头。我想把枕头拉开，可她简直力大无穷，跟她较劲真累人。乖乖，要是她想用枕头捂住头，那就谁也**拉不开**。"菲比，**求你了**，别捂着。"我一直在说，"好了，嗨……嗨，韦瑟菲尔德，别捂着了。"

可她还是不肯露出脑袋，有时候她根本不可理喻。最后我起身去了客厅，从桌子上的烟盒里取了几根塞进口袋，我的抽光了。

22

我回来时,她已经把枕头从脑袋上拿开了——我知道她会的——但还是不肯看我,就算仰面躺着也不肯。我走到床边又坐下后,她把她的破脸转过去,对我排斥得要命,就像我把破击剑器材丢在地铁上后,潘西的击剑队员对待我那样。

"黑兹尔·韦瑟菲尔德丫头怎么样了?"我说,"你有没有再写她的故事?我把你寄给我的那篇放在手提箱里,在火车站。那篇写得很好。"

"爸爸会**干掉**你的。"

乖乖,她要是脑子里惦记上什么事儿,那可就放不下了。

"不,他不会,最坏的局面无非是他臭骂我一顿而已,然后送我去上一所破军事学校。他只能这样对我。不过**首先**呢,我根本不会待在这儿,我要离开。我会——很可能会到科罗拉多州的一个农场。"

"别逗我笑了,你连马都不会骑呢。"

"谁不会?我当然会,我理所当然会。有人教,两分钟就能学会。"我说,"别抠。"她在抠她胳膊上的橡皮膏。"谁给你理的发?"我问她。我刚好注意到不知道谁给她理的头发,很难看,太短了。

"不关你事。"她说。她有时说话语气很躁,躁得不得了。"我看你又是每门课都考砸了吧?"她说——语气很躁,说起来多少有点儿滑稽,有时候她说话像个破老师,可她还只是个小孩儿而已。

"错了,我没有。"我说,"我语文及格了。"接着,纯粹是他妈觉得好玩,我拧了她屁股一下。她侧身躺着,屁股撅得老远。她的屁股上几乎没什么肉，我拧得也不重，可她还是想打我的手，但是没打着。

接着，她突然说："噢，你干吗要那样做？"她意思是说我怎么又被开除了，她问的语气让我有点儿不好受。

"噢，天哪，菲比，你别问我，我讨厌谁都来问这个。"我说，"原因有上百万。这所学校是我上过的学校中最差的，里面全是些装模作样的家伙，还有卑鄙的家伙，你这辈子也不会见到那么多卑鄙的家伙。比如说，要是你跟别人在一间宿舍里吹牛时有人想进来，假如这位有点儿笨，脸上又长粉刺，那谁也不会放他进来。有人想进来时，他们总是锁住门不开。还有什么破秘密联谊会，我胆子小，不得不加入。有个惹人烦、脸上还长粉刺的家伙，名叫罗伯特·阿克利，他想加入。他一直努力想加入，可是他们不让，就因为他惹人烦，脸上还长粉刺。我根本不想提这件事，这是所烂学校，相信我的话吧。"

菲比丫头什么也没说，但是在听，我能从她的脑后根看出她在听。跟她说什么事时，她老是在听着，而且有趣的是，一半时候，她明白你说的究竟是什么意思，她真的知道。

我一直跟她说潘西的事，我有点儿想说。

"就连那一两个在潘西还算不错的老师也虚伪。"我说，"有个老头儿，斯潘塞先生，他太太老是请人喝热巧克力什么的，他们两口子确实很不错。可是你该见识一下斯潘塞先生上历史课时，校长老瑟默走进教室坐在后排时他那副样子。老瑟默老是走进教室去后排坐上半小时，他本意是不声张，可是过了一会儿，他坐在那儿开始打断斯潘塞先生讲课，讲很多老掉牙的笑话。斯潘塞老先生笑得咯咯响，几乎呛死，还堆着一脸笑，就好像老瑟默是他妈亲王什么的。"

"别老是说脏话。"

"那会让你吐出来，我保证你会。"我说，"然后，在退伍军人节——学校里在退伍军人节这天，建国前后从潘西毕业的所有蠢材都会返校，带着老婆孩子什么的在校园里到处走。你该见识一下那个五十岁左右的老头儿。他所做的，是走进我们宿舍，敲着门，问**我们**介不介意让他用厕所，可厕所是在走廊尽头——我不知道他他妈的干吗要问我们。你知道他怎么说的？他说他想看看他几十年前刻在某一格厕所门上的名字缩写还在不在。他所做的，是大约九十年前把他愚不可及的破名字缩写刻在一格厕所门上，他想看看还在不在。我就和同屋的跟他去了厕所。他在一格格厕所门上找他的名字缩写时，我们只好一直站在那儿，而他一直跟我们说话。他说在潘西的日子是他一生中最快乐的时候，还给了我们许多关于前途之类的建议。乖乖，他可真让我觉得没劲！我不是说他是个坏蛋——不是的，不一定非得是个坏蛋才能让你觉得没劲儿——好人也能让你觉得特别没劲儿。只用一边在厕所门上找自己名字的缩写，一边给别人一大堆虚伪的建议，就能把你搞得特别没劲儿了，你只用这么做就能。我说不好。要不是他连气都喘不上来，也许还没那么严重。仅仅是爬楼梯上来，就能让他累得很是上气不接下气。找他的名字缩写时，他一直在大口大口喘气，他的鼻孔让人看着很好玩，也让人难受，而他一直对我和斯特拉雷德说，在潘西要尽可能多学些东西。老天，菲比！我没法解释，我就是不喜欢潘西那儿**发生的**一切，我没法解释。"

菲比丫头这时说了句什么，我没有听清。她半边嘴巴还堵在枕头上，我听不清楚她说什么。

"什么？"我说，"把你的嘴挪开，那样堵着我听不见你说什么。"

"你对发生的**任何事情**都不喜欢。"

她这句话让我甚至更沮丧了。

"我喜欢，喜欢的，我当然喜欢。别那么说，见鬼，你干吗要那么说？"

"因为你不喜欢，你不喜欢任何一所学校。你不喜欢的东西有上百万，你不喜欢。"

"我喜欢的！你错就错在这儿——刚好错在这儿！你干吗非得他妈的那么说？"我说。乖乖，她真让我感到沮丧。

"因为你不喜欢,"她说,"你就说一样事吧。"

"一样事?我喜欢的一样事?"我说,"好吧。"

问题是我没法很集中思想,有时候真的难以集中思想。

"你是说我很喜欢的一样事?"我问她。

可是她没理我,她斜坐在床对面跟我隔他妈很远的地方,有上千英里远。"好了,你说,"我说,"你要我说一样我很喜欢的事呢,还是一样我只是一般喜欢的?"

"你很喜欢的。"

"好吧。"我说。但问题是我没法集中思想,几乎只能想到那两个拿着破旧的草篮到处募捐的修女,尤其是戴铁边眼镜的那个,还有我在埃克顿岗中学认识的一个男生。埃克顿岗中学有这么一位男生,名叫詹姆斯·卡斯尔,他不肯收回他所说的关于一个狂妄自大、名叫菲尔·斯塔比尔的男生的话。詹姆斯·卡斯尔说他是个狂妄自大的家伙,斯塔比尔的一个混蛋朋友打了小报告,结果斯塔比尔领着六个无耻的家伙去了詹姆斯·卡斯尔的房间,进去后就锁上门,要他收回说过的话。他不肯,他们就动手了。我根本不会跟你说他们是怎么对待他的——太让人恶心了——可他**还是**不肯收回他的话,这个詹姆斯·卡斯尔。你该看看他那副样子。他瘦得皮包骨头,看上去就不壮实,小个子,手腕几乎细得像铅笔。最后他怎么样呢?他不收回他的话,而是从窗户跳了下去。我当时正在**洗澡**,连**我**都听见他摔到外面的声音,但只是以为有什么东西从窗户掉下去,收音机、书桌什么的,没想到是个**学生**。接着就听到大家跑过走廊、跑下楼梯的声音,我也穿上浴袍跑下去。詹姆斯·卡斯尔就躺在石阶上,死了,他的牙齿、鲜血哪儿都是,谁都不敢走近一步。他穿着我借给他的高翻领羊毛衫。学校只是把到他房间的那几个学生开除了事,他们根本没进监狱。

我想起来的差不多就是那些,就是早餐时碰到的两个修女,还有在埃克顿岗中学认识的学生詹姆斯·卡斯尔。说实话,奇怪的是,我根本不怎么认识詹姆斯·卡斯尔。他是那种很安静的人，跟我在一个班上数学课，可他远远地坐在教室的另一边。他几乎从来没站起来背过课文，或者上讲台在黑板上演算。有些人上学时，几乎从来没站起来背过课文，或者上讲台在黑板上演算还是怎么样。我记得唯一一次跟他说话，是他问我能不能借给他那件高翻领羊毛衫。他开口问我时，我他妈差点儿完蛋，真的是万分惊讶。我记得他问我时，我正在厕所刷牙，他说他表哥要来开车带他出去什么的，我根本不明白他怎么知道我有件高翻领羊毛衫。关于他，我仅仅知道点名时他的名字刚好在我前面，R.卡贝尔，W.卡贝尔，卡斯尔，考尔菲尔德——我现在还记得。实话跟你说，我差点儿没把羊毛衫借给他，就因为我跟他不是很熟。

"什么？"我问菲比丫头，她跟我说了句什么，我没听清。

"你根本一件事情也想不起来。"

"我能，我能。"

"那好，你想吧。"

"我喜欢艾里，"我说，"我喜欢我这会儿干的事，跟你坐在这儿，聊天，想事儿，还有——"

"艾里死了——你老是说这个！要是谁死了，上了天堂，那就不是真的——"

"我知道他死了！你以为我不知道？但是我仍然可以喜欢他，不行吗？就因为这人死了，你不可能马上不再喜欢他了，岂有此理——特别当这个人比你认识的活人要好上一千倍时。"

菲比丫头什么也没说，她要是想不出说什么话，可是一句破话都不会说。

"反正我喜欢现在，"我说，"我是说就这会儿，跟你坐这儿什么事也不干，只是吹吹牛，乐一乐——"

"这实际上不算是一件事！"

"这实际上就是一件事！当然是！他妈的怎么不是？人们从来不认

为有些事实际上就是事,我他妈嫌恶心。"

"别说脏话。好吧,说一样别的事吧。说说你希望当什么,比如科学家或律师什么的。"

"我当不了科学家,我在科学上根本不行。"

"那好,律师呢?像爸爸那样的。"

"律师还行,我想是吧——可是我也没兴趣。"我说,"我是说如果律师一天到晚到处去搭救无辜人们的性命什么的,那样倒还不算坏,可是真当了律师,你就不会去做那些事了。整天所做的,就是挣很多很多钞票,打打高尔夫球还有桥牌,买名车,喝马提尼酒,让自己的样子像是个有头有面的人物。况且,就算你真的到处去搭救别人的性命,你怎么知道那是因为你真的想那样做呢,还是之所以那样做,是因为你真正的想法是当个很厉害的律师,在他妈案子审完后,让那些记者什么的拍着你的背,当庭向你表示祝贺,就像那些破电影里演的?你怎么知道你不是个装模作样的家伙?问题就在这儿,你不会知道。"

我对菲比丫头到底听明白了没有我说的话,不是很有把握,我是说她还只是个小孩子,但至少她在听我说。如果至少有人听你说话,就不算太糟糕。

"爸爸会干掉你的,他会干掉你。"她说。

可我没听她说,而是在想别的事——离谱的事。"你知道我想当什么吗?"我说,"你知道我想当什么吗?我是说要是我他妈能选择的话。"

"什么?别说脏话。"

"你知道那首歌'如果有人抓到别人在穿越麦田'吗?我想——"

"那是'如果有人碰到别人在穿越麦田'!"菲比丫头说,"罗伯特·彭斯写的。"

"我知道是罗伯特·彭斯的诗。"

她说得没错,那一句的确是"如果有人碰到别人在穿越麦田",可我当时不知道。

"我还以为是'有人抓到别人'呢。"我说,"不管怎么样,我老是想象一大群小孩儿在一大块麦田里玩一种游戏,有几千个,旁边没人——我是说没有岁数大一点儿的——我是说只有我。我会站在一道破悬崖边上。我要做的,就是抓住每个跑向悬崖的孩子——我是说要是他们跑起来不看方向,我就得从哪儿过来抓住他们。我整天就干那种事,就当个麦田里的守望者得了。我知道这个想法很离谱,但这是我唯一真正想当的,我知道这个想法很离谱。"

菲比丫头很久没有说话,然后她开口时,还是那一句:"爸爸会干掉你的。"

"他真那么着,我他妈才无所谓呢。"我说着从床上站起身,因为我想站起来,想给在埃克顿岗中学教过我的语文老师打个电话,就是安托利尼先生。他现在住在纽约,辞了埃克顿岗中学的工作后,如今在纽约大学教语文。"我得打个电话,"我告诉菲比,"我马上回来,别睡着了。"我不想让她在我去客厅那会儿睡着了,我知道她不会,但我还是说了,只是为了保险起见。

我走向门口时,菲比丫头说:"霍尔顿!"我转过身。

她直挺挺地坐在床上,样子很漂亮。"我在跟一个叫菲莉斯·马古利斯的女孩儿学打嗝,"她说,"你听。"

我听了,还听到**有点儿声音**,可是也不算响。"好。"我说,然后就进了客厅,去给我以前的老师安托利尼先生打电话。

23

电话打得很简短,因为我害怕正在说话时,我爸妈会突然闯进来抓到我,可是他们没回来。安托利尼先生很好,他说如果我想,可以马上去他家。我想我很可能把他们两口子全吵醒了,因为过了他妈的很久,才有人接电话。他上来就问我是不是什么事搞砸了。我说没有,但说了被潘西开除的事,我想还是跟他说了吧。我告诉他时,他嘴里说着"好,好",他的幽默感还不错。他说我想的话,可以马上去他家。

安托利尼先生可能是教过我的老师中最好的一个。他很年轻,比我哥 D. B. 大不了多少,你可以跟他开玩笑,却对他仍不失敬意。是他最后抱起从窗户跳了楼的男生詹姆斯·卡斯尔,我说过的。安托利尼先生试了试他的脉搏,然后脱下外套盖着詹姆斯·卡斯尔,一直把他抱到校医务室。他根本他妈的不在乎他的外套上搞的全是血。

我回到 D. B. 的房间时,菲比这丫头开了收音机,播放的是舞曲,她把声音拧小一些,好不让女佣听到。你真该见识一下她当时的样子:她在床中间坐得笔直,就在被子外面,盘着腿,好像在练瑜伽。她在听音乐,她让我喜欢得要命。

"来吧,"我说,"你想不想跳舞?"她还是个小孩儿时,我教过她跳舞,她跳得很好,我是说我只教了她一点点,主要还是她自己学的。你不可能教会别人怎样跳得好。

"你还穿着鞋呢。"她说。

"我把鞋脱了,来吧。"

她几乎从床上一跃而下，然后等我脱鞋。接着我跟她跳了一会儿舞，她跳得真他妈棒。我不喜欢那些跟小孩儿跳舞的人，因为多数情况下跳得很难看。我是说你去餐厅吃饭时，要是看到一些老头和他家的小孩儿在舞池里跳舞，经常会看到他们老是不小心把小孩儿的衣服从后面扯起来，而且那个小孩儿总是跳得再差不过，难看极了。我和菲比从来不在公众场合跳舞，只是在家里闹着玩。跟她跳感觉不一样，因为她真的会跳，不管你怎么跳，她都跟得上。我是说如果把她搂得很近，你的腿长得多也没关系，她都跟得上你。你可以换位，或者来几个那种很俗套的突然弯腰，甚至跳点儿吉特巴舞，她都跟得上。天哪，你甚至能跟她跳探戈。

我们跳了有四首曲子，在曲子间隙，她也好玩得要命。她保持着姿势，甚至不跟你说话还是怎么样。我们两人只是原地不动等着乐队再次开始演奏，真要逗死我了。而且你也不应该笑还是怎么样。

不管怎么样，我们跳了有四首曲子，然后我把收音机关了，菲比丫头跳上床钻进被窝。"我有进步，对不对？"她问我。

"可不是嘛。"我说。我又挨着她坐到床上。我有点儿接不上来气，烟抽他妈太多。我几乎接不上气，她却根本连气也不喘。

"摸摸我额头。"她突然说。

"干吗？"

"摸摸，就摸一次。"

我摸了，可是没什么感觉。

"有没有感到很烫？"她问我。

"没有，应该很烫吗？"

"对——我在让它发烫，你再摸摸。"

我又摸了一次，还是感觉不到什么，但是我说："我觉得这会儿开始有点儿烫了。"我可不想让她有什么破自卑情结。

她点了点头："我能让它高得超过温度计上的最高刻度。"

"**温度计**，谁说的？"

"艾丽斯·霍尔姆堡教过我怎么做。你可以盘腿闭气，想些很热很热的东西，暖气片什么的，然后你整个额头就会变热，热得能把别人的手给烫了。"

真要逗死我了，我把手从她额头那儿拿开，就好像特别危险。"多谢你**告诉**我。"我说。

"噢，我不会烫着你的手，我在还没太热时就停了——嘘！"这时，她迅速得要命地在床上坐起身子。

她那样做，把我他妈吓得够呛。"怎么了？"我说。

"你听前门！"尽管她是小声说，可声音也够大的了，"是他们！"

我马上跳起来，跑去关了书桌上的灯，把烟在鞋上拧灭并装进口袋，然后手在空中猛扇，好把烟赶出去——老天，我根本不该抽烟。然后我抓起鞋钻进壁橱并关上橱门。乖乖，我的心跳得咚咚响。

我听到我妈进了这个房间。

"菲比？"她说，"喂，别装了，我刚才还看见灯亮着，大小姐。"

"嗨！"我听到菲比丫头说，"我睡不着。你们玩得好吗？"

"好极了。"我听到我妈说，可是听得出她言不由衷，她出去总是尽不了兴。"我想问问你怎么还不睡？够暖和吗？"

"够暖和的了，只是我睡不着。"

"菲比，你是不是在房间里抽过烟？大小姐，请你说实话。"

"什么？"菲比丫头问。

"你听到我问什么了。"

"我只是点着有一秒钟，才抽了**一口**，后来就把它扔出窗外了。"

"**为什么**？可以问问吗？"

"我睡不着。"

"我不喜欢你那样，菲比，我一点儿也不喜欢你那样。"我妈说，"想再加条毛毯吗？"

"不用了,谢谢您,晚安!"菲比丫头说。听得出,她想让我妈快点儿走。

"电影怎么样?"我妈问。

"很棒,就是艾丽斯她妈妈从头到尾老是歪过身子问艾丽斯感觉是不是得了流感。我们打的回来的。"

"让我摸摸你的头。"

"我什么也没得上,艾丽斯一点儿事也没有,只是她妈妈瞎操心。"

"好吧,现在睡觉。晚饭怎么样?"

"糟糕。"菲比说。

"你爸爸跟你说过别用那个词。有什么糟糕的?你吃了很好的羊排,我可是大老远走到列克星敦大道,就为——"

"羊排还行,可是查伦每次放下东西时,老是把气**哈**到我身上。她把气哈到所有吃的东西上,哪儿都给她的气哈到了。"

"好了,睡觉吧,给妈妈亲一个。你做祷告了吗?"

"我在浴室里做了。晚安!"

"晚安,现在马上睡觉。我的头疼得快要裂开了。"我妈说。她经常头疼,真的。

"吃几片阿司匹林吧。"菲比丫头说,"霍尔顿星期三回来,是吗?"

"据我所知是。现在睡觉,盖好点儿。"

我听到我妈出去并关上了门。我等了两分钟才从壁橱里出来。黑灯瞎火的,我一下子撞到菲比身上,她下床正要告诉我可以出来了。"我碰疼你了吗?"我问她,那时我只能悄声说话,因为他们全在家。"我得走了。"我说着在黑暗中摸到床沿,坐下来开始穿鞋。我得承认我很紧张。

"**现在**别走,"菲比悄悄说,"等他们睡了以后!"

"不,就是现在,现在是最好的时候,"我说,"妈妈会在浴室,爸爸会打开收音机听新闻什么的,这会儿时机最好。"我几乎绑不好鞋带,太他妈紧张了，倒不是害怕他们逮到我在家里会**干掉**我还是怎么样，而是如果那样的话，会很不愉快而已。"见鬼，你在哪儿？"我对菲比丫头说，这地方黑得很，看不到她。

"这儿。"她就站在我身边，我却根本没看到。

"我的破手提箱还在火车站。"我说，"喂，菲比，你有没有钱？我几乎一分钱也没有了。"

"只有过圣诞节的钱，为了买礼物什么的，我还**根本**没买东西呢。"

"噢。"我不想拿她的过节钱。

"你想要一点吗？"她问。

"我不想拿你过节的钱。"

"我可以借给你一点。"她说。接着，我听到她去 D. B. 的书桌那儿打开了无数抽屉，用手在里边摸索。屋里一片漆黑，伸手不见五指。"你要是走，就看不到我演戏了。"她说，声音听起来有点儿怪。

"不，我能看到，在那之前我不走，你以为我会错过看这场戏吗？"我说，"我会这么着，很可能会在安托利尼先生家一直待到也许星期二晚上吧，然后我会回家。有机会我给你打电话。"

"给你。"菲比丫头说。她想把钱递给我，可是找不到我的手。

"哪儿？"

她把钞票放到我手里。

"嗨，不需要这么多。"我说，"就给我两块吧，够了。不开玩笑——给你。"我想把钱还给她，可是她不肯接。

"你可以全拿着，以后再还我，看戏时带来。"

"老天，这有多少？"

"八块八毛五，不对，是**六毛五**，我花了一点。"

这时，我突然哭了起来，我忍不住。我哭得不让人听到，可真的是哭了。我哭起来时，菲比这丫头吓得够呛，她过来想让我别哭了，可是一旦哭起来，就他妈不可能**说停就停**。我哭的时候还坐在床沿，菲比搂住我的脖子,我也搂住她的,可还是过了很久才不哭,我觉得我要呛死了还是怎么样。乖乖,我真的把菲比这个可怜的丫头吓坏了。那扇破窗户开着,我能感到她在哆嗦,因为她只穿着睡衣。我想让她钻回被窝,她不肯。最后,我终于不哭了,但肯定哭了很久。然后我扣好外套什么的,跟她说我会跟她保持联系。她说我如果想,可以跟她睡一块儿。我说不必了,我最好还是走吧,安托利尼先生还等着呢。然后我把红猎帽从外套口袋里拿出来给了她,她喜欢那种古怪帽子。她不想要,我非让她收下。我敢打赌她睡觉还会戴着呢,她很喜欢那种帽子。接着我又说了遍有机会我给她打电话,然后就走了。

说起来,离家跟回家比起来太他妈容易了。首先就是我他妈不怎么在乎我爸妈逮住我,真的不在乎。我想,要逮就让他们逮吧,说起来,我还几乎希望他们会呢。

我一路走下楼梯,没坐电梯。我走的是后面的楼梯,那堆无数个垃圾桶差点让我摔断脖子,可我总算顺利出来了。电梯工甚至都没看到我,很可能还以为我在迪克斯坦家呢。

24

安托利尼先生和太太住在萨顿广场的一套非常豪华的公寓里,进门后到客厅还得下两级台阶,另外还有吧台什么的,我去过好几趟。我离开埃克顿岗中学后,安托利尼先生经常来我们家吃饭,来得挺多,因为他想看我过得怎么样,那时他还没结婚。后来他结婚后,我经常跟他和他太太在长岛福里斯特希尔的西区网球俱乐部打球,安托利尼太太是俱乐部的会员。她花钱大手大脚,岁数比安托利尼先生大很多,不过他们看样子过得挺不错。头一个原因,就是他们都是很聪明的人,特别是安托利尼先生,不过跟他相处时,会觉得他更显得谈吐诙谐,有点儿像 D. B. 那样。安托利尼太太一般情况下不苟言笑,她患有严重的哮喘病。他们都读过 D. B. 的所有短篇小说——安托利尼太太也全读过——D. B. 要去好莱坞时,安托利尼先生打电话要他别去,可他还是去了。安托利尼先生说不管是谁,如果能写得像 D. B. 那样好,就根本别去好莱坞。我差不多也是那么说的。

我本来应该走路去他们家,因为我想除非必要,就别动菲比的过节钱,可是我到了街上后,感觉有点儿不舒服,有点儿头晕,就打了辆的士。我也不想,但还是坐了。就连叫到一辆的士,我都真他妈费了老劲儿。

我按了门铃后,安托利尼先生来开门——是在电梯工终于让我上去后,那个杂种。安托利尼先生穿着浴袍和拖鞋,一只手里拿了杯高杯酒。他很老练,酒瘾也很大。"霍尔顿,好小伙子!"他说,"我的天,你又长高了半米吧？见到你真好。"

"您好，安托利尼先生，安托利尼太太好吗？"

"我们都好着呢，外套脱了吧。"他为我脱下外套并挂了起来。"我还以为会看到你抱着一个刚生下来的婴儿呢，走投无路，你的眼睫毛上沾着雪花。"他有时是个说话很风趣的人。他又转身对着厨房嚷："莉莲！咖啡好了吗？"莉莲是安托利尼太太的名字。

"好了，"她嚷回一嗓子，"是霍尔顿吗？你好，霍尔顿！"

"您好，安托利尼太太。"

他们家老是嚷来嚷去，因为他们从来不会同时在一个房间里，说起来也有点儿意思。

"坐下吧，霍尔顿。"安托利尼先生说。看得出，他还有点儿精神。房间里看样子好像刚刚举办过派对，到处都是杯子，还有盛着花生的盘子。"这里乱，将就一下吧，"他说，"我们招待了安托利尼太太的几个布法罗来的朋友……事实上，就是几头野牛。"

我笑了起来。安托利尼太太在厨房里对我嚷了句什么，我没听到。"她说什么？"我问安托利尼先生。

"她说进来时你别看她，她刚从被窝里出来。抽根烟吧，你现在抽烟吗？"

"谢谢。"我说着从他递给我的烟盒里抽出一根，"偶尔吧，我抽得不凶。"

"肯定如此。"他说着用桌上的一个大打火机帮我点着火。"这么说你跟潘西分道扬镳了？"他说。他老是这样说话，有时逗得我很开心，有时却不，他做得有点儿过头了。我不是说他不够风趣还是怎么样——他的确风趣——但有时你会烦别人老是跟你说"你跟潘西分道扬镳了"这种话。D. B.有时候也是，这种话说得太多。

"怎么了？"安托利尼先生说，"你的语文怎么样？你要是连语文都没及格，我可要马上送客了，你还是个作文高手呢。"

"噢,我语文过了,不过主要是文学方面。我这学期只写过两篇作文。"我说,"口头表达这门课我没及格。那儿有这门必修课,口头表达,这门我没及格。"

"为什么?"

"噢,我说不好。"我不太想谈这个,我感觉还有点儿头晕什么的,而且我他妈一下子头疼得要命,真的。可是看得出他想知道为什么,就多少跟他说了一点。"这门课是要求班上每个同学都得站起来发言,你也知道,全是自发的。要是哪个同学跑题了,别的同学都要在第一时间向他喊'跑题!'这几乎让我气得要命。这门课我得了个F。"

"为什么?"

"噢,我说不好。喊别人跑题这种事让我来气。我也说不好,问题是我喜欢别人跑题,那样更有趣。"

"别人跟你说什么时,你不在乎他是否紧扣主题吗?"

"噢,当然!我喜欢别人紧扣主题,可是我不喜欢他们过分紧扣主题。我说不好。我想我是不喜欢别人从头到尾紧扣主题吧。口头表达这门课得了高分的,全是从头到尾紧扣主题的——我承认,可是有个叫理查德·金塞拉的,他不会太紧扣主题,他们老是向他喊'跑题!'太可恶了。因为首先说来,他这个人很容易紧张——我是说他这个人确实容易变得很紧张——每次轮到他发言时,他嘴唇老哆嗦。你要是坐在教室里的最后一排,就几乎听不到他说什么。可是他嘴唇稍微没哆嗦得那么厉害时,比起其他人,我更喜欢听他说。可是他这门课也几乎没及格,得了个D+,因为他们老是在向他喊'跑题!'比方说,他有次说的是他爸爸在佛蒙特州买的一个农场。他发言的那段时间里从头到尾,他们一直向他喊'跑题!'这门课的老师文森先生给他打了F,因为他没能说明白农场上有什么动植物之类的玩意儿。这位理查德·金塞拉是怎么发言的呢?他一开始说的全是那种事——后来却突然说起他妈妈收到的一封信,他舅舅写的,还说他舅舅怎么在四十二岁时得了脊髓灰质炎,还有他不想让大家去医院看他，因为不想人看到他用支具。他的发言跟农场没多大关系——我承认——不过那样也**挺好**的，像这样听别人讲起他舅舅挺好，特别是他开始时说的是他爸爸的农场，后来突然就更想讲他舅舅。我是说如果他讲得挺好，还有点儿激动，像这样老是向他大喊'跑题！'也太不地道了……我说不好，很难解释。"我也不想试着解释，头一个原因，就是我一下子头疼得很厉害。我求天求地，安托利尼太太赶紧把咖啡端来吧，这件事让我恼火得够呛——我是说如果谁要是**嘴里说**咖啡好了，而实际上并没好。

"霍尔顿……跟你提个又小又有点儿乏味、关于教学方面的问题，你难道不认为干任何事，都要分时间、场合吗？你难道不认为既然他一开始说的是他爸爸的农场，就该紧扣主题，**然后**回头再说他舅舅的支具的事吗？**要么**，如果他觉得以他舅舅的支具作为话题很发人深思，那他是不是应该首先选择那个作为话题——而不是农场？"

我不太想思考，也不太想回答，我头疼，感觉糟糕，而且说实话，我甚至感觉胃有点儿疼。

"是吧——我说不好。我想他是该那样，我是说我想如果他对他舅舅最感兴趣，就应该以他舅舅为话题，而不是农场。可我是说，很多情况下，除非你开始说了**并非**让你最感兴趣的那一样，否则不会**知道**什么是你最感兴趣的，我是说有时候这无法避免。我的想法是这样，如果他说的至少还有点儿意思，而且他为什么事情变得很激动，就应该让他说下去。我喜欢看到别人为什么事激动，那样挺好。你只是不认识文森先生而已，他有时候真能把你气疯，就是他再加上他妈的整班人。我是说他老是从头到尾跟你说要**统一**、**简化**，可有些事你就是没办法那样**做**。我是说如果只因为别人**想让**你这样，那你几乎从来不能把有些事简化统一。你不知道这位文森先生，我是说他是很聪明，不过你也看得出，他也不是太有脑子。"

"咖啡，先生们，**终于**来了。"安托利尼太太说着进来了，用托盘端着咖啡、蛋糕之类的东西,"霍尔顿,绝对不准偷看我,我一团糟。"

"您好,安托利尼太太。"我说着要起身,可是安托利尼先生拽着我的上衣又让我坐下来。安托利尼太太夹了一头卷头发用的铁夹子,没抹口红什么的,样子不太漂亮,显得很老。

"我不陪两位了,你们开喝吧。"她说着把托盘放到茶几上,把玻璃杯全推到一边,"你妈妈好吧,霍尔顿?"

"她很好,谢谢。我最近没见她,但是上回——"

"亲爱的,霍尔顿需要什么,都在放铺盖的壁橱里,最上面一格。我要睡觉了,累坏了。"安托利尼太太说,她看样子也是如此,"你们两个男的能不能自己铺好沙发?"

"都让我们自己来,你赶快溜上床吧。"安托利尼先生说完亲了安托利尼太太一下。她跟我说了再见后就进了卧室。他们总是不避人地亲来亲去。

一杯咖啡我喝了一点,又吃了半块硬得像石头的什么蛋糕。安托利尼先生只是又倒了一杯酒,闻得出,这酒他调得很有劲儿,他不留神可能会变成酒鬼。

"我几周前跟你爸爸共进过一顿午餐,"他突然说,"你知道吗?"

"不,我不知道。"

"你当然也清楚,他为你操心得不得了。"

"我知道,我知道他是这样。"我说。

"显然,在给我打电话前,他刚刚收到你上一所学校的校长所写的一封让他很痛苦的长信,里面说你一点儿也不用功。逃学,每门课都不预习。总之,是个到处——"

"我没有逃学,学校不允许。倒是有几门我偶尔缺课,例如我跟您提过的口头表达课,可是我没有逃学。"

我根本不想讨论这件事。咖啡让我的胃感觉好受了一点儿,头还是疼得厉害。

安托利尼先生又点了根烟——他烟抽得像个瘾君子,然后他说:"说实话,霍尔顿,我也不知道到底该怎么跟你说。"

"我知道,我很是不可理喻,我意识到了。"

"我有种感觉你正在迈向一次很危险、很危险的跌落,再这样下去,会吃很大、很大的苦头,可我真的不知道是什么样……你在听我说吗?"

"对。"

看得出,他正在努力专心思考。

"可能是这样:到了三十岁时,你坐在一间酒吧里,讨厌每个走进来的看样子像是在大学里打过橄榄球的那种人;要么你可能刚好得到了足够的教育,讨厌那些说'这是咱俩之间的秘密'的人;要么你可能落脚在某一间商行的办公室,向坐得最近的速记员扔回形针。我真的不知道该怎么说,可是你究竟明不明白我的意思?"

"当然明白,"我说,我真的明白,"可是您对讨厌这件事说得不对,我是说讨厌那些球员什么的,您真的搞错了。我讨厌的人并不是很多,而可能是这样:我可能会讨厌他们一**小阵子**,就像在潘西认识的那个家伙,斯特拉雷德,还有另外一位罗伯特·阿克利。我偶尔讨厌**他们**——我承认——但是不太久,这就是我的意思。过上一阵子,如果看不到他们,如果他们不进我的房间,要么有几顿饭在食堂看不到他们,我就会有点儿想念他们,我是说我有点儿想念他们。"

安托利尼先生有一阵子没说话,他起身又取了一大块冰放进酒杯,接着又坐下来,看得出他在思考。可我一直希望他等到白天再接着说,而不是那时候,可他劲头十足。人们老是这样,你没精神讨论时,他们偏偏劲头十足。

"好吧,你现在听我说一会儿……我想说得能让你记住,可是不一定能。我这一两天会给你写封信,这样你就能理顺一切,不过现在还是听我说吧。"他又开始专心思考,然后又说,"我觉得你再这样下去,吃到的不是一般的苦头,是要命的苦头。吃苦头的人感觉不到,也听不到什么时候苦头就这么大了,而只是一直吃下去,吃下去。对一个人来说,一辈子里注定会不时去寻找一些他们自身周围所不能提供的东西,要么他们以为自身周围无法提供,所以放弃了寻找,他们甚至在还没有真正开始寻找前,就放弃了。你明白我的意思吗?"

"明白,先生。"

"肯定吗?"

"对。"

他又起身往杯子里倒了些酒,然后又坐下,过了很久,他什么也没说。

"我不想吓唬你,"他说,"可是我很清楚地看到,你就为了一个极不值得的理由,不是这样就是那样,正在轰轰烈烈地死去。"他怪怪地看了我一眼,"如果我给你写下一点东西,你会不会仔细看?而且保存下去?"

"我当然会。"我说。我真的是,到现在还保留着他写给我的那张纸呢。

他走到房间那边的书桌那儿,也没坐下,就在一张纸上写了些字,然后回来坐下,手里拿着那张纸。"很奇怪,这句话不是由一位职业诗人所写,而是由一位精神分析学家写的,他叫威廉·斯特克尔,这就是他所……你在听我说话吗?"

"对,当然,我在听。"

"这就是他所说的:'一个不成熟的人的标志是他愿意为了某个理由而轰轰烈烈地死去,而一个成熟的人的标志是他愿意为了某个理由而谦恭地活下去。'"

他侧身把那张纸递给我。我接过后马上看了一遍,向他道谢后放进口袋。难得他那么费事写下来,他真的挺好,可问题是我不太想专心听他讲。乖乖,我突然感到真他妈困。

看样子他根本不困,首先,他那会儿可以说是精神抖擞。"我觉得近期,"他说,"你一定得认识到自己想往哪个方向发展,然后一定要对准那个方向出发,要马上。你再也浪费不起多一秒的时间了,你浪费不起。"

我点点头,因为他正盯着我看,可是我不太肯定他话里的意思。我当时**很**肯定我知道,但不是百分之百有把握,我太他妈累了。

"我很不愿意这样跟你说,"他说,"可我认为你一旦对自己以后何去何从有了清晰的概念,首先就会在学校里用功学习,你必须这样。你是个学生——不管这点对你来说有没有吸引力。你追求的是知识。我想你会发现,一旦你见识过太多文塞斯先生那种人,还有他们的口头——"

"是文森先生。"我说。他是指太多文森先生那种人,不是文塞斯先生,可我还是不该打岔。

"好吧——文森先生那种人。你见识过太多文森先生那种人之后,你会开始越来越接近——也就是说,如果你**愿意**的话,如果你寻找和等待——接近你内心会非常、非常珍视的认识,首先你会发现,你不是第一个对人类行为感到困惑、害怕乃至反感的,在这方面,绝对不是只有你。了解这一点会让你激动,你还会得到激励。许许多多人跟你现在一样,在道德和精神上同样感到困惑。幸好,有些人对自己的苦恼做了记录,你愿意的话,就能向他们学习。同样会有一天,如果你有了可以教给别人的东西,他们就能从你这儿学到,这种方式是美好的,有来有往。这不是教育,而是历史,是诗歌。"他停下来喝了一大口高杯酒,然后又开始说了。乖乖,他可真够激动的,还好我没拦住不让他说。"我并不是想跟你说,"他说,"只有受过教育、有学识的人才能对这个世界做出重要贡献,并非如此。但我的确要说,对受过教育、有学识的人而言,如果他们首先也是才华横溢、具有创新精神的——不幸的是这种情况很少见——他们可能会比**仅仅**是才华横溢和有创新精神的人留下无限多更宝贵的记录,他们往往能更清晰地表达自己的意见,一般说来，他们也有顺着自己的想法坚持到底的热情。而且——最重要的是——他们十个里头有九个比那些没学识的思考者更谦恭。你到底明不明白我的意思？"

"明白，先生。"

他又是半天没说话，不知道你有没有遇到过这种情况，就是那样，坐着等别人一边想一边说，有点儿难受，真的。我一直在忍着别打哈欠，倒不是我烦了还是怎么样——我没烦——只是我他妈突然困得要命。

"学校教育还有另外一个作用，如果你接受学校教育相当长一段时间，它就开始让你对自己的心性如何有个认识，认识到什么适合自己的心性，还可能认识到什么不适合。经过一段时间，你就会了解哪些想法适合你独特的心性。首先，这有可能让你节省下大量时间，而不用试来试去对你来说不合适、不相称的观念，你会开始明白自己的真实心性如何，并且相应吸收合适的想法。"

这时，我突然打了个哈欠，我真是个**没礼貌的混蛋**，可我愣是没忍住！

安托利尼先生只是笑了。"来吧，"他说着站起身，"我们来给你铺沙发。"

我跟着他去到壁橱那儿，想把最上面一格的几条床单、毛毯之类的东西拿下来，可他手里还拿着高杯酒，他就喝光了酒，把杯子放到地板上，然后把那些东西抱下来。我帮他抱到沙发那儿，我们一块儿铺床。他不是很在行，什么都没掖好，不过我无所谓，我太困了，站着也能睡。

"你的女孩儿都好吧？"

"都还好。"我那会儿成了个很不会交谈的人，可是我不想聊。

"萨莉呢？"他认识萨莉·海斯这妞儿，我给他介绍过。

"还好，我今天下午才约她见过面。"乖乖，那好像是二十年前的事！"我们不再有很多共同点了。"

"很漂亮的女孩儿嘛。另外一个怎么样？你跟我说过的，在缅因州？"

"噢——简·加拉格尔，她挺好吧，我大概明天会给她打个电话。"

我们已经收拾好沙发。"你就睡这儿，"安托利尼先生说，"可是我不知道你的腿究竟该怎么放。"

"没关系，我睡惯了短床。"我说，"非常感谢，先生，您和您太太今天晚上真是救了我一命啊。"

"你知道洗手间在哪儿，想找什么，尽管喊我们。我要在厨房待一会儿——开灯不会影响你吧？"

"不——根本不会，非常感谢。"

"那好。晚安，帅哥。"

"晚安，先生，非常感谢。"

他进了厨房，我去厕所脱了衣服。没办法刷牙，因为我没带牙刷。也没带睡衣，安托利尼先生忘了借给我一套，所以我只好回到客厅，拧灭了沙发边上的一盏小灯，然后只穿着短裤就躺下了。沙发对我来说太短，但我真的可以眼也不合站着睡。我只是有几秒钟没睡着，在想安托利尼先生对我说的每一句话，就是关于发现自己心性如何什么的。他真是个很聪明的人，可是我他妈连眼睛都睁不开，就睡着了。

接着发生了一件事，我根本不想讲。

我突然醒了，不知道当时几点钟，可是我醒了。我感到头上有什么东西，是一个人的手。乖乖，真他妈把我吓得要死。原来是安托利尼先生的手，他在黑暗里，坐在沙发边的地板上，要么在抚弄，要么在拍我的头。乖乖，我当时肯定是一跳而起，跳得很高。

"你他妈在干吗？"

"什么也没有！我只是坐在这儿，欣赏——"

"你他妈到底在干吗？"我又说了一遍。我不知道他妈的该说什么——我是说这太他妈让人难堪了。

"你小声点好不好？我只是坐在这儿——"

"我反正得走了。"我说——乖乖，我太紧张了！我开始摸黑穿我的破裤子，几乎穿不上，我太他妈紧张了。我在学校认识的混账变态佬比你们谁见过的都多，他们老是趁我在场时，做出一些变态举动。

"你去哪儿？"安托利尼先生说。他尽量表现得很他妈若无其事，很冷静，可是他他妈的也根本不是太冷静，你得相信我的话。

"我把手提箱什么的全放在火车站了，我想我最好去取出来，我的东西全在里边。"

"到明天早上还会在那儿，现在继续睡吧，我也要去睡。你怎么回事？"

"我没事，只是我的钱什么的全在一个手提箱里。我很快就会回来，我会很快打的回来。"我说，乖乖，我摸着黑真是跌跌撞撞，"问题是钱不是我的，是我妈的，我还——"

"别瞎说了，霍尔顿，你继续睡吧，我也要去睡了，钱到明天早晨还会好好在那儿——"

"不，我不是开玩笑，我得走了，真的。"我他妈几乎穿好了衣服，只是找不到领带，忘了放在哪儿。我穿上夹克，也不打领带了。安托利尼先生坐在离我不远的一把椅子上，在看着我。屋里黑着，我看不清楚，可是我知道他在看着我，随他便。他还在喝酒，从不离手的酒杯还在手里拿着。

"你是个非常、非常奇怪的孩子。"

"我知道。"我说。我根本没有到处找领带，所以没打领带就走了。"再见，先生，"我说，"非常感谢，我不是开玩笑。"

我去门口时，他一直跟在我后面。我按了电梯铃后，他还是待在破门道那儿。他只是又说了遍我是个"非常、非常奇怪的孩子"那种话，奇怪个屁。然后他待在门道里，一直等到破电梯来。我他妈整个这辈子也没有那次等电梯的时间长，我敢发誓。

我等电梯时，他一直站在那儿，我他妈也不知道该说什么，就说："我要开始读些好书，真的要。"我是说总得说点儿**什么**，那场面真的让人很尴尬。

"你拿了手提箱马上回来，我门不闩。"

"非常感谢，"我说，"再见！"电梯终于来了，我乘电梯下楼。乖乖，我打战打个没完，还在冒汗。碰到这种变态事情，我会出汗出个没完。从小到大，这种事我遇到过有二十回，受不了。

25

到外面时,天色正在变亮,也很冷,不过因为我身上大汗淋漓,所以感觉还不错。

我他妈不知道该去哪儿,不想再去找家旅馆住,那样会把菲比的钱花光,所以最后只是走到列克星敦大道,然后坐地铁去了中央大火车站,我的手提箱还在那儿。我琢磨可以在破候车厅里睡,里面有很多长椅,我也是那么干的。那样睡上一阵子还不算太糟糕,因为里面没多少人,所以脚也能放到长椅上,可是这件事我不想多说,并非很舒服。你根本别去试,我不是开玩笑,会让你沮丧的。

我只睡到九点钟左右,因为有成千上万人开始拥进候车室,我不得不把脚放下来。因为脚放在地上,睡不好,所以坐了起来。我的头还疼,甚至更厉害了。而且,我想当时是我这辈子感觉最沮丧的时候。

我不愿意想,可还是开始想着安托利尼先生,不知道安托利尼太太看到我没在那儿睡觉时,他会怎样跟她解释。不过这点我倒不是太担心,因为我知道安托利尼先生是个很聪明的人,会编些话给她听,会说我回家了什么的,这我倒不是很担心。**真正**让我担心的,是我醒了发现他正在拍我的头那件事。我是说会不会也许只是我搞错了,以为他在对我有同性恋的举动。我怀疑或者可能他只是喜欢在别人睡着后轻轻拍他的头而已,我是说这种事情你怎么能很有把握?不可能。我甚至开始琢磨也许我**应该**取了手提箱再去他家,就像我跟他说过的那样。我是说就算他是个同性恋,不用说他一直对我很好。我想到我那么晚给他打电话，他没有见怪，还说我想的话，可以马上去他家。他还不嫌费事地给了我关于发现自己心性如何等建议。另外，他是詹姆斯·卡斯尔死后唯一一个走近他的人，我跟你说过那个男生的事。我想的尽是那些，越想越沮丧。我是说我开始琢磨也许应该回他家，也许他的确只是轻轻拍我的头而已，也不他妈为什么。可是我越想越沮丧，越是为此心里乱作一团。更糟糕的是我他妈眼睛酸得要命，因为我没怎么睡觉，所以又酸又痛。不仅如此，我还有点着凉，可是我他妈根本没手帕。手提箱里倒是有几条，可我不想把手提箱从保管箱里取出来，并在大庭广众之下打开。

我旁边的长椅上有本别人留下的杂志，我就读了起来，以为至少能有一小会儿不想安托利尼先生以及别的千头万绪的事情。可我开始读的这篇破文章几乎让我感觉更糟糕了。它写的全是关于荷尔蒙的事，里面描述了如果荷尔蒙正常，你的脸和眼睛等应该看起来怎么样，我没有一样对得上，我的外表正像文章里那个荷尔蒙大有问题的家伙，就开始担心我那不争气的荷尔蒙。接着又读到另外一篇文章，关于怎样判断自己有没有得上癌症的。里面说如果你嘴里的溃疡不能很快痊愈，那就是你很可能得了癌症的信号。我嘴里面有个地方溃疡，已经有两星期左右，所以我估计自己得了癌症。那本杂志可真能给人打气啊。我最后不读了，出去走一走。我琢磨既然我患了癌症，应该只有几个月的活头，我真的那样想，我甚至肯定自己快死了。那样想，肯定让自己感觉不太舒服。

当时好像有点儿要下雨的样子，我还是出去走了走，第一个原因是我琢磨该去吃点早餐。我根本不饿，可是琢磨至少该吃点东西，我是说至少吃点含维生素的东西。我就开始往东走，那边有很便宜的饭馆，因为我不想花很多钱。

走路时，我从两个家伙身边经过，他们正在把一棵大圣诞树卸下卡车。一个家伙老是对另一个说："把这个狗娘养的竖起来！竖起来，我的天!"这样说一棵圣诞树当然很过瘾,尽管粗鲁点,但还算有趣,我笑了起来。这可能是我最不该干的,因为在开始笑的那一刻,我觉得我要吐了,真的。我甚至开始要吐,可是那种感觉又没了。我不知道为什么,我是说我没吃什么不卫生还是怎么样的东西,而且我的胃功能通常很好。不管怎么样,呕吐的感觉过去了。我琢磨我要是吃点东西,感觉就会好一些,就进了一家看样子档次很低的餐馆,要了甜甜圈和咖啡,只是没吃甜甜圈,因为我几乎无法下咽。问题是你为什么事特别沮丧的时候,就真他妈无法下咽。不过那个侍者挺好,他把甜甜圈拿回去,没收钱,我只是喝了咖啡就离开了,开始朝第五大道走去。

那天是星期一,很快就到圣诞节了,店铺全开着,所以在第五大道上走一走也不算太糟糕。圣诞气氛已经很浓,那些样子瘦不拉叽的圣诞老人站在街角摇着那种铃铛,救世军的女孩儿——没涂口红之类的女孩儿——也在摇铃铛。我到处看了看,想找到前一天吃早餐时碰到的那两个修女,可是看不到。我知道不会看到,因为她们说过她们是到纽约当老师的,可是我一直在找她们。不管怎么样,一转眼,圣诞气氛就很浓了。无数小孩儿跟着他们的妈妈来到市中心,上上下下汽车,进进出出店铺。我希望菲比丫头也来了,她没那么小了,不会在玩具部死盯着玩具看,可是她喜欢到处胡闹和看人。前年圣诞节我带她去市中心买东西,我们玩够了心。我想那是在布鲁明代尔商店吧,在鞋类部,我们假装她——菲比丫头——想买双高帮风雪鞋,就是有无数鞋带孔的那种。我们把可怜的售货员折腾得晕头转向。菲比试了有二十双鞋,每试一双,那个可怜的家伙都要把鞋子的鞋带全穿好。那样做很捣蛋,菲比这丫头却开心得要命。我们最后买的是双软帮鞋,记账买的。售货员的态度很好,我想他也知道我们在胡闹,因为菲比丫头老是笑得咯咯响。

总之,我就顺着第五大道走啊走啊,也没打领带。突然,有件很怪异的事情发生了。每次我到了街区尽头走下该死的路沿时,我就有种感觉,就是我再也不了街对面。我想我只是继续走,走,走,没人会再次见到我。乖乖,我真是吓坏了,你想象不出。我开始出汗出得一塌糊涂——整件衬衫内衣什么的全是汗。接着,我做起另外一件事:走到街区尽头时,我就装作和弟弟艾里说话。我会跟他说:"艾里,别让我消失。艾里,别让我消失。艾里,别让我消失。求你了,艾里。"我到了街对面而没有消失时,就会谢谢他。然后一到下个街角,就全部重演一遍。但我一直在走着,我想我是有点儿害怕停下来——说实话,我不记得了。我记得我一口气走到第六十几街才停下来,已经过了动物园。然后,我坐到一条长椅上。我几乎接不上来气,而且还在出汗出得一塌糊涂。我坐在那儿,我想有一小时吧,最后决定了该怎么做。我决定离开,决定再也不回家了,永远不再上另外一所学校。我决定只跟菲比丫头见一面,算是跟她道个别,把她的过节钱还给她,然后就开始搭便车向西部出发。我琢磨该怎么办呢,我会去霍兰隧道,在那里请人搭我一程,然后再搭一程,再一程,再一程,要不了几天,我就会到达西部某个地方。那里风景很好,阳光明媚,而且谁也不认识我。我会找个活干,我琢磨我能在加油站找到活干,帮人给车加油。我不在乎干什么工作,只要谁都不认识我,我也不认识谁就好。我想我会怎么样呢?我会装得又聋又哑,这样就他妈不用跟谁做蠢而无用的交谈了。谁想跟我说什么,就不得不写在纸上拿给我看,这样一来二去,他们就会烦得要命,我下半辈子就不用再说什么话了。每个人都以为我只是个可怜的又聋又哑的混蛋,不再搭理我。他们让我给他们的破车加油,然后付我工资。我会用我挣的钞票盖座小木屋,余生就在那儿住。我会把木屋盖得靠近森林边上,但不是在森林中间,因为我他妈想一直有阳光高照。一日三餐全是我自己做,到后来,想结婚的话,我会去认识一个美丽的女孩儿,她也又聋又哑,我们就结婚。她会来和我一起住在木屋里,她想跟我说什么话,会像别人一样,写到一张破纸条上。我们要是有了小孩儿,会把他们藏起来,给他们买很多书本,自个儿教他们读书认字。

想着想着,我他妈变得万分激动,真的。我知道关于装扮成又聋又哑的人这个想法很离谱，可我还是喜欢那样想，我也真的决定去西部。我想干的第一件事，就是跟菲比这丫头告别。所以，我突然像个疯子似的跑过马路——说实话，那差点儿让我送了命——我进了一家文具店，买了本便笺簿和一支铅笔。我琢磨可以给她写张纸条，叫她去哪儿跟我见面，好让我跟她告别，顺便把过节钱还给她。我把纸条拿去她们的学校，找校长办公室的某个人转交。但我只是把便笺簿和铅笔装到口袋里，然后开始飞快地往她们的学校走去——我在文具店时太激动，没办法写纸条。我走得快，因为我想让她在回家吃午饭前看到纸条，我的时间不太多。

我当然知道她学校的位置，因为小时候我也在那儿上的学。到了后，我感觉怪怪的。一开始，我还不能肯定自己记不记得里面的样子，可是我真的还记得，跟我上学时一模一样。里面还是那个大院子，那儿老是有点儿暗，灯全用罩子罩着，好不被球打破。地上到处还是同样的用白漆画的圈子，用来玩游戏什么的。还是旧篮球筐，没球网——只有篮板和球筐。

那儿一个人也看不到，很可能是因为还没到休息时间，也没到午饭时间。我只看到一个小孩儿，一个有色人种小孩儿，他正往厕所走，屁股口袋里插了个木制许可牌，跟我们以前用的一样。有了那个，说明他得到了允许，可以上厕所。

我还在出汗，不过没那么厉害了。我走到楼梯那儿坐在第一级上，拿出买的便笺簿和铅笔。楼梯上有股跟我以前上学时一样的气味，好像有人刚在上边撒了一泡尿，学校里的楼梯上总有类似气味。不管怎么样，我坐下写了张纸条：

亲爱的菲比：

  我等不到星期三了，我很可能今天下午就开始搭便车去西部。你要是能出来，十二点一刻跟我在艺术博物馆门口附近见面，我会还你的过节钱，我没花多少。

爱你的，
霍尔顿

　　她上的这所学校实际上就在博物馆附近，反正她回家吃午饭也得经过那儿，所以我知道她完全能跟我见面。

　　后来我就走上楼梯找校长办公室，好找人把纸条送到她的班上交给她。我把纸条折了有十道，让谁也没法打开看。在他妈这种破学校，谁都靠不住，但是我知道如果我说我是她哥，他们会把纸条交给她。

　　上楼梯时，我一下子又感觉想呕吐，只是没吐出来。我坐了一下，感觉好了点儿。可是在我往下坐时，看到的东西又让我气得要命。有人在墙上写了"操你"两个字，他妈的快把我气疯了。我想象菲比和别的小孩儿都会看到，就会很纳闷那到底是他妈什么意思，最后，哪个下流的小孩儿就会告诉他们那两个字是什么意思，当然全是胡说八道。然后他们就会想着这件事，甚至可能好几天都会为此担心。我老是想着要干掉写那两个字的人，我琢磨会是哪个变态流浪汉深夜溜进学校撒了泡尿还是怎么样，然后在墙上写了那两个字。我老是想象我抓到他在写，我会把他的头往石阶上撞，直到他他妈的血流遍地，一命呜呼。可是我也知道，我没胆量做那种事，这我知道，所以更沮丧了。实话跟你说，我竟然几乎没胆量用手把它从墙上擦掉。我害怕哪个老师看到我在擦，会以为是我写的。但是不管怎么样，最后我还是把它擦掉了，然后就走进校长办公室。

　　校长好像不在，有位好像有一百岁上下的老太太在打字。我告诉她我是4B-1班菲比·考尔菲尔德的哥哥，请她把纸条转交给她。我说是件很重要的事，就是告诉她我妈病了，不能给她做饭，所以她得跟我去吃便餐。那位老太太很好，她从我手上接过纸条，叫来隔壁办公室的另外一位女士，那位女士就把纸条拿去给菲比。然后我跟这位上百岁的老太太闲聊了几句，她很和气。我告诉她我当年上的也是这所学校，我哥哥、弟弟也是。她问我现在在哪儿上学，我说是潘西，她说潘西是所很好的学校。就算我想，我也没有气力更正她。再说，既然她认为潘西是所很好的学校，就让她那么认为好了，你也会很不愿意告诉一位百岁上下的老人什么新东西的，说了她也听不进去。这样过了一会儿我就走了，好笑的是，她向我嚷了句："祝你好运！"像我离开潘西时斯潘塞老先生对我那样。天哪，我真不喜欢别人在我离开时向我嚷"祝你好运！"叫人沮丧。

下楼时，我走的是另外一道楼梯，又看到墙上写有"操你"两个字。我想把它擦掉，可这次是用小刀什么的刻在墙上，擦不掉，真是没治了。就算你有一百万年时间来擦"操你"这两个字，可是你连这世界上的一半也擦不完，不可能。

我望望课间休息处那儿的钟，才十一点四十分，到和菲比丫头见面，还有很多时间可以消磨，可我只是向博物馆走去，也没别的地方可去。我想搭便车去西部前，也许可以在某个电话间停一下，给简·加拉格尔这妞儿打个电话，可是我没心情，头一个原因就是我甚至不能肯定她是不是已经放假到家了，所以我只是到了博物馆，在那里转悠。

在博物馆等菲比时——我就站在大门里面——两个小孩儿走到我跟前，问我知不知道木乃伊在哪儿。那个小孩儿，就是问我话的小孩儿，裤扣没扣。我跟他说了，他就边跟我说话边扣上了——他竟然懒得跑到柱子后面那种地方扣上，逗死我了。我本来要笑出来，可是我害怕会再有想呕吐的感觉，所以没笑。"木乃伊在哪儿，哥们儿？"他又问了一遍，"你知道吗？"

我跟他们瞎扯了一会儿。"木乃伊？是什么？"我问那个小孩儿。

"你知道，木乃伊——那些死人，就是埋在风墓里的。"

风墓，逗死我了，他指的是坟墓。

"你们怎么不上学？"我问。

"今天没课。"那个一直说话的小孩儿说。他在撒谎,我百分之百肯定,这个小混蛋。反正菲比还没来,我也没什么事,就帮他们找放木乃伊的地方。乖乖,我以前知道准确的位置,但是我几年没来过这座博物馆了。

"你们对木乃伊很感兴趣吗?"我说。

"对。"

"你的朋友不会说话吗?"我问他。

"他不是我朋友,是我弟弟。"

"他不会说话吗?"我看着另外那个一句话也没说过的小孩儿。"你根本不会说话吗?"我问他。

"会。"他说,"我不想说。"

到最后,我们找到放木乃伊的地方走了进去。

"你知不知道埃及人是怎样埋死人的?"我问那个小孩儿。

"不知道。"

"好吧,你应该知道,很有趣。他们把死人的脸用布裹起来,那些布用神秘的化学物质处理过,这样,死人就能在坟墓里埋上几千年,他们的脸却不会腐烂还是怎么样。除了埃及人,谁也不知道他们是怎样做到这一点的,就算现代科学也做不到。"

要到达放木乃伊的地方,就得穿过一条很窄的走廊,两边全是从法老坟墓里搞来的石头。那里很瘆人,看得出,跟我在一起的那两个棒小子不是太喜欢。他们紧紧挨着我,根本不说话的那个小孩儿几乎是一直拽着我的袖子。"咱们走吧,"他对他哥说,"我已经看过了。嗨,走吧。"他转身就跑掉了。

"他的胆量比耗子还小。"另一个说,"再见。"他也跑掉了。

那样一来,坟墓里就只剩下我一个人。说起来,我还有点儿喜欢那样呢。那儿很不错,很安静。你永远猜不到这时我突然在墙上看到了什么,又是"操你"这两个字,是用红粉笔或者别的什么写的,就在墙上装了玻璃部分的下面，在石头下面。

这就是全部麻烦所在，你永远找不到一个不错而且安静的地方，因为不存在。可能你以为有，但是你到了那里后，趁你不注意，有人会溜进来，在你眼皮底下写上"操你"两个字，不信你什么时候试试。我甚至在想，如果有一天我死掉，他们会把我塞进一个坟墓，还立个碑，上面刻着"霍尔顿·考尔菲尔德"，还有我哪年出生，哪年死的，然后就在下面，会有"操你"这两个字。说实话，我对这件事有把握。

从放木乃伊的地方出来后，我不得不上厕所。说实话，我有点拉肚子。拉肚子我倒不太担心，可是还发生了别的事。我从厕所出来，快到大门口时，我可以说晕倒了。但我还算幸运，我是说摔到地上可能会让我送命，但我只是侧着身子摔了下来。说来有趣，晕倒后，我感觉好了些，真的。我手臂上有点儿小伤，就是摔到的地方，不过感觉没他妈那么晕了。

那时是十二点十分左右，所以我回去站在门口等菲比丫头。我想那可能是见她的最后一面，我是说和家里人的最后一面。我琢磨我很可能还会再见到他们，但几年内不会。我琢磨我可能在三十五岁左右回家，那是假如得知家里的谁快死了，想见我最后一面，那会是让我离开小屋回家的唯一原因。我甚至开始想象我回家时，会是怎样的场面。我知道我妈会紧张得要命，会哭起来，求我待在家里，别回我的小屋，但我还是要走。我会一副若无其事的样子，让她平静下来，然后到客厅的另一边掏出烟盒，点着一根烟，冷静得要命。我会让他们什么时候想的话就去看我，可是我也不坚持要他们去。我会让菲比丫头在夏天，还有圣诞节、复活节放假时过去看我。还有 D. B.，要是他想在一个舒适安静的地方写作，我会让他去我那里过一阵子，不过他不能在我的小屋里写电影剧本，只能写短篇小说和书。我要定下一条规矩，就是不管谁来看我，都不许做虚伪的事，谁要做就别待。

突然，我看到存物处的钟已经一点二十五。我开始害怕学校里那个老太太有可能让另外一个女士别把我的纸条交给菲比丫头，开始害怕她叫她把纸条烧掉还是怎么样。想到这里把我他妈吓坏了，我真的想在开路前见上菲比丫头一面，我是说，我还拿着她的过节钱呢。

终于，我看到她了，是透过门的玻璃部分看到她的。之所以能看到，是因为她戴着我的破猎帽——大约十英里外都能看到她。

我走出门口，开始顺着石阶往下走去接她。我不理解的是，她带了一只大手提箱。她正在穿过第五大道，拖着只破大手提箱，几乎拖不动。走近后，我发现那是我的旧手提箱，就是在伍顿中学上学时用过的那个。我想不通她究竟干吗要带着。"嗨。"她走近时说。因为那只破手提箱，她累得几乎上气不接下气。

"我还以为你不来了呢。"我说，"这只手提箱里到底他妈的装了什么？我什么也不需要，我就这么走了，连放在火车站的那两只手提箱也不带。里面到底他妈的装了什么？"

她放下手提箱。"我的衣服，"她说，"我要跟你一起走，行吗？好不好？"

"什么？"我说。她那样说差点儿让我摔了个跟头，真的，我可以向上帝发誓。我有点儿头晕，我觉得我又要晕过去了还是怎么样。

"我拿着东西从后面的电梯下来的，好不让查伦看到。箱子不重，我只装了两身衣服、软帮鞋、内衣、袜子，还有些别的东西。你拎一下，不重，拎一下嘛……我不能跟你一块儿走吗，霍尔顿？不行吗？**求你了**。"

"不行，闭嘴。"

我觉得我快要彻底晕倒了，我是说我原意不是让她闭嘴，可是我觉得我要再次晕倒了。

"为什么不行？**求你了**，霍尔顿！我不会干什么的——只要跟你一块儿走，如此而已！你要是不想让我带，我甚至可以一件衣服也不带——只带——"

"你什么也不能带，因为你走不成，我一个人走，你给我闭嘴。"

"**求你了**,霍尔顿。**请**你带我走,我会非常、非常、非常——你根本不用——"

"你走不成,现在给我闭嘴!箱子给我。"我说着从她手里夺过手提箱,我差点儿要揍她。有一秒钟工夫,我觉得我想揍她,真的。

她哭了起来。

"我还以为你会在学校的戏剧里面演出呢,我以为你要在那出戏里演本内迪克特·阿诺德呢。"我说得很难听,"你想干吗?岂有此理,你不演戏了吗?"这让她哭得更凶了,我却高兴起来。突然,我想让她眼珠子哭掉才好呢。我几乎讨厌起她来,我觉得我讨厌她的最主要的原因,是她如果跟我一起走就演不成戏了。

"来吧。"我说着开始在博物馆的台阶上往上走。我琢磨可以这样,我去把她带来的破手提箱放到存物处,她可以在放学后三点钟时再取出来,我知道她没法把它拖回学校。"来吧,快点儿。"我说。

可她没跟我一起上台阶,她不肯。我还是上去了,把手提箱拿去寄存,然后我又下来了。她还站在人行道上,但是在我走向她时,她背过身。她会那样的,她想么干就会把身子转过去,不对着你。"我哪儿也不去,我改变主意了。你别哭,闭嘴。"我说。好笑的是,我那样说时,她根本没在哭。"走吧,我跟你走回学校,快点儿,你要迟到了。"

她不肯理我还是怎么样。我试了下想抓住她的手,可她不让,她不断转过身背对着我。

"你吃过午饭没有?你没吃午饭吗?"

她不肯理我,只是取下了我的红猎帽——我给她的那顶——几乎正好摔到我脸上,然后她又背过身子。我快被气死了,但什么也没说,只是捡起猎帽塞进我的外套口袋。

"嗨,走吧,我跟你走回学校。"我说。

"我不回学校。"

她那样说,让我不知道说什么才好,只是在那儿站了几分钟。

"你**必须**回学校。你想在那出戏里演出,不是吗?你想演本内迪克特·阿诺德,不是吗?"

"不想。"

"你当然想,理所当然你想。走吧,我们一块儿走。"我说,"首先嘛,我哪儿也不去,跟你说过了。我要回家,你一回学校我就回家。我先去火车站取我的手提箱,然后直接——"

"我说过我不回学校,你想干吗就干吗,我不回学校。"她说,"你就闭嘴吧。"这是我头一次听到她说让我闭嘴,太难听了。天哪,太难听了,比骂我还难听。她还是不肯看我,每次我想把手搭到她肩膀上还是哪儿,她总不让。

"喂,你想不想走一走?"我问她,"想不想去动物园走一走?要是我让你今天下午不回学校,而是去走一走,别再这么胡闹了好不好?"

她不肯回答我,所以我又说了一遍:"如果我让你下午逃课去走一会儿,你别再胡闹了好不好?明天再上学,当个好孩子,好吗?"

"我也许会,也许不会。"她说完径直穿过街道跑到对面,根本不看有没有车过来,她有时候可真是个疯子。

我没有跟着她,我知道她会跟着**我**,所以我开始沿靠近公园的这边街道往闹市区方向走,去动物园。她也开始在他妈街道**对面**往闹市区方向走。她根本不看我,但是我看得出,她很可能在用眼角瞄我往哪儿走。总之,我们就那样一直走到了动物园,唯一让我烦的是双层巴士开过时,因为那会儿我看不到街对面,也就看不到她。可是我们到了动物园时,我喊她:"菲比!我要进动物园了!马上过来!"她还是不肯看我,但我看得出她听到了。我开始走下台阶进动物园时,转过身看到她正在穿过街道,跟着我走来。

动物园里的人不太多,因为天气有点糟糕,可是海狮游泳池边有几个人。我走过那儿,倒是菲比丫头停下脚步,装作看喂海狮——有人扔鱼给它们吃——我就走回头,我琢磨那是个逮住她的好机会。我走过去站在她身后，把手轻轻搭在她肩上，但她屈膝让我的手滑开——她想负气还真能显得很负气的样子。别人喂海狮时，她一直站在那儿，我就站在她身后。我没再把手往她肩膀上搭还是怎么样，因为要是我搭了，她**真的会**撂下我走掉。小孩儿很有趣，你干什么都得留神。

我们看完海狮后，她不肯挨着我走，但也离我不远。她走人行道那边，我走这边，不太好，不过比刚才和我隔着差不多一英里走好点。我们走上一座小山看熊，看了一会儿，可是也没什么好看的。只有一头熊在外边，是头北极熊。另一头棕熊待在洞里不肯出来，只能看到它的屁股。我旁边站着一个小孩儿，头上戴的牛仔帽几乎盖住耳朵，他一个劲儿叫他爸爸："把它弄**出来**，爸爸，把它弄出来。"我看着菲比丫头，可她不笑。你也知道小孩儿生你气时的样子，他们不会笑出来还是怎么样。

离开那两头熊之后，我们就离开动物园，穿过公园里的一条小街，然后又穿过一条小隧道，里面总是有股谁在里面撒了尿的气味，它通向旋转木马。菲比丫头还是不肯跟我说话，但那会儿可以说走在我身边。我抓住她外衣后面的腰带，只是他妈的觉得好玩而已，可她不让。她说："不介意的话，请把手拿开。"她还在生我的气，只是不像以前那样生气了。总之，我们一直在走，离旋转木马越来越近，开始能听到总是在播放的那首古怪的曲子，是《噢，玛丽！》，放了五十年了，我还是个小孩儿时，他们放的也是这同一首曲子。旋转木马这点还不错，他们总是放同样的曲子。

"我还以为到冬天旋转木马就**关掉**了呢。"菲比丫头说。这几乎是她第一次开口说话，她大概忘了该对我生气才对。

"可能因为是圣诞期间吧。"我说。

我说完后她没说话，她大概想起来该生我的气才对。

"你想不想坐一下？"我说。我知道她很可能想。她还很小时，艾里、D.B.，还有我经常带她去公园，她对旋转木马喜欢得要命，上了那个破玩意儿，拉都拉不下来。

"我太大了。"她说。我以为她不会理我，但是她理了。

"不，你不大。去吧，我等你，去吧。"我说。我们刚好到了那儿，有几个小孩儿在坐，多数是很小的孩子，有几位当父母的在外边等，坐在长椅上等。我所做的，是去售票窗口那儿给菲比丫头买了一张票，然后把票给她。她就站在我身边。"给你，"我说，"等等——剩下的也拿着，你的。"我要把她借给我的钱剩下的还给她。

"你拿着吧，替我保管。"她说，紧接着她又说，"请你保管。"

别人对我说"请"时，真让我沮丧，我是说要是菲比或者别的什么人对我这样说，会让我他妈沮丧得要命，不过我还是把钱放进了口袋。

"你不上来吗？"她问我。她看着我的表情有点儿好玩，看得出，她不再那么生我的气了。

"下次吧，也许。我看你坐。"我说，"你拿票了吗？"

"拿了。"

"去吧，那——我就坐那张椅子上，会看着你。"我过去坐到长椅上。她走上旋转木马台子，绕着旋转木马走了一圈，我是说她绕着走了一整圈，然后她坐到一匹又旧又破的褐色大木马上。接着旋转木马开动了，我看她转了一圈又一圈。只有五六个小孩儿在骑。那会儿放的歌曲是《烟雾迷住了你的眼睛》，爵士味很浓，也很有趣。那几个小孩儿都老是想抓住金环，菲比丫头也是。我有点儿害怕她会从那匹破马上摔下来，但我没说什么，也没做什么。对小孩儿就该那样，他们要是想抓金环，你就让他们抓好了，别说什么。他们摔下来就摔吧，可你要是对他们说什么就不好了。

转完后，她从木马上下来走到我面前。"这次你也坐吧。"她说。

"不，我就看着你，我想我还是看吧。"我说着又给了她一点钱，还是她的钱，"拿着，再去多买几张票。"

她从我手里拿了钱。"我不生你的气了。"她说。

"我知道,快点儿——又要开始转了。"

这时,她突然亲了我一下,然后伸出手说:"下雨了,开始下雨了。"

"我知道。"

接着她所做的——让我他妈差点儿开心死了——她把手伸进我的口袋取出猎帽,并把它戴在我头上。

"你不想要了吗?"我问她。

"你可以戴一会儿。"

"好吧,快点去,你要坐不上了,你会找不到你那匹马。"

可她还是不肯走。

"你说话算不算数?真的哪儿都不去了?等会儿你真的回家?"她问我。

"对。"我说,而且说的是真话,没有撒谎,后来我真的回家了。"快点儿去,快点儿,"我说,"又要转了。"

她跑去买了票,刚好能赶上再坐。然后她绕着它走了一整圈,直到找到她的木马坐上去。她向我挥手,我也向她挥手。

乖乖,下起大雨了,向上帝发誓,雨下得**瓢泼一般**。那些当爹当妈的还有别的所有人全一窝蜂站到旋转木马的棚下,免得被淋得浑身湿透还是怎么样,可我继续在长椅上坐了很久。我几乎被淋透了,尤其是脖子和裤子上。说起来,我的猎帽真的起了不少保护作用,可我还是浑身湿透,我无所谓。看着菲比转了一圈又一圈,我突然感到太他妈开心了。说实话,我他妈几乎要大喊大叫,感到太他妈开心了,也不知道为什么。只能说菲比太他妈**可爱**了,就是她穿着蓝色大衣,在木马上转了一圈又一圈的样子。天哪,我真希望你也在场。

26

  我想说的就这么多。我大概也能跟你说说回家后我都做了什么事,还有我怎么生病的, 等等, 还有我离开这儿后, 下学期准备上哪所学校的事, 可是我不想说了, 真的。对那些事, 我现在不是很有兴趣。

  好多人, 特别是这儿一个搞精神分析的家伙, 老是问我九月份上学后会不会用功。我看这话问得真蠢, 我是说在还没做一件事情之前, 又怎么会知道将来怎么做呢? 我的回答是: 不知道。我觉得我会, 可是我又怎么能知道? 我敢说, 这话问得蠢。

  D. B. 不像别人那样差劲, 可他也老是问我很多问题。上星期六他开车来了, 带着一个英国妞儿, 她要在他正在编剧的那部电影里演出。她很做作, 不过很漂亮。有一次, 趁她去了那边侧楼很他妈远的厕所时, D. B. 问我经历过我刚刚跟你说过的那些事情后, 心里怎么想, 我他妈不知道该怎么说。说实话, 我不知道我对此怎么想。我后悔跟这么多人说过, 我所知道的, 差不多就是我有点儿想念我提到过的每一个人, 例如甚至斯特拉雷德和阿克利这两个家伙。我觉得我甚至想念那个混蛋莫里斯呢, 有意思。千万别跟人说事儿, 说了你就会想念起每一个人。

图书在版编目（CIP）数据

麦田里的守望者：汉英对照／（美）J.D.塞林格（J. D. Salinger）著；孙仲旭译． -- 南京：译林出版社，2025.3（2025.4重印）． -- ISBN 978-7-5753-0271-5

Ⅰ．I712.45

中国国家版本馆CIP数据核字第2024MV4442号

THE CATCHER IN THE RYE by J.D. Salinger
Copyright © 1945, 1946, 1951 by J.D. Salinger,
renewed 1973, 1974, 1979 by J.D. Salinger
This edition arranged with the J.D. Salinger Literary Trust
through Andrew Nurnberg Associates International Limited
Bilingual edition copyright © 2025 by Yilin Press, Ltd
All rights reserved.

著作权合同登记号　图字：10-2019-707 号

麦田里的守望者 ［美国］J.D. 塞林格／著　孙仲旭／译

责任编辑	於　梅
装帧设计	所以设计馆
校　　对	王　敏
责任印制	董　虎

原文出版	Little, Brown and Company, 2001
出版发行	译林出版社
地　　址	南京市湖南路 1 号 A 楼
邮　　箱	yilin@yilin.com
网　　址	www.yilin.com
市场热线	025-86633278
排　　版	南京展望文化发展有限公司
印　　刷	河北鹏润印刷有限公司
开　　本	880 毫米×1230 毫米　1/32
印　　张	13
版　　次	2025 年 3 月第 1 版
印　　次	2025 年 4 月第 2 次印刷
书　　号	ISBN 978-7-5753-0271-5
定　　价	65.00 元

版权所有·侵权必究

译林版图书若有印装错误可向出版社调换。质量热线：025-83658316

The Catcher in the Rye

J. D. Salinger

译林出版社

To My Mother

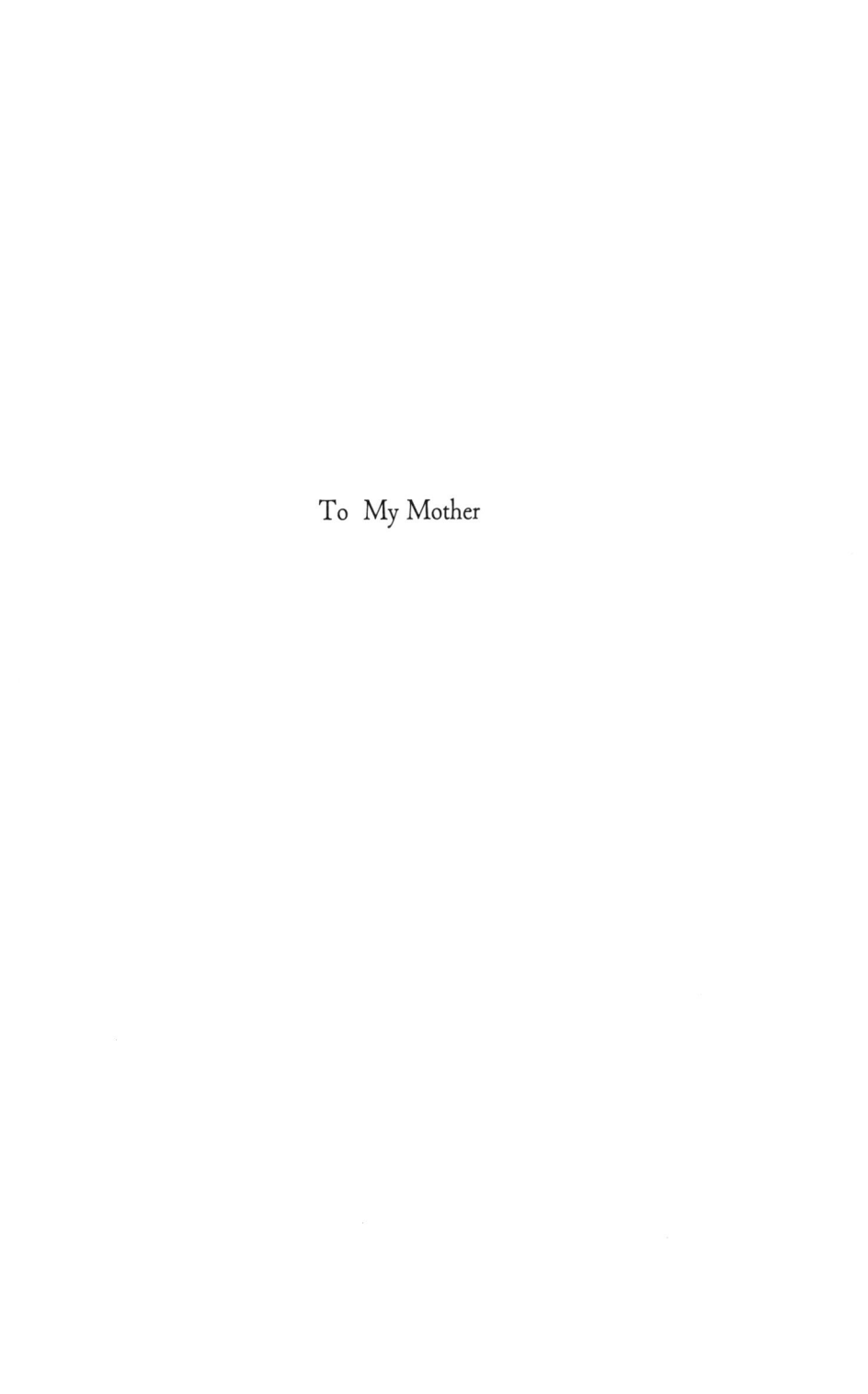

1

If you really want to hear about it, the first thing you'll probably want to know is where I was born, and what my lousy childhood was like, and how my parents were occupied and all before they had me, and all that David Copperfield kind of crap, but I don't feel like going into it, if you want to know the truth. In the first place, that stuff bores me, and in the second place, my parents would have about two hemorrhages apiece if I told anything pretty personal about them. They're quite touchy about anything like that, especially my father. They're *nice* and all—I'm not saying that—but they're also touchy as hell. Besides, I'm not going to tell you my whole goddam autobiography or anything. I'll just tell you about this madman stuff that happened to me around last Christmas just before I got pretty run-down and had to come out here and take it easy. I mean that's all I told D.B. about, and he's my *brother* and all. He's in Hollywood. That isn't too far from this crumby place, and he comes over and visits me practically every week end. He's going to drive me home when I go home next month maybe. He just got a Jaguar. One of those little English jobs that can do around two hundred miles an hour. It cost him damn near four thousand bucks. He's got a lot of dough, now. He didn't *use* to. He used to be just a regular writer, when he was home. He wrote this terrific book of short stories, *The Secret Goldfish*, in case you never heard of him. The best one in it was "The Secret Goldfish." It was about this little kid that wouldn't let anybody look at his goldfish because he'd bought it with his own money. It killed me. Now he's out in Hollywood, D.B., being a prostitute. If there's one thing I hate, it's the movies. Don't even mention them to me.

Where I want to start telling is the day I left Pencey Prep. Pencey Prep is this school that's in Agerstown, Pennsylvania. You probably heard of it. You've probably seen the ads, anyway. They advertise in about a thousand magazines, always showing some hot-shot guy on a horse jumping over a fence. Like as if all you ever did at Pencey was play polo all the time. I never even once saw a horse anywhere *near* the place. And underneath the guy on the horse's picture, it always says: "Since 1888 we have been molding boys into splendid, clear-thinking young men." Strictly for the birds. They don't do any damn more *molding* at Pencey than they do at any other school. And I didn't know anybody there that was splendid and clear-thinking and all. Maybe two guys. If that many. And they probably *came* to Pencey that way.

Anyway, it was the Saturday of the football game with Saxon Hall. The game with Saxon Hall was supposed to be a very big deal around Pencey. It was the last game of the year, and you were supposed to commit suicide or something if old Pencey didn't win. I remember around three o'clock that afternoon I was standing way the hell up on top of Thomsen Hill, right next to this crazy cannon that was in the Revolutionary War and all. You could see the whole field from there, and you could see the two teams bashing each other all over the place. You couldn't see the grandstand too hot, but you could hear them all yelling, deep and terrific on the Pencey side, because practically the whole school except me was there, and scrawny and faggy on the Saxon Hall side, because the visiting team hardly ever brought many people with them.

There were never many girls at all at the football games. Only seniors were allowed to bring girls with them. It was a terrible school, no matter how you looked at it. I like to be somewhere at least where you can see a few girls around once in a while, even if they're only scratching their arms or blowing their noses or even just giggling or something. Old Selma Thurmer—she was the headmaster's daughter—showed up at the games quite often, but she wasn't exactly the type that drove you mad with desire. She was a pretty nice girl, though. I sat next to her once in the bus from Agerstown and we sort of struck up a conversation. I liked her. She had a big nose and her nails were all bitten down and bleedy-looking and she had on those damn falsies that point all over the place, but you felt sort of sorry for her. What I liked about her, she didn't give you a lot of horse manure about what a great guy her father was. She probably knew what a phony slob he was.

The reason I was standing way up on Thomsen Hill, instead of down at the game, was because I'd just got back from New York with the fencing team. I was the goddam manager of the fencing team. Very big deal. We'd gone in to New York that morning for this fencing meet with McBurney School. Only, we didn't have the meet. I left all the foils and equipment and stuff on the goddam subway. It wasn't all my fault. I had to keep getting up to look at this map, so we'd know where to get off. So we got back to Pencey around two-thirty instead of around dinnertime. The whole team ostracized me the whole way back on the train. It was pretty funny, in a way.

The other reason I wasn't down at the game was because I was on my way to say good-by to old Spencer, my history teacher. He had the grippe, and I figured I probably wouldn't see him again till Christmas vacation started. He wrote me this note saying he wanted to see me before I went home. He knew I wasn't coming back to Pencey.

I forgot to tell you about that. They kicked me out. I wasn't supposed to come back after Christmas vacation, on account of I was flunking four subjects and not applying myself and all. They gave me frequent warning to start applying myself—especially around mid-terms, when my parents came up for a conference with old

Thurmer—but I didn't do it. So I got the ax. They give guys the ax quite frequently at Pencey. It has a very good academic rating, Pencey. It really does.

Anyway, it was December and all, and it was cold as a witch's teat, especially on top of that stupid hill. I only had on my reversible and no gloves or anything. The week before that, somebody'd stolen my camel's-hair coat right out of my room, with my fur-lined gloves right in the pocket and all. Pencey was full of crooks. Quite a few guys came from these very wealthy families, but it was full of crooks anyway. The more expensive a school is, the more crooks it has—I'm not kidding. Anyway, I kept standing next to that crazy cannon, looking down at the game and freezing my ass off. Only, I wasn't watching the game too much. What I was really hanging around for, I was trying to feel some kind of a good-by. I mean I've left schools and places I didn't even know I was leaving them. I hate that. I don't care if it's a sad good-by or a bad good-by, but when I leave a place I like to *know* I'm leaving it. If you don't, you feel even worse.

I was lucky. All of a sudden I thought of something that helped make me know I was getting the hell out. I suddenly remembered this time, in around October, that I and Robert Tichener and Paul Campbell were chucking a football around, in front of the academic building. They were nice guys, especially Tichener. It was just before dinner and it was getting pretty dark out, but we kept chucking the ball around anyway. It kept getting darker and darker, and we could hardly *see* the ball any more, but we didn't want to stop doing what we were doing. Finally we had to. This teacher that taught biology, Mr. Zambesi, stuck his head out of this window in the academic building and told us to go back to the dorm and get ready for dinner. If I get a chance to remember that kind of stuff, I can get a good-by when I need one—at least, most of the time I can. As soon as I got it, I turned around and started running down the other side of the hill, toward old Spencer's house. He didn't live on the campus. He lived on Anthony Wayne Avenue.

I ran all the way to the main gate, and then I waited a second till I got my breath. I have no wind, if you want to know the truth. I'm quite a heavy smoker, for one thing—that is, I used to be. They made me cut it out. Another thing, I *grew* six and a half inches last year. That's also how I practically got t.b. and came out here for all these goddam checkups and stuff. I'm pretty healthy, though.

Anyway, as soon as I got my breath back I ran across Route 204. It was icy as hell and I damn near fell down. I don't even know what I was running for—I guess I just felt like it. After I got across the road, I felt like I was sort of disappearing. It was that kind of a crazy afternoon, terrifically cold, and no sun out or anything, and you felt like you were disappearing every time you crossed a road.

Boy, I rang that doorbell fast when I got to old Spencer's house. I was really frozen. My ears were hurting and I could hardly move my fingers at all. "C'mon, c'mon," I said right out loud, almost, "somebody open the *door*." Finally old Mrs. Spencer opened it. They didn't have a maid or anything, and they always opened the door themselves. They didn't have too much dough.

"Holden!" Mrs. Spencer said. "How lovely to see you! Come in, dear! Are you frozen to death?" I think she was glad to see me. She liked me. At least, I think she did.

Boy, did I get in that house fast. "How are you, Mrs. Spencer?" I said. "How's Mr. Spencer?"

"Let me take your coat, dear," she said. She didn't hear me ask her how Mr. Spencer was. She was sort of deaf.

She hung up my coat in the hall closet, and I sort of brushed my hair back with my hand. I wear a crew cut quite frequently and I never have to comb it much. "How've you been, Mrs. Spencer?" I said again, only louder, so she'd hear me.

"I've been just fine, Holden." She closed the closet door. "How have *you* been?" The way she asked me, I knew right away old Spencer'd told her I'd been kicked out.

"Fine," I said. "How's Mr. Spencer? He over his grippe yet?"

"Over it! Holden, he's behaving like a perfect—I don't know *what* ... He's in his room, dear. Go right in."

II

They each had their own room and all. They were both around seventy years old, or even more than that. They got a bang out of things, though—in a half-assed way, of course. I know that sounds mean to say, but I don't mean it mean. I just mean that I used to think about old Spencer quite a lot, and if you thought about him *too* much, you wondered what the heck he was still living for. I mean he was all stooped over, and he had very terrible posture, and in class, whenever he dropped a piece of chalk at the blackboard, some guy in the first row always had to get up and pick it up and hand it to him. That's awful, in my opinion. But if you thought about him just enough and not *too* much, you could figure it out that he wasn't doing too bad for himself. For instance, one Sunday when some other guys and I were over there for hot chocolate, he showed us this old beat-up Navajo blanket that he and Mrs. Spencer'd bought off some Indian in Yellowstone Park. You could tell old Spencer'd got a big bang out of buying it. That's what I mean. You take somebody old as hell, like old Spencer, and they can get a big bang out of buying a blanket.

His door was open, but I sort of knocked on it anyway, just to be polite and all. I could see where he was sitting. He was sitting in a big leather chair, all wrapped up in that blanket I just told you about. He looked over at me when I knocked. "Who's that?" he yelled. "Caulfield? Come in, boy." He was always yelling, outside class. It got on your nerves sometimes.

The minute I went in, I was sort of sorry I'd come. He was reading the *Atlantic Monthly*, and there were pills and medicine all over the place, and everything smelled like Vicks Nose Drops. It was pretty depressing. I'm not too crazy about sick people, anyway. What made it even more depressing, old Spencer had on this very sad, ratty old bathrobe that he was probably born in or something. I don't much like to see old guys in their pajamas and bathrobes anyway. Their bumpy old chests are always showing. And their legs. Old guys' legs, at beaches and places, always look so white and unhairy. "Hello, sir," I said. "I got your note. Thanks a lot." He'd written me this note asking me to stop by and say good-by before vacation started, on account of I wasn't coming back. "You didn't have to do all that. I'd have come over to say good-by anyway."

"Have a seat there, boy," old Spencer said. He meant the bed.

I sat down on it. "How's your grippe, sir?"

"M'boy, if I felt any better I'd have to send for the doctor," old Spencer said. That knocked him out. He started chuckling like a madman. Then he finally straightened himself out and said, "Why aren't you down at the game? I thought this was the day of the big game."

"It is. I was. Only, I just got back from New York with the fencing team," I said. Boy, his bed was like a rock.

He started getting serious as hell. I knew he would. "So you're leaving us, eh?" he said.

"Yes, sir. I guess I am."

He started going into this nodding routine. You never saw anybody nod as much in your life as old Spencer did. You never knew if he was nodding a lot because he was thinking and all, or just because he was a nice old guy that didn't know his ass from his elbow.

"What did Dr. Thurmer say to you, boy? I understand you had quite a little chat."

"Yes, we did. We really did. I was in his office for around two hours, I guess."

"What'd he say to you?"

"Oh ... well, about Life being a game and all. And how you should play it according to the rules. He was pretty nice about it. I mean he didn't hit the ceiling or anything. He just kept talking about Life being a game and all. You know."

"Life *is* a game, boy. Life *is* a game that one plays according to the rules."

"Yes, sir. I know it is. I know it."

Game, my ass. Some game. If you get on the side where all the hot-shots are, then it's a game, all right—I'll admit that. But if you get on the other side, where there aren't any hot-shots, then what's a game about it? Nothing. No game. "Has Dr. Thurmer written to your parents yet?" old Spencer asked me.

"He said he was going to write them Monday."

"Have you yourself communicated with them?"

"No, sir, I haven't communicated with them, because I'll probably see them Wednesday night when I get home."

"And how do you think they'll take the news?"

"Well... they'll be pretty irritated about it," I said. "They really will. This is about the fourth school I've gone to." I shook my head. I shake my head quite a lot. "Boy!" I said. I also say "Boy!" quite a lot. Partly because I have a lousy vocabulary and partly because I act quite young for my age sometimes. I was sixteen then, and I'm seventeen now, and sometimes I act like I'm about thirteen. It's really ironical, because I'm six foot two and a half and I have gray hair. I really do. The one side of my head—the right side—is full of millions of gray hairs. I've had them ever since I was a kid. And yet I still act sometimes like I was only about twelve. Everybody says that, especially my father. It's partly true, too, but it isn't *all* true. People always think something's *all* true. I don't give a damn, except that I get bored sometimes when people tell me to act my age. Sometimes I act a lot older than I am—I really do—but people never notice it. People never notice anything.

Old Spencer started nodding again. He also started picking his nose. He made out like he was only pinching it, but he was really getting the old thumb right in there. I guess he thought it was all right to do because it was only me that was in the room. I didn't *care*, except that it's pretty disgusting to watch somebody pick their nose.

Then he said, "I had the privilege of meeting your mother and dad when they had their little chat with Dr. Thurmer some weeks ago. They're grand people."

"Yes, they are. They're very nice."

Grand. There's a word I really hate. It's a phony. I could puke every time I hear it.

Then all of a sudden old Spencer looked like he had something very good, something sharp as a tack, to say to me. He sat up more in his chair and sort of moved around. It was a false alarm, though. All he did was lift the *Atlantic Monthly* off his lap and try to chuck it on the bed, next to me. He missed. It was only about two inches away, but he missed anyway. I got up and picked it up and put it down on the bed. All of a sudden then, I wanted to get the hell out of the room. I could feel a terrific lecture coming on. I didn't mind the idea so much, but I didn't feel like being lectured to and smell Vicks Nose Drops and look at old Spencer in his pajamas and bathrobe all at the same time. I really didn't.

It started, all right. "What's the matter with you, boy?" old Spencer said. He said it pretty tough, too, for him. "How many subjects did you carry this term?"

"Five, sir."

"Five. And how many are you failing in?"

"Four." I moved my ass a little bit on the bed. It was the hardest bed I ever sat on. "I passed English all right," I said, "because I had all that Beowulf and Lord Randal My

Son stuff when I was at the Whooton School. I mean I didn't have to do any work in English at all hardly, except write compositions once in a while."

He wasn't even listening. He hardly ever listened to you when you said something.

"I flunked you in history because you knew absolutely nothing."

"I know that, sir. Boy, I know it. You couldn't help it."

"Absolutely nothing," he said over again. That's something that drives me crazy. When people say something twice that way, after you *admit* it the first time. Then he said it *three* times. "But absolutely nothing. I doubt very much if you opened your textbook even once the whole term. Did you? Tell the truth, boy."

"Well, I sort of glanced through it a couple of times," I told him. I didn't want to hurt his feelings. He was mad about history.

"You glanced through it, eh?" he said—very sarcastic. "Your, ah, *exam* paper is over there on top of my chiffonier. On top of the pile. Bring it here, please."

It was a very dirty trick, but I went over and brought it over to him—I didn't have any alternative or anything. Then I sat down on his cement bed again. Boy, you can't imagine how sorry I was getting that I'd stopped by to say good-by to him.

He started handling my exam paper like it was a turd or something. "We studied the Egyptians from November 4th to December 2nd," he said. "You *chose* to write about them for the optional essay question. Would you care to hear what you had to say?"

"No, sir, not very much," I said.

He read it anyway, though. You can't stop a teacher when they want to do something. They just *do* it.

The Egyptians were an ancient race of Caucasians residing in one of the northern sections of Africa. The latter as we all know is the largest continent in the Eastern Hemisphere.

I had to sit there and *listen* to that crap. It certainly was a dirty trick.

The Egyptians are extremely interesting to us today for various reasons. Modern science would still like to know what the secret ingredients were that the Egyptians used when they wrapped up dead people so that their faces would not rot for innumerable centuries. This interesting riddle is still quite a challenge to modern science in the twentieth century.

He stopped reading and put my paper down. I was beginning to sort of hate him. "Your *essay*, shall we say, ends there," he said in this very sarcastic voice. You wouldn't think such an old guy would be so sarcastic and all. "However, you dropped me a little note, at the bottom of the page," he said.

"I know I did," I said. I said it very fast because I wanted to stop him before he started reading *that* out loud. But you couldn't stop him. He was hot as a firecracker.

DEAR MR. SPENCER [he read out loud]. That is all I know about the Egyptians. I can't seem to get very interested in them although your lectures are very interesting. It is all right with me if you flunk me though as I am flunking everything else except English anyway. Respectfully yours, HOLDEN CAULFIELD.

He put my goddam paper down then and looked at me like he'd just beaten hell out of me in ping-pong or something. I don't think I'll ever forgive him for reading me that crap out loud. I wouldn't've read it out loud to *him* if *he'd* written it—I really wouldn't. In the first place, I'd only *writ*ten that damn note so that he wouldn't feel too bad about flunking me.

"Do you blame me for flunking you, boy?" he said.

"No, sir! I certainly don't," I said. I wished to hell he'd stop calling me "boy" all the time.

He tried chucking my exam paper on the bed when he was through with it. Only, he missed again, naturally. I had to get up again and pick it up and put it on top of the *Atlantic Monthly*. It's *boring* to do that every two minutes.

"What would you have done in my place?" he said. "Tell the truth, boy."

Well, you could see he really felt pretty lousy about flunking me. So I shot the bull for a while. I told him I was a real moron, and all that stuff. I told him how I would've done exactly the same thing if I'd been in his place, and how most people didn't appreciate how tough it is being a teacher. That kind of stuff. The old bull.

The funny thing is, though, I was sort of thinking of something else while I shot the bull. I live in New York, and I was thinking about the lagoon in Central Park, down near Central Park South. I was wondering if it would be frozen over when I got home, and if it was, where did the ducks go. I was wondering where the ducks went when the lagoon got all icy and frozen over. I wondered if some guy came in a truck and took them away to a zoo or something. Or if they just flew away.

I'm lucky, though. I mean I could shoot the old bull to old Spencer and think about those ducks at the same time. It's funny. You don't have to think too hard when you talk to a teacher. All of a sudden, though, he interrupted me while I was shooting the bull. He was always interrupting you.

"How do you *feel* about all this, boy? I'd be very interested to know. Very interested."

"You mean about my flunking out of Pencey and all?" I said. I sort of wished he'd cover up his bumpy chest. It wasn't such a beautiful view.

"If I'm not mistaken, I believe you also had some difficulty at the Whooton School and at Elkton Hills." He didn't say it just sarcastic, but sort of nasty, too.

"I didn't have too much difficulty at Elkton Hills," I told him. "I didn't exactly flunk out or anything. I just quit, sort of."

"Why, may I ask?"

"Why? Oh, well it's a long story, sir. I mean it's pretty complicated." I didn't feel like going into the whole thing with him. He wouldn't have understood it anyway. It wasn't up his alley at all. One of the biggest reasons I left Elkton Hills was because I was surrounded by phonies. That's all. They were coming in the goddam window. For instance, they had this headmaster, Mr. Haas, that was the phoniest bastard I ever met in my life. Ten times worse than old Thurmer. On Sundays, for instance, old Haas went around shaking hands with everybody's parents when they drove up to school. He'd be charming as hell and all. Except if some boy had little old funny-looking parents. You should've seen the way he did with my roommate's parents. I mean if a boy's mother was sort of fat or cornylooking or something, and if somebody's father was one of those guys that wear those suits with very big shoulders and corny black-and-white shoes, then old Haas would just shake hands with them and give them a phony smile and then he'd go talk, for maybe a half an *hour*, with somebody else's parents. I can't stand that stuff. It drives me crazy. It makes me so depressed I go crazy. I hated that goddam Elkton Hills.

Old Spencer asked me something then, but I didn't hear him. I was thinking about old Haas. "What, sir?" I said.

"Do you have any particular *qualms* about leaving Pencey?"

"Oh, I have a few qualms, all right. Sure ... but not too many. Not yet, anyway. I guess it hasn't really hit me yet. It takes things a while to hit me. All I'm doing right now is thinking about going home Wednesday. I'm a moron."

"Do you feel absolutely no concern for your future, boy?"

"Oh, I feel some concern for my future, all right. Sure. Sure, I do." I thought about it for a minute. "But not too much, I guess. Not too much, I guess."

"You *will*," old Spencer said. "You will, boy. You will when it's too late."

I didn't like hearing him say that. It made me sound dead or something. It was very depressing. "I guess I will," I said.

"I'd like to put some sense in that head of yours, boy. I'm trying to help you. I'm trying to *help* you, if I can."

He really was, too. You could see that. But it was just that we were too much on opposite sides of the pole, that's all. "I know you are, sir," I said. "Thanks a lot. No kidding. I appreciate it. I really do." I got up from the bed then. Boy, I couldn't've sat there another ten minutes to save my life. "The thing is, though, I have to get going now. I have quite a bit of equipment at the gym I have to get to take home with me. I really do." He looked up at me and started nodding again, with this very serious look on his face. I felt sorry as hell for him, all of a sudden. But I just couldn't hang around there any longer, the way we were on opposite sides of the pole, and the way he kept missing the bed whenever he chucked something at it, and his sad old bathrobe with his chest showing, and that grippy smell of Vicks Nose Drops all over the place. "Look, sir. Don't worry about me," I said. "I mean it. I'll be all right. I'm just going through a phase right now. Everybody goes through phases and all, don't they?"

"I don't know, boy. I don't know."

I hate it when somebody answers that way. "Sure. Sure, they do," I said. "I mean it, sir. Please don't worry about me." I sort of put my hand on his shoulder. "Okay?" I said.

"Wouldn't you like a cup of hot chocolate before you go? Mrs. Spencer would be—"

"I would, I really would, but the thing is, I have to get going. I have to go right to the gym. Thanks, though. Thanks a lot, sir."

Then we shook hands. And all that crap. It made me feel sad as hell, though.

"I'll drop you a line, sir. Take care of your grippe, now."

"Good-by, boy."

After I shut the door and started back to the living room, he yelled something at me, but I couldn't exactly hear him. I'm pretty sure he yelled "Good luck!" at me, I hope not. I hope to hell not. I'd never yell "Good luck!" at anybody. It sounds terrible, when you think about it.

III

I'm the most terrific liar you ever saw in your life. It's awful. If I'm on my way to the store to buy a magazine, even, and somebody asks me where I'm going, I'm liable to say I'm going to the opera. It's terrible. So when I told old Spencer I had to go to the gym to get my equipment and stuff, that was a sheer lie. I don't even keep my goddam equipment in the gym.

Where I lived at Pencey, I lived in the Ossenburger Memorial Wing of the new dorms. It was only for juniors and seniors. I was a junior. My roommate was a senior. It was named after this guy Ossenburger that went to Pencey. He made a pot of dough in the undertaking business after he got out of Pencey. What he did, he started these undertaking parlors all over the country that you could get members of your family buried for about five bucks apiece. You should see old Ossenburger. He probably just shoves them in a sack and dumps them in the river. Anyway, he gave Pencey a pile of dough, and they named our wing after him. The first football game of the year, he came up to school in this big goddam Cadillac, and we all had to stand up in the grandstand and give him a locomotive—that's a cheer. Then, the next morning, in chapel, he made a speech that lasted about ten hours. He started off with about fifty corny jokes, just to show us what a regular guy he was. Very big deal. Then he started telling us how he was never ashamed, when he was in some kind of trouble or something, to get right down on his knees and pray to God. He told us we should always pray to God—talk to Him and all—

wherever we were. He told us we ought to think of Jesus as our buddy and all. He said *he* talked to Jesus all the time. Even when he was driving his car. That killed me. I can just see the big phony bastard shifting into first gear and asking Jesus to send him a few more stiffs. The only good part of his speech was right in the middle of it. He was telling us all about what a swell guy he was, what a hotshot and all, then all of a sudden this guy sitting in the row in front of me, Edgar Marsalla, laid this terrific fart. It was a very crude thing to do, in chapel and all, but it was also quite amusing. Old Marsalla. He damn near blew the roof off. Hardly anybody laughed out loud, and old Ossenburger made out like he didn't even hear it, but old Thurmer, the headmaster, was sitting right next to him on the rostrum and all, and you could tell *he* heard it. *Boy*, was he sore. He didn't say anything then, but the next night he made us have compulsory study hall in the academic building and he came up and made a speech. He said that the boy that had created the disturbance in chapel wasn't fit to go to Pencey. We tried to get old Marsalla to rip off another one, right while old Thurmer was making his speech, but he wasn't in the right mood. Anyway, that's where I lived at Pencey. Old Ossenburger Memorial Wing, in the new dorms.

It was pretty nice to get back to my room, after I left old Spencer, because everybody was down at the game, and the heat was on in our room, for a change. It felt sort of cosy. I took off my coat and my tie and unbuttoned my shirt collar, and then I put on this hat that I'd bought in New York that morning. It was this red hunting hat, with one of those very, very long peaks. I saw it in the window of this sports store when we got out of the subway, just after I noticed I'd lost all the goddam foils. It only cost me a buck. The way I wore it, I swung the old peak way around to the back—very corny, I'll admit, but I liked it that way. I looked good in it that way. Then I got this book I was reading and sat down in my chair. There were two chairs in every room. I had one and my roommate, Ward Stradlater, had one. The arms were in sad shape, because everybody was always sitting on them, but they were pretty comfortable chairs.

The book I was reading was this book I took out of the library by mistake. They gave me the wrong book, and I didn't notice it till I got back to my room. They gave me *Out of Africa*, by Isak Dinesen. I thought it was going to stink, but it didn't. It was a very good book. I'm quite illiterate, but I read a lot. My favorite author is my brother D.B., and my next favorite is Ring Lardner. My brother gave me a book by Ring Lardner for my birthday, just before I went to Pencey. It had these very funny, crazy plays in it, and then it had this one story about a traffic cop that falls in love with this very cute girl that's always speeding. Only, he's married, the cop, so be can't marry her or anything. Then this girl gets killed, because she's always speeding. That story just about killed me. What I like best is a book that's at least funny once in a while. I read a lot of classical books, like *The Return of the Native* and all, and I like them, and I read a lot of war books and mysteries and all, but they don't knock me out too much. What really knocks me out is a book that, when you're all done reading it, you wish the author that wrote it was a terrific friend of yours and you could call him up on the phone whenever you felt like it. That doesn't happen much, though. I wouldn't mind calling this Isak Dinesen up. And Ring Lardner, except that D.B. told me he's dead. You take that book *Of Human Bondage*, by Somerset Maugham, though. I read it last summer. It's a pretty good book and all, but I wouldn't want to call Somerset Maugham up. I don't know. He just isn't the kind of a guy I'd want to call up, that's all. I'd rather call old Thomas Hardy up. I like that Eustacia Vye.

Anyway, I put on my new hat and sat down and started reading that book *Out of Africa*. I'd read it already, but I wanted to read certain parts over again. I'd only read about three pages, though, when I heard somebody coming through the shower curtains. Even without looking up, I knew right away who it was. It was Robert Ackley, this guy that roomed right next to me. There was a shower right between every two rooms in our wing, and about eighty-five times a day old Ackley barged in on me. He was probably the only guy in the whole dorm, besides me, that wasn't down at the game. He hardly ever went *any*where. He was a very peculiar guy. He was a senior, and he'd been at Pencey the whole four years and all, but nobody ever called him anything except "Ackley." Not even Herb Gale, his own roommate, ever called him "Bob" or even "Ack." If he ever gets married, his own wife'll probably call him "Ackley." He was one of these very, very tall, round-shouldered guys—he was about six four—with lousy teeth. The whole time he roomed next to me, I never even once saw him brush his teeth. They always looked mossy and awful, and he damn near made you sick if you saw him in the dining room with his mouth full of mashed potatoes and peas or something. Besides that, he had a lot of pimples. Not just on his forehead or his chin, like most guys, but all over his whole face. And not only that, he had a terrible personality. He was also sort of a nasty guy. I wasn't too crazy about him, to tell you the truth.

I could feel him standing on the shower ledge, right behind my chair, taking a look to see if Stradlater was around. He hated Stradlater's guts and he never came in the room if Stradlater was around. He hated everybody's guts, damn near.

He came down off the shower ledge and came in the room. "Hi," he said. He always said it like he was terrifically bored or terrifically tired. He didn't want you to think he was *vis*iting you or anything. He wanted you to think he'd come in by mis*take*, for God's sake.

"Hi," I said, but I didn't look up from my book. With a guy like Ackley, if you looked up from your book you were a goner. You were a goner *any*way, but not as quick if you didn't look up right away.

He started walking around the room, very slow and all, the way he always did, picking up your personal stuff off your desk and chiffonier. He always picked up your personal stuff and looked at it. Boy, could he get on your nerves sometimes. "How was the fencing?" he said. He just wanted me to quit reading and enjoying myself. He didn't give a damn about the fencing. "We win, or what?" he said.

"Nobody won," I said. Without looking up, though.

"What?" he said. He always made you say everything twice.

"Nobody won," I said. I sneaked a look to see what he was fiddling around with on my chiffonier. He was looking at this picture of this girl I used to go around with in New York, Sally Hayes. He must've picked up that goddam picture and looked at it at least five thousand times since I got it. He always put it back in the wrong place, too, when he was finished. He did it on purpose. You could tell.

"*No*body won," he said. "How come?"

"I left the goddam foils and stuff on the subway." I still didn't look up at him.

"On the *sub*way, for Chrissake! Ya *lost* them, ya mean?"

"We got on the wrong subway. I had to keep getting up to look at a goddam map on the wall."

He came over and stood right in my light. "Hey," I said. "I've read this same sentence about twenty times since you came in."

Anybody else except Ackley would've taken the goddam hint. Not him, though. "Think they'll make *you* pay for 'em?" he said.

"I don't know, and I don't give a damn. How 'bout sitting *down* or something, Ackley kid? You're right in my goddam light." He didn't like it when you called him "Ackley kid." He was always telling me I was a goddam kid, because I was sixteen and he was eighteen. It drove him mad when I called him "Ackley kid."

He kept standing there. He was *exact*ly the kind of a guy that wouldn't get out of your light when you asked him to. He'd *do* it, finally, but it took him a lot longer if you *asked* him to. "What the hellya reading?" he said.

"Goddam book."

He shoved my book back with his hand so that he could see the name of it. "Any good?" he said.

"This *sen*tence I'm reading is terrific." I can be quite sarcastic when I'm in the mood. He didn't get it, though. He started walking around the room again, picking up all my personal stuff, and Stradlater's. Finally, I put my book down on the floor. You couldn't read anything with a guy like Ackley around. It was impossible.

I slid way the hell down in my chair and watched old Ackley making himself at home. I was feeling sort of tired from the trip to New York and all, and I started yawning. Then I started horsing around a little bit. Sometimes I horse around quite a lot, just to keep from getting bored. What I did was, I pulled the old peak of my hunting hat around to the front, then pulled it way down over my eyes. That way, I couldn't see a goddam thing. "I think I'm going blind," I said in this very hoarse voice. "Mother darling, everything's getting so *dark* in here."

"You're nuts. I swear to God," Ackley said.

"Mother darling, give me your *hand*. Why won't you give me your *hand?*"

"For Chrissake, grow up."

I started groping around in front of me, like a blind guy, but without getting up or anything. I kept saying, "Mother darling, why won't you give me your *hand?*" I was only horsing around, naturally. That stuff gives me a bang sometimes. Besides, I know it annoyed hell out of old Ackley. He always brought out the old sadist in me. I was pretty sadistic with him quite often. Finally, I quit, though. I pulled the peak around to the back again, and relaxed.

"Who belongsa this?" Ackley said. He was holding my roommate's knee supporter up to show me. That guy Ackley'd pick up *any*thing. He'd even pick up your jock strap or something. I told him it was Stradlater's. So he chucked it on Stradlater's bed. He got it off Stradlater's *chiffonier*, so he chucked it on the *bed*.

He came over and sat down on the arm of Stradlater's chair. He never sat down *in* a chair. Just always on the arm. "Where the hellja get that hat?" he said.

"New York."

"How much?"

"A buck."

"You got robbed." He started cleaning his goddam fingernails with the end of a match. He was always cleaning his fingernails. It was funny, in a way. His teeth were always mossy-looking, and his ears were always dirty as hell, but he was always cleaning his fingernails. I guess he thought that made him a very *neat* guy. He took another look at my hat while he was cleaning them. "Up home we wear a hat like that to shoot *deer* in, for Chrissake," he said. "That's a deer shooting hat."

"Like hell it is." I took it off and looked at it. I sort of closed one eye, like I was taking aim at it. "This is a people shooting hat," I said. "I shoot people in this hat."

"Your folks know you got kicked out yet?"

"Nope."

"Where the hell's Stradlater at, anyway?"

"Down at the game. He's got a date." I yawned. I was yawning all over the place. For one thing, the room was too damn hot. It made you sleepy. At Pencey, you either froze to death or died of the heat.

"The great Stradlater," Ackley said. "—Hey. Lend me your scissors a second, willya? Ya got 'em handy?"

"No. I packed them already. They're way in the top of the closet."

"Get 'em a second, willya?" Ackley said. "I got this hangnail I want to cut off."

He didn't care if you'd packed something or not and had it way in the top of the closet. I got them for him though. I nearly got killed doing it, too. The second I opened the closet door, Stradlater's tennis racket—in its wooden press and all—

fell right on my head. It made a big *clunk*, and it hurt like hell. It damn near killed old Ackley, though. He started laughing in this very high falsetto voice. He kept laughing the whole time I was taking down my suitcase and getting the scissors out for him. Something like that—a guy getting hit on the head with a rock or something—tickled the pants off Ackley. "You have a damn good sense of humor, Ackley kid," I told him. "You know that?" I handed him the scissors. "Lemme be your manager. I'll get you on the goddam radio." I sat down in my chair again, and he started cutting his big horny-looking nails. "How 'bout using the table or something?" I said. "Cut'em over the table, willya? I don't feel like walking on your crumby nails in my bare feet tonight." He kept right on cutting them over the floor, though. What lousy manners. I mean it.

"Who's Stradlater's date?" he said. He was always keeping tabs on who Stradlater was dating, even though he hated Stradlater's guts.

"I don't know. Why?"

"No reason. Boy, I can't stand that sonuvabitch. He's one sonuvabitch I really can't stand."

"He's crazy about *you*. He told me he thinks you're a goddam prince," I said. I call people a "prince" quite often when I'm horsing around. It keeps me from getting bored or something.

"He's got this superior *at*titude all the time," Ackley said. "I just can't stand the sonuvabitch. You'd think he—"

"Do you mind cutting your nails over the *table*, hey?" I said. "I've asked you about fifty—"

"He's got this goddam superior attitude all the time," Ackley said. "I don't even think the sonuvabitch is intelligent. He *thinks* he is. He thinks he's about the most—"

"*Ack*ley! For Chrissake. Willya *please* cut your crumby nails over the table? I've asked you fifty times."

He started cutting his nails over the table, for a change. The only way he ever did anything was if you yelled at him.

I watched him for a while. Then I said, "The reason you're sore at Stradlater is because he said that stuff about brushing your teeth once in a while. He didn't mean to insult you, for cryin' out loud. He didn't *say* it right or anything, but he didn't mean anything insulting. All he meant was you'd look better and *feel* better if you sort of brushed your teeth once in a while."

"I brush my teeth. Don't gimme *that*."

"No, you don't. I've seen you, and you don't," I said. I didn't say it nasty, though. I felt sort of sorry for him, in a way. I mean it isn't too nice, naturally, if somebody tells you you don't brush your teeth. "Stradlater's all right. He's not too bad," I said. "You don't know him, that's the trouble."

"I still say he's a sonuvabitch. He's a conceited sonuvabitch."

"He's conceited, but he's very generous in some things. He really is," I said. "Look. Suppose, for instance, Stradlater was wearing a tie or something that you liked. Say he had a tie on that you liked a helluva lot—I'm just giving you an example, now. You know what he'd do? He'd probably take it off and give it to you. He really would. Or—you know what he'd do? He'd leave it on your bed or something. But he'd *give* you the goddam tie. Most guys would probably just—"

"*Hell*," Ackley said. "If I had his dough, I would, too."

"No, you wouldn't." I shook my head. "No, you wouldn't, Ackley kid. If you had his dough, you'd be one of the biggest—"

"Stop calling me 'Ackley kid,' God damn it. I'm old enough to be your lousy father."

"No, you're not." Boy, he could really be aggravating sometimes. He never missed a chance to let you know you were sixteen and he was eighteen. "In the first place, I wouldn't let you *in* my goddam family," I said.

"Well, just cut out calling me—"

All of a sudden the door opened, and old Stradlater barged in, in a big hurry. He was always in a big hurry. Everything was a very big deal. He came over to me and gave me these two playful as hell slaps on both cheeks—which is something that can be very annoying. "Listen," he said. "You going out anywheres special tonight?"

"I don't know. I might. What the hell's it doing out—snowing?" He had snow all over his coat.

"Yeah. Listen. If you're not going out anyplace special, how 'bout lending me your hound's-tooth jacket?"

"Who won the game?" I said.

"It's only the half. We're leaving," Stradlater said. "No kidding, you gonna use your hound's-tooth tonight or not? I spilled some crap all over my gray flannel."

"No, but I don't want you stretching it with your goddam shoulders and all," I said. We were practically the same heighth, but he weighed about twice as much as I did. He had these very broad shoulders.

"I won't stretch it." He went over to the closet in a big hurry. "How'sa boy, Ackley?" he said to Ackley. He was at least a pretty friendly guy, Stradlater. It was partly a phony kind of friendly, but at least he always said hello to Ackley and all.

Ackley just sort of grunted when he said "How'sa boy?" He wouldn't *answer* him, but he didn't have guts enough not to at least grunt. Then he said to me, "I think I'll get going. See ya later."

"Okay," I said. He never exactly broke your heart when he went back to his own room.

Old Stradlater started taking off his coat and tie and all. "I think maybe I'll take a fast shave," he said. He had a pretty heavy beard. He really did.

"Where's your date?" I asked him.

"She's waiting in the Annex." He went out of the room with his toilet kit and towel under his arm. No shirt on or anything. He always walked around in his bare torso because he thought he had a damn good build. He did, too. I have to admit it.

IV

I didn't have anything special to do, so I went down to the can and chewed the rag with him while he was shaving. We were the only ones in the can, because everybody was still down at the game. It was hot as hell and the windows were all steamy. There were about ten washbowls, all right against the wall. Stradlater had the middle one. I sat down on the one right next to him and started turning the cold water on and off—this nervous habit I have. Stradlater kept whistling "Song of India" while he shaved. He had one of those very piercing whistles that are practically never in tune, and he always picked out some song that's hard to whistle even if you're a *good* whistler, like "Song of India" or "Slaughter on Tenth Avenue." He could really mess a song up.

You remember I said before that Ackley was a slob in his personal habits? Well, so was Stradlater, but in a different way. Stradlater was more of a secret slob. He always *looked* all right, Stradlater, but for instance, you should've seen the razor he shaved himself with. It was always rusty as hell and full of lather and hairs and crap. He never cleaned it or anything. He always *looked* good when he was finished fixing himself up, but he was a secret slob anyway, if you knew him the way I did. The reason he fixed himself up to look good was because he was madly in love with himself. He thought he was the handsomest guy in the Western Hemisphere. He *was* pretty handsome, too—I'll admit it. But he was mostly the kind of a handsome guy that if your parents saw his picture in your Year Book, they'd right away say, "Who's *this* boy?" I mean he was mostly a Year Book kind of handsome guy. I knew a lot of guys at Pencey I thought were a lot handsomer than Stradlater, but they wouldn't look handsome if you saw their pictures in the Year Book. They'd look like they had big noses or their ears stuck out. I've had that experience frequently.

Anyway, I was sitting on the washbowl next to where Stradlater was shaving, sort of turning the water on and off. I still had my red hunting hat on, with the peak around to the back and all. I really got a bang out of that hat.

"Hey," Stradlater said. "Wanna do me a big favor?"

"What?" I said. Not too enthusiastic. He was always asking you to do him a big favor. You take a very handsome guy, or a guy that thinks he's a real hot-shot, and they're always asking you to do them a big favor. Just because *they're* crazy about themself, they think *you're* crazy about them, too, and that you're just dying to do them a favor. It's sort of funny, in a way.

"You goin' out tonight?" he said.

"I might. I might not. I don't know. Why?"

"I got about a hundred pages to read for history for Monday," he said. "How' bout writing a composition for me, for English? I'll be up the creek if I don't get the goddam thing in by Monday, the reason I ask. How 'bout it?"

It was very ironical. It really was.

"*I'm* the one that's flunking out of the goddam place, and *you're* asking me to write you a goddam composition," I said.

"Yeah, I know. The thing is, though, I'll be up the creek if I don't get it in. Be a buddy. Be a buddyroo. Okay?"

I didn't answer him right away. Suspense is good for some bastards like Stradlater.

"What on?" I said.

"*Any*thing. Anything descriptive. A room. Or a house. Or something you once lived in or something—*you* know. Just as long as it's descriptive as hell." He gave out a big yawn while he said that. Which is something that gives me a royal pain in the ass. I mean if somebody *yawns* right while they're asking you to do them a goddam favor. "Just don't do it *too* good, is all," he said. "That sonuvabitch Hartzell thinks you're a hot-shot in English, and he knows you're my roommate. So I mean don't stick all the commas and stuff in the right place."

That's something else that gives me a royal pain. I mean if you're good at writing compositions and somebody starts talking about commas. Stradlater was always doing that. He wanted you to think that the only reason *he* was lousy at writing compositions was because he stuck all the commas in the wrong place. He was a little bit like Ackley, that way. I once sat next to Ackley at this basketball game. We had a terrific guy on the team, Howie Coyle, that could sink them from the middle of the floor, without even touching the backboard or anything. Ackley kept saying, the whole goddam game, that Coyle had a perfect *build* for basketball. God, how I hate that stuff.

I got bored sitting on that washbowl after a while, so I backed up a few feet and started doing this tap dance, just for the hell of it. I was just amusing myself. I can't really tap-dance or anything, but it was a stone floor in the can, and it was good for tap-dancing. I started imitating one of those guys in the movies. In one of those *musicals*. I hate the movies like poison, but I get a bang imitating them. Old Stradlater watched me in the mirror while he was shaving. All I need's an audience. I'm an exhibitionist. "I'm the goddam Governor's son," I said. I was knocking myself out. Tap-dancing all over the place. "He doesn't want me to be a tap dancer. He wants me to go to Oxford. But it's in my goddam blood, tap-dancing." Old Stradlater laughed. He didn't have too bad a sense of humor. "It's the opening night of the *Ziegfeld Follies*." I was getting out of breath. I have hardly any wind at all. "The leading man can't go on. He's drunk as a bastard. So who do they get to take his place? Me, that's who. The little ole goddam Governor's son."

"Where'dja get that hat?" Stradlater said. He meant my hunting hat. He'd never seen it before.

I was out of breath anyway, so I quit horsing around. I took off my hat and looked at it for about the ninetieth time. "I got it in New York this morning. For a buck. Ya like it?"

Stradlater nodded. "Sharp," he said. He was only flattering me, though, because right away he said, "Listen. Are ya gonna write that composition for me? I have to know."

"If I get the time, I will. If I don't, I won't," I said. I went over and sat down on the washbowl next to him again. "Who's your date?" I asked him. "Fitzgerald?"

"Hell, no! I told ya, I'm through with that pig."

"Yeah? Give her to me, boy. No kidding. She's my type."

"Take her ... She's too old for you."

All of a sudden—for no good reason, really, except that I was sort of in the mood for horsing around—I felt like jumping off the washbowl and getting old Stradlater in a half nelson. That's a wrestling hold, in case you don't know, where you get the other guy around the neck and choke him to death, if you feel like it. So I did it. I landed on him like a goddam panther.

"Cut it out, Holden, for Chrissake!" Stradlater said. He didn't feel like horsing around. He was shaving and all. "Wuddaya wanna make me do—cut my goddam head off?"

I didn't let go, though. I had a pretty good half nelson on him. "Liberate yourself from my viselike grip." I said.

"Je-sus *Christ*." He put down his razor, and all of a sudden jerked his arms up and sort of broke my hold on him. He was a very strong guy. I'm a very weak guy. "Now, cut out the crap," he said. He started shaving himself all over again. He always shaved himself twice, to look gorgeous. With his crumby old razor.

"Who *is* your date if it isn't Fitzgerald?" I asked him. I sat down on the washbowl next to him again. "That Phyllis Smith babe?"

"No. It was supposed to be, but the arrangements got all screwed up. I got Bud Thaw's girl's roommate now ... Hey. I almost forgot. She knows *you*."

"Who does?" I said.

"My date."

"Yeah?" I said. "What's her name?" I was pretty interested.

"I'm thinking ... Uh. Jean Gallagher."

Boy, I nearly dropped *dead* when he said that.

"*Jane* Gallagher," I said. I even got up from the washbowl when he said that. I damn near dropped dead. "You're damn right I know her. She practically lived right next *door* to me, the summer before last. She had this big damn Doberman pinscher. That's how I met her. Her dog used to keep coming over in our—"

"You're right in my light, Holden, for Chrissake," Stradlater said. "Ya have to stand right there?"

Boy, was I excited, though. I really was.

"Where is she?" I asked him. "I oughta go down and say hello to her or something. Where is she? In the Annex?"

"Yeah."

"How'd she happen to mention me? Does she go to B.M. now? She said she might go there. She said she might go to Shipley, too. I thought she went to Shipley. How'd she happen to mention me?" I was pretty excited. I really was.

"*I* don't know, for Chrissake. Lift up, willya? You're on my towel," Stradlater said. I was sitting on his stupid towel.

"Jane Gallagher," I said. I couldn't get over it. "Jesus H. Christ."

Old Stradlater was putting Vitalis on his hair. *My* Vitalis.

"She's a dancer," I said. "Ballet and all. She used to practice about two hours every day, right in the middle of the hottest weather and all. She was worried that it might make her legs lousy—all thick and all. I used to play checkers with her all the time."

"You used to play *what* with her all the time?"

"Checkers."

"*Checkers*, for Chrissake!"

"Yeah. She wouldn't move any of her kings. What she'd do, when she'd get a king, she wouldn't move it. She'd just leave it in the back row. She'd get them all lined up in the back row. Then she'd never use them. She just liked the way they looked when they were all in the back row."

Stradlater didn't say anything. That kind of stuff doesn't interest most people.

"Her mother belonged to the same club we did," I said. "I used to caddy once in a while, just to make some dough. I caddy'd for her mother a couple of times. She went around in about a hundred and seventy, for nine holes."

Stradlater wasn't hardly listening. He was combing his gorgeous locks.

"I oughta go down and at least say hello to her," I said.

"Why don'tcha?"

"I will, in a minute."

He started parting his hair all over again. It took him about an hour to comb his hair.

"Her mother and father were divorced. Her mother was married again to some booze hound," I said. "Skinny guy with hairy legs. I remember him. He wore shorts all the time. Jane said he was supposed to be a playwright or some goddam thing, but all *I* ever saw him do was booze all the time and listen to every single goddam mystery program on the radio. And run around the goddam house, naked.

With *Jane* around, and all."

"Yeah?" Stradlater said. That really interested him. About the booze hound running around the house naked, with Jane around. Stradlater was a very sexy bastard.

"She had a lousy childhood. I'm not kidding."

That didn't interest Stradlater, though. Only very sexy stuff interested him.

"Jane Gallagher. Jesus." I couldn't get her off my mind. I really couldn't. "I oughta go down and say hello to her, at least."

"Why the hell *don't*cha, instead of keep saying it?" Stradlater said.

I walked over to the window, but you couldn't see out of it, it was so steamy from all the heat in the can. "I'm not in the mood right now," I said. I wasn't, either. You have to be in the mood for those things. "I thought she went to Shipley. I could've sworn she went to Shipley." I walked around the can for a little while. I didn't have anything else to do. "Did she enjoy the game?" I said.

"Yeah, I guess so. I don't know."

"Did she tell you we used to play checkers all the time, or anything?"

"I don't know. For Chrissake, I only just *met* her," Stradlater said. He was finished combing his goddam gorgeous hair. He was putting away all his crumby toilet articles.

"Listen. Give her my regards, willya?"

"Okay," Stradlater said, but I knew he probably wouldn't. You take a guy like Stradlater, they never give your regards to people.

He went back to the room, but I stuck around in the can for a while, thinking about old Jane. Then I went back to the room, too.

Stradlater was putting on his tie, in front of the mirror, when I got there. He spent around half his goddam life in front of the mirror. I sat down in my chair and sort of watched him for a while.

"Hey," I said. "Don't tell her I got kicked out, willya?"

"Okay."

That was one good thing about Stradlater. You didn't have to explain every goddam little thing with him, the way you had to do with Ackley. Mostly, I guess, because he wasn't too interested. That's really why. Ackley, it was different. Ackley was a very nosy bastard.

He put on my hound's-tooth jacket.

"Jesus, now, try not to stretch it all over the place," I said. I'd only worn it about twice.

"I won't. Where the hell's my cigarettes?"

"On the desk." He never knew where he left anything. "Under your muffler." He put them in his coat pocket—*my* coat pocket.

I pulled the peak of my hunting hat around to the front all of a sudden, for a change. I was getting sort of nervous, all of a sudden. I'm quite a nervous guy. "Listen, where ya going on your date with her?" I asked him. "Ya know yet?"

"I don't know. New York, if we have time. She only signed out for nine-thirty, for Chrissake."

I didn't like the way he said it, so I said, "The reason she did that, she probably just didn't know what a handsome, charming bastard you are. If she'd *known*, she probably would've signed out for nine-thirty in the *morning*."

"Goddam right," Stradlater said. You couldn't rile him too easily. He was too conceited. "No kidding, now. Do that composition for me," he said. He had his coat on, and he was all ready to go. "Don't knock yourself out or anything, but just make it descriptive as hell. Okay?"

I didn't answer him. I didn't feel like it. All I said was, "Ask her if she still keeps all her kings in the back row."

"Okay," Stradlater said, but I knew he wouldn't. "Take it easy, now." He banged the hell out of the room.

I sat there for about a half hour after he left. I mean I just sat in my chair, not doing anything. I kept thinking about Jane, and about Stradlater having a date with her and all. It made me so nervous I nearly went crazy. I already told you what a sexy bastard Stradlater was.

All of a sudden, Ackley barged back in again, through the damn shower curtains, as usual. For once in my stupid life, I was really glad to see him. He took my mind off the other stuff.

He stuck around till around dinnertime, talking about all the guys at Pencey that he hated their guts, and squeezing this big pimple on his chin. He didn't even use his handkerchief. I don't even think the bastard *had* a handkerchief, if you want to know the truth. I never saw him use one, anyway.

V

We always had the same meal on Saturday nights at Pencey. It was supposed to be a big deal, because they gave you steak. I'll bet a thousand bucks the reason they did that was because a lot of guys' parents came up to school on Sunday, and old Thurmer probably figured everybody's mother would ask their darling boy what he had for dinner last night, and he'd say, "Steak." What a racket. You should've seen the steaks. They were these little hard, dry jobs that you could hardly even cut. You always got these very lumpy mashed potatoes on steak night, and for dessert you got Brown Betty, which nobody ate, except maybe the little kids in the lower school that didn't know any better—and guys like Ackley that ate *ev*erything.

It was nice, though, when we got out of the dining room. There were about three inches of snow on the ground, and it was still coming down like a madman. It looked pretty as hell, and we all started throwing snowballs and horsing around all over the place. It was very childish, but everybody was really enjoying themselves.

I didn't have a date or anything, so I and this friend of mine, Mal Brossard, that was on the wrestling team, decided we'd take a bus into Agerstown and have a hamburger and maybe see a lousy movie. Neither of us felt like sitting around on our ass all night. I asked Mal if he minded if Ackley came along with us. The reason I asked was because Ackley never did *any*thing on Saturday night, except stay in his room and squeeze his pimples or something. Mal said he didn't *mind* but that he wasn't too crazy about the idea. He didn't like Ackley much. Anyway, we both went to our rooms to get ready and all, and while I was putting on my galoshes and crap, I yelled over and asked old Ackley if he wanted to go to the movies. He could hear me all right through the shower curtains, but he didn't answer me right away. He was the kind of a guy that hates to answer you right away. Finally he came over, through the goddam curtains, and stood on the shower ledge and asked who was going besides me. He always had to know who was going. I swear, if that guy was shipwrecked somewhere, and you rescued him in a goddam boat, he'd want to know who the guy was that was rowing it before he'd even get in. I told him Mal Brossard was going. He said, "*That* bastard ... All right. Wait a second." You'd think he was doing you a big favor.

It took him about five hours to get ready. While he was doing it, I went over to my window and opened it and packed a snowball with my bare hands. The snow was very good for packing. I didn't throw it at anything, though. I *start*ed to throw it. At a car that was parked across the street. But I changed my mind. The car looked so nice and white. Then I started to throw it at a hydrant, but that looked too nice and white, too. Finally I didn't throw it at anything. All I did was close the window and walk around the room with the snowball, packing it harder. A little while later, I still had it with me when I and Brossard and Ackley got on the bus. The bus driver opened the doors and made me throw it out. I *told* him I wasn't going to chuck it at anybody, but he wouldn't believe me. People never believe you.

Brossard and Ackley both had seen the picture that was playing, so all we did, we just had a couple of hamburgers and played the pinball machine for a little while, then took the bus back to Pencey. I didn't care about not seeing the movie, anyway. It was supposed to be a comedy, with Cary Grant in it, and all that crap. Besides, I'd been to the movies with Brossard and Ackley before. They both laughed like hyenas at stuff that wasn't even funny. I didn't even enjoy sitting next to them in the movies.

It was only about a quarter to nine when we got back to the dorm. Old Brossard was a bridge fiend, and he started looking around the dorm for a game. Old Ackley parked himself in my room, just for a change. Only, instead of sitting on the arm of Stradlater's chair, he laid down on my bed, with his face right on my pillow and all. He started talking in this very monotonous voice, and picking at all his pimples. I dropped about a thousand hints, but I couldn't get rid of him. All he did was keep talking in this very monotonous voice about some babe he was supposed to have had sexual intercourse with the summer before. He'd already told me about it about a hundred times. Every time he told it, it was different. One minute he'd be giving it to her in his cousin's Buick, the next minute he'd be giving it to her under some boardwalk. It was all a lot of crap, naturally. He was a virgin if ever I saw one. I doubt if he ever even gave anybody a feel. Anyway, finally I had to come right out and tell him that I had to write a composition for Stradlater, and that he had to clear the hell out, so I could concentrate. He finally did, but he took his time about it, as usual. After he left, I put on my pajamas and bathrobe and my old hunting hat, and started writing the composition.

The thing was, I couldn't think of a room or a house or anything to describe the way Stradlater said he had to have. I'm not too crazy about describing rooms and houses anyway. So what I did, I wrote about my brother Allie's baseball mitt. It was a very descriptive subject. It really was. My brother Allie had this left-handed fielder's mitt. He was left-handed. The thing that was descriptive about it, though, was that he had poems written all over the fingers and the pocket and everywhere. In green ink. He wrote them on it so that he'd have something to read when he was in the field and nobody was up at bat. He's dead now. He got leukemia and died when we were up in Maine, on July 18, 1946. You'd have liked him. He was two years younger than I was, but he was about fifty times as intelligent. He was terrifically intelligent. His teachers were always writing letters to my mother, telling her what a pleasure it was having a boy like Allie in their class. And they weren't just shooting the crap. They really meant it. But it wasn't just that he was the most intelligent member in the family. He was also the nicest, in lots of ways. He never got mad at anybody. People with red hair are supposed to get mad very easily, but Allie never did, and he had very red hair. I'll tell you what kind of red hair he had. I started playing golf when I was only ten years old. I remember once, the summer I was around twelve, teeing off and all, and having a hunch that if I turned around all of a sudden, I'd see Allie. So I did, and sure enough, he was sitting on his bike outside the fence—there was this fence that went all around the course—and he was sitting there, about a hundred and fifty yards behind me, watching me tee off. That's the kind of red hair he had. God, he was a nice kid, though. He used to laugh so hard at something he thought of at the dinner table that he just about fell off his chair. I was only thirteen, and they were going to have me psychoanalyzed and all, because I broke all the windows in the garage. I don't blame them. I really don't. I slept in the garage the night he died, and I broke all the goddam windows with my fist, just for the hell of it. I even tried to break all the windows on the station wagon we had that summer, but my hand was already broken and everything by that time, and I couldn't do it. It was a very stupid thing to do, I'll admit, but I hardly didn't even know I was doing it, and you didn't know Allie. My hand still hurts me once in a while when it rains and all, and I can't make a real fist any more—not a tight one, I mean—but outside of that I don't care much. I mean I'm not going to be a goddam surgeon or a violinist or anything anyway.

Anyway, that's what I wrote Stadlater's composition about. Old Allie's baseball mitt. I happened to have it with me, in my suitcase, so I got it out and copied down the poems that were written on it. All I had to do was change Allie's name so that nobody would know it was my brother and not Stradlater's. I wasn't too crazy about doing it, but I couldn't think of anything else descriptive. Besides, I sort of liked writing about it. It took me about an hour, because I had to use Stradlater's lousy typewriter, and it kept jamming on me. The reason I didn't use my own was because I'd lent it to a guy down the hall.

It was around ten-thirty, I guess, when I finished it. I wasn't tired, though, so I looked out the window for a while. It wasn't snowing out any more, but every once in a while you could hear a car somewhere not being able to get started. You could also hear old Ackley snoring. Right through the goddam shower curtains you could hear him. He had sinus trouble and he couldn't breathe too hot when he was asleep. That guy had just about everything. Sinus trouble, pimples, lousy teeth, halitosis, crumby fingernails. You had to feel a little sorry for the crazy sonuvabitch.

VI

Some things are hard to remember. I'm thinking now of when Stradlater got back from his date with Jane. I mean I can't remember exactly what I was doing when I heard his goddam stupid footsteps coming down the corridor. I probably was still looking out the window, but I swear I can't remember. I was so damn worried, that's why. When I really worry about something, I don't just fool around. I even have to go to the bathroom when I worry about something. Only, I don't go. I'm too worried to go. I don't want to interrupt my worrying to go. If you knew Stradlater, you'd have been worried, too. I'd double-dated with that bastard a couple of times, and I know what I'm talking about. He was unscrupulous. He really was.

Anyway, the corridor was all linoleum and all, and you could hear his goddam footsteps coming right towards the room. I don't even remember where I was sitting when he came in—at the window, or in my chair or his. I swear I can't remember.

He came in griping about how cold it was out. Then he said, "Where the hell is everybody? It's like a goddam morgue around here." I didn't even bother to answer him. If he was so goddam stupid not to realize it was Saturday night and everybody was out or asleep or home for the week end, I wasn't going to break my neck telling him. He started getting undressed. He didn't say one goddam word about Jane. Not one. Neither did I. I just watched him. All he did was thank me for letting him wear my hound's-tooth. He hung it up on a hanger and put it in the closet.

Then, when he was taking off his tie, he asked me if I'd written his goddam composition for him. I told him it was over on his goddam bed. He walked over and read it while he was unbuttoning his shirt. He stood there, reading it, and sort of stroking his bare chest and stomach, with this very stupid expression on his face. He was always stroking his stomach or his chest. He was mad about himself.

All of a sudden, he said, "For Chris*sake*, Holden. This is about a goddam *base*ball glove."

"So what?" I said. Cold as hell.

"Wuddaya mean *so what?* I told ya it had to be about a goddam *room* or a house or something."

"You said it had to be descriptive. What the hell's the difference if it's about a baseball glove?"

"God damn it." He was sore as hell. He was really furious. "You always do everything backasswards." He looked at me. "No wonder you're flunking the hell out of here," he said. "You don't do *one damn thing* the way you're supposed to. I mean it. Not one damn thing."

"All right, give it back to me, then," I said. I went over and pulled it right out of his goddam hand. Then I tore it up.

"What the hellja do *that* for?" he said.

I didn't even answer him. I just threw the pieces in the wastebasket. Then I lay down on my bed, and we both didn't say anything for a long time. He got all undressed, down to his shorts, and I lay on my bed and lit a cigarette. You weren't allowed to smoke in the dorm, but you could do it late at night when everybody was asleep or out and nobody could smell the smoke. Besides, I did it to annoy Stradlater. It drove him crazy when you broke any rules. He never smoked in the dorm. It was only me.

He still didn't say one single solitary word about Jane. So finally I said, "You're back pretty goddam late if she only signed out for nine-thirty. Did you make her be late signing in?"

He was sitting on the edge of his bed, cutting his goddam toenails, when I asked him that. "Coupla minutes," he said. "Who the hell signs out for nine-thirty on a Saturday night?" *God*, how I hated him.

"Did you go to New York?" I said.

"Ya crazy? How the hell could we go to New York if she only signed out for nine-thirty?"

"That's tough."

He looked up at me. "Listen," he said, "if you're gonna smoke in the room, how 'bout going down to the can and do it? You may be getting the hell out of here, but I have to stick around long enough to graduate."

I ignored him. I really did. I went right on smoking like a madman. All I did was sort of turn over on my side and watched him cut his damn toenails. What a school. You were always watching somebody cut their damn toenails or squeeze their pimples or something.

"Did you give her my regards?" I asked him.

"Yeah."

The hell he did, the bastard.

"What'd she say?" I said. "Did you ask her if she still keeps all her kings in the back row?"

"*No*, I didn't ask her. What the hell ya think we did all night—play checkers, for Chrissake?"

I didn't even answer him. God, how I hated him.

"If you didn't go to New York, where'd ya go with her?" I asked him, after a little while. I could hardly keep my voice from shaking all over the place. Boy, was I getting nervous. I just had a *feeling* something had gone funny.

He was finished cutting his damn toenails. So he got up from the bed, in just his damn shorts and all, and started getting very damn playful. He came over to my bed and started leaning over me and taking these playful as hell socks at my shoulder. "Cut it out," I said. "Where'd you go with her if you didn't go to New York?"

"Nowhere. We just sat in the goddam car." He gave me another one of those playful stupid little socks on the shoulder.

"Cut it *out*," I said. "Whose car?"

"Ed Banky's."

Ed Banky was the basketball coach at Pencey. Old Stradlater was one of his pets, because he was the center on the team, and Ed Banky always let him borrow his car when he wanted it. It wasn't allowed for students to borrow faculty guys' cars, but all the athletic bastards stuck together. In every school I've gone to, all the athletic bastards stick together.

Stradlater kept taking these shadow punches down at my shoulder. He had his toothbrush in his hand, and he put it in his mouth. "What'd you do?" I said. "Give her the time in Ed Banky's goddam car?" My voice was shaking something awful.

"What a thing to say. Want me to wash your mouth out with soap?"

"*Did* you?"

"That's a professional secret, buddy."

This next part I don't remember so hot. All I know is I got up from the bed, like I was going down to the can or something, and then I tried to sock him, with all my might, right smack in the toothbrush, so it would split his goddam throat open. Only, I missed. I didn't connect. All I did was sort of get him on the side of the head or something. It probably hurt him a little bit, but not as much as I wanted.

It probably would've hurt him a lot, but I did it with my right hand, and I can't make a good fist with that hand. On account of that injury I told you about.

Anyway, the next thing I knew, I was on the goddam floor and he was sitting on my chest, with his face all red. That is, he had his goddam *knees* on my chest, and he weighed about a ton. He had hold of my wrists, too, so I couldn't take another sock at him. I'd've killed him.

"What the hell's the matter with you?" he kept saying, and his stupid face kept getting redder and redder.

"Get your lousy *knees* off my *chest*," I told him. I was almost bawling. I really was. "Go on, get *offa* me, ya crumby bastard."

He wouldn't do it, though. He kept holding onto my wrists and I kept calling him a sonuvabitch and all, for around ten hours. I can hardly even remember what all I said to him. I told him he thought he could give the time to anybody he felt like. I told him he didn't even care if a girl kept all her kings in the back row or not, and the reason he didn't care was because he was a goddam stupid moron. He hated it when you called him a moron. All morons hate it when you call them a moron.

"Shut up, now, Holden," he said with his big stupid red face. "just shut up, now."

"You don't even know if her first name is Jane or *Jean*, ya goddam moron!"

"Now, *shut up*, Holden, God damn it—I'm *warning* ya," he said—I really had him going. "If you don't shut up, I'm gonna slam ya one."

"Get your dirty stinking moron knees off my chest."

"If I letcha up, will you keep your mouth shut?"

I didn't even answer him.

He said it over again. "Holden. If I letcha up, willya keep your mouth shut?"

"Yes."

He got up off me, and I got up, too. My chest hurt like hell from his dirty knees. "You're a dirty stupid sonuvabitch of a moron," I told him.

That got him *really* mad. He shook his big stupid finger in my face. "Holden, God damn it, I'm *warning* you, now. For the last time. If you don't keep your yap shut, I'm gonna—"

"Why should I?" I said—I was practically yelling. "That's just the trouble with all you morons. You never want to discuss anything. That's the way you can always tell a moron. They never want to discuss anything intellig—"

Then he really let one go at me, and the next thing I knew I was on the goddam floor again. I don't remember if he knocked me out or not, but I don't think so. It's pretty hard to knock a guy out, except in the goddam movies. But my nose was bleeding all over the place. When I looked up, old Stradlater was standing practically right on top of me. He had his goddam toilet kit under his arm. "Why the hell don'tcha shut *up* when I tellya to?" he said. He sounded pretty nervous. He probably was scared he'd fractured my skull or something when I hit the floor. It's too bad I didn't. "You asked for it, God damn it," he said. Boy, did he look worried.

I didn't even bother to get up. I just lay there on the floor for a while, and kept calling him a moron sonuvabitch. I was so mad, I was practically bawling.

"Listen. Go wash your face," Stradlater said. "Ya hear me?"

I told him to go wash his own moron face—which was a pretty childish thing to say, but I was mad as hell. I told him to stop off on the way to the can and give Mrs. Schmidt the time. Mrs. Schmidt was the janitor's wife. She was around sixty-five.

I kept sitting there on the floor till I heard old Stradlater close the door and go down the corridor to the can. Then I got up. I couldn't find my goddam hunting hat anywhere. Finally I found it. It was under the bed. I put it on, and turned the old peak around to the back, the way I liked it, and then I went over and took a look at my stupid face in the mirror. You never saw such gore in your life. I had blood all over my mouth and chin and even on my pajamas and bathrobe. It partly scared me and it partly fascinated me. All that blood and all sort of made me look tough. I'd only been in about two fights in my life, and I lost *both* of them. I'm not too tough. I'm a pacifist, if you want to know the truth.

I had a feeling old Ackley'd probably heard all the racket and was awake. So I went through the shower curtains into his room, just to see what the hell he was doing. I hardly ever went over to his room. It always had a funny stink in it, because he was so crumby in his personal habits.

VII

A tiny bit of light came through the shower curtains and all from our room, and I could see him lying in bed. I knew damn well he was wide awake. "Ackley?" I said. "Y'awake?"

"Yeah."

It was pretty dark, and I stepped on somebody's shoe on the floor and damn near fell on my head. Ackley sort of sat up in bed and leaned on his arm. He had a lot of white stuff on his face, for his pimples. He looked sort of spooky in the dark. "What the hellya doing, anyway?" I said.

"Wuddaya mean what the hell am I doing? I was tryna *sleep* before you guys started making all that noise. What the hell was the fight about, anyhow?"

"Where's the light?" I couldn't find the light. I was sliding my hand all over the wall.

"Wuddaya want the light for? ... Right next to your hand."

I finally found the switch and turned It on. Old Ackley put his hand up so that the light wouldn't hurt his eyes.

"*Je*sus!" he said. "What the hell happened to *you*?" He meant all the blood and all.

"I had a little goddam tiff with Stradlater," I said. Then I sat down on the floor. They never had any chairs in their room. I don't know what the hell they did with their chairs. "Listen," I said, "do you feel like playing a little Canasta?" He was a

Canasta fiend.

"You're still *bleed*ing, for Chrissake. You better put something on it."

"It'll stop. Listen. Ya wanna play a little Canasta or don'tcha?"

"Ca*nas*ta, for Chrissake. Do you know what time it is, by any chance?"

"It isn't late. It's only around eleven, eleven-thirty."

"*On*ly around!" Ackley said. "Listen. I gotta get up and go to *Mass* in the morning, for Chrissake. You guys start hollering and fighting in the middle of the goddam—What the hell was the fight about, anyhow?"

"It's a long story. I don't wanna bore ya, Ackley. I'm thinking of your welfare," I told him. I never discussed my personal life with him. In the first place, he was even more stupid than Stradlater. Stradlater was a goddam genius next to Ackley. "Hey," I said, "is it okay if I sleep in Ely's bed tonight? He won't be back till tomorrow night, will he?" I knew damn well he wouldn't. Ely went home damn near every week end.

"*I* don't know when the hell he's coming back," Ackley said.

Boy, did that annoy me. "What the hell do you mean you don't know when he's coming back? He never comes back till Sunday *night*, does he?"

"No, but for Chrissake, I can't just tell somebody they can sleep in his goddam *bed* if they want to."

That killed me. I reached up from where I was sitting on the floor and patted him on the goddam shoulder. "You're a prince, Ackley kid," I said. "You know that?"

"No, I mean it—I can't just tell somebody they can sleep in—"

"You're a real prince. You're a gentleman and a scholar, kid," I said. He really was, too. "Do you happen to have any cigarettes, by any chance?—Say 'no' or I'll drop dead."

"No, I don't, as a matter of fact. Listen, what the hell was the fight about?"

I didn't answer him. All I did was, I got up and went over and looked out the window. I felt so lonesome, all of a sudden. I almost wished I was dead.

"What the hell was the fight about, anyhow?" Ackley said, for about the fiftieth time. He certainly was a bore about that.

"About you," I said.

"About *me*, for Chrissake?"

"Yeah. I was defending your goddam honor. Stradlater said you had a lousy personality. I couldn't let him get away with that stuff."

That got him excited. "He did? No kidding? He did?"

I told him I was only kidding, and then I went over and laid down on Ely's bed. Boy, did I feel rotten. I felt so damn lonesome.

"This room stinks," I said. "I can smell your socks from way over here. Don'tcha ever send them to the laundry?"

"If you don't like it, you know what you can do," Ackley said. What a witty guy. "How 'bout turning off the goddam light?"

I didn't turn it off right away, though. I just kept laying there on Ely's bed, thinking about Jane and all. It just drove me stark staring mad when I thought about her and Stradlater parked somewhere in that fat-assed Ed Banky's car. Every time I thought about it, I felt like jumping out the window. The thing is, you didn't know Stradlater. I knew him. Most guys at Pencey just *talked* about having sexual intercourse with girls all the time—like Ackley, for instance—but old Stradlater really did it. I was personally acquainted with at least two girls he gave the time to. That's the truth.

"Tell me the story of your fascinating life, Ackley kid," I said.

"How 'bout turning off the goddam light? I gotta get up for Mass in the morning."

I got up and turned it off, if it made him happy. Then I laid down on Ely's bed again.

"What're ya gonna do—sleep in Ely's bed?" Ackley said. He was the perfect host, boy.

"I may. I may not. Don't worry about it."

"I'm not *wor*ried about it. Only, I'd hate like hell if Ely came in all of a sudden and found some guy—"

"Relax. I'm not gonna sleep here. I wouldn't abuse your goddam hospitality."

A couple of minutes later, he was snoring like mad. I kept laying there in the dark anyway, though, trying not to think about old Jane and Stradlater in that goddam Ed Banky's car. But it was almost impossible. The trouble was, I knew that guy Stradlater's technique. That made it even worse. We once double-dated, in Ed Banky's car, and Stradlater was in the back, with his date, and I was in the front with mine. What a technique that guy had. What he'd do was, he'd start snowing his date in this very quiet, *sincere* voice—like as if he wasn't only a very handsome guy but a nice, *sincere* guy, too. I damn near puked, listening to him. His date kept saying, "No—*please*. Please, don't. Please." But old Stradlater kept snowing her in this Abraham Lincoln, sincere voice, and finally there'd be this terrific silence in the back of the car. It was really embarrassing. I don't think he gave that girl the time that night—but damn near. *Damn* near.

While I was laying there trying not to think, I heard old Stradlater come back from the can and go in our room. You could hear him putting away his crumby toilet articles and all, and opening the window. He was a fresh-air fiend. Then, a little while later, he turned off the light. He didn't even look around to see where I was at.

It was even depressing out in the street. You couldn't even hear any cars any more. I got feeling so lonesome and rotten, I even felt like waking Ackley up.

"Hey, Ackley," I said, in sort of a whisper, so Stradlater couldn't hear me through the shower curtain.

Ackley didn't hear me, though.

"Hey, Ackley!"

He still didn't hear me. He slept like a rock.

"Hey, *Ackley!*"

He heard that, all right.

"What the hell's the matter with you?" he said. "I was asleep, for Chrissake."

"Listen. What's the routine on joining a monastery?" I asked him. I was sort of toying with the idea of joining one. "Do you have to be a Catholic and all?"

"*Cert*ainly you have to be a Catholic. You bastard, did you wake me just to ask me a dumb ques—"

"Aah, go back to sleep. I'm not gonna join one anyway. The kind of luck I have, I'd probably join one with all the wrong kind of monks in it. All stupid bastards. Or just bastards."

When I said that, old Ackley sat way the hell up in bed. "Listen," he said, "I don't care what you say about *me* or anything, but if you start making cracks about my goddam re*ligion*, for Chrissake—"

"Relax," I said. "Nobody's making any cracks about your goddam religion." I got up off Ely's bed, and started towards the door. I didn't want to hang around in that stupid atmosphere any more. I stopped on the way, though, and picked up Ackley's hand, and gave him a big, phony handshake. He pulled it away from me. "What's the idea?" he said.

"No idea. I just want to thank you for being such a goddam prince, that's all," I said. I said it in this very sincere voice. "You're aces, Ackley kid," I said. "You know that?"

"Wise guy. Someday somebody's gonna bash your—"

I didn't even bother to listen to him. I shut the damn door and went out in the corridor.

Everybody was asleep or out or home for the week end, and it was very, very quiet and depressing in the corridor. There was this empty box of Kolynos toothpaste outside Leahy and Hoffman's door, and while I walked down towards the stairs, I kept giving it a boot with this sheep-lined slipper I had on. What I thought I'd do, I thought I might go down and see what old Mal Brossard was doing. But all of a sudden, I changed my mind. All of a sudden, I decided what I'd really do, I'd get the hell out of Pencey—right that same night and all. I mean not wait till Wednesday or anything. I just didn't want to hang around any more. It made me too sad and lonesome. So what I decided to do, I decided I'd take a room in a hotel in New York—some very inexpensive hotel and all—and just take it easy till Wednesday. Then, on Wednesday, I'd go home all rested up and feeling swell. I figured my parents probably wouldn't get old Thurmer's letter saying I'd been given the ax till maybe Tuesday or Wednesday. I didn't want to go home or anything till they got it and thoroughly digested it and all. I didn't want to be around when they *first* got it. My mother gets very hysterical. She's not too bad after she gets something thoroughly digested, though. Besides, I sort of needed a little vacation. My nerves were shot. They really were.

Anyway, that's what I decided I'd do. So I went back to the room and turned on the light, to start packing and all. I already had quite a few things packed. Old Stradlater didn't even wake up. I lit a cigarette and got all dressed and then I packed these two Gladstones I have. It only took me about two minutes. I'm a very rapid packer.

One thing about packing depressed me a little. I had to pack these brand-new ice skates my mother had practically just sent me a couple of days before. That depressed me. I could see my mother going in Spaulding's and asking the salesman a million dopy questions—and here I was getting the ax again. It made me feel pretty sad. She bought me the wrong kind of skates—I wanted racing skates and she bought hockey—but it made me sad anyway. Almost every time somebody gives me a present, it ends up making me sad.

After I got all packed, I sort of counted my dough. I don't remember exactly how much I had, but I was pretty loaded. My grandmother'd just sent me a wad about a week before. I have this grandmother that's quite lavish with her dough. She doesn't have all her marbles any more—she's old as hell—and she keeps sending me money for my birthday about four times a year. Anyway, even though I was pretty loaded, I figured I could always use a few extra bucks. You never know. So what I did was, I went down the hail and woke up Frederick Woodruff, this guy I'd lent my typewriter to. I asked him how much he'd give me for it. He was a pretty wealthy guy. He said he didn't know. He said he didn't much want to buy it. Finally he bought it, though. It cost about ninety bucks, and all he bought it for was twenty. He was sore because I'd woke him up.

When I was all set to go, when I had my bags and all, I stood for a while next to the stairs and took a last look down the goddam corridor. I was sort of crying. I don't know why. I put my red hunting hat on, and turned the peak around to the back, the way I liked it, and then I yelled at the top of my goddam voice, "*Sleep tight, ya morons!*" I'll bet I woke up every bastard on the whole floor. Then I got the hell out. Some stupid guy had thrown peanut shells all over the stairs, and I damn near broke my crazy neck.

VIII

It was too late to call up for a cab or anything, so I walked the whole way to the station. It wasn't too far, but it was cold as hell, and the snow made it hard for walking, and my Gladstones kept banging hell out of my legs. I sort of enjoyed the air and all, though. The only trouble was, the cold made my nose hurt, and right under my upper lip, where old Stradlater'd laid one on me. He'd smacked my lip right on my teeth, and it was pretty sore. My ears were nice and warm, though. That hat I bought had earlaps in it, and I put them on—I didn't give a damn how I looked. Nobody was around anyway. Everybody was in the sack.

I was quite lucky when I got to the station, because I only had to wait about ten minutes for a train. While I waited, I got some snow in my hand and washed my face with it. I still had quite a bit of blood on.

Usually I like riding on trains, especially at night, with the lights on and the windows so black, and one of those guys coming up the aisle selling coffee and sandwiches and magazines. I usually buy a ham sandwich and about four magazines. If I'm on a train at night, I can usually even read one of those dumb stories in a magazine without puking. You know. One of those stories with a lot of phony, lean-jawed guys named David in it, and a lot of phony girls named Linda or Marcia that are always lighting all the goddam Davids' pipes for them. I can even read one of those lousy stories on a train at night, usually. But this time, it was different. I just didn't feel like it. I just sort of sat and not did anything. All I did was take off my hunting hat and put it in my pocket.

All of a sudden, this lady got on at Trenton and sat down next to me. Practically the whole car was empty, because it was pretty late and all, but she sat down next to me, instead of an empty seat, because she had this big bag with her and I was sitting in the front seat. She stuck the bag right out in the middle of the aisle, where the conductor and everybody could trip over it. She had these orchids on, like she'd just been to a big party or something. She was around forty or forty-five, I guess, but she was very good-looking. Women kill me. They really do. I don't mean I'm oversexed or anything like that—although I am quite sexy. I just like them, I mean. They're always leaving their goddam bags out in the middle of the aisle.

Anyway, we were sitting there, and all of a sudden she said to me, "Excuse me, but isn't that a Pencey Prep sticker?" She was looking up at my suitcases, up on the rack.

"Yes, it is," I said. She was right. I did have a goddam Pencey sticker on one of my Gladstones. Very corny, I'll admit.

"Oh, do you go to Pencey?" she said. She had a nice voice. A nice telephone voice, mostly. She should've carried a goddam telephone around with her.

"Yes, I do," I said.

"Oh, how lovely! Perhaps you know my son, then, Ernest Morrow? He goes to Pencey."

"Yes, I do. He's in my class."

Her son was doubtless the biggest bastard that ever went to Pencey, in the whole crumby history of the school. He was always going down the corridor, after he'd had a shower, snapping his soggy old wet towel at people's asses. That's exactly the kind of a guy he was.

"Oh, how nice!" the lady said. But not corny. She was just nice and all. "I must tell Ernest we met," she said. "May I ask your name, dear?"

"Rudolf Schmidt," I told her. I didn't feel like giving her my whole life history. Rudolf Schmidt was the name of the janitor of our dorm.

"Do you like Pencey?" she asked me.

"Pencey? It's not too bad. It's not *par*adise or anything, but it's as good as most schools. Some of the faculty are pretty conscientious."

"Ernest just adores it."

"I know he does," I said. Then I started shooting the old crap around a little bit. "He adapts himself very well to things. He really does. I mean he really knows how to adapt himself."

"Do you think so?" she asked me. She sounded interested as hell.

"Ernest? Sure," I said. Then I watched her take off her gloves. Boy, was she lousy with rocks.

"I just broke a nail, getting out of a cab," she said. She looked up at me and sort of smiled. She had a terrifically nice smile. She really did. Most people have hardly any smile at all, or a lousy one. "Ernest's father and I sometimes worry about him," she said. "We sometimes feel he's not a terribly good mixer."

"How do you mean?"

"Well. He's a very sensitive boy. He's really never been a terribly good mixer with other boys. Perhaps he takes things a little more seriously than he should at his age."

Sensitive. That killed me. That guy Morrow was about as sensitive as a goddam toilet seat.

I gave her a good look. She didn't look like any dope to me. She looked like she might have a pretty damn good idea what a bastard she was the mother of. But you can't always tell—with somebody's mother, I mean. Mothers are all slightly insane. The thing is, though, I liked old Morrow's mother. She was all right. "Would you care for a cigarette?" I asked her.

She looked all around. "I don't believe this is a smoker, Rudolf," she said. Rudolf. That killed me.

"That's all right. We can smoke till they start screaming at us," I said. She took a cigarette off me, and I gave her a light.

She looked nice, smoking. She inhaled and all, but she didn't *wolf* the smoke down, the way most women around her age do. She had a lot of charm. She had quite a lot of sex appeal, too, if you really want to know.

She was looking at me sort of funny. "I may be wrong, but I believe your nose is bleeding, dear," she said, all of a sudden.

I nodded and took out my handkerchief. "I got hit with a snowball," I said. "One of those very icy ones." I probably would've told her what really happened, but it would've taken too long. I liked her, though. I was beginning to feel sort of sorry I'd told her my name was Rudolf Schmidt. "Old Ernie," I said. "He's one of the most popular boys at Pencey. Did you know that?"

"No, I didn't."

I nodded. "It really took everybody quite a long time to get to know him. He's a funny guy. A *strange* guy, in lots of ways—know what I mean? Like when I first met him. When I first met him, I thought he was kind of a snobbish person. That's what I thought. But he isn't. He's just got this very original personality that takes you a little while to get to know him."

Old Mrs. Morrow didn't say anything, but boy, you should've seen her. I had her glued to her seat. You take somebody's mother, all they want to hear about is what a hot-shot their son is.

Then I *real*ly started chucking the old crap around. "Did he tell you about the elections?" I asked her. "The class elections?"

She shook her head. I had her in a trance, like. I really did.

"Well, a bunch of us wanted old Ernie to be president of the class. I mean he was the unanimous choice. I mean he was the only boy that could really handle the job," I said—boy, was I chucking it. "But this other boy—Harry Fencer—was elected. And the *reason* he was elected, the simple and obvious reason, was because Ernie wouldn't let us nominate him. Because he's so darn shy and modest and all. He *refused* ... Boy, he's *really* shy. You oughta make him try to get over that." I looked at her. "Didn't he tell you about it?"

"No, he didn't."

I nodded. "That's Ernie. He wouldn't. That's the one fault with him—he's too shy and modest. You really oughta get him to try to relax occasionally."

Right that minute, the conductor came around for old Mrs. Morrow's ticket, and it gave me a chance to quit shooting it. I'm glad I shot it for a while, though. You take a guy like Morrow that's always snapping their towel at people's asses—really trying to *hurt* somebody with it—they don't just stay a rat while they're a kid. They stay a rat their whole life. But I'll bet, after all the crap I shot, Mrs. Morrow'll keep thinking of him now as this very shy, modest guy that wouldn't let us nominate him for president. She might. You can't tell. Mothers aren't too sharp about that stuff.

"Would you care for a cocktail?" I asked her. I was feeling in the mood for one myself. "We can go in the club car. All right?"

"Dear, are you allowed to order drinks?" she asked me. Not snotty, though. She was too charming and all to be snotty.

"Well, no, not exactly, but I can usually get them on account of my heighth," I said. "And I have quite a bit of gray hair." I turned sideways and showed her my gray hair. It fascinated hell out of her. "C'mon, join me, why don't you?" I said. I'd've enjoyed having her.

"I really don't think I'd better. Thank you so much, though, dear," she said. "Anyway, the club car's most likely closed. It's quite late, you know." She was right. I'd forgotten all about what time it was.

Then she looked at me and asked me what I was afraid she was going to ask me. "Ernest wrote that he'd be home on Wednesday, that Christmas vacation would start on *Wednes*day," she said. "I hope you weren't called home suddenly because of illness in the family." She really looked worried about it. She wasn't just being nosy, you could tell.

"No, everybody's fine at home," I said. "It's me. I have to have this operation."

"Oh! I'm so sorry," she said. She really was, too. I was right away sorry I'd said it, but it was too late.

"It isn't very serious. I have this tiny little tumor on the brain."

"Oh, *no!*" She put her hand up to her mouth and all.

"Oh, I'll be all right and everything! It's right near the outside. And it's a very tiny one. They can take it out in about two minutes."

Then I started reading this timetable I had in my pocket. Just to stop lying. Once I get started, I can go on for hours if I feel like it. No kidding. *Hours.*

We didn't talk too much after that. She started reading this *Vogue* she had with her, and I looked out the window for a while. She got off at Newark. She wished me a lot of luck with the operation and all. She kept calling me Rudolf. Then she invited me to visit Ernie during the summer, at Gloucester, Massachusetts. She said their house was right on the beach, and they had a tennis court and all, but I just thanked her and told her I was going to South America with my grandmother. Which was really a hot one, because my grandmother hardly ever even goes out of the *house*, except maybe to go to a goddam matinee or something. But I wouldn't visit that sonuvabitch Morrow for all the dough in the world, even if I was desperate.

IX

The first thing I did when I got off at Penn Station, I went into this phone booth. I felt like giving somebody a buzz. I left my bags right outside the booth so that I could watch them, but as soon as I was inside, I couldn't think of anybody to call up. My brother D.B. was in Hollywood. My kid sister Phoebe goes to bed around nine o'clock—so I couldn't call *her* up. She wouldn't've cared if I'd woke her up, but the trouble was, she wouldn't've been the one that answered the phone. My parents would be the ones. So that was out. Then I thought of giving Jane Gallagher's mother a buzz, and find out when Jane's vacation started, but I didn't feel like it. Besides, it was pretty late to call up. Then I thought of calling this girl I used to go around with quite frequently, Sally Hayes, because I knew her Christmas vacation had started already—she'd written me this long, phony letter, inviting me over to help her trim the Christmas tree Christmas Eve and all—but I was afraid her mother'd answer the phone. Her mother knew my mother, and I could picture her breaking a goddam leg to get to the phone and tell my mother I was in New York. Besides, I wasn't crazy about talking to old Mrs. Hayes on the phone. She once told Sally I was wild. She said I was wild and that I had no direction in life. Then I thought of calling up this guy that went to the Whooton School when I was there, Carl Luce, but I didn't like him much. So I ended up not calling anybody. I came out of the booth, after about twenty minutes or so, and got my bags and walked over to that tunnel where the cabs are and got a cab.

I'm so damn absent-minded, I gave the driver my regular address, just out of habit and all—I mean I completely forgot I was going to shack up in a hotel for a couple of days and not go home till vacation started. I didn't think of it till we were halfway through the park. Then I said, "Hey, do you mind turning around when you get a chance? I gave you the wrong address. I want to go back downtown."

The driver was sort of a wise guy. "I can't turn around here, Mac. This here's a one-way. I'll have to go all the way to Ninedieth Street now."

I didn't want to start an argument. "Okay," I said. Then I thought of something, all of a sudden. "Hey, listen," I said. "You know those ducks in that lagoon right near Central Park South? That little lake? By any chance, do you happen to know where they go, the ducks, when it gets all frozen over? Do you happen to know, by any chance?" I realized it was only one chance in a million.

He turned around and looked at me like I was a madman. "What're ya tryna do, bud?" he said. "Kid me?"

"*No*—I was just interested, that's all."

He didn't say anything more, so I didn't either. Until we came out of the park at Ninetieth Street. Then he said, "All right, buddy. Where to?"

"Well, the thing is, I don't want to stay at any hotels on the East Side where I might run into some acquaintances of mine. I'm traveling incognito," I said. I hate saying corny things like "traveling incognito." But when I'm with somebody that's corny, I always act corny too. "Do you happen to know whose band's at the Taft or the New Yorker, by any chance?"

"No idear, Mac."

"Well—take me to the Edmont, then," I said. "Would you care to stop on the way and join me for a cocktail? On me. I'm loaded."

"Can't do it, Mac. Sorry." He certainly was good company. Terrific personality.

We got to the Edmont Hotel, and I checked in. I'd put on my red hunting cap when I was in the cab, just for the hell of it, but I took it off before I checked in. I didn't want to look like a screwball or something. Which is really ironic. I didn't *know* then that the goddam hotel was full of perverts and morons. Screwballs all over the place.

They gave me this very crumby room, with nothing to look out of the window at except the other side of the hotel. I didn't care much. I was too depressed to care whether I had a good view or not. The bellboy that showed me to the room was this very old guy around sixty-five. He was even more depressing than the room was. He was one of those bald guys that comb all their hair over from the side to cover up the baldness. I'd rather be bald than do that. Anyway, what a gorgeous job for a guy around sixty-five years old. Carrying people's suitcases and waiting around for a tip. I suppose he wasn't too intelligent or anything, but it was terrible anyway.

After he left, I looked out the window for a while, with my coat on and all. I didn't have anything else to do. You'd be surprised what was going on on the other side of the hotel. They didn't even bother to pull their shades down. I saw one guy, a gray-haired, very distinguished-looking guy with only his shorts on, do something you wouldn't believe me if I told you. First he put his suitcase on the bed. Then he took out all these women's clothes, and put them on. Real women's clothes—silk stockings, high-heeled shoes, brassière, and one of those corsets with the straps hanging down and all. Then he put on this very tight black evening dress. I swear to God. Then he started walking up and down the room, taking these very small steps, the way a woman does, and smoking a cigarette and looking at himself in the mirror. He was all alone, too. Unless somebody was in the bathroom—I couldn't see that much. Then, in the window almost right over his, I saw a man and a woman squirting water out of their mouths at each other. It probably was highballs, not water, but I couldn't see what they had in their glasses. Anyway, first he'd take a swallow and squirt it all over *her*, then she did it to *him*—they took *turns*, for God's sake. You should've seen them. They were in hysterics the whole time, like it was the funniest thing that ever happened. I'm not kidding, that hotel was lousy with perverts. I was probably the only normal bastard in the whole place—and that isn't saying much. I damn near sent a telegram to old Stradlater telling him to take the first train to New York. He'd have been the king of the hotel.

The trouble was, that kind of junk is sort of fascinating to watch, even if you don't want it to be. For instance, that girl that was getting water squirted all over her face, she was pretty good-looking. I mean that's my big trouble. In my *mind*, I'm probably the biggest sex maniac you ever saw. Sometimes I can think of *very* crumby stuff I wouldn't mind doing if the opportunity came up. I can even see how it might be quite a lot of fun, in a crumby way, and if you were both sort of drunk and all, to get a girl and squirt water or something all over each other's face. The thing is, though, I don't *like* the idea. It stinks, if you analyze it. I think if you don't really like a girl, you shouldn't horse around with her at all, and if you *do* like her, then you're supposed to like her face, and if you like her face, you ought to be careful about doing crumby stuff to it, like squirting water all over it. It's really too bad that so much crumby stuff is a lot of fun sometimes. Girls aren't too much help, either, when you start trying not to get *too* crumby, when you start trying not to spoil anything really good. I knew this one girl, a couple of years ago, that was even crumbier than I was. Boy, was she crumby! We had a lot of fun, though, for a while, in a crumby way. Sex is something I really don't understand too hot. You never know *where* the hell you are. I keep making up these sex rules for myself, and then I break them right away. Last year I made a rule that I was going to quit horsing around with girls that, deep down, gave me a pain in the ass. I broke it, though, the same week I made it—the same *night*, as a matter of fact. I spent the whole night necking with a terrible phony named Anne Louise Sherman. Sex is something I just don't understand. I swear to God I don't.

I started toying with the idea, while I kept standing there, of giving old Jane a buzz—I mean calling her long distance at B.M., where she went, instead of calling up her mother to find out when she was coming home. You weren't supposed to call students up late at night, but I had it all figured out. I was going to tell whoever answered the phone that I was her uncle. I was going to say her aunt had just got killed in a car accident and I had to speak to her immediately. It would've worked, too. The only reason I didn't do it was because I wasn't in the mood. If you're not in the mood, you can't do that stuff right.

After a while I sat down in a chair and smoked a couple of cigarettes. I was feeling pretty horny. I have to admit it. Then, all of a sudden, I got this idea. I took out my wallet and started looking for this address a guy I met at a party last summer, that went to Princeton, gave me. Finally I found it. It was all a funny color from my wallet, but you could still read it. It was the address of this girl that wasn't exactly a whore or anything but that didn't mind doing it once in a while, this Princeton guy told me. He brought her to a dance at Princeton once, and they nearly kicked him out for bringing her. She used to be a burlesque stripper or something. Anyway, I went over to the phone and gave her a buzz. Her name was Faith Cavendish, and she lived at the Stanford Arms Hotel on Sixty-fifth and Broadway. A dump, no doubt.

For a while, I didn't think she was home or something. Nobody kept answering. Then, finally, somebody picked up the phone.

"Hello?" I said. I made my voice quite deep so that she wouldn't suspect my age or anything. I have a pretty deep voice anyway.

"Hello," this woman's voice said. None too friendly, either.

"Is this Miss Faith Cavendish?"

"Who's *this?*" she said. "Who's calling me up at this crazy goddam hour?"

That sort of scared me a little bit. "Well, I know it's quite late," I said, in this very mature voice and all. "I hope you'll forgive me, but I was very anxious to get in touch with you." I said it suave as hell. I really did.

"Who *is* this?" she said.

"Well, you don't know me, but I'm a friend of Eddie Birdsell's. He suggested that if I were in town sometime, we ought to get together for a cocktail or two."

"*Who?* You're a friend of *who?*" Boy, she was a real tigress over the phone. She was damn near yelling at me.

"Edmund Birdsell. Eddie Birdsell," I said. I couldn't remember if his name was Edmund or Edward. I only met him once, at a goddam stupid party.

"I don't know anybody by that name, Jack. And if you think I enjoy bein' woke up in the middle—"

"Eddie *Bird*sell? From Princeton?" I said.

You could tell she was running the name over in her mind and all.

"Birdsell, Birdsell ... from Princeton ... Princeton College?"

"That's right," I said.

"You from Princeton College?"

"Well, approximately."

"Oh ... How *is* Eddie?" she said. "This is certainly a peculiar time to call a person up, though. Jesus Christ."

"He's fine. He asked to be remembered to you."

"Well, thank you. Remember me to *him*," she said. "He's a grand person. What's he doing now?" She was getting friendly as hell, all of a sudden.

"Oh, you know. Same old stuff," I said. How the hell did *I* know what he was doing? I hardly knew the guy. I didn't even know if he was still at Princeton. "Look,"

I said. "Would you be interested in meeting me for a cocktail somewhere?"

"By any chance do you have any idea what *time* it is?" she said. "What's your name, anyhow, may I ask?" She was getting an English accent, all of a sudden. "You sound a little on the young side."

I laughed. "Thank you for the compliment," I said—suave as hell. "Holden Caulfield's my name." I should've given her a phony name, but I didn't think of it.

"Well, look, Mr. Cawffle. I'm not in the habit of making engagements in the middle of the night. I'm a working gal."

"Tomorrow's Sunday," I told her.

"Well, *any*way. I gotta get my beauty sleep. You know how it is."

"I thought we might have just one cocktail together. It isn't too late."

"Well. You're very sweet," she said. "Where ya callin' from? Where ya at now, anyways?"

"Me? I'm in a phone booth."

"Oh," she said. Then there was this very long pause. "Well, I'd like awfully to get together with you sometime, Mr. Cawffle. You sound very attractive. You sound like a very attractive person. But it is late."

"I could come up to your place."

"Well, ordinary, I'd say grand. I mean I'd love to have you drop up for a cocktail, but my roommate happens to be ill. She's been laying here all night without a wink of sleep. She just this minute closed her eyes and all. I mean."

"Oh. That's too bad."

"Where ya stopping at? Perhaps we could get together for cocktails tomorrow."

"I can't make it tomorrow," I said. "Tonight's the only time I can make it." What a dope I was. I shouldn't've said that.

"Oh. Well, I'm awfully sorry."

"I'll say hello to Eddie for you."

"Willya do that? I hope you enjoy your stay in New York. It's a grand place."

"I know it is. Thanks. Good night," I said. Then I hung up.

Boy, I *real*ly fouled that up. I should've at least made it for cocktails or something.

X

It was still pretty early. I'm not sure what time it was, but it wasn't too late. The one thing I hate to do is go to bed when I'm not even tired. So I opened my suitcases and took out a clean shirt, and then I went in the bathroom and washed and changed my shirt. What I thought I'd do, I thought I'd go downstairs and see what the hell was going on in the Lavender Room. They had this night club, the Lavender Room, in the hotel.

While I was changing my shirt, I damn near gave my kid sister Phoebe a buzz, though. I certainly felt like talking to her on the phone. Somebody with sense and all. But I couldn't take a chance on giving her a buzz, because she was only a little kid and she wouldn't have been up, let alone anywhere near the phone. I thought of maybe hanging up if my parents answered, but that wouldn't've worked, either. They'd know it was me. My mother always knows it's me. She's psychic. But I certainly wouldn't have minded shooting the crap with old Phoebe for a while.

You should see her. You never saw a little kid so pretty and smart in your whole life. She's really smart. I mean she's had all A's ever since she started school. As a matter of fact, I'm the only dumb one in the family. My brother D.B.'s a writer and all, and my brother Allie, the one that died, that I told you about, was a wizard. I'm the only really dumb one. But you ought to see old Phoebe. She has this sort of red hair, a little bit like Allie's was, that's very short in the summertime. In the summertime, she sticks it behind her ears. She has nice, pretty little ears.

In the wintertime, it's pretty long, though. Sometimes my mother braids it and sometimes she doesn't. It's really nice, though. She's only ten. She's quite skinny, like me, but nice skinny. Roller-skate skinny. I watched her once from the window when she was crossing over Fifth Avenue to go to the park, and that's what she is, roller-skate skinny. You'd like her. I mean if you tell old Phoebe something, she knows exactly what the hell you're talking about. I mean you can even take her anywhere with you. If you take her to a lousy movie, for instance, she knows it's a lousy movie. If you take her to a pretty good movie, she knows it's a pretty good movie. D.B. and I took her to see this French movie, The *Baker's Wife*, with Raimu in it. It killed her. Her favorite is *The 39 Steps*, though, with Robert Donat. She knows the whole goddam movie by heart, because I've taken her to see it about ten times. When old Donat comes up to this Scotch farmhouse, for instance, when he's running away from the cops and all, Phoebe'll say right out loud in the movie—right when the Scotch guy in the picture says it—"Can you eat the herring?" She knows all the talk by heart. And when this professor in the picture, that's really a German spy, sticks up his little finger with part of the middle joint missing, to show Robert Donat, old Phoebe beats him to it—she holds up *her* little finger at me in the dark, right in front of my face. She's all right. You'd like her. The only trouble is, she's a little too affectionate sometimes. She's very emotional, for a child. She really is. Something else she does, she writes books all the time. Only, she doesn't finish them. They're all about some kid named Hazel Weatherfield—only old Phoebe spells it "Hazle." Old Hazle Weatherfield is a girl detective. She's supposed to be an orphan, but her old man keeps showing up. Her old man's always a "tall attractive gentleman about 20 years of age." That kills me. Old Phoebe. I swear to God you'd like her. She was smart even when she was a very tiny little kid. When she was a very tiny little kid, I and Allie used to take her to the park with us, especially on Sundays. Allie had this sailboat he used to like to fool around with on Sundays, and we used to take old Phoebe with us. She'd wear white gloves and walk right between us, like a lady and all. And when Allie and I were having some conversation about things in general, old Phoebe'd be listening. Sometimes you'd forget she was around, because she was such a little kid, but *she'd* let you know. She'd interrupt you all the time. She'd give Allie or I a push or something, and say, "*Who*? Who said that? Bobby or the lady?" And we'd tell her who said it, and she'd say, "Oh," and go right on listening and all. She killed Allie, too. I mean he liked her, too. She's ten now, and not such a tiny little kid any more, but she still kills everybody—everybody with any sense, anyway.

Anyway, she was somebody you always felt like talking to on the phone. But I was too afraid my parents would answer, and then they'd find out I was in New York and kicked out of Pencey and all. So I just finished putting on my shirt. Then I got all ready and went down in the elevator to the lobby to see what was going on.

Except for a few pimpy-looking guys, and a few whory-looking blondes, the lobby was pretty empty. But you could hear the band playing in the Lavender Room, and so I went in there. It wasn't very crowded, but they gave me a lousy table anyway—way in the back. I should've waved a buck under the head-waiter's nose. In New York, boy, money really talks—I'm not kidding.

The band was putrid. Buddy Singer. Very brassy, but not good brassy—corny brassy. Also, there were very few people around my age in the place. In fact, nobody was around my age. They were mostly old, show-offy-looking guys with their dates. Except at the table right next to me. At the table right next to me, there were these three girls around thirty or so. The whole three of them were pretty ugly, and they all had on the kind of hats that you knew they didn't really live in New York, but one of them, the blonde one, wasn't too bad. She was sort of cute, the blonde one, and I started giving her the old eye a little bit, but just then the waiter came up for my order. I ordered a Scotch and soda, and told him not to mix it—I said it fast as hell, because if you hem and haw, they think you're under twenty-one and won't sell you any intoxicating liquor. I had trouble with him anyway, though. "I'm sorry, sir," he said, "but do you have some verification of your age? Your driver's license, perhaps?"

I gave him this very cold stare, like he'd insulted the hell out of me, and asked him, "Do I look like I'm under twenty-one?"

"I'm sorry, sir, but we have our—"

"Okay, okay," I said. I figured the hell with it. "Bring me a Coke." He started to go away, but I called him back. "Can'tcha stick a little rum in it or something?" I asked him. I asked him very nicely and all. "I can't sit in a corny place like this cold *sober*. Can'tcha stick a little rum in it or something?"

"I'm very sorry, sir ..." he said, and beat it on me. I didn't hold it against him, though. They lose their jobs if they get caught selling to a minor. I'm a goddam minor.

I started giving the three witches at the next table the eye again. That is, the blonde one. The other two were strictly from hunger. I didn't do it crudely, though. I just gave all three of them this very cool glance and all. What they did, though, the three of them, when I did it, they started giggling like morons. They probably thought I was too young to give anybody the once-over. That annoyed hell out of me—you'd've thought I wanted to *marry* them or something. I should've given them the freeze, after they did that, but the trouble was, I really felt like dancing. I'm very fond of dancing, sometimes, and that was one of the times. So all of a sudden, I sort of leaned over and said, "Would any of you girls care to dance?" I didn't ask them crudely or anything. Very suave, in fact. But God damn it, they thought *that* was a panic, too. They started giggling some more. I'm not kidding, they were three real morons. "C'mon," I said. "I'll dance with you one at a time. All right? How 'bout it? C'mon!" I really felt like dancing.

Finally, the blonde one got up to dance with me, because you could tell I was really talking to *her*, and we walked out to the dance floor. The other two grools nearly had hysterics when we did. I certainly must've been very hard up to even bother with any of them.

But it was worth it. The blonde was some dancer. She was one of the best dancers I ever danced with. I'm not kidding, some of these very stupid girls can really knock you out on a dance floor. You take a really smart girl, and half the time she's trying to lead *you* around the dance floor, or else she's such a lousy dancer, the best thing to do is stay at the table and just get drunk with her.

"You really can dance," I told the blonde one. "You oughta be a pro. I mean it. I danced with a pro once, and you're twice as good as she was. Did you ever hear of Marco and Miranda?"

"What?" she said. She wasn't even listening to me. She was looking all around the place.

"I said did you ever hear of Marco and Miranda?"

"I don't know. No. I don't know."

"Well, they're dancers, she's a dancer. She's not too hot, though. She does everything she's sup*posed* to, but she's not so hot anyway. You know when a girl's really a terrific dancer?"

"Wudga say?" she said. She wasn't listening to me, even. Her mind was wandering all over the place.

"I said do you know when a girl's really a terrific dancer?"

"Uh-uh."

"Well—where I have my hand on your back. If I think there isn't anything underneath my hand—no can, no legs, no feet, no *any*thing—then the girl's really a terrific dancer."

She wasn't listening, though. So I ignored her for a while. We just danced.

God, could that dopey girl dance. Buddy Singer and his stinking band was playing "Just One of Those Things" and even *they* couldn't ruin it entirely. It's a swell song. I didn't try any trick stuff while we danced—I hate a guy that does a lot of show-off tricky stuff on the dance floor—but I was moving her around plenty, and she stayed right with me. The funny thing is, I thought she was enjoying it, too, till all of a sudden she came out with this very dumb remark. "I and my girl friends saw Peter Lorre last night," she said. "The movie actor. In person. He was buyin' a newspaper. He's *cute*."

"You're lucky," I told her. "You're really lucky. You know that?" She was really a moron. But what a dancer. I could hardly stop myself from sort of giving her a kiss on the top of her dopey head—you know—right where the part is, and all. She got sore when I did it.

"Hey! What's the idea?"

"Nothing. No idea. You really can dance," I said. "I have a kid sister that's only in the goddam fourth grade. You're about as good as she is, and she can dance better than anybody living or dead."

"Watch your language, if you don't mind."

What a lady, boy. A *queen*, for Chrissake.

"Where you girls from?" I asked her.

She didn't answer me, though. She was busy looking around for old Peter Lorre to show up, I guess.

"Where you girls from?" I asked her again.

"What?" she said.

"Where you girls from? Don't answer if you don't feel like it. I don't want you to strain yourself."

"Seattle, Washington," she said. She was doing me a big favor to tell me.

"You're a very good conversationalist," I told her. "You know that?"

"What?"

I let it drop. It was over her head, anyway. "Do you feel like jitterbugging a little bit, if they play a fast one? Not corny jitterbug, not jump or anything—just nice and easy. Everybody'll all sit down when they play a fast one, except the old guys and the fat guys, and we'll have plenty of room. Okay?"

"It's immaterial to me," she said. "Hey—how old are you, anyhow?"

That annoyed me, for some reason. "Oh, Christ. Don't spoil it," I said. "I'm twelve, for Chrissake. I'm big for my age."

"*Lis*ten. I toleja about that. I don't like that type language," she said. "If you're gonna use that type language, I can go sit down with my girl friends, you know."

I apologized like a madman, because the band was starting a fast one. She started jitterbugging with me—but just very nice and easy, not corny. She was really good. All you had to do was touch her. And when she turned around, her pretty little butt twitched so nice and all. She knocked me out. I mean it. I was about half in love with her by the time we sat down. That's the thing about girls. Every time they do something pretty, even if they're not much to look at, or even if they're sort of stupid, you fall half in love with them, and then you never know *where* the hell you are. Girls. Jesus Christ. They can drive you crazy. They really can.

They didn't invite me to sit down at their table—mostly because they were too ignorant—but I sat down anyway. The blonde I'd been dancing with's name was Bernice something—Crabs or Krebs. The two ugly ones' names were Marty and Laverne. I told them my name was Jim Steele, just for the hell of it. Then I tried to get them in a little intelligent conversation, but it was practically impossible. You had to twist their arms. You could hardly tell which was the stupidest of the three of them. And the whole three of them kept looking all around the goddam room, like as if they expected a flock of goddam *movie* stars to come in any minute. They probably thought movie stars always hung out in the Lavender Room when they came to New York, instead of the Stork Club or El Morocco and all. Anyway, it took me about a half hour to find out where they all worked and all in Seattle. They all worked in the same insurance office. I asked them if they liked it, but do you think you could get an intelligent answer out of those three dopes? I thought the two ugly ones, Marty and Laverne, were sisters, but they got very insulted when I asked them. You could tell neither one of them wanted to look like the other one, and you couldn't blame them, but it was very amusing anyway.

I danced with them all—the whole three of them—one at a time. The one ugly one, Laverne, wasn't too bad a dancer, but the other one, old Marty, was murder. Old Marty was like dragging the Statue of Liberty around the floor. The only way I could even half enjoy myself dragging her around was if I amused myself a little. So I told her I just saw Gary Cooper, the movie star, on the other side of the floor.

"*Where?*" she asked me—excited as hell. "*Where?*"

"Aw, you just missed him. He just went out. Why didn't you look when I told you?"

She practically stopped dancing, and started looking over everybody's heads to see if she could see him. "Oh, shoot!" she said. I'd just about broken her heart—I really had. I was sorry as hell I'd kidded her. Some people you shouldn't kid, even if they deserve it.

Here's what was very funny, though. When we got back to the table, old Marty told the other two that Gary Cooper had just gone out. Boy, old Laverne and Bernice nearly committed suicide when they heard that. They got all excited and asked Marty if she'd seen him and all. Old Mart said she'd only caught a glimpse of him. That killed me.

The bar was closing up for the night, so I bought them all two drinks apiece quick before it closed, and I ordered two more Cokes for myself. The goddam table was lousy with glasses. The one ugly one, Laverne, kept kidding me because I was only drinking Cokes. She had a sterling sense of humor. She and old Marty were drinking Tom Collinses—in the middle of December, for God's sake. They didn't know any better. The blonde one, old Bernice, was drinking bourbon and water. She was really putting it away, too. The whole three of them kept looking for movie stars the whole time. They hardly talked—even to each other. Old Marty talked more than the other two. She kept saying these very corny, boring things, like calling the can the "little girls' room," and she thought Buddy Singer's poor old beat-up clarinet player was really terrific when he stood up and took a couple of ice-cold hot licks. She called his clarinet a "licorice stick." Was she corny. The other ugly one, Laverne, thought she was a very witty type. She kept asking me to call up my father and ask him what he was doing tonight. She kept asking me if my father had a date or not. *Four times* she asked me that—she was certainly witty. Old Bernice, the blonde one, didn't say hardly anything at all. Every time I'd ask her something, she said "What?" That can get on your nerves after a while.

All of a sudden, when they finished their drink, all three of them stood up on me and said they had to get to bed. They said they were going to get up early to see the first show at Radio City Music Hall. I tried to get them to stick around for a while, but they wouldn't. So we said good-by and all. I told them I'd look them up in Seattle sometime, if I ever got there, but I doubt if I ever will. Look them up, I mean.

With cigarettes and all, the check came to about thirteen bucks. I think they should've at least *of*fered to pay for the drinks they had before I joined them— I wouldn't've *let* them, naturally, but they should've at least offered. I didn't care much, though. They were so ignorant, and they had those sad, fancy hats on and all. And that business about getting up early to see the first show at Radio City Music Hall depressed me. If somebody, some girl in an awful-looking hat, for instance, comes all the way to New York—from Seattle, *Wash*ington, for God's sake—and ends up getting up early in the morning to see the goddam first show at Radio City Music Hall, it makes me so depressed I can't stand it. I'd've bought the whole three of them a *hundred* drinks if only they hadn't told me that.

 I left the Lavender Room pretty soon after they did. They were closing it up anyway, and the band had quit a long time ago. In the first place, it was one of those places that are very terrible to be in unless you have somebody good to dance with, or unless the waiter lets you buy real drinks instead of just Cokes. There isn't any night club in the world you can sit in for a long time unless you can at least buy some liquor and get drunk. Or unless you're with some girl that really knocks you out.

XI

All of a sudden, on my way out to the lobby, I got old Jane Gallagher on the brain again. I got her on, and I couldn't get her off. I sat down in this vomity-looking chair in the lobby and thought about her and Stradlater sitting in that goddam Ed Banky's car, and though I was pretty damn sure old Stradlater hadn't given her the time—I know old Jane like a book—I still couldn't get her off my brain. I knew her like a book. I really did. I mean, besides checkers, she was quite fond of all athletic sports, and after I got to know her, the whole summer long we played tennis together almost every morning and golf almost every afternoon. I really got to know her quite intimately. I don't mean it was anything *physical* or anything—it wasn't—but we saw each other all the time. You don't always have to get too sexy to get to know a girl.

The way I met her, this Doberman pinscher she had used to come over and relieve himself on our lawn, and my mother got very irritated about it. She called up Jane's mother and made a big stink about it. My mother can make a very big stink about that kind of stuff. Then what happened, a couple of days later I saw Jane laying on her stomach next to the swimming pool, at the club, and I said hello to her. I knew she lived in the house next to ours, but I'd never conversed with her before or anything. She gave me the big freeze when I said hello that day, though. I had a helluva time convincing her that *I* didn't give a good goddam *where* her dog relieved himself. He could do it in the living room, for all I cared. Anyway, after that, Jane and I got to be friends and all. I played golf with her that same afternoon. She lost eight balls, I remember. *Eight*. I had a terrible time getting her to at least open her eyes when she took a swing at the ball. I improved her game immensely, though. I'm a very good golfer. If I told you what I go around in, you probably wouldn't believe me. I almost was once in a movie short, but I changed my mind at the last minute. I figured that anybody that hates the movies as much as I do, I'd be a phony if I let them stick me in a movie short.

She was a funny girl, old Jane. I wouldn't exactly describe her as strictly beautiful. She knocked me out, though. She was sort of muckle-mouthed. I mean when she was talking and she got excited about something, her mouth sort of went in about fifty directions, her lips and all. That killed me. And she never really closed it all the way, her mouth. It was always just a little bit open, especially when she got in her golf stance, or when she was reading a book. She was always reading, and she read very good books. She read a lot of poetry and all. She was the only one, outside my family, that I ever showed Allie's baseball mitt to, with all the poems written on it. She'd never met Allie or anything, because that was her first summer in Maine—before that, she went to Cape Cod—but I told her quite a lot about him. She was interested in that kind of stuff.

My mother didn't like her too much. I mean my mother always thought Jane and her mother were sort of snubbing her or something when they didn't say hello. My mother saw them in the village a lot, because Jane used to drive to market with her mother in this LaSalle convertible they had. My mother didn't think Jane was pretty, even. I did, though. I just liked the way she looked, that's all.

I remember this one afternoon. It was the only time old Jane and I ever got close to necking, even. It was a Saturday and it was raining like a bastard out, and I was over at her house, on the porch—they had this big screened-in porch. We were playing checkers. I used to kid her once in a while because she wouldn't take her kings out of the back row. But I didn't kid her much, though. You never wanted to kid Jane too much. I think I really like it best when you can kid the pants off a girl when the opportunity arises, but it's a funny thing. The girls I like best are the ones I never feel much like kidding. Sometimes I think they'd *like* it if you kidded them—in fact, I *know* they would—but it's hard to get started, once you've known them a pretty long time and never kidded them. Anyway, I was telling you about that afternoon Jane and I came close to necking. It was raining like hell and we were out on her porch, and all of a sudden this booze hound her mother was married to came out on the porch and asked Jane if there were any cigarettes in the house. I didn't know him too well or anything, but he looked like the kind of a guy that wouldn't talk to you much unless he wanted something off you. He had a lousy personality. Anyway, old Jane wouldn't answer him when he asked her if she knew where there was any cigarettes. So the guy asked her again, but she still wouldn't answer him. She didn't even look up from the game. Finally the guy went inside the house. When he did, I asked Jane what the hell was going on. She wouldn't even answer *me*, then. She made out like she was concentrating on her next move in the game and all. Then all of a sudden, this tear plopped down on the checkerboard. On one of the red squares—boy, I can still see it. She just rubbed it into the board with her finger. I don't know why, but it bothered hell out of me. So what I did was, I went over and made her move over on the glider so that I could sit down next to her—I practically sat down in her *lap*, as a matter of fact. Then she *really* started to cry, and the next thing I knew, I was kissing her all over—*any*where—her eyes, her *nose*, her forehead, her eyebrows and all, her *ears*—her whole face except her mouth and all. She sort of wouldn't let me get to her mouth. Anyway, it was the closest we ever got to necking. After a while, she got up and went in and put on this red and white sweater she had, that knocked me out, and we went to a goddam movie. I asked her, on the way, if Mr. Cudahy—that was the booze hound's name—had ever tried to get wise with her. She was pretty young, but she had this terrific figure, and I wouldn't've put it past that Cudahy bastard. She said no, though. I never did find out what the hell was the matter. Some girls you practically never find out what's the matter.

I don't want you to get the idea she was a goddam *icicle* or something, just because we never necked or horsed around much. She wasn't. I held hands with her all the time, for instance. That doesn't sound like much, I realize, but she was terrific to hold hands with. Most girls if you hold hands with them, their goddam hand *dies* on you, or else they think they have to keep *moving* their hand all the time, as if they were afraid they'd bore you or something. Jane was different. We'd get into a goddam movie or something, and right away we'd start holding hands, and we wouldn't quit till the movie was over. And without changing the position or making a big deal out of it. You never even worried, with Jane, whether your hand was sweaty or not. All you knew was, you were happy. You really were.

One other thing I just thought of. One time, in this movie, Jane did something that just about knocked me out. The newsreel was on or something, and all of a sudden I felt this hand on the back of my neck, and it was Jane's. It was a funny thing to do. I mean she was quite young and all, and most girls if you see them putting their hand on the back of somebody's neck, they're around twenty-five or thirty and usually they're doing it to their husband or their little kid—I do it to my kid sister Phoebe once in a while, for instance. But if a girl's quite young and all and she does it, it's so pretty it just about kills you.

Anyway, that's what I was thinking about while I sat in that vomity-looking chair in the lobby. Old Jane. Every time I got to the part about her out with Stradlater in that damn Ed Banky's car, it almost drove me crazy. I knew she wouldn't let him get to first base with her, but it drove me crazy anyway. I don't even like to talk about it, if you want to know the truth.

There was hardly anybody in the lobby any more. Even all the whory-looking blondes weren't around any more, and all of a sudden I felt like getting the hell out of the place. It was too depressing. And I wasn't tired or anything. So I went up to my room and put on my coat. I also took a look out the window to see if all the perverts were still in action, but the lights and all were out now. I went down in the elevator again and got a cab and told the driver to take me down to Ernie's. Ernie's is this night club in Greenwich Village that my brother D.B. used to go to quite frequently before he went out to Hollywood and prostituted himself. He used to take me with him once in a while. Ernie's a big fat colored guy that plays the piano. He's a terrific snob and he won't hardly even talk to you unless you're a big shot or a celebrity or something, but he can really play the piano. He's so good he's almost corny, in fact. I don't exactly know what I mean by that, but I mean it. I certainly like to hear him play, but sometimes you feel like turning his goddam piano over. I think it's because sometimes when he plays, he *sounds* like the kind of a guy that won't talk to you unless you're a big shot.

XII

The cab I had was a real old one that smelled like someone'd just tossed his cookies in it. I always get those vomity kind of cabs if I go anywhere late at night. What made it worse, it was so quiet and lonesome out, even though it was Saturday night. I didn't see hardly anybody on the street. Now and then you just saw a man and a girl crossing a street, with their arms around each other's waists and all, or a bunch of hoodlumy-looking guys and their dates, all of them laughing like hyenas at something you could bet wasn't funny. New York's terrible when somebody laughs on the street very late at night. You can hear it for miles. It makes you feel so lonesome and depressed. I kept wishing I could go home and shoot the bull for a while with old Phoebe. But finally, after I was riding a while, the cab driver and I sort of struck up a conversation. His name was Horwitz. He was a much better guy than the other driver I'd had. Anyway, I thought maybe he might know about the ducks.

"Hey, Horwitz," I said. "You ever pass by the lagoon in Central Park? Down by Central Park South?"

"The *what?*"

"The lagoon. That little lake, like, there. Where the ducks are. You know."

"Yeah, what about it?"

"Well, you know the ducks that swim around in it? In the springtime and all? Do you happen to know where they go in the wintertime, by any chance?"

"Where *who* goes?"

"The ducks. Do you know, by any chance? I mean does somebody come around in a truck or something and take them away, or do they fly away by themselves—go south or something?"

Old Horwitz turned all the way around and looked at me. He was a very impatient-type guy. He wasn't a bad guy, though. "How the hell should I know?" he said. "How the hell should I know a stupid thing like that?"

"Well, don't get *sore* about it," I said. He was sore about it or something.

"Who's sore? Nobody's sore."

I stopped having a conversation with him, if he was going to get so damn touchy about it. But he started it up again himself. He turned all the way around again, and said, "The *fish* don't go no place. They stay right where they are, the fish. Right in the goddam lake."

"The fish—that's different. The fish is different. I'm talking about the *ducks*," I said.

"What's *dif*ferent about it? Nothin's *dif*ferent about it," Horwitz said. Everything he said, he sounded sore about something. "It's tougher for the *fish*, the winter and all, than it is for the ducks, for Chrissake. Use your head, for Chrissake."

I didn't say anything for about a minute. Then I said, "All right. What do they do, the fish and all, when that whole little lake's a solid block of ice, people *skating* on it and all?"

Old Horwitz turned around again. "What the hellaya mean what do they do?" he yelled at me. "They stay right where they are, for Chrissake."

"They can't just ignore the ice. They can't just ig*nore* it."

"Who's ignoring it? Nobody's ig*nor*ing it!" Horwitz said. He got so damn excited and all, I was afraid he was going to drive the cab right into a lamppost or something. "They live right *in* the goddam ice. It's their nature, for Chrissake.

They get frozen right in one position for the whole winter."

"Yeah? What do they eat, then? I mean if they're frozen *solid*, they can't swim around looking for *food* and all."

"Their *bodies*, for Chrissake—what's a matter with ya? Their bodies take in nutrition and all, right through the goddam seaweed and crap that's in the ice. They got their *pores* open the whole time. That's their *nature*, for Chrissake. See what I mean?" He turned way the hell around again to look at me.

"Oh," I said. I let it drop. I was afraid he was going to crack the damn taxi up or something. Besides, he was such a touchy guy, it wasn't any pleasure discussing anything with him. "Would you care to stop off and have a drink with me somewhere?" I said.

He didn't answer me, though. I guess he was still thinking. I asked him again, though. He was a pretty good guy. Quite amusing and all.

"I ain't got no time for no liquor, bud," he said. "How the hell old are you, anyways? Why ain't cha home in bed?"

"I'm not tired."

When I got out in front of Ernie's and paid the fare, old Horwitz brought up the fish again. He certainly had it on his mind. "Listen," he said. "If you was a fish, Mother Nature'd take care of *you*, wouldn't she? Right? You don't think them fish just *die* when it gets to be winter, do ya?"

"No, but—"

"You're goddam right they don't," Horwitz said, and drove off like a bat out of hell. He was about the touchiest guy I ever met. Everything you said made him sore.

Even though it was so late, old Ernie's was jam-packed. Mostly with prep school jerks and college jerks. Almost every damn school in the world gets out earlier for Christmas vacation than the schools *I* go to. You could hardly check your coat, it was so crowded. It was pretty quiet, though, because Ernie was playing the piano. It was supposed to be something *holy*, for God's sake, when he sat down at the piano. Nobody's *that* good. About three couples, besides me, were waiting for tables, and they were all shoving and standing on tiptoes to get a look at old Ernie while he played. He had a big damn mirror in front of the piano, with this big spotlight on him, so that everybody could watch his face while he played. You couldn't see his *fingers* while he played—just his big old face. Big deal. I'm not too sure what the name of the song was that he was playing when I came in, but whatever it was, he was really stinking it up. He was putting all these dumb, show-offy ripples in the high notes, and a lot of other very tricky stuff that gives me a pain in the ass. You should've heard the crowd, though, when he was finished. You would've puked. They went mad. They were exactly the same morons that laugh like hyenas in the movies at stuff that isn't funny. I swear to God, if I were a piano player or an actor or something and all those dopes thought I was terrific, I'd hate it. I wouldn't even want them to *clap* for me. People always clap for the wrong things. If I were a piano player, I'd play it in the goddam closet. Anyway, when he was finished, and everybody was clapping their heads off, old Ernie turned around on his stool and gave this very phony, *humble* bow. Like as if he was a helluva humble guy, besides being a terrific piano player. It was very phony—I mean him being such a big snob and all. In a funny way, though, I felt sort of sorry for him when he was finished. I don't even think he *knows* any more when he's playing right or not. It isn't all his fault. I partly blame all those dopes that clap their heads off—they'd foul up *any*body, if you gave them a chance. Anyway, it made me feel depressed and lousy again, and I damn near got my coat back and went back to the hotel, but it was too early and I didn't feel much like being all alone.

They finally got me this stinking table, right up against a wall and behind a goddam post, where you couldn't see anything. It was one of those tiny little tables that if the people at the next table don't get up to let you by—and they never *do*, the bastards—you practically have to *climb* into your chair. I ordered a Scotch and soda, which is my favorite drink, next to frozen Daiquiris. If you were only around six years old, you could get liquor at Ernie's, the place was so dark and all, and besides, nobody cared how old you were. You could even be a dope fiend and nobody'd care.

I was surrounded by jerks. I'm not kidding. At this other tiny table, right to my left, practically on *top* of me, there was this funny-looking guy and this funny-looking girl. They were around my age, or maybe just a little older. It was funny. You could see they were being careful as hell not to drink up the minimum too fast. I listened to their conversation for a while, because I didn't have anything else to do. He was telling her about some pro football game he'd seen that afternoon. He gave her every single goddam play in the whole game—I'm not kidding. He was the most boring guy I ever listened to. And you could tell his date wasn't even interested in the goddam game, but she was even funnier-looking than *he* was, so I guess she *had* to listen. Real ugly girls have it tough. I feel so sorry for them sometimes. Sometimes I can't even look at them, especially if they're with some dopey guy that's telling them all about a goddam football game. On my *right*, the conversation was even worse, though. On my right there was this very Joe Yale-looking guy, in a gray flannel suit and one of those flitty-looking Tattersall vests. All those Ivy League bastards look alike. My father wants me to go to Yale, or maybe Princeton, but I swear, I wouldn't go to one of those Ivy League colleges if I was *dy*ing, for God's sake. Anyway, this Joe Yale-looking guy had a terrific-looking girl with him. Boy, she was good-looking. But you should've heard the conversation they were having. In the first place, they were both slightly crocked. What he was doing, he was giving her a feel under the table, and at the same time telling her all about some guy in his dorm that had eaten a whole bottle of aspirin and nearly committed suicide. His date kept saying to him, "How *hor*rible ... Don't, darling. Please, don't. Not here." Imagine giving somebody a feel and telling them about a guy committing suicide at the same time! They killed me.

I certainly began to feel like a prize horse's ass, though, sitting there all by myself. There wasn't anything to do except smoke and drink. What I did do, though, I told the waiter to ask old Ernie if he'd care to join me for a drink. I told him to tell him I was D.B.'s brother. I don't think he ever even gave him my message, though. Those bastards never give your message to anybody.

All of a sudden, this girl came up to me and said, "Holden Caulfield!" Her name was Lillian Simmons. My brother D.B. used to go around with her for a while. She had very big knockers.

"Hi," I said. I tried to get up, naturally, but it was some job getting up, in a place like that. She had some Navy officer with her that looked like he had a poker up his ass.

"How marvelous to see you!" old Lillian Simmons said. Strictly a phony. "How's your big brother?" That's all she really wanted to know.

"He's fine. He's in Hollywood."

"In *Hol*lywood! How *marvelous*! What's he *do*ing?"

"I don't know. Writing," I said. I didn't feel like discussing it. You could tell she thought it was a big deal, his being in Hollywood. Almost everybody does. Mostly people who've never read any of his stories. It drives me crazy, though.

"How exc*i*ting," old Lillian said. Then she introduced me to the Navy guy. His name was Commander Blop or something. He was one of those guys that think they're being a pansy if they don't break around forty of your fingers when they shake hands with you. God, I hate that stuff. "Are you all alone, baby?" old Lillian asked me. She was blocking up the *whole goddam traffic* in the aisle. You could tell she liked to block up a lot of traffic. This waiter was waiting for her to move out of the way, but she didn't even notice him. It was funny. You could tell the waiter didn't like her much, you could tell even the Navy guy didn't like her much, even though he was dating her. And *I* didn't like her much. Nobody did. You had to feel sort of sorry for her, in a way. "Don't you have a date, baby?" she asked me. I was standing up now, and she didn't even tell me to sit down. She was the type that keeps you standing up for hours. "Isn't he handsome?" she said to the Navy guy. "Holden, you're getting handsomer by the minute." The Navy guy told her to come on. He told her they were blocking up the whole aisle. "Holden, come join us," old Lillian said. "Bring your drink."

"I was just leaving," I told her. "I have to meet somebody." You could tell she was just trying to get in good with me. So that I'd tell old D.B. about it.

"Well, you little so-and-so. All right for you. Tell your big brother I hate him, when you see him."

Then she left. The Navy guy and I told each other we were glad to've met each other. Which always kills me. I'm always saying "Glad to've met you" to somebody I'm not at *all* glad I met. If you want to stay alive, you have to say that stuff, though.

After I'd told her I had to meet somebody, I didn't have any goddam choice except to *leave*. I couldn't even stick around to hear old Ernie play something halfway decent. But I certainly wasn't going to sit down at a table with old Lillian Simmons and that Navy guy and be bored to death. So I left. It made me mad, though, when I was getting my coat. People are always ruining things for you.

XIII

I walked all the way back to the hotel. Forty-one gorgeous blocks. I didn't do it because I felt like walking or anything. It was more because I didn't feel like getting in and out of another taxicab. Sometimes you get tired of riding in taxicabs the same way you get tired riding in elevators. All of a sudden, you have to walk, no matter how far or how high up. When I was a kid, I used to walk all the way up to our apartment very frequently. Twelve stories.

You wouldn't even have known it had snowed at all. There was hardly any snow on the sidewalks. But it was freezing cold, and I took my red hunting hat out of my pocket and put it on—I didn't give a damn how I looked. I even put the earlaps down. I wished I knew who'd swiped my gloves at Pencey, because my hands were freezing. Not that I'd have done much about it even if I had known. I'm one of these very yellow guys. I try not to show it, but I am. For instance, if I'd found out at Pencey who'd stolen my gloves, I probably would've gone down to the crook's room and said, "Okay. How 'bout handing over those gloves?" Then the crook that had stolen them probably would've said, his voice very innocent and all, "What gloves?" Then what I probably would've done, I'd have gone in his closet and found the gloves somewhere. Hidden in his goddam galoshes or something, for instance. I'd have taken them out and showed them to the guy and said, "I suppose these are *your* goddam gloves?" Then the crook probably would've given me this very phony, innocent look, and said, "I never saw those gloves before in my life. If they're yours, take 'em. I don't want the goddam things." Then I probably would've just stood there for about five minutes. I'd have the damn gloves right in my hand and all, but I'd feel I ought to sock the guy in the jaw or something—break his goddam jaw. Only, I wouldn't have the guts to do it. I'd just *stand* there, trying to look tough. What I might do, I might say something very cutting and snotty, to rile him up—*instead* of socking him in the jaw. Anyway, if I did say something very cutting and snotty, he'd probably get up and come over to me and say, "Listen, Caulfield. Are you calling me a crook?" *Then*, instead of saying, "You're goddam right I am, you dirty crooked bastard!" all I probably would've said would be, "All I know is my goddam gloves were in *your* goddam galoshes." Right away then, the guy would know for sure that I wasn't going to take a sock at him, and he probably would've said, "Listen. Let's get this straight. Are you calling me a thief?" Then I probably would've said, "Nobody's calling anybody a thief. All I know is my gloves were in your goddam galoshes." It could go on like that for *hours*. Finally, though, I'd leave his room without even taking a sock at him. I'd probably go down to the can and sneak a cigarette and watch myself getting tough in the mirror. Anyway, that's what I thought about the whole way back to the hotel. It's no fun to be yellow. Maybe I'm not *all* yellow. I don't know. I think maybe I'm just partly yellow and partly the type that doesn't give much of a damn if they lose their gloves. One of my troubles is, I never care too much when I lose something—it used to drive my mother crazy when I was a kid. Some guys spend *days* looking for something they lost. I never seem to have anything that if I lost it I'd care too much. Maybe that's why I'm partly yellow. It's no excuse, though. It really isn't. What you should be is not yellow at all. If you're supposed to sock somebody in the jaw, and you sort of feel like doing it, you should do it. I'm just no good at it, though. I'd rather push a guy out the window or chop his head off with an ax than sock him in the jaw. I hate fist fights. I don't mind getting hit so much—although I'm not crazy about it, naturally—but what scares me most in a fist fight is the guy's face. I can't stand looking at the other guy's face, is my trouble. It wouldn't be so bad if you could both be blindfolded or something. It's a funny kind of yellowness, when you come to think of it, but it's yellowness, all right. I'm not kidding myself.

The more I thought about my gloves and my yellowness, the more depressed I got, and I decided, while I was walking and all, to stop off and have a drink somewhere. I'd only had three drinks at Ernie's, and I didn't even finish the last one. One thing I have, it's a terrific capacity. I can drink all night and not even show it, if I'm in the mood. Once, at the Whooton School, this other boy, Raymond Goldfarb, and I bought a pint of Scotch and drank it in the chapel one Saturday night, where nobody'd see us. He got stinking, but I hardly didn't even show it. I just got very cool and nonchalant. I puked before I went to bed, but I didn't really have to—I forced myself.

Anyway, before I got to the hotel, I started to go in this dumpy-looking bar, but two guys came out, drunk as hell, and wanted to know where the subway was. One of them was this very Cuban-looking guy, and he kept breathing his stinking breath in my face while I gave him directions. I ended up not even going in the damn bar. I just went back to the hotel.

The whole lobby was empty. It smelled like fifty million dead cigars. It really did. I wasn't sleepy or anything, but I was feeling sort of lousy. Depressed and all. I almost wished I was dead.

Then, all of a sudden, I got in this big mess.

The first thing when I got in the elevator, the elevator guy said to me, "Innarested in having a good time, fella? Or is it too late for you?"

"How do you mean?" I said. I didn't know what he was driving at or anything.

"Innarested in a little tail t'night?"

"Me?" I said. Which was a very dumb answer, but it's quite embarrassing when somebody comes right up and asks you a question like that.

"How old are you, chief?" the elevator guy said.

"Why?" I said. "Twenty-two."

"Uh huh. Well, how 'bout it? Y'innarested? Five bucks a throw. Fifteen bucks the whole night." He looked at his wrist watch. "Till noon. Five bucks a throw, fifteen bucks till noon."

"Okay," I said. It was against my principles and all, but I was feeling so depressed I didn't even *think*. That's the whole trouble. When you're feeling very depressed, you can't even think.

"Okay *what?* A throw, or till noon? I gotta know."

"Just a throw."

"Okay, what room ya in?"

I looked at the red thing with my number on it, on my key. "Twelve twenty-two," I said. I was already sort of sorry I'd let the thing start rolling, but it was too late now.

"Okay. I'll send a girl up in about fifteen minutes." He opened the doors and I got out.

"Hey, is she good-looking?" I asked him. "I don't want any old bag."

"No old bag. Don't worry about it, chief."

"Who do I pay?"

"Her," he said. "Let's go, chief." He shut the doors, practically right in my face.

I went to my room and put some water on my hair, but you can't really comb a crew cut or anything. Then I tested to see if my breath stank from so many cigarettes and the Scotch and sodas I drank at Ernie's. All you do is hold your hand under your mouth and blow your breath up toward the old nostrils. It didn't seem to stink much, but I brushed my teeth anyway. Then I put on another clean shirt. I knew I didn't have to get all dolled up for a prostitute or anything, but it sort of gave me something to do. I was a little nervous. I was starting to feel pretty sexy and all, but I was a little nervous anyway. If you want to know the truth, I'm a virgin. I really am. I've had quite a few opportunities to lose my virginity and all, but I've never got around to it yet. Something always happens. For instance, if you're at a girl's house, her parents always come home at the wrong time—or you're afraid they will. Or if you're in the back seat of somebody's car, there's always somebody's date in the front seat—some girl, I mean—that always wants to know what's going on *all over* the whole goddam car. I mean some girl in front keeps turning around to see what the hell's going on. Anyway, something always happens. I came quite close to doing it a couple of times, though. One time in particular, I remember. Something went wrong, though — I don't even remember what any more. The thing is, most of the time when you're coming pretty close to doing it with a girl—a girl that isn't a prostitute or anything, I mean—she keeps telling you to stop. The trouble with me is, I stop. Most guys don't. I can't help it. You never know whether they really *want* you to stop, or whether they're just scared as hell, or whether they're just telling you to stop so that if you *do* go through with it, the blame'll be on *you*, not them. Anyway, I keep stopping. The trouble is, I get to feeling sorry for them. I mean most girls are so dumb and all. After you neck them for a while, you can really *watch* them losing their brains. You take a girl when she really gets passionate, she just hasn't any brains. I don't know. They tell me to stop, so I stop. I always wish I *hadn't*, after I take them home, but I keep doing it anyway.

Anyway, while I was putting on another clean shirt, I sort of figured this was my big chance, in a way. I figured if she was a prostitute and all, I could get in some practice on her, in case I ever get married or anything. I worry about that stuff sometimes. I read this book once, at the Whooton School, that had this very sophisticated, suave, sexy guy in it. Monsieur Blanchard was his name, I can still remember. It was a lousy book, but this Blanchard guy was pretty good. He had this big château and all on the Riviera, in Europe, and all he did in his spare time was beat women off with a club. He was a real rake and all, but he knocked women out. He said, in this one part, that a woman's body is like a violin and all, and that it takes a terrific musician to play it right. It was a very corny book—I realize that—but I couldn't get that violin stuff out of my mind anyway. In a way, that's why I sort of wanted to get some practice in, in case I ever get married. Caulfield and his Magic Violin, boy. It's corny, I realize, but it isn't *too* corny. I wouldn't mind being pretty good at that stuff. Half the time, if you really want to know the truth, when I'm horsing around with a girl, I have a helluva lot of trouble just *find*ing what I'm looking for, for God's sake, if you know what I mean. Take this girl that I just missed having sexual intercourse with, that I told you about. It took me about an *hour* to just get her goddam brassière off. By the time I did get it off, she was about ready to spit in my eye.

Anyway, I kept walking around the room, waiting for this prostitute to show up. I kept hoping she'd be good-looking. I didn't care too much, though. I sort of just wanted to get it over with. Finally, somebody knocked on the door, and when I went to open it, I had my suitcase right in the way and I fell over it and damn near broke my knee. I always pick a gorgeous time to fall over a suitcase or something.

When I opened the door, this prostitute was standing there. She had a polo coat on, and no hat. She was sort of a blonde, but you could tell she dyed her hair. She wasn't any old bag, though. "How do you do," I said. Suave as hell, boy.

"You the guy Maurice said?" she asked me. She didn't seem too goddam friendly.

"Is he the elevator boy?"

"Yeah," she said.

"Yes, I am. Come in, won't you?" I said. I was getting more and more nonchalant as it went along. I really was.

She came in and took her coat off right away and sort of chucked it on the bed. She had on a green dress underneath. Then she sort of sat down sideways on the chair that went with the desk in the room and started jiggling her foot up and down. She crossed her legs and started jiggling this one foot up and down. She was very nervous, for a prostitute. She really was. I think it was because she was young as hell. She was around my age. I sat down in the big chair, next to her, and offered her a cigarette. "I don't smoke," she said. She had a tiny little wheeny-whiny voice. You could hardly hear her. She never said thank you, either, when you offered her something. She just didn't know any better.

"Allow me to introduce myself. My name is Jim Steele," I said.

"Ya got a watch on ya?" she said. She didn't care what the hell my name was, naturally. "Hey, how old are you, anyways?"

"Me? Twenty-two."

"Like fun you are."

It was a funny thing to say. It sounded like a real kid. You'd think a prostitute and all would say "Like hell you are" or "Cut the crap" instead of "Like fun you are."

"How old are *you*?" I asked her.

"Old enough to know better," she said. She was really witty. "Ya got a watch on ya?" she asked me again, and then she stood up and pulled her dress over her head.

I certainly felt peculiar when she did that. I mean she did it so *sudden* and all. I know you're supposed to feel pretty sexy when somebody gets up and pulls their dress over their head, but I didn't. Sexy was about the *last* thing I was feeling. I felt much more depressed than sexy.

"Ya got a watch on ya, hey?"

"No. No, I don't," I said. *Boy*, was I feeling peculiar. "What's your name?"

I asked her. All she had on was this pink slip. It was really quite embarrassing. It really was.

"Sunny," she said. "Let's go, hey."

"Don't you feel like talking for a while?" I asked her. It was a childish thing to say, but I was feeling so damn peculiar. "Are you in a very big hurry?"

She looked at me like I was a madman. "What the heck ya wanna talk about?" she said.

"I don't know. Nothing special. I just thought perhaps you might care to chat for a while."

She sat down in the chair next to the desk again. She didn't like it, though, you could tell. She started jiggling her foot again—boy, she was a nervous girl.

"Would you care for a cigarette now?" I said. I forgot she didn't smoke.

"I don't smoke. Listen, if you're gonna talk, *do* it. I got things to do."

I couldn't think of anything to talk about, though. I thought of asking her how she got to be a prostitute and all, but I was scared to ask her. She probably wouldn't've told me anyway.

"You don't come from New York, do you?" I said finally. That's all I could think of.

"Hollywood," she said. Then she got up and went over to where she'd put her dress down, on the bed. "Ya got a hanger? I don't want to get my dress all wrinkly. It's brand-clean."

"Sure," I said right away. I was only too glad to get up and do something. I took her dress over to the closet and hung it up for her. It was funny. It made me feel sort of sad when I hung it up. I thought of her going in a store and buying it, and nobody in the store knowing she was a prostitute and all. The salesman probably just thought she was a regular girl when she bought it. It made me feel sad as hell—I don't know why exactly.

I sat down again and tried to keep the old conversation going. She was a lousy conversationalist. "Do you work every night?" I asked her—it sounded sort of awful, after I'd said it.

"Yeah." She was walking all around the room. She picked up the menu off the desk and read it.

"What do you do during the day?"

She sort of shrugged her shoulders. She was pretty skinny. "Sleep. Go to the show." She put down the menu and looked at me. "Let's go, hey. I haven't got all—"

"Look," I said. "I don't feel very much like myself tonight. I've had a rough night. Honest to God. I'll pay you and all, but do you mind very much if we don't do it? Do you mind very much?" The trouble was, I just didn't want to do it. I felt more depressed than sexy, if you want to know the truth. *She* was depressing. Her green dress hanging in the closet and all. And besides, I don't think I could *ever* do it with somebody that sits in a stupid movie all day long. I really don't think I could.

She came over to me, with this funny look on her face, like as if she didn't believe me. "What's a matter?" she said.

"Nothing's the matter." Boy, was I getting nervous. "The thing is, I had an operation very recently."

"Yeah? Where?"

"On my wuddayacallit—my clavichord."

"Yeah? Where the hell's that?"

"The clavichord?" I said. "Well, actually, it's in the spinal canal. I mean it's quite a ways down in the spinal canal."

"Yeah?" she said. "That's tough." Then she sat down on my goddam lap. "You're cute."

She made me so nervous, I just kept on lying my head off. "I'm still recuperating," I told her.

"You look like a guy in the movies. You know. Whosis. *You* know who I mean. What the heck's his name?"

"I don't know," I said. She wouldn't get off my goddam lap.

"Sure you know. He was in that pitcher with Mel-vine Douglas? The one that was Mel-vine Douglas's kid brother? That falls off this boat? *You* know who I mean."

"No, I don't. I go to the movies as seldom as I can."

Then she started getting funny. Crude and all.

"Do you mind cutting it out?" I said. "I'm not in the mood, I just told you. I just had an operation."

She didn't get up from my lap or anything, but she gave me this terrifically dirty look. "Listen," she said. "I was *sleep*in' when that crazy Maurice woke me up. If you think I'm—"

"I *said* I'd pay you for coming and all. I really will. I have plenty of dough. It's just that I'm practically just recovering from a very serious—"

"What the heck did you tell that crazy Maurice you wanted a *gir*l for, then? If you just had a goddam operation on your goddam wuddayacallit. *Huh?*"

"I thought I'd be feeling a lot better than I do. I was a little premature in my calculations. No kidding. I'm sorry. If you'll just get up a second, I'll get my wallet. I mean it."

She was sore as hell, but she got up off my goddam lap so that I could go over and get my wallet off the chiffonier. I took out a five-dollar bill and handed it to her. "Thanks a lot," I told her. "Thanks a million."

"This is a five. It costs ten."

She was getting funny, you could tell. I was afraid something like that would happen—I really was.

"Maurice said five," I told her. "He said fifteen till noon and only five for a throw."

"Ten for a throw."

"He said five. I'm sorry—I really am—but that's all I'm gonna shell out."

She sort of shrugged her shoulders, the way she did before, and then she said, very cold, "Do you mind getting me my frock? Or would it be too much trouble?" She was a pretty spooky kid. Even with that little bitty voice she had, she could sort of scare you a little bit. If she'd been a big old prostitute, with a lot of makeup on her face and all, she wouldn't have been half as spooky.

I went and got her dress for her. She put it on and all, and then she picked up her polo coat off the bed. "So long, crumb-bum," she said.

"So long," I said. I didn't thank her or anything. I'm glad I didn't.

XIV

After Old Sunny was gone, I sat in the chair for a while and smoked a couple of cigarettes. It was getting daylight outside. Boy, I felt miserable. I felt so depressed, you can't imagine. What I did, I started talking, sort of out loud, to Allie. I do that sometimes when I get very depressed. I keep telling him to go home and get his bike and meet me in front of Bobby Fallon's house. Bobby Fallon used to live quite near us in Maine—this is, years ago. Anyway, what happened was, one day Bobby and I were going over to Lake Sedebego on our bikes. We were going to take our lunches and all, and our BB guns—we were kids and all, and we thought we could shoot something with our BB guns. Anyway, Allie heard us talking about it, and he wanted to go, and I wouldn't let him. I told him he was a child. So once in a while, now, when I get very depressed, I keep saying to him, "Okay. Go home and get your bike and meet me in front of Bobby's house. Hurry up." It wasn't that I didn't use to take him with me when I went somewhere. I did. But that one day, I didn't. He didn't get sore about it—he never got sore about anything—but I keep thinking about it anyway, when I get very depressed.

Finally, though, I got undressed and got in bed. I felt like praying or something, when I was in bed, but I couldn't do it. I can't always pray when I feel like it. In the first place, I'm sort of an atheist. I like Jesus and all, but I don't care too much for most of the other stuff in the Bible. Take the Disciples, for instance. They annoy the hell out of me, if you want to know the truth. They were all right after Jesus was dead and all, but while He was alive, they were about as much use to Him as a hole in the head. All they did was keep letting Him down. I like almost anybody in the Bible better than the Disciples. If you want to know the truth, the guy I like best in the Bible, next to Jesus, was that lunatic and all, that lived in the tombs and kept cutting himself with stones. I like him ten times as much as the Disciples, that poor bastard. I used to get in quite a few arguments about it, when I was at the Whooton School, with this boy that lived down the corridor, Arthur Childs. Old Childs was a Quaker and all, and he read the Bible all the time. He was a very nice kid, and I liked him, but I could never see eye to eye with him on a lot of stuff in the Bible, especially the Disciples. He kept telling me if I didn't like the Disciples, then I didn't like Jesus and all. He said that because Jesus *picked* the Disciples, you were supposed to like them. I said I knew He picked them, but that He picked them at *random*. I said He didn't have time to go around analyzing everybody. I said I wasn't blaming Jesus or anything. It wasn't His fault that He didn't have any time. I remember I asked old Childs if he thought Judas, the one that betrayed Jesus and all, went to Hell after he committed suicide. Childs said certainly. That's exactly where I disagreed with him. I said I'd bet a thousand bucks that Jesus never sent old Judas to Hell. I still would, too, if I had a thousand bucks. I think any one of the Dis*cip*les would've sent him to Hell and all—and fast, too—but I'll bet anything Jesus didn't do it. Old Childs said the trouble with me was that I didn't go to church or anything. He was right about that, in a way. I don't. In the first place, my parents are different religions, and all the children in our family are atheists. If you want to know the truth, I can't even stand ministers. The ones they've had at every school I've gone to, they all have these Holy Joe voices when they start giving their sermons. God, I hate that. I don't see why the hell they can't talk in their natural voice. They sound so phony when they talk.

Anyway, when I was in bed, I couldn't pray worth a damn. Every time I got started, I kept picturing old Sunny calling me a crumb-bum. Finally, I sat up in bed and smoked another cigarette. It tasted lousy. I must've smoked around two packs since I left Pencey.

All of a sudden, while I was laying there smoking, somebody knocked on the door. I kept hoping it wasn't *my* door they were knocking on, but I knew damn well it was. I don't know *how* I knew, but I knew. I knew *who* it was, too. I'm psychic.

"Who's there?" I said. I was pretty scared. I'm very yellow about those things.

They just knocked again, though. Louder.

Finally I got out of bed, with just my pajamas on, and opened the door. I didn't even have to turn the light on in the room, because it was already daylight. Old Sunny and Maurice, the pimpy elevator guy, were standing there.

"What's the matter? Wuddaya want?" I said. Boy, my voice was shaking like hell.

"Nothin' much," old Maurice said. "Just five bucks." He did all the talking for the two of them. Old Sunny just stood there next to him, with her mouth open and all.

"I paid her already. I gave her five bucks. Ask her," I said. Boy, was my voice shaking.

"It's ten bucks, chief. I tole ya that. Ten bucks for a throw, fifteen bucks till noon. I tole ya that."

"You did not tell me that. You said *five* bucks a throw. You said fifteen bucks till noon, all right, but I distinctly heard you—"

"Open up, chief."

"What *for*?" I said. God, my old heart was damn near beating me out of the room. I wished I was *dressed* at least. It's terrible to be just in your pajamas when something like that happens.

"Let's go, chief," old Maurice said. Then he gave me a big shove with his crumby hand. I damn near fell over on my can—he was a huge sonuvabitch. The next thing I knew, he and old Sunny were both in the room. They acted like they owned the damn place. Old Sunny sat down on the window sill. Old Maurice sat down in the big chair and loosened his collar and all—he wearing this elevator operator's uniform. *Boy*, was I nervous.

"All right, chief, let's have it. I gotta get back to work."

"I told you about ten times, I don't owe you a cent. I already gave her the five—"

"Cut the crap, now. Let's have it."

"Why should I give her another five bucks?" I said. My voice was cracking all over the place. "You're trying to chisel me."

Old Maurice unbuttoned his whole uniform coat. All he had on underneath was a phony shirt collar, but no shirt or anything. He had a big fat hairy stomach. "Nobody's tryna chisel nobody," he said. "Let's have it, chief."

"*No.*"

When I said that, he got up from his chair and started walking towards me and all. He looked like he was very, very tired or very, very bored. God, was I scared. I sort of had my arms folded, I remember. It wouldn't have been so bad, I don't think, if I hadn't had just my goddam *pajamas* on.

"Let's have it, chief." He came right up to where I was standing. That's all he could say. "Let's have it, chief." He was a real moron.

"*No.*"

"Chief, you're gonna force me inna roughin' ya up a little bit. I don't wanna do it, but that's the way it looks," he said. "You owe us five bucks."

"I *don't* owe you five bucks," I said. "If you rough me up, I'll yell like hell. I'll wake up everybody in the hotel. The police and all." My voice was shaking like a bastard.

"Go ahead. Yell your goddam head off. Fine," old Maurice said. "Want your parents to know you spent the night with a whore? High-class kid like you?" He was pretty sharp, in his crumby way. He really was.

"Leave me alone. If you'd *said* ten, it'd be different. But you distinctly—"

"Are ya gonna let us have it?" He had me right up against the damn door. He was almost standing on top of me, his crumby old hairy stomach and all.

"Leave me alone. Get the hell out of my room," I said. I still had my arms folded and all. God, what a jerk I was.

Then Sunny said something for the first time. "Hey, Maurice. Want me to get his wallet?" she said. "It's right on the wutchamacallit."

"Yeah, get it."

"Leave my wallet alone!"

"I awreddy got it," Sunny said. She waved five bucks at me. "See? All I'm takin' is the five you owe me. I'm no crook."

All of a sudden I started to cry. I'd give anything if I hadn't, but I did. "No, you're no crooks," I said. "You're just stealing five—"

"Shut up," old Maurice said, and gave me a shove.

"Leave him alone, hey," Sunny said. "C'mon, hey. We got the dough he owes us. Let's go. C'mon, hey."

"I'm comin'," old Maurice said. But he didn't.

"I mean it, Maurice, hey. Leave him alone."

"Who's hurtin' anybody?" he said, innocent as hell. Then what he did, he snapped his finger very hard on my pajamas. I won't tell you *where* he snapped it, but it hurt like hell. I told him he was a goddam dirty moron. "What's that?" he said. He put his hand behind his ear, like a deaf guy. "What's that? What am I?"

I was still sort of crying. I was so damn mad and nervous and all. "You're a dirty moron," I said. "You're a stupid chiseling moron, and in about two years you'll be one of those scraggy guys that come up to you on the street and ask for a dime for coffee. You'll have snot all over your dirty filthy overcoat, and you'll be—"

Then he smacked me. I didn't even try to get out of the way or duck or anything. All I felt was this terrific punch in my stomach.

I wasn't knocked out or anything, though, because I remember looking up from the floor and seeing them both go out the door and shut it. Then I stayed on the floor a fairly long time, sort of the way I did with Stradlater. Only, this time I thought I was dying. I really did. I thought I was drowning or something. The trouble was, I could hardly breathe. When I did finally get up, I had to walk to the bathroom all doubled up and holding onto my stomach and all.

But I'm crazy. I swear to God I am. About halfway to the bathroom, I sort of started pretending I had a bullet in my guts. Old Maurice had plugged me. Now I was on the way to the bathroom to get a good shot of bourbon or something to steady my nerves and help me *really* go into action. I pictured myself coming out of the goddam bathroom, dressed and all, with my automatic in my pocket, and staggering around a little bit. Then I'd walk downstairs, instead of using the elevator. I'd hold onto the banister and all, with this blood trickling out of the side of my mouth a little at a time. What I'd do, I'd walk down a few floors—holding onto my guts, blood leaking all over the place—and then I'd ring the elevator bell. As soon as old Maurice opened the doors, he'd see me with the automatic in my hand and he'd start screaming at me, in this very high-pitched, yellow-belly voice, to leave him alone. But I'd plug him anyway. Six shots right through his fat hairy belly. Then I'd throw my automatic down the elevator shaft—after I'd wiped off all the finger prints and all. Then I'd crawl back to my room and call up Jane and have her come over and bandage up my guts. I pictured her holding a cigarette for me to smoke while I was bleeding and all.

The goddam movies. They can ruin you. I'm not kidding.

I stayed in the bathroom for about an hour, taking a bath and all. Then I got back in bed. It took me quite a while to get to sleep—I wasn't even tired—but finally I did. What I really felt like, though, was committing suicide. I felt like jumping out the window. I probably would've done it, too, if I'd been sure somebody'd cover me up as soon as I landed. I didn't want a bunch of stupid rubbernecks looking at me when I was all gory.

XV

I didn't sleep too long, because I think it was only around ten o'clock when I woke up. I felt pretty hungry as soon as I had a cigarette. The last time I'd eaten was those two hamburgers I had with Brossard and Ackley when we went in to Agerstown to the movies. That was a long time ago. It seemed like fifty years ago. The phone was right next to me, and I started to call down and have them send up some breakfast, but I was sort of afraid they might send it up with old Maurice. If you think I was dying to see him again, you're crazy. So I just laid around in bed for a while and smoked another cigarette. I thought of giving old Jane a buzz, to see if she was home yet and all, but I wasn't in the mood.

What I did do, I gave old Sally Hayes a buzz. She went to Mary A. Woodruff, and I knew she was home because I'd had this letter from her a couple of weeks ago. I wasn't too crazy about her, but I'd known her for years. I used to think she was quite intelligent, in my stupidity. The reason I did was because she knew quite a lot about the theater and plays and literature and all that stuff. If somebody knows quite a lot about those things, it takes you quite a while to find out whether they're really stupid or not. It took me years to find it out, in old Sally's case. I think I'd have found it out a lot sooner if we hadn't necked so damn much. My big trouble is, I always sort of think whoever I'm necking is a pretty intelligent person. It hasn't got a goddam thing to do with it, but I keep thinking it anyway.

Anyway, I gave her a buzz. First the maid answered. Then her father. Then she got on. "Sally?" I said.

"Yes—who is this?" she said. She was quite a little phony. I'd already told her father who it was.

"Holden Caulfield. How are ya?"

"Holden! I'm fine! How are you?"

"Swell. Listen. How are ya, anyway? I mean how's school?"

"Fine," she said. "I mean—you know."

"Swell. Well, listen. I was wondering if you were busy today. It's Sunday, but there's always one or two matinees going on Sunday. Benefits and that stuff. Would you care to go?"

"I'd love to. Grand."

Grand. If there's one word I hate, it's grand. It's so phony. For a second, I was tempted to tell her to forget about the matinee. But we chewed the fat for a while. That is, she chewed it. You couldn't get a word in edgewise. First she told me about some Harvard guy— it probably was a freshman, but she didn't say, naturally—that was rushing hell out of her. Calling her up *night and day*. Night and day—that killed me. Then she told me about some other guy, some West Point cadet, that was cutting his throat over her too. Big deal. I told her to meet me under the clock at the Biltmore at two o'clock, and not to be late, because the show probably started at two-thirty. She was always late. Then I hung up. She gave me a pain in the ass, but she was very good-looking.

After I made the date with old Sally, I got out of bed and got dressed and packed my bag. I took a look out the window before I left the room, though, to see how all the perverts were doing, but they all had their shades down. They were the heighth of modesty in the morning. Then I went down in the elevator and checked out. I didn't see old Maurice around anywhere. I didn't break my neck looking for him, naturally, the bastard.

I got a cab outside the hotel, but I didn't have the faintest damn idea where I was going. I had no place to go. It was only Sunday, and I couldn't go home till Wednesday—or Tuesday the *soon*est. And I certainly didn't feel like going to another hotel and getting my brains beat out. So what I did, I told the driver to take me to Grand Central Station. It was right near the Biltmore, where I was meeting Sally later, and I figured what I'd do, I'd check my bags in one of those strong boxes that they give you a key to, then get some breakfast. I was sort of hungry. While I was in the cab, I took out my wallet and sort of counted my money. I don't remember exactly what I had left, but it was no fortune or anything. I'd spent a king's ransom in about two lousy weeks. I really had. I'm a goddam spendthrift at heart. What I don't spend, I lose. Half the time I sort of even forget to pick up my change, at restaurants and night clubs and all. It drives my parents crazy. You can't blame them. My father's quite wealthy, though. I don't know how much he makes—he's never discussed that stuff with me—but I imagine quite a lot. He's a corporation lawyer. Those boys really haul it in. Another reason I know he's quite well off, he's always investing money in shows on Broadway. They always flop, though, and it drives my mother crazy when he does it. She hasn't felt too healthy since my brother Allie died. She's very nervous. That's another reason why I hated like hell for her to know I got the ax again.

After I put my bags in one of those strong boxes at the station, I went into this little sandwich bar and had breakfast. I had quite a large breakfast, for me—orange juice, bacon and eggs, toast and coffee. Usually I just drink some orange juice. I'm a very light eater. I really am. That's why I'm so damn skinny. I was supposed to be on this diet where you eat a lot of starches and crap, to gain weight and all, but I didn't ever do it. When I'm out somewhere, I generally just eat a Swiss cheese sandwich and a malted milk. It isn't much, but you get quite a lot of vitamins in the malted milk. H. V. Caulfield. Holden Vitamin Caulfield.

While I was eating my eggs, these two nuns with suitcases and all—I guessed they were moving to another convent or something and were waiting for a train—came in and sat down next to me at the counter. They didn't seem to know what the hell to do with their suitcases, so I gave them a hand. They were these very inexpensive-looking suitcases—the ones that aren't genuine leather or anything. It isn't important, I know, but I hate it when somebody has cheap suitcases. It sounds terrible to say it, but I can even get to hate somebody, just *look*ing at them, if they have cheap suitcases with them. Something happened once. For a while when I was at Elkton Hills, I roomed with this boy, Dick Slagle, that had these very inexpensive suitcases. He used to keep them under the bed, instead of on the rack, so that nobody'd see them standing next to mine. It depressed holy hell out of me, and I kept wanting to throw mine out or something, or even *trade* with him. Mine came from Mark Cross, and they were genuine cowhide and all that crap, and I guess they cost quite a pretty penny. But it was a funny thing. Here's what happened. What I did, I finally put *my* suitcases under *my* bed, instead of on the rack, so that old Slagle wouldn't get a goddam inferiority complex about it. But here's what he did. The day after I put mine under my bed, he took them out and put them back on the rack. The reason he did it, it took me a while to find out, was because he wanted people to think my bags were his. He really did. He was a very funny guy, that way. He was always saying snotty things about them, my suitcases, for instance. He kept saying they were too new and bourgeois. That was his favorite goddam word. He read it somewhere or heard it somewhere. Everything I had was bourgeois as hell. Even my fountain pen was bourgeois. He borrowed it off me all the time, but it was bourgeois anyway. We only roomed together about two months. Then we both asked to be moved. And the funny thing was, I sort of missed him after we moved, because he had a helluva good sense of humor and we had a lot of fun sometimes. I wouldn't be surprised if he missed me, too. At first he only used to be kidding when he called my stuff bourgeois, and I didn't give a damn—it *was* sort of funny, in fact. Then, after a while, you could tell he wasn't kidding any more. The thing is, it's really hard to be roommates with people if your suitcases are much better than theirs—if yours are really *good* ones and theirs aren't. You think if they're intelligent and all, the other person, and have a good sense of humor, that they don't give a damn whose suitcases are better, but they do. They really do. It's one of the reasons why I roomed with a stupid bastard like Stradlater. At least his suitcases were as good as mine.

Anyway, these two nuns were sitting next to me, and we sort of struck up a conversation. The one right next to me had one of those straw baskets that you see nuns and Salvation Army babes collecting dough with around Christmas time. You see them standing on corners, especially on Fifth Avenue, in front of the big department stores and all. Anyway, the one next to me dropped hers on the floor and I reached down and picked it up for her. I asked her if she was out collecting money for charity and all. She said no. She said she couldn't get it in her suitcase when she was packing it and she was just carrying it. She had a pretty nice smile when she looked at you. She had a big nose, and she had on those glasses with sort of iron rims that aren't too attractive, but she had a helluva kind face. "I thought if you were taking up a collection," I told her, "I could make a small contribution. You could keep the money for when you do take up a collection."

"Oh, how very kind of you," she said, and the other one, her friend, looked over at me. The other one was reading a little black book while she drank her coffee. It looked like a Bible, but it was too skinny. It was a Bible-type book, though. All the two of them were eating for breakfast was toast and coffee. That depressed me. I hate it if I'm eating bacon and eggs or something and somebody else is only eating toast and coffee.

They let me give them ten bucks as a contribution. They kept asking me if I was sure I could afford it and all. I told them I had quite a bit of money with me, but they didn't seem to believe me. They took it, though, finally. The both of them kept thanking me so much it was embarrassing. I swung the conversation around to general topics and asked them where they were going. They said they were schoolteachers and that they'd just come from Chicago and that they were going to start teaching at some convent on 168th Street or 186th Street or one of those streets way the hell uptown. The one next to me, with the iron glasses, said she taught English and her friend taught history and American government. Then I started wondering like a bastard what the one sitting next to me, that taught English, thought about, being a nun and all, when she read certain books for English. Books not necessarily with a lot of sexy stuff in them, but books with lovers and all in them. Take old Eustacia Vye, in *The Return of the Native* by Thomas Hardy. She wasn't too sexy or anything, but even so you can't help wondering what a nun maybe thinks about when she reads about old Eustacia. I didn't say anything, though, naturally. All I said was English was my best subject.

"Oh, really? Oh, I'm so glad!" the one with the glasses, that taught English, said. "What have you read this year? I'd be very interested to know." She was really nice.

"Well, most of the time we were on the Anglo-Saxons. Beowulf, and old Grendel, and Lord Randal My Son, and all those things. But we had to read outside books for extra credit once in a while. I read *The Return of the Native* by Thomas Hardy, and *Romeo and Juliet* and *Julius*—"

"Oh, *Romeo and Juliet*! Lovely! Didn't you just love it?" She certainly didn't sound much like a nun.

"Yes. I did. I liked it a lot. There were a few things I didn't like about it, but it was quite moving, on the whole."

"What didn't you like about it? Can you remember?"

To tell you the truth, it was sort of embarrassing, in a way, to be talking about *Romeo and Juliet* with her. I mean that play gets pretty sexy in some parts, and she was a nun and all, but she *asked* me, so I discussed it with her for a while. "Well, I'm not too crazy about Romeo and Juliet," I said. "I mean I like them, but—I don't know. They get pretty annoying sometimes. I mean I felt much sorrier when old Mercutio got killed than when Romeo and Juliet did. The thing is, I never liked Romeo too much after Mercutio gets stabbed by that other man— Juliet's cousin— what's his name?"

"Tybalt."

"That's right. Tybalt," I said—I always forget that guy's name. "It was Romeo's fault. I mean I liked him the best in the play, old Mercutio. I don't know. All those Montagues and Capulets, they're all right—especially Juliet—but Mercutio, he was—it's hard to explain. He was very smart and entertaining and all. The thing is, it drives me crazy if somebody gets killed—especially somebody very smart and entertaining and all—and it's somebody else's fault. Romeo and Juliet, at least it was their own fault."

"What school do you go to?" she asked me. She probably wanted to get off the subject of Romeo and Juliet.

I told her Pencey, and she'd heard of it. She said it was a very good school. I let it pass, though. Then the other one, the one that taught history and government, said they'd better be running along. I took their check off them, but they wouldn't let me pay it. The one with the glasses made me give it back to her.

"You've been more than generous," she said. "You're a very sweet boy." She certainly was nice. She reminded me a little bit of old Ernest Morrow's mother, the one I met on the train. When she smiled, mostly. "We've enjoyed talking to you so much," she said.

I said I'd enjoyed talking to them a lot, too. I meant it, too. I'd have enjoyed it even more though, I think, if I hadn't been sort of afraid, the whole time I was talking to them, that they'd all of a sudden try to find out if I was a Catholic. Catholics are always trying to find out if you're a Catholic. It happens to me a lot, I know, partly because my last name is Irish, and most people of Irish descent are Catholics. As a matter of fact, my father *was* a Catholic once. He quit, though, when he married my mother. But Catholics are always trying to find out if you're a Catholic even if they don't know your last name. I knew this one Catholic boy, Louis Shaney, when I was at the Whooton School. He was the first boy I ever met there. He and I were sitting in the first two chairs outside the goddam infirmary, the day school opened, waiting for our physicals, and we sort of struck up this conversation about tennis. He was quite interested in tennis, and so was I. He told me he went to the Nationals at Forest Hills every summer, and I told him I did too, and then we talked about certain hot-shot tennis players for quite a while. He knew quite a lot about tennis, for a kid his age. He really did. Then, after a while, right in the middle of the goddam conversation, he asked me, "Did you happen to notice where the Catholic church is in town, by any chance?" The thing was, you could tell by the way he asked me that he was trying to find out if I was a Catholic. He really was. Not that he was prejudiced or anything, but he just wanted to know. He was enjoying the conversation about tennis and all, but you could tell he would've enjoyed it *more* if I was a Catholic and all. That kind of stuff drives me crazy. I'm not saying it ruined our conversation or anything—it didn't—but it sure as hell didn't do it any good. That's why I was glad those two nuns didn't ask me if I was a Catholic. It wouldn't have *spoiled* the conversation if they had, but it would've been different, probably. I'm not saying I *blame* Catholics. I don't. I'd be the same way, probably, if I was a Catholic. It's just like those suitcases I was telling you about, in a way. All I'm saying is that it's no good for a nice conversation. That's all I'm saying.

When they got up to go, the two nuns, I did something very stupid and embarrassing. I was smoking a cigarette, and when I stood up to say good-by to them, by mistake I blew some smoke in their face. I didn't mean to, but I did it. I apologized like a madman, and they were very polite and nice about it, but it was very embarrassing anyway.

After they left, I started getting sorry that I'd only given them ten bucks for their collection. But the thing was, I'd made that date to go to a matinee with old Sally Hayes, and I needed to keep some dough for the tickets and stuff. I was sorry anyway, though. Goddam money. It always ends up making you blue as hell.

XVI

After I had my breakfast, it was only around noon, and I wasn't meeting old Sally till two o'clock, so I started taking this long walk. I couldn't stop thinking about those two nuns. I kept thinking about that beat-up old straw basket they went around collecting money with when they weren't teaching school. I kept trying to picture my mother or somebody, or my aunt, or Sally Hayes's crazy mother, standing outside some department store and collecting dough for poor people in a beat-up old straw basket. It was hard to picture. Not so much my mother, but those other two. My aunt's pretty charitable—she does a lot of Red Cross work and all—but she's very well-dressed and all, and when she does anything charitable she's always very well-dressed and has lipstick on and all that crap. I couldn't picture her doing anything for charity if she had to wear black clothes and no lipstick while she was doing it. And old Sally Hayes's mother. Jesus Christ. The only way *she* could go around with a basket collecting dough would be if everybody kissed her ass for her when they made a contribution. If they just dropped their dough in her basket, then walked away without saying anything to her, ignoring her and all, she'd quit in about an hour. She'd get bored. She'd hand in her basket and then go someplace swanky for lunch. That's what I liked about those nuns. You could tell, for one thing, that they never went anywhere swanky for lunch. It made me so damn sad when I thought about it, their never going anywhere swanky for lunch or anything. I knew it wasn't too important, but it made me sad anyway.

I started walking over toward Broadway, just for the hell of it, because I hadn't been over there in years. Besides, I wanted to find a record store that was open on Sunday. There was this record I wanted to get for Phoebe, called "Little Shirley Beans." It was a very hard record to get. It was about a little kid that wouldn't go out of the house because two of her front teeth were out and she was ashamed to. I heard it at Pencey. A boy that lived on the next floor had it, and I tried to buy it off him because I knew it would knock old Phoebe out, but he wouldn't sell it. It was a very old, terrific record that this colored girl singer, Estelle Fletcher, made about twenty years ago. She sings it very Dixieland and whorehouse, and it doesn't sound at all mushy. If a white girl was singing it, she'd make it sound *cute* as hell, but old Estelle Fletcher knew what the hell she was doing, and it was one of the best records I ever heard. I figured I'd buy it in some store that was open on Sunday and then I'd take it up to the park with me. It was Sunday and Phoebe goes roller-skating in the park on Sundays quite frequently. I knew where she hung out mostly.

It wasn't as cold as it was the day before, but the sun still wasn't out, and it wasn't too nice for walking. But there was one nice thing. This family that you could tell just came out of some church were walking right in front of me—a father, a mother, and a little kid about six years old. They looked sort of poor. The father had on one of those pearl-gray hats that poor guys wear a lot when they want to look sharp. He and his wife were just walking along, talking, not paying any attention to their kid. The kid was swell. He was walking in the street, instead of on the sidewalk, but right next to the curb. He was making out like he was walking a very straight line, the way kids do, and the whole time he kept singing and humming. I got up closer so I could hear what he was singing. He was singing that song, "If a body catch a body coming through the rye." He had a pretty little voice, too. He was just singing for the hell of it, you could tell. The cars zoomed by, brakes screeched all over the place, his parents paid no attention to him, and he kept on walking next to the curb and singing "If a body catch a body coming through the rye." It made me feel better. It made me feel not so depressed any more.

Broadway was mobbed and messy. It was Sunday, and only about twelve o'clock, but it was mobbed anyway. Everybody was on their way to the movies—the Paramount or the Astor or the Strand or the Capitol or one of those crazy places. Everybody was all dressed up, because it was Sunday, and that made it worse. But the worst part was that you could tell they all *wanted* to go to the movies. I couldn't stand looking at them. I can understand somebody going to the movies because there's nothing else to do, but when somebody really *wants* to go, and even walks fast so as to get there quicker, then it depresses hell out of me. Especially if I see millions of people standing in one of those long, terrible lines, all the way down the block, waiting with this terrific patience for seats and all. Boy, I couldn't get off that goddam Broadway fast enough. I was lucky. The first record store I went into had a copy of "Little Shirley Beans." They charged me five bucks for it, because it was so hard to get, but I didn't care. Boy, it made me so happy all of a sudden. I could hardly wait to get to the park to see if old Phoebe was around so that I could give it to her.

When I came out of the record store, I passed this drugstore, and I went in. I figured maybe I'd give old Jane a buzz and see if she was home for vacation yet. So I went in a phone booth and called her up. The only trouble was, her mother answered the phone, so I had to hang up. I didn't feel like getting involved in a long conversation and all with her. I'm not crazy about talking to girls' mothers on the phone anyway. I should've at *least* asked her if Jane was home yet, though. It wouldn't have killed me. But I didn't feel like it. You really have to be in the mood for that stuff.

I still had to get those damn theater tickets, so I bought a paper and looked up to see what shows were playing. On account of it was Sunday, there were only about three shows playing. So what I did was, I went over and bought two orchestra seats for *I Know My Love*. It was a benefit performance or something. I didn't much want to see it, but I knew old Sally, the queen of the phonies, would start drooling all over the place when I told her I had tickets for that, because the Lunts were in it and all. She liked shows that are supposed to be very sophisticated and dry and all, with the Lunts and all. I don't. I don't like any shows very much, if you want to know the truth. They're not as bad as movies, but they're certainly nothing to rave about. In the first place, I hate actors. They never act like people. They just think they do. Some of the good ones do, in a very slight way, but not in a way that's fun to watch. And if any actor's really good, you can always tell he *knows* he's good, and that spoils it. You take Sir Laurence Olivier, for example. I saw him in *Hamlet*. D.B. took Phoebe and I to see it last year. He treated us to lunch first, and then he took us. He'd already seen it, and the way he talked about it at lunch, I was anxious as hell to see it, too. But I didn't enjoy it much. I just don't see what's so marvelous about Sir Laurence Olivier, that's all. He has a terrific voice, and he's a helluva handsome guy, and he's very nice to watch when he's walking or dueling or something, but he wasn't at all the way D.B. said Hamlet was. He was too much like a goddam general, instead of a sad, screwed-up type guy. The best part in the whole picture was when old Ophelia's brother—the one that gets in the duel with Hamlet at the very end—was going away and his father was giving him a lot of advice. While the father kept giving him a lot of advice, old Ophelia was sort of horsing around with her brother, taking his dagger out of the holster, and teasing him and all while he was trying to look interested in the bull his father was shooting. That was nice. I got a big bang out of that. But you don't see that kind of stuff much. The only thing old Phoebe liked was when Hamlet patted this dog on the head. She thought that was funny and nice, and it was. What I'll have to do is, I'll have to read that play. The trouble with me is, I always have to read that stuff by myself. If an actor acts it out, I hardly listen. I keep worrying about whether he's going to do something phony every minute.

After I got the tickets to the Lunts' show, I took a cab up to the park. I should've taken a subway or something, because I was getting slightly low on dough, but I wanted to get off that damn Broadway as fast as I could.

It was lousy in the park. It wasn't too cold, but the sun still wasn't out, and there didn't look like there was anything in the park except dog crap and globs of spit and cigar butts from old men, and the benches all looked like they'd be wet if you sat down on them. It made you depressed, and every once in a while, for no reason, you got goose flesh while you walked. It didn't seem at all like Christmas was coming soon. It didn't seem like *any*thing was coming. But I kept walking over to the Mall anyway, because that's where Phoebe usually goes when she's in the park. She likes to skate near the bandstand. It's funny. That's the same place I used to like to skate when I was a kid.

When I got there, though, I didn't see her around anywhere. There were a few kids around, skating and all, and two boys were playing Flys Up with a soft ball, but no Phoebe. I saw one kid about her age, though, sitting on a bench all by herself, tightening her skate. I thought maybe she might know Phoebe and could tell me where she was or something, so I went over and sat down next to her and asked her, "Do you know Phoebe Caulfield, by any chance?"

"Who?" she said. All she had on was jeans and about twenty sweaters. You could tell her mother made them for her, because they were lumpy as hell.

"Phoebe Caulfield. She lives on Seventy-first Street. She's in the fourth grade, over at—"

"You know Phoebe?"

"Yeah, I'm her brother. You know where she is?"

"She's in Miss Callon's class, isn't she?" the kid said.

"I don't know. Yes, I think she is."

"She's prob'ly in the museum, then. *We* went last Saturday," the kid said.

"Which museum?" I asked her.

She shrugged her shoulders, sort of. "I don't know," she said. "The museum."

"I know, but the one where the pictures are, or the one where the Indians are?"

"The one where the Indians."

"Thanks a lot," I said. I got up and started to go, but then I suddenly remembered it was Sunday. "This is *Sun*day," I told the kid.

She looked up at me. "Oh. Then she isn't."

She was having a helluva time tightening her skate. She didn't have any gloves on or anything and her hands were all red and cold. I gave her a hand with it. Boy, I hadn't had a skate key in my hand for years. It didn't feel funny, though. You could put a skate key in my hand fifty years from now, in pitch dark, and I'd still know what it is. She thanked me and all when I had it tightened for her. She was a very nice, polite little kid. God, I love it when a kid's nice and polite when you tighten their skate for them or something. Most kids are. They really are. I asked her if she'd care to have a hot chocolate or something with me, but she said no, thank you. She said she had to meet her friend. Kids always have to meet their friend. That kills me.

Even though it was Sunday and Phoebe wouldn't be there with her class or anything, and even though it was so damp and lousy out, I walked all the way through the park over to the Museum of Natural History. I knew that was the museum the kid with the skate key meant. I knew that whole museum routine like a book. Phoebe went to the same school I went to when I was a kid, and we used to go there all the time. We had this teacher, Miss Aigletinger, that took us there damn near every Saturday. Sometimes we looked at the animals and sometimes we looked at the stuff the Indians had made in ancient times. Pottery and straw baskets and all stuff like that. I get very happy when I think about it. Even now. I remember after we looked at all the Indian stuff, usually we went to see some movie in this big auditorium. Columbus. They were always showing Columbus discovering America, having one helluva time getting old Ferdinand and Isabella to lend him the dough to buy ships with, and then the sailors mutinying on him and all. Nobody gave too much of a damn about old Columbus, but you always had a lot of candy and gum and stuff with you, and the inside of that auditorium had such a nice smell. It always smelled like it was raining outside, even if it wasn't, and you were in the only nice, dry, cosy place in the world. I loved that damn museum. I remember you had to go through the Indian Room to get to the auditorium. It was a long, long room, and you were only supposed to whisper. The teacher would go first, then the class. You'd be two rows of kids, and you'd have a partner. Most of the time my partner was this girl named Gertrude Levine. She always wanted to hold your hand, and her hand was always sticky or sweaty or something. The floor was all stone, and if you had some marbles in your hand and you dropped them, they bounced like madmen all over the floor and made a helluva racket, and the teacher would hold up the class and go back and see what the hell was going on. She never got sore, though, Miss Aigletinger. Then you'd pass by this long, long Indian war canoe, about as long as three goddam Cadillacs in a row, with about twenty Indians in it, some of them paddling, some of them just standing around looking tough, and they all had war paint all over their faces. There was one very spooky guy in the back of the canoe, with a mask on. He was the witch doctor. He gave me the creeps, but I liked him anyway. Another thing, if you touched one of the paddles or anything while you were passing, one of the guards would say to you, "Don't touch anything, children," but he always said it in a nice voice, not like a goddam cop or anything. Then you'd pass by this big glass case, with Indians inside it rubbing sticks together to make a fire, and a squaw weaving a blanket. The squaw that was weaving the blanket was sort of bending over, and you could see her bosom and all. We all used to sneak a good look at it, even the girls, because they were only little kids and they didn't have any more bosom than *we* did. Then, just before you went inside the auditorium, right near the doors, you passed this Eskimo. He was sitting over a hole in this icy lake, and he was fishing through it. He had about two fish right next to the hole, that he'd already caught. Boy, that museum was full of glass cases. There were even more upstairs, with deer inside them drinking at water holes, and birds flying south for the winter. The birds nearest you were all stuffed and hung up on wires, and the ones in back were just painted on the wall, but they all looked like they were really flying south, and if you bent your head down and sort of looked at them upside down, they looked in an even bigger hurry to fly south. The best thing, though, in that museum was that everything always stayed right where it was. Nobody'd move. You could go there a hundred thousand times, and that Eskimo would still be just finished catching those two fish, the birds would still be on their way south, the deers would still be drinking out of that water hole, with their pretty antlers and their pretty, skinny legs, and that squaw with the naked bosom would still be weaving that same blanket. Nobody'd be different. The only thing that would be different would be *you*. Not that you'd be so much older or anything. It wouldn't be that, exactly. You'd just be different, that's all. You'd have an overcoat on this time. Or the kid that was your partner in line the last time had got scarlet fever and you'd have a new partner. Or you'd have a substitute taking the class, instead of Miss Aigletinger. Or you'd heard your mother and father having a terrific fight in the bathroom. Or you'd just passed by one of those puddles in the street with gasoline rainbows in them. I mean you'd be *dif*ferent in some way—I can't explain what I mean. And even if I could, I'm not sure I'd feel like it.

I took my old hunting hat out of my pocket while I walked, and put it on. I knew I wouldn't meet anybody that knew me, and it was pretty damp out. I kept walking and walking, and I kept thinking about old Phoebe going to that museum on Saturdays the way I used to. I thought how she'd see the same stuff I used to see, and how *she'd* be different every time she saw it. It didn't exactly depress me to think about it, but it didn't make me feel gay as hell, either. Certain things they should stay the way they are. You ought to be able to stick them in one of those big glass cases and just leave them alone. I know that's impossible, but it's too bad anyway. Anyway, I kept thinking about all that while I walked.

I passed by this playground and stopped and watched a couple of very tiny kids on a seesaw. One of them was sort of fat, and I put my hand on the skinny kid's end, to sort of even up the weight, but you could tell they didn't want me around, so I let them alone.

Then a funny thing happened. When I got to the museum, all of a sudden I wouldn't have gone inside for a million bucks. It just didn't appeal to me—and here I'd walked through the whole goddam park and looked forward to it and all. If Phoebe'd been there, I probably would have, but she wasn't. So all I did, in front of the museum, was get a cab and go down to the Biltmore. I didn't feel much like going. I'd made that damn date with Sally, though.

XVII

I was way early when I got there, so I just sat down on one of those leather couches right near the clock in the lobby and watched the girls. A lot of schools were home for vacation already, and there were about a million girls sitting and standing around waiting for their dates to show up. Girls with their legs crossed, girls with their legs not crossed, girls with terrific legs, girls with lousy legs, girls that looked like swell girls, girls that looked like they'd be bitches if you knew them. It was really nice sightseeing, if you know what I mean. In a way, it was sort of depressing, too, because you kept wondering what the hell would *happen* to all of them. When they got out of school and college, I mean. You figured most of them would probably marry dopey guys. Guys that always talk about how many miles they get to a gallon in their goddam cars. Guys that get sore and childish as hell if you beat them at golf, or even just some stupid game like ping-pong. Guys that are very mean. Guys that never read books. Guys that are very boring—But I have to be careful about that. I mean about calling certain guys bores. I don't understand boring guys. I really don't. When I was at Elkton Hills, I roomed for about two months with this boy, Harris Macklin. He was very intelligent and all, but he was one of the biggest bores I ever met. He had one of these very raspy voices, and he never stopped talking, practically. He never stopped talking, and what was awful was, he never said anything you wanted to hear in the first place. But he could do one thing. The sonuvabitch could whistle better than anybody

I ever heard. He'd be making his bed, or hanging up stuff in the closet—he was always hanging up stuff in the closet—it drove me crazy—and he'd be whistling while he did it, if he wasn't talking in this raspy voice. He could even whistle classical stuff, but most of the time he just whistled jazz. He could take something very jazzy, like "Tin Roof Blues," and whistle it so nice and easy—right while he was hanging stuff up in the closet—that it could kill you. Naturally, I never *told* him I thought he was a terrific whistler. I mean you don't just go up to somebody and say, "You're a terrific whistler." But I roomed with him for about two whole months, even though he bored me till I was half crazy, just because he was such a terrific whistler, the best I ever heard. So I don't know about bores. Maybe you shouldn't feel too sorry if you see some swell girl getting married to them. They don't hurt anybody, most of them, and maybe they're secretly all terrific whistlers or something. Who the hell knows? Not me.

Finally, old Sally started coming up the stairs, and I started down to meet her. She looked terrific. She really did. She had on this black coat and sort of a black beret. She hardly ever wore a hat, but that beret looked nice. The funny part is, I felt like marrying her the minute I saw her. I'm crazy. I didn't even *like* her much, and yet all of a sudden I felt like I was in love with her and wanted to marry her. I swear to God I'm crazy. I admit it.

"Holden!" she said. "It's marvelous to see you! It's been *ages*." She had one of these very loud, embarrassing voices when you met her somewhere. She got away with it because she was so damn good-looking, but it always gave me a pain in the ass.

"Swell to see *you*," I said. I meant it, too. "How are ya, anyway?"

"Absolutely marvelous. Am I late?"

I told her no, but she was around ten minutes late, as a matter of fact. I didn't give a damn, though. All that crap they have in cartoons in the *Saturday Evening*

Post and all, showing guys on street corners looking sore as hell because their dates are late—that's bunk. If a girl looks swell when she meets you, who gives a damn if she's late? Nobody. "We better hurry," I said. "The show starts at two-forty." We started going down the stairs to where the taxis are.

"What are we going to see?" she said.

"I don't know. The Lunts. It's all I could get tickets for."

"The Lunts! Oh, marvelous!"

I told you she'd go mad when she heard it was for the Lunts.

We horsed around a little bit in the cab on the way over to the theater. At first she didn't want to, because she had her lipstick on and all, but I was being seductive as hell and she didn't have any alternative. Twice, when the goddam cab stopped short in traffic, I damn near fell off the seat. Those damn drivers never even look where they're going, I swear they don't. Then, just to show you how crazy I am, when we were coming out of this big clinch, I told her I loved her and all. It was a lie, of course, but the thing is, I *meant* it when I said it. I'm crazy. I swear to God I am.

"Oh, darling, I love you too," she said. Then, right in the same damn breath, she said, "Promise me you'll let your hair grow. Crew cuts are getting corny. And your hair's so lovely."

Lovely my ass.

The show wasn't as bad as some I've seen. It was on the crappy side, though. It was about five hundred thousand years in the life of this one old couple. It starts out when they're young and all, and the girl's parents don't want her to marry the boy, but she marries him anyway. Then they keep getting older and older. The husband goes to war, and the wife has this brother that's a drunkard. I couldn't get very interested. I mean I didn't care too much when anybody in the family died or anything. They were all just a bunch of actors. The husband and wife were a pretty nice old couple—very witty and all—but I couldn't get too interested in them. For one thing, they kept drinking tea or some goddam thing all through the play. Every time you saw them, some butler was shoving some tea in front of them, or the wife was pouring it for somebody. And everybody kept coming *in* and going *out* all the time—you got dizzy watching people sit down and stand up. Alfred Lunt and Lynn Fontanne were the old couple, and they were very good, but I didn't like them much. They were different, though, I'll say that. They didn't act like people and they didn't act like actors. It's hard to explain. They acted more like they knew they were celebrities and all. I mean they were good, but they were *too* good. When one of them got finished making a speech, the other one said something very fast right after it. It was supposed to be like people really talking and interrupting each other and all. The trouble was, it was *too* much like people talking and interrupting each other. They acted a little bit the way old Ernie, down in the Village, plays the piano. If you do something *too* good, then, after a while, if you don't watch it, you start showing off. And then you're not as good any more. But anyway, they were the only ones in the show—the Lunts, I mean—that looked like they had any real brains. I have to admit it.

At the end of the first act we went out with all the other jerks for a cigarette. What a deal that was. You never saw so many phonies in all your life, everybody smoking their ears off and talking about the play so that everybody could hear and know how sharp they were. Some dopey movie actor was standing near us, having a cigarette. I don't know his name, but he always plays the part of a guy in a war movie that gets yellow before it's time to go over the top. He was with some gorgeous blonde, and the two of them were trying to be very blas and all, like as if he didn't even know people were looking at him. Modest as hell. I got a big bang out of it. Old Sally didn't talk much, except to rave about the Lunts, because she was busy rubbering and being charming. Then all of a sudden, she saw some jerk she knew on the other side of the lobby. Some guy in one of those very dark gray flannel suits and one of those checkered vests. Strictly Ivy League. Big deal. He was standing next to the wall, smoking himself to death and looking bored as hell. Old Sally kept saying, "I *know* that boy from somewhere." She always *knew* somebody, any place you took her, or thought she did. She kept saying that till I got bored as hell, and I said to her, "Why don't you go on over and give him a big soul kiss, if you know him? He'll enjoy it." She got sore when I said that. Finally, though, the jerk noticed her and came over and said hello. You should've seen the way they said hello. You'd have thought they hadn't seen each other in twenty years. You'd have thought they'd taken baths in the same bathtub or something when they were little kids. Old buddyroos. It was nauseating. The funny part was, they probably met each other just *once*, at some phony party. Finally, when they were all done slobbering around, old Sally introduced us. His name was George something—I don't even remember—and he went to Andover. Big, big deal. You should've seen him when old Sally asked him how he liked the play. He was the kind of a phony that have to give themselves *room* when they answer somebody's question. He stepped back, and stepped right on the lady's foot behind him. He probably broke every toe in her body. He said the play *itself* was no masterpiece, but that the Lunts, of course, were absolute angels. Angels. For Chrissake. *Angels*. That killed me. Then he and old Sally started talking about a lot of people they both knew. It was the phoniest conversation you ever heard in your life. They both kept thinking of places as fast as they could, then they'd think of somebody that lived there and mention their name. I was all set to puke when it was time to go sit down again. I really was. And then, when the next act was over, they *continued* their goddam boring conversation. They kept thinking of more places and more names of people that lived there. The worst part was, the jerk had one of those very phony, Ivy League voices, one of those very tired, snobby voices. He sounded just like a girl. He didn't *hes*itate to horn in on my date, the bastard. I even thought for a minute that he was going to get in the goddam cab with us when the show was over, because he walked about two blocks with us, but he had to meet a bunch of phonies for cocktails, he said. I could see them all sitting around in some bar, with their goddam checkered vests, criticizing shows and books and women in those tired, snobby voices. They kill me, those guys.

I sort of hated old Sally by the time we got in the cab, after listening to that phony Andover bastard for about ten hours. I was all set to take her home and all—I really was—but she said, "I have a marvelous idea!" She was always having a marvelous idea. "Listen," she said. "What time do you have to be home for dinner? I mean are you in a terrible hurry or anything? Do you have to be home any special time?"

"Me? No. No special time," I said. Truer word was never spoken, boy. "Why?"

"Let's go ice-skating at Radio City!"

That's the kind of ideas she always had.

"Ice-skating at Radio City? You mean right now?"

"Just for an hour or so. Don't you want to? If you don't *want* to—"

"I didn't say I didn't want to," I said. "Sure. If you want to."

"Do you mean it? Don't just *say* it if you don't mean it. I mean I don't *give* a darn, one way or the other."

Not much she didn't.

"You can rent those darling little skating skirts," old Sally said. "Jeannette Cultz did it last week."

That's why she was so hot to go. She wanted to see herself in one of those little skirts that just come down over their butt and all.

So we went, and after they gave us our skates, they gave Sally this little blue butt-twitcher of a dress to wear. She really did look damn good in it, though. I have to admit it. And don't think she didn't know it. She kept walking ahead of me, so that I'd see how cute her little ass looked. It did look pretty cute, too. I have to admit it.

The funny part was, though, we were the worst skaters on the whole goddam rink. I mean the *worst*. And there were some lulus, too. Old Sally's ankles kept bending in till they were practically on the ice. They not only looked stupid as hell, but they probably hurt like hell, too. I know mine did. Mine were killing me. We must've looked gorgeous. And what made it worse, there were at least a couple of hundred rubbernecks that didn't have anything better to do than stand around and watch everybody falling all over themselves.

"Do you want to get a table inside and have a drink or something?" I said to her finally.

"That's the most marvelous idea you've had all day," she said. She was *killing* herself. It was brutal. I really felt sorry for her.

We took off our goddam skates and went inside this bar where you can get drinks and watch the skaters in just your stocking feet. As soon as we sat down, old Sally took off her gloves, and I gave her a cigarette. She wasn't looking too happy. The waiter came up, and I ordered a Coke for her—she didn't drink—and a Scotch and soda for myself, but the sonuvabitch wouldn't bring me one, so I had a Coke, too. Then I sort of started lighting matches. I do that quite a lot when I'm in a certain mood. I sort of let them burn down till I can't hold them any more, then I drop them in the ashtray. It's a nervous habit.

Then all of a sudden, out of a clear blue sky, old Sally said, "Look. I have to know. Are you or aren't you coming over to help me trim the tree Christmas Eve? I have to know." She was still being snotty on account of her ankles when she was skating.

"I wrote you I would. You've asked me that about twenty times. Sure, I am."

"I mean I have to know," she said. She started looking all around the goddam room.

All of a sudden I quit lighting matches, and sort of leaned nearer to her over the table. I had quite a few topics on my mind. "Hey, Sally," I said.

"What?" she said. She was looking at some girl on the other side of the room.

"Did you ever get fed up?" I said. "I mean did you ever get scared that everything was going to go lousy unless you did something? I mean do you like school, and all that stuff?"

"It's a terrific *bore*."

"I mean do you hate it? I know it's a terrific bore, but do you *hate* it, is what I mean."

"Well, I don't exactly *hate* it. You always have to—"

"Well, *I* hate it. Boy, do I hate it," I said. "But it isn't just that. It's everything. I hate living in New York and all. Taxicabs, and Madison Avenue buses, with the drivers and all always yelling at you to get out at the rear door, and being introduced to phony guys that call the Lunts angels, and going up and down in elevators when you just want to go outside, and guys fitting your pants all the time at Brooks, and people always—"

"Don't shout, please," old Sally said. Which was very funny, because I wasn't even shouting.

"Take cars," I said. I said it in this very quiet voice. "Take most people, they're crazy about cars. They worry if they get a little scratch on them, and they're always talking about how many miles they get to a gallon, and if they get a brand-new car already they start thinking about trading it in for one that's even newer. I don't even like *old* cars. I mean they don't even interest me. I'd rather have a goddam horse. A horse is at least *human*, for God's sake. A horse you can at least—"

"I don't know what you're even talking about," old Sally said. "You jump from one—"

"You know something?" I said. "You're probably the only reason I'm in New York right now, or anywhere. If you weren't around, I'd probably be someplace way the hell off. In the woods or some goddam place. You're the only reason I'm around, practically."

"You're sweet," she said. But you could tell she wanted me to change the damn subject.

"You ought to go to a boys' school sometime. Try it sometime," I said. "It's full of phonies, and all you do is study so that you can learn enough to be smart enough to be able to buy a goddam Cadillac some day, and you have to keep making believe you give a damn if the football team loses, and all you do is talk about girls and liquor and sex all day, and everybody sticks together in these dirty little goddam cliques. The guys that are on the basketball team stick together, the Catholics stick together, the goddam intellectuals stick together, the guys that play bridge stick together. Even the guys that belong to the goddam Book-of-the-*Month* Club stick together. If you try to have a little intelligent—"

"Now, *lis*ten," old Sally said. "Lots of boys get more out of school than *that*."

"I agree! I agree they do, some of them! But that's all *I* get out of it. See? That's my point. That's exactly my goddam point," I said. "I don't get hardly anything out of anything. I'm in bad shape. I'm in *lousy* shape."

"You certainly are."

Then, all of a sudden, I got this idea.

"Look," I said. "Here's my idea. How would you like to get the hell out of here? Here's my idea. I know this guy down in Greenwich Village that we can borrow his car for a couple of weeks. He used to go to the same school I did and he still owes me ten bucks. What we could do is, tomorrow morning we could drive up to Massachusetts and Vermont, and all around there, see. It's beautiful as hell up there, It really is." I was getting excited as hell, the more I thought about it, and I sort of reached over and took old Sally's goddam hand. What a goddam *fool* I was. "No kidding," I said. "I have about a hundred and eighty bucks in the bank. I can take it out when it opens in the morning, and then I could go down and get this guy's car. No kidding. We'll stay in these cabin camps and stuff like that till the dough runs out. Then, when the dough runs out, I could get a job somewhere and we could live somewhere with a brook and all and, later on, we could get married or something. I could chop all our own wood in the wintertime and all. Honest to God, we could have a terrific time! Wuddaya say? C'mon! Wuddaya say? Will you do it with me? Please!"

"You can't just *do* something like that," old Sally said. She sounded sore as hell.

"Why not? Why the hell not?"

"Stop screaming at me, please," she said. Which was crap, because I wasn't even screaming at her.

"Why can'tcha? Why not?"

"Because you can't, that's all. In the first place, we're both practically *child*ren. And did you ever stop to think what you'd do if you *didn't* get a job when your money ran out? We'd *starve* to death. The whole thing's so fan*tastic*, it isn't even—"

"It isn't fantastic. I'd get a job. Don't worry about that. You don't have to worry about that. What's the matter? Don't you want to go with me? Say so, if you don't."

"It isn't *that*. It isn't that at *all*," old Sally said. I was beginning to hate her, in a way. "We'll have oodles of time to do those things—all those things. I mean after you go to college and all, and if we should get married and all. There'll be oodles of marvelous places to go to. You're just—"

"No, there wouldn't be. There wouldn't be oodles of places to go to at all. It'd be entirely different," I said. I was getting depressed as hell again.

"What?" she said. "I can't hear you. One minute you scream at me, and the next you—"

"I said no, there wouldn't be marvelous places to go to after I went to college and all. Open your ears. It'd be entirely different. We'd have to go downstairs in elevators with suitcases and stuff. We'd have to phone up everybody and tell 'em good-by and send 'em postcards from hotels and all. And I'd be working in some office, making a lot of dough, and riding to work in cabs and Madison Avenue buses, and reading newspapers, and playing bridge all the time, and going to the movies and seeing a lot of stupid shorts and coming attractions and newsreels. Newsreels. Christ almighty. There's always a dumb horse race, and some dame breaking a bottle over a ship, and some chimpanzee riding a goddam bicycle with pants on. It wouldn't be the same at all. You don't see what I mean at all."

"Maybe I don't! Maybe *you* don't, either," old Sally said. We both hated each other's guts by that time. You could see there wasn't any sense trying to have an intelligent conversation. I was sorry as hell I'd started it.

"C'mon, let's get outa here," I said. "You give me a royal pain in the ass, if you want to know the truth."

Boy, did she hit the ceiling when I said that. I know I shouldn't've said it, and I probably wouldn't've ordinarily, but she was depressing the hell out of me. Usually I never say crude things like that to girls. *Boy*, did she hit the ceiling. I apologized like a madman, but she wouldn't accept my apology. She was even crying. Which scared me a little bit, because I was a little afraid she'd go home and tell her father I called her a pain in the ass. Her father was one of those big silent bastards, and he wasn't too crazy about me anyhow. He once told old Sally I was too goddam noisy.

"No kidding. I'm sorry," I kept telling her.

"You're sorry. You're sorry. That's very funny," she said. She was still sort of crying, and all of a sudden I *did* feel sort of sorry I'd said it.

"C'mon, I'll take ya home. No kidding."

"I can go home by myself, thank you. If you think I'd let *you* take me home, you're mad. No boy ever said that to me in my entire life."

The whole thing was sort of funny, in a way, if you thought about it, and all of a sudden I did something I shouldn't have. I laughed. And I have one of these very loud, stupid laughs. I mean if I ever sat behind myself in a movie or something, I'd probably lean over and tell myself to please shut up. It made old Sally madder than ever.

I stuck around for a while, apologizing and trying to get her to excuse me, but she wouldn't. She kept telling me to go away and leave her alone. So finally I did it. I went inside and got my shoes and stuff, and left without her. I shouldn't've, but I was pretty goddam fed up by that time.

If you want to know the truth, I don't even know why I started all that stuff with her. I mean about going away somewhere, to Massachusetts and Vermont and all. I probably wouldn't've taken her even if she'd wanted to go with me. She wouldn't have been anybody to go with. The terrible part, though, is that I *meant* it when I asked her. That's the terrible part. I swear to God I'm a madman.

XVIII

When I left the skating rink I felt sort of hungry, so I went in this drugstore and had a Swiss cheese sandwich and a malted, and then I went in a phone booth. I thought maybe I might give old Jane another buzz and see if she was home yet. I mean I had the whole evening free, and I thought I'd give her a buzz and, if she was home yet, take her dancing or something somewhere. I never danced with her or anything the whole time I knew her. I saw her dancing once, though. She looked like a very good dancer. It was at this Fourth of July dance at the club. I didn't know her too well then, and I didn't think I ought to cut in on her date. She was dating this terrible guy, Al Pike, that went to Choate. I didn't know him too well, but he was always hanging around the swimming pool. He wore those white Lastex kind of swimming trunks, and he was always going off the high dive. He did the same lousy old half gainer all day long. It was the only dive he could do, but he thought he was very hot stuff. All muscles and no brains. Anyway, that's who Jane dated that night. I couldn't understand it. I swear I couldn't. After we started going around together, I asked her how come she could date a show-off bastard like Al Pike. Jane said he wasn't a show-off. She said he had an inferiority complex. She acted like she felt sorry for him or something, and she wasn't just putting it on. She meant it. It's a funny thing about girls. Every time you mention some guy that's strictly a bastard—very mean, or very conceited and all—and when you mention it to the girl, she'll tell you he has an inferiority complex.

Maybe he *has*, but that still doesn't keep him from being a bastard, in my opinion. Girls. You never know what they're going to think. I once got this girl Roberta Walsh's roommate a date with a friend of mine. His name was Bob Robinson and *he really* had an inferiority complex. You could tell he was very ashamed of his parents and all, because they said "he don't" and "she don't" and stuff like that and they weren't very wealthy. But he wasn't a bastard or anything. He was a very nice guy. But this Roberta Walsh's roommate didn't like him at all. She told Roberta he was too conceited—and the *reason* she thought he was conceited was because he happened to mention to her that he was captain of the debating team. A little thing like that, and she thought he was conceited! The trouble with girls is, if they like a boy, no matter how big a bastard he is, they'll say he has an inferiority complex, and if they *don't* like him, no matter how nice a guy he is, or how big an inferiority complex he has, they'll say he's conceited. Even smart girls do it.

Anyway, I gave old Jane a buzz again, but her phone didn't answer, so I had to hang up. Then I had to look through my address book to see who the hell might be available for the evening. The trouble was, though, my address book only has about three people in it. Jane, and this man, Mr. Antolini, that was my teacher at Elkton Hills, and my father's office number. I keep forgetting to put people's names in. So what I did finally, I gave old Carl Luce a buzz. He graduated from the Whooton School after I left. He was about three years older than I was, and I didn't like him too much, but he was one of these very intellectual guys—he had the highest I.Q. of any boy at Whooton—and I thought he might want to have dinner with me somewhere and have a slightly intellectual conversation. He was very enlightening sometimes. So I gave him a buzz. He went to Columbia now, but he lived on 65th Street and all, and I knew he'd be home. When I got him on the phone, he said he couldn't make it for dinner but that he'd meet me for a drink at ten o'clock at the Wicker Bar, on 54th. I think he was pretty surprised to hear from me. I once called him a fat-assed phony.

I had quite a bit of time to kill till ten o'clock, so what I did, I went to the movies at Radio City. It was probably the worst thing I could've done, but it was near, and I couldn't think of anything else.

I came in when the goddam stage show was on. The Rockettes were kicking their heads off, the way they do when they're all in line with their arms around each other's waist. The audience applauded like mad, and some guy behind me kept saying to his wife, "You know what that is? That's precision." He killed me. Then, after the Rockettes, a guy came out in a tuxedo and roller skates on, and started skating under a bunch of little tables, and telling jokes while he did it. He was a very good skater and all, but I couldn't enjoy it much because I kept picturing him *pract*icing to be a guy that roller-skates on the stage. It seemed so stupid. I guess I just wasn't in the right mood. Then, after him, they had this Christmas thing they have at Radio City every year. All these angels start coming out of the boxes and everywhere, guys carrying crucifixes and stuff all over the place, and the whole bunch of them—*thousands* of them—singing "Come All Ye Faithful!" like mad. Big deal. It's supposed to be religious as hell, I know, and very pretty and all, but I can't see anything religious or pretty, for God's sake, about a bunch of actors carrying crucifixes all over the stage. When they were all finished and started going out the boxes again, you could tell they could hardly wait to get a cigarette or something. I saw it with old Sally Hayes the year before, and she kept saying how beautiful it was, the costumes and all. I said old Jesus probably would've puked if He could see it—all those fancy costumes and all. Sally said I was a sacrilegious atheist. I probably am. The thing Jesus *really* would've liked would be the guy that plays the kettle drums in the orchestra. I've watched that guy since I was about eight years old. My brother Allie and I, if we were with our parents and all, we used to move our seats and go way down so we could watch him. He's the best drummer I ever saw. He only gets a chance to bang them a couple of times during a whole piece, but he never looks bored when he isn't doing it. Then when he does bang them, he does it so nice and sweet, with this nervous expression on his face. One time when we went to Washington with my father, Allie sent him a postcard, but I'll bet he never got it. We weren't too sure how to address it.

After the Christmas thing was over, the goddam picture started. It was so putrid I couldn't take my eyes off it. It was about this English guy, Alec something, that was in the war and loses his memory in the hospital and all. He comes out of the hospital carrying a cane and limping all over the place, all over London, not knowing who the hell he is. He's really a duke, but he doesn't know it. Then he meets this nice, homey, sincere girl getting on a bus. Her goddam hat blows off and he catches it, and then they go upstairs and sit down and start talking about Charles Dickens. He's both their favorite author and all. He's carrying this copy of *Oliver Twist* and so's she. I could've puked. Anyway, they fall in love right away, on account of they're both so nuts about Charles Dickens and all, and he helps her run her publishing business. She's a publisher, the girl. Only, she's not doing so hot, because her brother's a drunkard and he spends all their dough. He's a very bitter guy, the brother, because he was a doctor in the war and now he can't operate any more because his nerves are shot, so he boozes all the time, but he's pretty witty and all. Anyway, old Alec writes a book, and this girl publishes it, and they both make a hatful of dough on it. They're all set to get married when this other girl, old Marcia, shows up. Marcia was Alec's fiancée before he lost his memory, and she recognizes him when he's in this store autographing books. She tells old Alec he's really a duke and all, but he doesn't believe her and doesn't want to go with her to visit his mother and all. His mother's blind as a bat. But the other girl, the homey one, makes him go. She's very noble and all. So he goes. But he still doesn't get his memory back, even when his great Dane jumps all over him and his mother sticks her fingers all over his face and brings him this teddy bear he used to slobber around with when he was a kid. But then, one day, some kids are playing cricket on the lawn and he gets smacked in the head with a cricket ball. Then right away he gets his goddam memory back and he goes in and kisses his mother on the forehead and all. Then he starts being a regular duke again, and he forgets all about the homey babe that has the publishing business. I'd tell you the rest of the story, but I might puke if I did. It isn't that I'd *spoil* it for you or anything. There isn't anything to *spoil*, for Chrissake. Anyway, it ends up with Alec and the homey babe getting married, and the brother that's a drunkard gets his nerves back and operates on Alec's mother so she can see again, and then the drunken brother and old Marcia go for each other. It ends up with everybody at this long dinner table laughing their asses off because the great Dane comes in with a bunch of puppies. Everybody thought it was a male, I suppose, or some goddam thing. All I can say is, don't see it if you don't want to puke all over yourself.

The part that got me was, there was a lady sitting next to me that cried all through the goddam picture. The phonier it got, the more she cried. You'd have thought she did it because she was kindhearted as hell, but I was sitting right next to her, and she wasn't. She had this little kid with her that was bored as hell and had to go to the bathroom, but she wouldn't take him. She kept telling him to sit still and behave himself. She was about as kindhearted as a goddam wolf. You take somebody that cries their goddam eyes out over phony stuff in the movies, and nine times out of ten they're mean bastards at heart. I'm not kidding.

After the movie was over, I started walking down to the Wicker Bar, where I was supposed to meet old Carl Luce, and while I walked I sort of thought about war and all. Those war movies always do that to me. I don't think I could stand it if I had to go to war. I really couldn't. It wouldn't be too bad if they'd just take you out and shoot you or something, but you have to stay in the *Army* so goddam long. That's the whole trouble. My brother D.B. was in the Army for four goddam years. He was in the war, too—he landed on D-Day and all—but I really think he hated the Army worse than the war. I was practically a child at the time, but I remember when he used to come home on furlough and all, all he did was lie on his bed, practically. He hardly ever even came in the living room. Later, when he went overseas and was in the war and all, he didn't get wounded or anything and he didn't have to shoot anybody. All he had to do was drive some cowboy general around all day in a command car. He once told Allie and I that if he'd had to shoot anybody, he wouldn't've known which direction to shoot in. He said the Army was practically as full of bastards as the Nazis were. I remember Allie once asked him wasn't it sort of good that he was in the war because he was a writer and it gave him a lot to write about and all. He made Allie go get his baseball mitt and then he asked him who was the best war poet, Rupert Brooke or Emily Dickinson. Allie said Emily Dickinson. I don't know too much about it myself, because I don't read much poetry, but I *do* know it'd drive me crazy if I had to be in the Army and be with a bunch of guys like Ackley and Stradlater and old Maurice all the time, marching with them and all. I was in the Boy Scouts once, for about a week, and I couldn't even stand looking at the back of the guy's neck in front of me. They kept telling you to look at the back of the guy's neck in front of you. I swear if there's ever another war, they better just take me out and stick me in front of a firing squad. I wouldn't object. What gets me about D.B., though, he hated the war so much, and yet he got me to read this book *A Farewell to Arms* last summer. He said it was so terrific. That's what I can't understand. It had this guy in it named Lieutenant Henry that was supposed to be a nice guy and all. I don't see how D.B. could hate the Army and war and all so much and still like a phony like that. I mean, for instance, I don't see how he could like a phony book like that and still like that one by Ring Lardner, or that other one he's so crazy about, *The Great Gatsby*. D.B. got sore when I said that, and said I was too young and all to appreciate it, but I don't think so. I told him I liked Ring Lardner and *The Great Gatsby* and all. I did, too. I was crazy about *The Great Gatsby*. Old Gatsby. Old sport. That killed me. Anyway, I'm sort of glad they've got the atomic bomb invented. If there's ever another war, I'm going to sit right the hell on top of it. I'll volunteer for it, I swear to God I will.

XIX

In case you don't live in New York, the Wicker Bar is in this sort of swanky hotel, the Seton Hotel. I used to go there quite a lot, but I don't any more. I gradually cut it out. It's one of those places that are supposed to be very sophisticated and all, and the phonies are coming in the window. They used to have these two French babes, Tina and Janine, come out and play the piano and sing about three times every night. One of them played the piano—strictly lousy—and the other one sang, and most of the songs were either pretty dirty or in French. The one that sang, old Janine, was always whispering into the goddam microphone before she sang. She'd say, "And now we like to geeve you our impression of Vooly Voo Fransay. Eet ees the story of a leetle Fransh girl who comes to a beeg ceety, just like New York, and falls een love wees a leetle boy from Brookleen. We hope you like eet." Then, when she was all done whispering and being cute as hell, she'd sing some dopey song, half in English and half in French, and drive all the phonies in the place mad with joy. If you sat around there long enough and heard all the phonies applauding and all, you got to hate everybody in the world, I swear you did. The bartender was a louse, too. He was a big snob. He didn't talk to you at all hardly unless you were a big shot or a celebrity or something. If you *were* a big shot or a celebrity or something, then he was even more nauseating. He'd go up to you and say, with this big charming smile, like he was a helluva swell guy if you knew him, "Well! How's Connecticut?" or "How's Florida?" It was a terrible place, I'm not kidding. I cut out going there entirely, gradually.

It was pretty early when I got there. I sat down at the bar—it was pretty crowded—and had a couple of Scotch and sodas before old Luce even showed up. I stood up when I ordered them so they could see how tall I was and all and not think I was a goddam minor. Then I watched the phonies for a while. Some guy next to me was snowing hell out of the babe he was with. He kept telling her she had aristocratic hands. That killed me. The other end of the bar was full of flits. They weren't too flitty-looking—I mean they didn't have their hair too long or anything—but you could tell they were flits anyway. Finally old Luce showed up.

Old Luce. What a guy. He was supposed to be my Student Adviser when I was at Whooton. The only thing he ever did, though, was give these sex talks and all, late at night when there was a bunch of guys in his room. He knew quite a bit about sex, especially perverts and all. He was always telling us about a lot of creepy guys that go around having affairs with sheep, and guys that go around with girls' pants sewed in the lining of their hats and all. And flits and Lesbians. Old Luce knew who every flit and Lesbian in the United States was. All you had to do was mention somebody—*any*body—and old Luce'd tell you if he was a flit or not. Sometimes it was hard to believe, the people he said were flits and Lesbians and all, movie actors and like that. Some of the ones he said were flits were even married, for God's sake. You'd keep saying to him, "You mean Joe Blow's a flit? Joe *Blow*? That big, tough guy that plays gangsters and cowboys all the time?" Old Luce'd say, "Certainly." He was always saying "Certainly." He said it didn't matter if a guy was married or not. He said half the married guys in the world were flits and didn't even know it. He said you could turn into one practically overnight, if you had all the traits and all. He used to scare the hell out of us. I kept waiting to turn into a flit or something. The funny thing about old Luce, I used to think he was sort of flitty himself, in a way. He was always saying, "Try this for size," and then he'd goose the hell out of you while you were going down the corridor. And whenever he went to the can, he always left the goddam door open and *talked* to you while you were brushing your teeth or something. That stuff's sort of flitty. It really is. I've known quite a few real flits, at schools and all, and they're always doing stuff like that, and that's why I always had my doubts about old Luce. He was a pretty intelligent guy, though. He really was.

He never said hello or anything when he met you. The first thing he said when he sat down was that he could only stay a couple of minutes. He said he had a date. Then he ordered a dry Martini. He told the bartender to make it very dry, and no olive.

"Hey, I got a flit for you," I told him. "At the end of the bar. Don't look now. I been saving him for ya."

"Very funny," he said. "Same old Caulfield. When are you going to grow up?"

I bored him a lot. I really did. He amused me, though. He was one of those guys that sort of amuse me a lot.

"How's your sex life?" I asked him. He hated you to ask him stuff like that.

"Relax," he said. "Just sit back and relax, for Chrissake."

"I'm relaxed," I said. "How's Columbia? Ya like it?"

"Certainly I like it. If I didn't like it I wouldn't have gone there," he said. He could be pretty boring himself sometimes.

"What're you majoring in?" I asked him. "Perverts?" I was only horsing around.

"What're you trying to be—funny?"

"No. I'm only kidding," I said. "Listen, hey, Luce. You're one of these intellectual guys. I need your advice. I'm in a terrific—"

He let out this big groan on me. "*Lis*ten, Caulfield. If you want to sit here and have a quiet, peaceful drink and a *quiet*, peaceful conver—"

"All right, all right," I said. "Relax." You could tell he didn't feel like discussing anything serious with me. That's the trouble with these intellectual guys. They never want to discuss anything serious unless *they* feel like it. So all I did was, I started discussing topics in general with him. "No kidding, how's your sex life?" I asked him. "You still going around with that same babe you used to at Whooton? The one with the terrffic—"

"Good God, no," he said.

"How come? What happened to her?"

"I haven't the *faint*est idea. For all I know, since you ask, she's probably the Whore of New Hampshire by this time."

"That isn't nice. If she was decent enough to let you get sexy with her all the time, you at least shouldn't talk about her that way."

"Oh, God!" old Luce said. "Is this going to be a typical Caulfield conversation? I want to know right now."

"No," I said, "but it isn't nice anyway. If she was decent and nice enough to let you—"

"*Must* we pursue this horrible trend of thought?"

I didn't say anything. I was sort of afraid he'd get up and leave on me if I didn't shut up. So all I did was, I ordered another drink. I felt like getting stinking drunk.

"Who're you going around with now?" I asked him. "You feel like telling me?"

"Nobody you know."

"Yeah, but who? I might know her."

"Girl lives in the Village. Sculptress. If you must know."

"Yeah? No kidding? How old is she?"

"I've never *asked* her, for God's sake."

"Well, around how old?"

"I should imagine she's in her late thirties," old Luce said.

"In her late *thirties*? Yeah? You like that?" I asked him. "You like 'em that old?" The reason I was asking was because he really knew quite a bit about sex and all. He was one of the few guys I knew that did. He lost his virginity when he was only fourteen, in Nantucket. He really did.

"I like a mature person, if that's what you mean. Certainly."

"You do? Why? No kidding, they better for sex and all?"

"Listen. Let's get one thing straight. I refuse to answer any typical Caulfield questions tonight. When in *hell* are you going to grow up?"

I didn't say anything for a while. I let it drop for a while. Then old Luce ordered another Martini and told the bartender to make it a lot dryer.

"Listen. How long you been going around with her, this sculpture babe?" I asked him. I was really interested. "Did you know her when you were at Whooton?"

"Hardly. She just arrived in this country a few months ago."

"She did? Where's she from?"

"She happens to be from Shanghai."

"No kidding! She Chi*nese*, for Chrissake?"

"Obviously."

"No kidding! Do you like that? Her being Chinese?"

"Obviously."

"Why? I'd be interested to know—I really would."

"I simply happen to find Eastern philosophy more satisfactory than Western. Since you *ask*."

"You do? Wuddaya mean 'philosophy'? Ya mean sex and all? You mean it's better in China? That what you mean?"

"Not necessarily in *China*, for God's sake. The *East* I said. Must we go on with this inane conversation?"

"Listen, I'm serious," I said. "No kidding. Why's it better in the East?"

"It's too involved to go into, for God's sake," old Luce said. "They simply happen to regard sex as both a physical and a spiritual experience. If you think I'm—"

"So do I! So do I regard it as a wuddayacallit—a physical and spiritual experience and all. I really do. But it depends on who the hell I'm doing it with. If I'm doing it with somebody I don't even—"

"Not so *loud*, for God's sake, Caulfield. If you can't manage to keep your voice down, let's drop the whole—"

"All right, but listen," I said. I was getting excited and I *was* talking a little too loud. Sometimes I talk a little loud when I get excited. "This is what I mean, though," I said. "I know it's supposed to be physical and spiritual, and artistic and all. But what I mean is, you can't do it with *everybody*—every girl you neck with and all—and make it come out that way. Can you?"

"Let's drop it," old Luce said. "Do you mind?"

"All right, but listen. Take you and this Chinese babe. What's so good about you two?"

"*Drop* it, I said."

I was getting a little too personal. I realize that. But that was one of the annoying things about Luce. When we were at Whooton, he'd make you describe the most personal stuff that happened to *you*, but if you started asking *him* questions about *him*self, he got sore. These intellectual guys don't like to have an intellectual conversation with you unless they're running the whole thing. They always want you to shut up when *they* shut up, and go back to your room when they go back to *their* room. When I was at Whooton old Luce used to hate it—you really could tell he did—when after he was finished giving this sex talk to a bunch of us in his room we stuck around and chewed the fat by ourselves for a while. I mean the other guys and myself. In somebody else's room. Old Luce hated that. He always wanted everybody to go back to their own room and shut up when he was finished being the big shot. The thing he was afraid of, he was afraid somebody'd say something smarter than *he* had. He really amused me.

"Maybe I'll go to China. My sex life is lousy," I said.

"Naturally. Your mind is immature."

"It is. It really is. I know it," I said. "You know what the trouble with me is? I can never get really sexy—I mean *really* sexy—with a girl I don't like a lot. I mean I have to *like* her a lot. If I don't, I sort of lose my goddam desire for her and all. Boy, it really screws up my sex life something awful. My sex life stinks."

"Naturally it does, for God's sake. I told you the last time I saw you what you need."

"You mean to go to a psychoanalyst and all?" I said. That's what he'd told me I ought to do. His father was a psychoanalyst and all.

"It's up to you, for God's sake. It's none of my goddam business what you do with your life."

I didn't say anything for a while. I was thinking.

"Supposing I went to your father and had him psychoanalyze me and all," I said. "What would he do to me? I mean what would he do to me?"

"He wouldn't do a goddam thing to you. He'd simply talk to you, and you'd talk to him, for God's sake. For one thing, he'd help you to recognize the patterns of your mind."

"That what?"

"The patterns of your mind. Your mind runs in—Listen. I'm not giving an elementary course in psychoanalysis. If you're interested, call him up and make an appointment. If you're not, don't. I couldn't care less, frankly."

I put my hand on his shoulder. Boy, he amused me. "You're a real friendly bastard," I told him. "You know that?"

He was looking at his wrist watch. "I have to tear," he said, and stood up. "Nice seeing you." He got the bartender and told him to bring him his check.

"Hey," I said, just before he beat it. "Did your father ever psychoanalyze you?"

"Me? Why do you ask?"

"No reason. Did he, though? Has he?"

"Not exactly. He's helped me to ad*just* myself to a certain extent, but an extensive analysis hasn't been necessary. Why do you ask?"

"No reason. I was just wondering."

"Well. Take it easy," he said. He was leaving his tip and all and he was starting to go.

"Have just one more drink," I told him. "Please. I'm lonesome as hell. No kidding."

He said he couldn't do it, though. He said he was late now, and then he left.

Old Luce. He was strictly a pain in the ass, but he certainly had a good vocabulary. He had the largest vocabulary of any boy at Whooton when I was there. They gave us a test.

XX

I kept sitting there getting drunk and waiting for old Tina and Janine to come out and do their stuff, but they weren't there. A flitty-looking guy with wavy hair came out and played the piano, and then this new babe, Valencia, came out and sang. She wasn't any good, but she was better than old Tina and Janine, and at least she sang good songs. The piano was right next to the bar where I was sitting and all, and old Valencia was standing practically right next to me. I sort of gave her the old eye, but she pretended she didn't even see me. I probably wouldn't have done it, but I was getting drunk as hell. When she was finished, she beat it out of the room so fast I didn't even get a chance to invite her to join me for a drink, so I called the headwaiter over. I told him to ask old Valencia if she'd care to join me for a drink. He said he would, but he probably didn't even give her my message. People never give your message to anybody.

Boy, I sat at that goddam bar till around one o'clock or so, getting drunk as a bastard. I could hardly see straight. The one thing I did, though, I was careful as hell not to get boisterous or anything. I didn't want anybody to notice me or anything or ask how old I was. But, boy, I could hardly see straight. When I was *really* drunk, I started that stupid business with the bullet in my guts again. I was the only guy at the bar with a bullet in their guts. I kept putting my hand under my jacket, on my stomach and all, to keep the blood from dripping all over the place. I didn't want anybody to know I was even wounded. I was con*ceal*ing the fact that

I was a wounded sonuvabitch. Finally what I felt like, I felt like giving old Jane a buzz and see if she was home yet. So I paid my check and all. Then I left the bar and went out where the telephones were. I kept keeping my hand under my jacket to keep the blood from dripping. Boy, was I drunk.

But when I got inside this phone booth, I wasn't much in the mood any more to give old Jane a buzz. I was too drunk, I guess. So what I did, I gave old Sally Hayes a buzz.

I had to dial about twenty numbers before I got the right one. Boy, was I blind.

"Hello," I said when somebody answered the goddam phone. I sort of yelled it, I was so drunk.

"Who is this?" this very cold lady's voice said.

"This is me. Holden Caulfield. Lemme speaka Sally, please."

"Sally's *asleep*. This is Sally's grandmother. Why are you calling at this hour, Holden? Do you know what time it is?"

"Yeah. Wanna talka Sally. Very important. Put her on."

"Sally's *asleep*, young man. Call her tomorrow. Good night."

"Wake 'er up! Wake 'er up, hey. Attaboy."

Then there was a different voice. "Holden, this is me." It was old Sally. "What's the big idea?"

"Sally? That you?"

"Yes—stop screaming. Are you drunk?"

"Yeah. Listen. Listen, hey. I'll come over Christmas Eve. Okay? Trimma goddam tree for ya. Okay? Okay, hey, Sally?"

"Yes. You're drunk. Go to bed now. Where are you? Who's with you?"

"Sally? I'll come over and trimma tree for ya, okay? Okay, hey?"

"*Yes.* Go to bed now. Where are you? Who's with you?"

"Nobody. Me, myself and I." Boy was I drunk! I was even still holding onto my guts. "They got me. Rocky's mob got me. You know that? Sally, you know that?"

"I can't hear you. Go to bed now. I have to go. Call me tomorrow."

"Hey, Sally! You want me trimma tree for ya? Ya want me to? *Huh?*"

"Yes. Good night. Go home and go to bed."

She hung up on me.

"G'night. G'night, Sally baby. Sally sweetheart darling," I said. Can you imagine how drunk I was? I hung up too, then. I figured she probably just came home from a date. I pictured her out with the Lunts and all somewhere, and that Andover jerk. All of them swimming around in a goddam pot of tea and saying sophisticated stuff to each other and being charming and phony. I wished to God I hadn't even phoned her. When I'm drunk, I'm a madman.

I stayed in the damn phone booth for quite a while. I kept holding onto the phone, sort of, so I wouldn't pass out. I wasn't feeling too marvelous, to tell you the truth. Finally, though, I came out and went in the men's room, staggering around like a moron, and filled one of the washbowls with cold water. Then I dunked my head in it, right up to the ears. I didn't even bother to dry it or anything. I just let the sonuvabitch drip. Then I walked over to this radiator by the window and sat down on it. It was nice and warm. It felt good because I was shivering like a bastard. It's a funny thing, I always shiver like hell when I'm drunk.

I didn't have anything else to do, so I kept sitting on the radiator and counting these little white squares on the floor. I was getting soaked. About a gallon of water was dripping down my neck, getting all over my collar and tie and all, but I didn't give a damn. I was too drunk to give a damn. Then, pretty soon, the guy that played the piano for old Valencia, this very wavy-haired, flitty-looking guy, came in to comb his golden locks. We sort of struck up a conversation while he was combing it, except that he wasn't too goddam friendly.

"Hey. You gonna see that Valencia babe when you go back in the bar?" I asked him.

"It's highly probable," he said. Witty bastard. All I ever meet is witty bastards.

"Listen. Give her my compliments. Ask her if that goddam waiter gave her my message, willya?"

"Why don't you go home, Mac? How old are you, anyway?"

"Eighty-six. Listen. Give her my compliments. Okay?"

"Why don't you go home, Mac?"

"Not me. Boy, you can play that goddam piano." I told him. I was just flattering him. He played the piano stinking, if you want to know the truth. "You oughta go on the radio," I said. "Handsome chap like you. All those goddam golden locks. Ya need a manager?"

"Go home, Mac, like a good guy. Go home and hit the sack."

"No home to go to. No kidding—you need a manager?"

He didn't answer me. He just went out. He was all through combing his hair and patting it and all, so he left. Like Stradlater. All these handsome guys are the same. When they're done combing their goddam hair, they beat it on you.

When I finally got down off the radiator and went out to the hat-check room, I was crying and all. I don't know why, but I was. I guess it was because I was feeling so damn depressed and lonesome. Then, when I went out to the checkroom, I couldn't find my goddam check. The hat-check girl was very nice about it, though. She gave me my coat anyway. And my "Little Shirley Beans" record—I still had it with me and all. I gave her a buck for being so nice, but she wouldn't take it. She kept telling me to go home and go to bed. I sort of tried to make a date with her for when she got through working, but she wouldn't do it. She said she was old enough to be my mother and all. I showed her my goddam gray hair and told her I was forty-two—I was only horsing around, naturally. She was nice, though. I showed her my goddam red hunting hat, and she liked it. She made me put it on before I went out, because my hair was still pretty wet. She was all right.

I didn't feel too drunk any more when I went outside, but it was getting very cold out again, and my teeth started chattering like hell. I couldn't make them stop. I walked over to Madison Avenue and started to wait around for a bus because I didn't have hardly any money left and I had to start economizing on cabs and all. But I didn't feel like getting on a damn bus. And besides, I didn't even know where I was supposed to go. So what I did, I started walking over to the park. I figured I'd go by that little lake and see what the hell the ducks were doing, see if they were around or not, I still didn't know if they were around or not. It wasn't far over to the park, and I didn't have anyplace else special to go to—I didn't even know where I was going to *sleep* yet—so I went. I wasn't tired or anything. I just felt blue as hell.

Then something terrible happened just as I got in the park. I dropped old Phoebe's record. It broke into about fifty pieces. It was in a big envelope and all, but it broke anyway. I damn near cried, it made me feel so terrible, but all I did was, I took the pieces out of the envelope and put them in my coat pocket. They weren't any good for anything, but I didn't feel like just throwing them away. Then I went in the park. Boy, was it dark.

I've lived in New York all my life, and I know Central Park like the back of my hand, because I used to roller-skate there all the time and ride my bike when I was a kid, but I had the most terrific trouble finding that lagoon that night. I *knew* right where it was—it was right near Central Park South and all—but I still couldn't find it. I must've been drunker than I thought. I kept walking and walking, and it kept getting darker and darker and spookier and spookier. I didn't see one person the whole time I was in the park. I'm just as glad. I probably would've jumped about a mile if I had. Then, finally, I found it. What it was, it was partly frozen and partly not frozen. But I didn't see any ducks around. I walked all around the whole damn lake—I damn near fell *in* once, in fact—but I didn't see a single duck. I thought maybe if there *were* any around, they might be asleep or something near the edge of the water, near the grass and all. That's how I nearly fell in. But I couldn't find any.

Finally I sat down on this bench, where it wasn't so goddam dark. Boy, I was still shivering like a bastard, and the back of my hair, even though I had my hunting hat on, was sort of full of little hunks of ice. That worried me. I thought probably I'd get pneumonia and die. I started picturing millions of jerks coming to my funeral and all. My grandfather from Detroit, that keeps calling out the numbers of the streets when you ride on a goddam bus with him, and my aunts—I have about fifty aunts—and all my lousy cousins. What a mob'd be there. They all came when Allie died, the whole goddam stupid bunch of them. I have this one stupid aunt with halitosis that kept saying how *peace*ful he looked lying there, D.B. told me. I wasn't there. I was still in the hospital. I had to go to the hospital and all after I hurt my hand. Anyway, I kept worrying that I was getting pneumonia, with all those hunks of ice in my hair, and that I was going to die. I felt sorry as hell for my mother and father. Especially my mother, because she still isn't over my brother Allie yet. I kept picturing her not knowing what to do with all my suits and athletic equipment and all. The only good thing, I knew she wouldn't let old Phoebe come to my goddam funeral because she was only a little kid. That was the only good part. Then I thought about the whole bunch of them sticking me in a goddam cemetery and all, with my name on this tombstone and all. Surrounded by dead guys. Boy, when you're dead, they really fix you up. I hope to hell when I *do* die somebody has sense enough to just dump me in the river or something. Anything except sticking me in a goddam cemetery. People coming and putting a bunch of flowers on your stomach on Sunday, and all that crap. Who wants flowers when you're dead? Nobody.

When the weather's nice, my parents go out quite frequently and stick a bunch of flowers on old Allie's grave. I went with them a couple of times, but I cut it out. In the first place, I certainly don't enjoy seeing him in that crazy cemetery. Surrounded by dead guys and tombstones and all. It wasn't too bad when the sun was out, but twice—*twice*—we were there when it started to rain. It was awful. It rained on his lousy tombstone, and it rained on the grass on his stomach. It rained all over the place. All the visitors that were visiting the cemetery started running like hell over to their cars. That's what nearly drove me crazy. All the visitors could get in their cars and turn on their radios and all and then go someplace nice for dinner—everybody except Allie. I couldn't stand it. I know it's only his body and all that's in the cemetery, and his soul's in Heaven and all that crap, but I couldn't stand it anyway. I just wish he wasn't there. You didn't know him. If you'd known him, you'd know what I mean. It's not too bad when the sun's out, but the sun only comes out when it feels like coming out.

After a while, just to get my mind off getting pneumonia and all, I took out my dough and tried to count it in the lousy light from the street lamp. All I had was three singles and five quarters and a nickel left—boy, I spent a fortune since I left Pencey. Then what I did, I went down near the lagoon and I sort of skipped the quarters and the nickel across it, where it wasn't frozen. I don't know why I did it, but I did it. I guess I thought it'd take my mind off getting pneumonia and dying. It didn't, though.

I started thinking how old Phoebe would feel if I got pneumonia and died. It was a childish way to think, but I couldn't stop myself. She'd feel pretty bad if something like that happened. She likes me a lot. I mean she's quite fond of me. She really is. Anyway, I couldn't get that off my mind, so finally what I figured I'd do, I figured I'd better sneak home and see her, in case I died and all. I had my door key with me and all, and I figured what I'd do, I'd sneak in the apartment, very quiet and all, and just sort of chew the fat with her for a while. The only thing that worried me was our front door. It creaks like a bastard. It's a pretty old apartment house, and the superintendent's a lazy bastard, and everything creaks and squeaks. I was afraid my parents might hear me sneaking in. But I decided I'd try it anyhow.

So I got the hell out of the park, and went home. I walked all the way. It wasn't too far, and I wasn't tired or even drunk any more. It was just very cold and nobody around anywhere.

XXI

The best break I had in years, when I got home the regular night elevator boy, Pete, wasn't on the car. Some new guy I'd never seen was on the car, so I figured that if I didn't bump smack into my parents and all I'd be able to say hello to old Phoebe and then beat it and nobody'd even know I'd been around. It was really a terrific break. What made it even better, the new elevator boy was sort of on the stupid side. I told him, in this very casual voice, to take me up to the Dicksteins'. The Dicksteins were these people that had the other apartment on our floor. I'd already taken off my hunting hat, so as not to look suspicious or anything. I went in the elevator like I was in a terrific hurry.

He had the elevator doors all shut and all, and was all set to take me up, and then he turned around and said, "They ain't in. They're at a party on the fourteenth floor."

"That's all right," I said. "I'm supposed to wait for them. I'm their nephew."

He gave me this sort of stupid, suspicious look. "You better wait in the lobby, fella," he said.

"I'd like to—I really would," I said. "But I have a bad leg. I have to hold it in a certain position. I think I'd better sit down in the chair outside their door."

He didn't know what the hell I was talking about, so all he said was "Oh" and took me up. Not bad, boy. It's funny. All you have to do is say something nobody understands and they'll do practically anything you want them to.

I got off at our floor—limping like a bastard—and started walking over toward the Dicksteins' side. Then, when I heard the elevator doors shut, I turned around and went over to our side. I was doing all right. I didn't even feel drunk anymore. Then I took out my door key and opened our door, quiet as hell. Then, very, very carefully and all, I went inside and closed the door. I really should've been a crook.

It was dark as hell in the foyer, naturally, and naturally I couldn't turn on any lights. I had to be careful not to bump into anything and make a racket. I certainly knew I was home, though. Our foyer has a funny smell that doesn't smell like anyplace else. I don't know what the hell it is. It isn't cauliflower and it isn't perfume—I don't know what the hell it is—but you always know you're home. I started to take off my coat and hang it up in the foyer closet, but that closet's full of hangers that rattle like madmen when you open the door, so I left it on. Then I started walking very, very slowly back toward old Phoebe's room. I knew the maid wouldn't hear me because she had only one eardrum. She had this brother that stuck a straw down her ear when she was a kid, she once told me. She was pretty deaf and all. But my *par*ents, especially my mother, she has ears like a goddam bloodhound. So I took it very, very easy when I went past their door. I even held my breath, for God's sake. You can hit my father over the head with a chair and he won't wake up, but my mother, all you have to do to my mother is cough somewhere in Siberia and she'll hear you. She's nervous as hell. Half the time she's up all night smoking cigarettes.

Finally, after about an hour, I got to old Phoebe's room. She wasn't there, though. I forgot about that. I forgot she always sleeps in D.B.'s room when he's away in Hollywood or some place. She likes it because it's the biggest room in the house. Also because it has this big old madman desk in it that D.B. bought off some lady alcoholic in Philadelphia, and this big, gigantic bed that's about ten miles wide and ten miles long. I don't know where he bought that bed. Anyway, old Phoebe likes to sleep in D.B.'s room when he's away, and he lets her. You ought to see her doing her homework or something at that crazy desk. It's almost as big as the bed. You can hardly see her when she's doing her homework. That's the kind of stuff she likes, though. She doesn't like her own room because it's too little, she says. She says she likes to spread out. That kills me. What's old Phoebe got to spread out? Nothing.

Anyway, I went into D.B.'s room quiet as hell, and turned on the lamp on the desk. Old Phoebe didn't even wake up. When the light was on and all, I sort of looked at her for a while. She was laying there asleep, with her face sort of on the side of the pillow. She had her mouth way open. It's funny. You take adults, they look lousy when they're asleep and they have their mouths way open, but kids don't. Kids look all right. They can even have spit all over the pillow and they still look all right.

I went around the room, very quiet and all, looking at stuff for a while. I felt swell, for a change. I didn't even feel like I was getting pneumonia or anything any more. I just felt good, for a change. Old Phoebe's clothes were on this chair right next to the bed. She's very neat, for a child. I mean she doesn't just throw her stuff around, like some kids. She's no slob. She had the jacket to this tan suit my mother bought her in Canada hung up on the back of the chair. Then her blouse and stuff were on the seat. Her shoes and socks were on the floor, right underneath the chair, right next to each other. I never saw the shoes before. They were new. They were these dark brown loafers, sort of like this pair I have, and they went swell with that suit my mother bought her in Canada. My mother dresses her nice. She really does. My mother has terrific taste in some things. She's no good at buying ice skates or anything like that, but clothes, she's perfect. I mean Phoebe always has some dress on that can kill you. You take most little kids, even if their parents are wealthy and all, they usually have some terrible dress on. I wish you could see old Phoebe in that suit my mother bought her in Canada. I'm not kidding.

I sat down on old D.B.'s desk and looked at the stuff on it. It was mostly Phoebe's stuff, from school and all. Mostly books. The one on top was called *Arithmetic Is Fun!* I sort of opened the first page and took a look at it. This is what old Phoebe had on it:

Phoebe Weatherfield Caulfield

4B-1

That killed me. Her middle name is Josephine, for God's sake, not Weatherfield. She doesn't like it, though. Every time I see her she's got a new middle name for herself.

The book underneath the arithmetic was a geography, and the book under the geography was a speller. She's very good in spelling. She's very good in all her subjects, but she's best in spelling. Then, under the speller, there were a bunch of notebooks. She has about five thousand notebooks. You never saw a kid with so many notebooks. I opened the one on top and looked at the first page. It had on it:

> *Bernice meet me at recess I have something*
> *very very important to tell you.*

That was all there was on that page. The next one had on it:

> *Why has south eastern Alaska so many caning factories?*
> *Because theres so much salmon*
> *Why has it valuable forests?*

because it has the right climate.
What has our government done to make
life easier for the alaskan eskimos?
look it up for tomorrow!!!
Phoebe Weatherfield Caulfield
Phoebe Weatherfield Caulfield
Phoebe Weatherfield Caulfield
Phoebe W. Caulfield
Phoebe Weatherfield Caulfield, Esq.
Please pass to Shirley!!!!
Shirley you said you were sagitarius
but your only taurus bring your skates
when you come over to my house

I sat there on D.B.'s desk and read the whole notebook. It didn't take me long, and I can read that kind of stuff, some kid's notebook, Phoebe's or anybody's, all day and all night long. Kids' notebooks kill me. Then I lit another cigarette—it was my last one. I must've smoked about three cartons that day. Then, finally, I woke her up. I mean I couldn't sit there on that desk for the rest of my life, and besides, I was afraid my parents might barge in on me all of a sudden and I wanted to at least say hello to her before they did. So I woke her up.

She wakes up very easily. I mean you don't have to yell at her or anything. All you have to do, practically, is sit down on the bed and say, "Wake up, Phoeb," and bingo, she's awake.

"*Holden!*" she said right away. She put her arms around my neck and all. She's very affectionate. I mean she's quite affectionate, for a child. Sometimes she's even too affectionate. I sort of gave her a kiss, and she said, "Whenja get *home?*"

She was glad as hell to see me. You could tell.

"Not so loud. Just now. How are ya anyway?"

"I'm fine. Did you get my letter? I wrote you a five-page—"

"Yeah—not so loud. Thanks."

She wrote me this letter. I didn't get a chance to answer it, though. It was all about this play she was in in school. She told me not to make any dates or anything for Friday so that I could come see it.

"How's the play?" I asked her. "What'd you say the name of it was?"

"'A Christmas Pageant for Americans.' It stinks, but I'm Benedict Arnold. I have practically the biggest part," she said. Boy, was she wide-awake. She gets very excited when she tells you that stuff. "It starts out when I'm dying. This ghost comes in on Christmas Eve and asks me if I'm ashamed and everything. You know. For betraying my country and everything. Are you coming to it?" She was sitting way the hell up in the bed and all. "That's what I wrote you about. Are you?"

"Sure I'm coming. Certainly I'm coming."

"Daddy can't come. He has to fly to California," she said. Boy, was she wide-awake. It only takes her about two seconds to get wide-awake. She was sitting—sort of kneeling—way up in bed, and she was holding my goddam hand. "Listen. Mother said you'd be home *Wednes*day," she said. "She said *Wednes*day."

"I got out early. Not so loud. You'll wake everybody up."

"What time is it? They won't be home till very late, Mother said. They went to a party in Norwalk, Connecticut," old Phoebe said. "Guess what I did this afternoon! What movie I saw. Guess!"

"I don't know—Listen. Didn't they say what time they'd—"

"*The Doctor*," old Phoebe said. "It's a special movie they had at the Lister Foundation. Just this one day they had it—today was the only day. It was all about this doctor in Kentucky and everything that sticks a blanket over this child's face that's a cripple and can't walk. Then they send him to jail and everything. It was excellent."

"Listen a second. Didn't they say what time they'd—"

"He feels sorry for it, the doctor. That's why he sticks this blanket over her face and everything and makes her suffocate. Then they make him go to jail for life imprisonment, but this child that he stuck the blanket over its head comes to visit him all the time and thanks him for what he did. He was a mercy killer. Only, he knows he deserves to go to jail because a doctor isn't supposed to take things away from God. This girl in my class's mother took us. Alice Holmborg. She's my best friend. She's the only girl in the whole—"

"Wait a second, *willya*?" I said. "I'm asking you a question. Did they say what time they'd be back, or didn't they?"

"No, but not till very late. Daddy took the car and everything so they wouldn't have to worry about trains. We have a radio in it now! Except that Mother said nobody can play it when the car's in traffic."

I began to relax, sort of. I mean I finally quit *wor*rying about whether they'd catch me home or not. I figured the hell with it. If they did, they did.

You should've seen old Phoebe. She had on these blue pajamas with red elephants on the collars. Elephants knock her out.

"So it was a good picture, huh?" I said.

"Swell, except Alice had a cold, and her mother kept asking her all the time if she felt grippy. Right in the middle of the *pic*ture. Always in the middle of something important, her mother'd lean all over me and everything and ask Alice if she felt grippy. It got on my nerves."

Then I told her about the record. "Listen, I bought you a record," I told her. "Only I broke it on the way home." I took the pieces out of my coat pocket and showed her. "I was plastered," I said.

"Gimme the pieces," she said. "I'm saving them." She took them right out of my hand and then she put them in the drawer of the night table. She kills me.

"D.B. coming home for Christmas?" I asked her.

"He may and he may not, Mother said. It all depends. He may have to stay in Hollywood and write a picture about Annapolis."

"Annapolis, for God's sake!"

"It's a love story and everything. Guess who's going to be in it! What movie star. Guess!"

"I'm not interested. An*nap*olis, for God's sake. What's D.B. know about An*nap*olis, for God's sake? What's that got to do with the kind of stories he writes?" I said. Boy, that stuff drives me crazy. That goddam Hollywood. "What'd you do to your arm?" I asked her. I noticed she had this big hunk of adhesive tape on her elbow. The reason I noticed it, her pajamas didn't have any sleeves.

"This boy, Curtis Weintraub, that's in my class, pushed me while I was going down the stairs in the park," she said. "Wanna see?" She started taking the crazy adhesive tape off her arm.

"Leave it alone. Why'd he push you down the stairs?"

"I don't know. I think he hates me," old Phoebe said. "This other girl and me, Selma Atterbury, put ink and stuff all over his windbreaker."

"That isn't nice. What are you—a child, for God's sake?"

"No, but every time I'm in the park, he follows me everywhere. He's always following me. He gets on my nerves."

"He probably likes you. That's no reason to put ink all—"

"I don't want him to like me," she said. Then she started looking at me funny. "Holden," she said, "how come you're not home *Wednes*day?"

"What?"

Boy, you have to watch her every minute. If you don't think she's smart, you're mad.

"How come you're not home *Wednes*day?" she asked me. "You didn't get kicked out or anything, did you?"

"I told you. They let us out early. They let the whole—"

"You did get kicked out! You did!" old Phoebe said. Then she hit me on the leg with her fist. She gets very fisty when she feels like it. "You *did!* Oh, *Hol*den!" She had her hand on her mouth and all. She gets very emotional, I swear to God.

"Who said I got kicked out? Nobody said I—"

"You *did*. You *did*," she said. Then she smacked me again with her fist. If you don't think that hurts, you're crazy. "Daddy'll *kill* you!" she said. Then she flopped on her stomach on the bed and put the goddam pillow over her head. She does that quite frequently. She's a true madman sometimes.

"Cut it out, now," I said. "Nobody's gonna kill me. Nobody's gonna even— C'*mon*, Phoeb, take that goddam thing off your head. Nobody's gonna kill me."

She wouldn't take it off, though. You can't make her do something if she doesn't want to. All she kept saying was, "Daddy's gonna kill you." You could hardly understand her with that goddam pillow over her head.

"Nobody's gonna kill me. Use your head. In the first place, I'm going away. What I may do, I may get a job on a ranch or something for a while. I know this guy whose grandfather's got a ranch in Colorado. I may get a job out there," I said. "I'll keep in touch with you and all when I'm gone, if I go. C'mon. Take that off your head. C'mon, hey, Phoeb. Please. Please, willya?"

She wouldn't take it off, though I tried pulling it off, but she's strong as hell. You get tired fighting with her. Boy, if she wants to keep a pillow over her head, she *keeps* it. "Phoebe, *please*. C'mon outa there," I kept saying. "C'mon, hey ...

Hey, Weatherfield. C'mon out."

She wouldn't come out, though. You can't even reason with her sometimes. Finally, I got up and went out in the living room and got some cigarettes out of the box on the table and stuck some in my pocket. I was all out.

XXII

When I came back, she had the pillow off her head all right—I knew she would—but she still wouldn't look at me, even though she was laying on her back and all. When I came around the side of the bed and sat down again, she turned her crazy face the other way. She was ostracizing the hell out of me. Just like the fencing team at Pencey when I left all the goddam foils on the subway.

"How's old Hazel Weatherfield?" I said. "You write any new stories about her? I got that one you sent me right in my suitcase. It's down at the station. It's very good."

"Daddy'll *kill* you."

Boy, she really gets something on her mind when she gets something on her mind.

"No, he won't. The worst he'll do, he'll give me hell again, and then he'll send me to that goddam military school. That's all he'll do to me. And in the *first* place, I won't even be around. I'll be away. I'll be—I'll probably be in Colorado on this ranch."

"Don't make me laugh. You can't even ride a horse."

"Who can't? Sure I can. Certainly I can. They can teach you in about two minutes," I said. "Stop picking at that." She was picking at that adhesive tape on her arm. "Who gave you that haircut?" I asked her. I just noticed what a stupid haircut somebody gave her. It was way too short.

"None of your business," she said. She can be very snotty sometimes. She can be quite snotty. "I suppose you failed in every single subject again," she said—very snotty. It was sort of funny, too, in a way. She sounds like a goddam schoolteacher sometimes, and she's only a little child.

"No, I didn't," I said. "I passed English." Then, just for the hell of it, I gave her a pinch on the behind. It was sticking way out in the breeze, the way she was laying on her side. She has hardly any behind. I didn't do it hard, but she tried to hit my hand anyway, but she missed.

Then all of a sudden, she said, "Oh, why did you *do* it?" She meant why did I get the ax again. It made me sort of sad, the way she said it.

"Oh, God, Phoebe, don't ask me. I'm sick of everybody asking me that," I said. "A million reasons why. It was one of the worst schools I ever went to. It was full of phonies. And mean guys. You never saw so many mean guys in your life. For instance, if you were having a bull session in somebody's room, and somebody wanted to come in, nobody'd let them in if they were some dopey, pimply guy. Everybody was always *lock*ing their door when somebody wanted to come in. And they had this goddam secret fraternity that I was too yellow not to join. There was this one pimply, boring guy, Robert Ackley, that wanted to get in. He kept trying to join, and they wouldn't let him. Just because he was boring and pimply. I don't even feel like talking about it. It was a stinking school. Take my word."

Old Phoebe didn't say anything, but she was listening. I could tell by the back of her neck that she was listening. She always listens when you tell her something. And the funny part is she knows, half the time, what the hell you're talking about. She really does.

I kept talking about old Pencey. I sort of felt like it.

"Even the couple of *nice* teachers on the faculty, they were phonies, too," I said. "There was this one old guy, Mr. Spencer. His wife was always giving you hot chocolate and all that stuff, and they were really pretty nice. But you should've seen him when the headmaster, old Thurmer, came in the history class and sat down in the back of the room. He was always coming in and sitting down in the back of the room for about a half an hour. He was supposed to be incognito or something. After a while, he'd be sitting back there and then he'd start interrupting what old Spencer was saying to crack a lot of corny jokes. Old Spencer'd practically kill himself chuckling and smiling and all, like as if Thurmer was a goddam prince or something."

"Don't swear so much."

"It would've made you puke, I swear it would," I said. "Then, on Veterans' Day. They have this day, Veterans' Day, that all the jerks that graduated from Pencey around 1776 come back and walk all over the place, with their wives and children and everybody. You should've seen this one old guy that was about fifty. What he did was, he came in our room and knocked on the door and asked us if we'd mind if he used the bathroom. The bathroom was at the end of the corridor—I don't know why the hell he asked *us*. You know what he said? He said he wanted to see if his initials were still in one of the can doors. What he did, he carved his goddam stupid sad old initials in one of the can doors about ninety years ago, and he wanted to see if they were still there. So my roommate and I walked him down to the bathroom and all, and we had to stand there while he looked for his initials in all the can doors. He kept talking to us the whole time, telling us how when he was at Pencey they were the happiest days of his life, and giving us a lot of advice for the future and all. Boy, did he depress me! I don't mean he was a bad guy—he wasn't. But you don't have to be a bad guy to depress somebody—you can be a *good* guy and do it. All you have to do to depress somebody is give them a lot of phony advice while you're looking for your initials in some can door—that's all you have to do. I don't know. Maybe it wouldn't have been so bad if he hadn't been all out of breath. He was all out of breath from just climbing up the stairs, and the whole time he was looking for his initials he kept breathing hard, with his nostrils all funny and sad, while he kept telling Stradlater and I to get all we could out of Pencey. God, Phoebe! I can't explain. I just didn't like anything that was *hap*pening at Pencey. I can't explain."

Old Phoebe said something then, but I couldn't hear her. She had the side of her mouth right smack on the pillow, and I couldn't hear her.

"What?" I said. "Take your mouth away. I can't hear you with your mouth that way."

"You don't like *any*thing that's happening."

It made me even more depressed when she said that.

"Yes I do. Yes I do. *Sure* I do. Don't say that. Why the hell do you say that?"

"Because you don't. You don't like any schools. You don't like a million things. You *don't*."

"I do! That's where you're wrong—that's exactly where you're wrong! Why the hell do you have to say that?" I said. Boy, was she depressing me.

"Because you don't," she said. "Name one thing."

"One thing? One thing I like?" I said. "Okay."

The trouble was, I couldn't concentrate too hot. Sometimes it's hard to concentrate.

"One thing I like a lot you mean?" I asked her.

She didn't answer me, though. She was in a cockeyed position way the hell over the other side of the bed. She was about a thousand miles away. "C'mon, answer me," I said. "One thing I like a lot, or one thing I just like?"

"You like a lot."

"All right," I said. But the trouble was, I couldn't concentrate. About all I could think of were those two nuns that went around collecting dough in those beat-up old straw baskets. Especially the one with the glasses with those iron rims. And this boy I knew at Elkton Hills. There was this one boy at Elkton Hills, named James Castle, that wouldn't take back something he said about this very conceited boy, Phil Stabile. James Castle called him a very conceited guy, and one of Stabile's lousy friends went and squealed on him to Stabile. So Stabile, with about six other dirty bastards, went down to James Castle's room and went in and locked the goddam door and tried to make him take back what he said, but he wouldn't do it. So they started in on him. I won't even tell you what they did to him—it's too repulsive—but he *still* wouldn't take it back, old James Castle. And you should've seen him. He was a skinny little weak-looking guy, with wrists about as big as pencils. Finally, what he did, instead of taking back what he said, he jumped out the window. I was in the *shower* and all, and even *I* could hear him land outside. But I just thought something fell out the window, a radio or a desk or something, not a *boy* or anything. Then I heard everybody running through the corridor and down the stairs, so I put on my bathrobe and I ran downstairs too, and there was old James Castle laying right on the stone steps and all. He was dead, and his teeth, and blood, were all over the place, and nobody would even go near him. He had on this turtleneck sweater I'd lent him. All they did with the guys that were in the room with him was expel them. They didn't even go to jail.

That was about all I could think of, though. Those two nuns I saw at breakfast and this boy James Castle I knew at Elkton Hills. The funny part is, I hardly even know James Castle, if you want to know the truth. He was one of these very quiet guys. He was in my math class, but he was way over on the other side of the room, and he hardly ever got up to recite or go to the blackboard or anything. Some guys in school hardly ever get up to recite or go to the blackboard. I think the only time I ever even had a conversation with him was that time he asked me if he could borrow this turtleneck sweater I had. I damn near dropped dead when he asked me,

I was so surprised and all. I remember I was brushing my teeth, in the can, when he asked me. He said his cousin was coming up to take him for a drive and all. I didn't even know he knew I *had* a turtleneck sweater. All I knew about him was that his name was always right ahead of me at roll call. Cabel, R., Cabel, W., Castle, Caulfield—I can still remember it. If you want to know the truth, I almost didn't *lend* him my sweater. Just because I didn't know him too well.

"What?" I said to old Phoebe. She said something to me, but I didn't hear her.

"You can't even think of one thing."

"Yes, I can. Yes, I can."

"Well, do it, then."

"I like Allie," I said. "And I like doing what I'm doing right now. Sitting here with you, and talking, and thinking about stuff, and—"

"Allie's *dead*—You always say that! If somebody's dead and everything, and in *Heaven*, then it isn't really—"

"I know he's dead! Don't you think I know that? I can still like him, though, can't I? Just because somebody's dead, you don't just stop liking them, for God's sake—especially if they were about a thousand times nicer than the people you know that're *alive* and all."

Old Phoebe didn't say anything. When she can't think of anything to say, she doesn't say a goddam word.

"Anyway, I like it now," I said. "I mean right now. Sitting here with you and just chewing the fat and horsing—"

"That isn't anything *real*ly!"

"It is so something *real*ly! Certainly it is! Why the hell isn't it? People never think anything is anything *really*. I'm getting goddam sick of it."

"Stop swearing. All right, name something else. Name something you'd like to *be*. Like a scientist. Or a *law*yer or something."

"I couldn't be a scientist. I'm no good in science."

"Well, a lawyer—like Daddy and all."

"Lawyers are all right, I guess—but it doesn't appeal to me," I said. "I mean they're all right if they go around saving innocent guys' lives all the time, and like that, but you don't *do* that kind of stuff if you're a lawyer. All you do is make a lot of dough and play golf and play bridge and buy cars and drink Martinis and look like a hot-shot. And besides. Even if you *did* go around saving guys' lives and all, how would you know if you did it because you really *wanted* to save guys' lives, or because you did it because what you *real*ly wanted to do was be a terrific lawyer, with everybody slapping you on the back and congratulating you in court when the goddam trial was over, the reporters and everybody, the way it is in the dirty movies? How would you know you weren't being a phony? The trouble is, you *wouldn't*."

I'm not too sure old Phoebe knew what the hell I was talking about. I mean she's only a little child and all. But she was listening, at least. If somebody at least listens, it's not too bad.

"Daddy's going to kill you. He's going to *kill* you," she said.

I wasn't listening, though. I was thinking about something else—something crazy. "You know what I'd like to be?" I said. "You know what I'd like to be? I mean if I had my goddam choice?"

"What? Stop *swear*ing."

"You know that song 'If a body catch a body comin' through the rye'? I'd like—"

"It's 'If a body *meet* a body coming through the rye'!" old Phoebe said. "It's a poem. By Robert *Burns*."

"I *know* it's a poem by Robert Burns."

She was right, though. It *is* "If a body meet a body coming through the rye." I didn't know it then, though.

"I thought it was 'If a body catch a body,'" I said. "Anyway, I keep picturing all these little kids playing some game in this big field of rye and all. Thousands of little kids, and nobody's around—nobody big, I mean—except me. And I'm standing on the edge of some crazy cliff. What I have to do, I have to catch everybody if they start to go over the cliff—I mean if they're running and they don't look where they're going I have to come out from somewhere and *catch* them. That's all I'd do all day. I'd just be the catcher in the rye and all. I know it's crazy, but that's the only thing I'd really like to be. I know it's crazy."

Old Phoebe didn't say anything for a long time. Then, when she said something, all she said was, "Daddy's going to kill you."

"I don't give a damn if he does," I said. I got up from the bed then, because what I wanted to do, I wanted to phone up this guy that was my English teacher at Elkton Hills, Mr. Antolini. He lived in New York now. He quit Elkton Hills. He took this job teaching English at N.Y.U. "I have to make a phone call," I told Phoebe. "I'll be right back. Don't go to sleep." I didn't want her to go to sleep while I was in the living room. I knew she wouldn't, but I said it anyway, just to make sure.

While I was walking toward the door, old Phoebe said, "Holden!" and I turned around.

She was sitting way up in bed. She looked so pretty. "I'm taking belching lessons from this girl, Phyllis Margulies," she said. "Listen."

I listened, and I heard *some*thing, but it wasn't much. "Good," I said. Then I went out in the living room and called up this teacher I had, Mr. Antolini.

XXIII

I made it very snappy on the phone because I was afraid my parents would barge in on me right in the middle of it. They didn't, though. Mr. Antolini was very nice. He said I could come right over if I wanted to. I think I probably woke he and his wife up, because it took them a helluva long time to answer the phone. The first thing he asked me was if anything was wrong, and I said no. I said I'd flunked out of Pencey, though. I thought I might as well tell him. He said "Good God," when I said that. He had a good sense of humor and all. He told me to come right over if I felt like it.

He was about the best teacher I ever had, Mr. Antolini. He was a pretty young guy, not much older than my brother D.B., and you could kid around with him without losing your respect for him. He was the one that finally picked up that boy that jumped out the window I told you about, James Castle. Old Mr. Antolini felt his pulse and all, and then he took off his coat and put it over James Castle and carried him all the way over to the infirmary. He didn't even give a damn if his coat got all bloody.

When I got back to D.B.'s room, old Phoebe'd turned the radio on. This dance music was coming out. She'd turned it on low, though, so the maid wouldn't hear it. You should've seen her. She was sitting smack in the middle of the bed, outside the covers, with her legs folded like one of those Yogi guys. She was listening to the music. She kills me.

"C'mon," I said. "You feel like dancing?" I taught her how to dance and all when she was a tiny little kid. She's a very good dancer. I mean I just taught her a few things. She learned it mostly by herself. You can't teach somebody how to *really* dance.

"You have shoes on," she said.

"I'll take 'em off. C'mon."

She practically jumped off the bed, and then she waited while I took my shoes off, and then I danced with her for a while. She's really damn good. I don't like people that dance with little kids, because most of the time it looks terrible. I mean if you're out at a restaurant somewhere and you see some old guy take his little kid out on the dance floor. Usually they keep yanking the kid's dress up in the back by mistake, and the kid can't dance worth a damn *any*way, and it looks terrible, but I don't do it out in public with Phoebe or anything. We just horse around in the house. It's different with her anyway, because she can *dance*. She can follow anything you do. I mean if you hold her in close as hell so that it doesn't matter that your legs are so much longer. She stays right with you. You can cross over, or do some corny dips, or even jitterbug a little, and she stays right with you. You can even *tango*, for God's sake.

We danced about four numbers. In between numbers she's funny as hell. She stays right in position. She won't even talk or anything. You both have to stay right in position and wait for the orchestra to start playing again. That kills me. You're not supposed to laugh or anything, either.

Anyway, we danced about four numbers, and then I turned off the radio. Old Phoebe jumped back in bed and got under the covers. "I'm improving, aren't I?" she asked me.

"And how," I said. I sat down next to her on the bed again. I was sort of out of breath. I was smoking so damn much, I had hardly any wind. She wasn't even out of breath.

"Feel my forehead," she said all of a sudden.

"Why?"

"*Feel* it. Just feel it once."

I felt it. I didn't feel anything, though.

"Does it feel very feverish?" she said.

"No. Is it supposed to?"

"Yes—I'm making it. Feel it again."

I felt it again, and I still didn't feel anything, but I said, "I think it's starting to, now." I didn't want her to get a goddam inferiority complex.

She nodded. "I can make it go up to over the thermoneter."

"Ther*mome*ter. Who said so?"

"Alice Holmborg showed me how. You cross your legs and hold your breath and think of something very, very hot. A radiator or something. Then your whole forehead gets so hot you can burn somebody's hand."

That killed me. I pulled my hand away from her forehead, like I was in terrific danger. "Thanks for *tell*ing me," I said.

"Oh, I wouldn't've burned *your* hand. I'd've stopped before it got too—*Shhh!*" Then, quick as hell, she sat way the hell up in bed.

She scared hell out of me when she did that. "What's the matter?" I said.

"The front door!" she said in this loud whisper. "It's them!"

I quick jumped up and ran over and turned off the light over the desk. Then I jammed out my cigarette on my shoe and put it in my pocket. Then I fanned hell out of the air, to get the smoke out—I shouldn't even have been smoking, for God's sake. Then I grabbed my shoes and got in the closet and shut the door. Boy, my heart was beating like a bastard.

I heard my mother come in the room.

"Phoebe?" she said. "Now, stop that. I saw the light, young lady."

"Hello!" I heard old Phoebe say. "I couldn't sleep. Did you have a good time?"

"Marvelous," my mother said, but you could tell she didn't mean it. She doesn't enjoy herself much when she goes out. "Why are you awake, may I ask? Were you warm enough?"

"I was warm enough, I just couldn't sleep."

"Phoebe, have you been smoking a cigarette in here? Tell me the truth, please, young lady."

"What?" old Phoebe said.

"You heard me."

"I just lit one for one second. I just took *one puff*. Then I threw it out the window."

"*Why*, may I ask?"

"I couldn't sleep."

"I don't like that, Phoebe. I don't like that at all," my mother said. "Do you want another blanket?"

"No, thanks. G'night!" old Phoebe said. She was trying to get rid of her, you could tell.

"How was the movie?" my mother said.

"Excellent. Except Alice's mother. She kept leaning over and asking her if she felt grippy during the whole entire movie. We took a taxi home."

"Let me feel your forehead."

"I didn't catch anything. She didn't have anything. It was just her mother."

"Well. Go to sleep now. How was your dinner?"

"Lousy," Phoebe said.

"You heard what your father said about using that word. What was lousy about it? You had a lovely lamb chop. I walked all over Lexington Avenue just to—"

"The lamb chop was all right, but Charlene always *breathes* on me whenever she puts something down. She breathes all over the food and everything. She *breathes* on everything."

"Well. Go to sleep. Give Mother a kiss. Did you say your prayers?"

"I said them in the bathroom. G'night!"

"Good night. Go right to sleep now. I have a splitting headache," my mother said. She gets headaches quite frequently. She really does.

"Take a few aspirins," old Phoebe said. "Holden'll be home on Wednesday, won't he?"

"So far as I know. Get under there, now. Way down."

I heard my mother go out and close the door. I waited a couple of minutes. Then I came out of the closet. I bumped smack into old Phoebe when I did it, because it was so dark and she was out of bed and coming to tell me. "I hurt you?" I said. You had to whisper now, because they were both home. "I gotta get a move on," I said. I found the edge of the bed in the dark and sat down on it and started putting on my shoes. I was pretty nervous. I admit it.

"Don't go *now*," Phoebe whispered. "Wait'll they're asleep!"

"No. Now. Now's the best time," I said. "She'll be in the bathroom and Daddy'll turn on the news or something. Now's the best time." I could hardly tie my shoelaces, I was so damn nervous. Not that they would've *killed* me or anything if they'd caught me home, but it would've been very unpleasant and all. "Where the hell are ya?" I said to old Phoebe. It was so dark I couldn't see her.

"Here." She was standing right next to me. I didn't even see her.

"I got my damn bags at the station," I said. "Listen. You got any dough, Phoeb? I'm practically broke."

"Just my Christmas dough. For presents and all. I haven't done any shopping at *all* yet."

"Oh." I didn't want to take her Christmas dough.

"You want some?" she said.

"I don't want to take your Christmas dough."

"I can lend you *some*," she said. Then I heard her over at D.B.'s desk, opening a million drawers and feeling around with her hand. It was pitch-black, it was so dark in the room. "If you go away, you won't see me in the play," she said. Her voice sounded funny when she said it.

"Yes, I will. I won't go way before that. You think I wanna miss the play?" I said. "What I'll do, I'll probably stay at Mr. Antolini's house till maybe Tuesday night. Then I'll come home. If I get a chance, I'll phone ya."

"Here," old Phoebe said. She was trying to give me the dough, but she couldn't find my hand.

"Where?"

She put the dough in my hand.

"Hey, I don't need all this," I said. "Just give me two bucks, is all. No kidding—Here." I tried to give it back to her, but she wouldn't take it.

"You can take it all. You can pay me back. Bring it to the play."

"How much is it, for God's sake?"

"Eight dollars and eighty-five cents. *Six*ty-five cents. I spent some."

Then, all of a sudden, I started to cry. I couldn't help it. I did it so nobody could hear me, but I did it. It scared hell out of old Phoebe when I started doing it, and she came over and tried to make me stop, but once you get started, you can't just stop on a goddam *dime*. I was still sitting on the edge of the bed when I did it, and she put her old arm around my neck, and I put my arm around her, too, but I still couldn't stop for a long time. I thought I was going to choke to death or something. Boy, I scared hell out of poor old Phoebe. The damn window was open and everything, and I could feel her shivering and all, because all she had on was her pajamas. I tried to make her get back in bed, but she wouldn't go. Finally I stopped. But it certainly took me a long, long time. Then I finished buttoning my coat and all. I told her I'd keep in touch with her. She told me I could sleep with her if I wanted to, but I said no, that I'd better beat it, that Mr. Antolini was waiting for me and all. Then I took my hunting hat out of my coat pocket and gave it to her. She likes those kind of crazy hats. She didn't want to take it, but I made her. I'll bet she slept with it on. She really likes those kind of hats. Then I told her again I'd give her a buzz if I got a chance, and then I left.

It was a helluva lot easier getting out of the house than it was getting in, for some reason. For one thing, I didn't give much of a damn any more if they caught me. I really didn't. I figured if they caught me, they caught me. I almost wished they did, in a way.

I walked all the way downstairs, instead of taking the elevator. I went down the back stairs. I nearly broke my neck on about ten million garbage pails, but I got out all right. The elevator boy didn't even see me. He probably *still* thinks I'm up at the Dicksteins'.

XXIV

Mr. and Mrs. Antolini had this very swanky apartment over on Sutton Place, with two steps that you go down to get in the living room, and a bar and all. I'd been there quite a few times, because after I left Elkton Hills Mr. Antoilni came up to our house for dinner quite frequently to find out how I was getting along. He wasn't married then. Then when he got married, I used to play tennis with he and Mrs. Antolini quite frequently, out at the West Side Tennis Club, in Forest Hills, Long Island. Mrs. Antolini belonged there. She was lousy with dough. She was about sixty years older than Mr. Antolini, but they seemed to get along quite well. For one thing, they were both very intellectual, especially Mr. Antolini, except that he was more witty than intellectual when you were with him, sort of like D.B. Mrs. Antolini was mostly serious. She had asthma pretty bad. They both read all D.B.'s stories—Mrs. Antolini, too—and when D.B. went to Hollywood, Mr. Antolini phoned him up and told him not to go. He went anyway, though. Mr. Antolini said that anybody that could write like D.B. had no business going out to Hollywood. That's exactly what I said, practically.

I would have walked down to their house, because I didn't want to spend any of Phoebe's Christmas dough that I didn't have to, but I felt funny when I got outside. Sort of dizzy. So I took a cab. I didn't want to, but I did. I had a helluva time even *find*ing a cab.

Old Mr. Antolini answered the door when I rang the bell—after the elevator boy *fina*lly let me up, the bastard. He had on his bathrobe and slippers, and he had a highball in one hand. He was a pretty sophisticated guy, and he was a pretty heavy drinker. "Holden, m'boy!" he said. "My God, he's grown another twenty inches. Fine to see you."

"How are you, Mr. Antolini? How's Mrs. Antolini?"

"We're both just dandy. Let's have that coat." He took my coat off me and hung it up. "I expected to see a day-old infant in your arms. Nowhere to turn. Snowflakes in your eyelashes." He's a very witty guy sometimes. He turned around and yelled out to the kitchen, "Lillian! How's the coffee coming?" Lillian was Mrs. Antolini's first name.

"It's all ready," she yelled back. "Is that Holden? Hello, Holden!"

"Hello, Mrs. Antolini!"

You were always yelling when you were there. That's because the both of them were never in the same room at the same time. It was sort of funny.

"Sit down, Holden," Mr. Antolini said. You could tell he was a little oiled up. The room looked like they'd just had a party. Glasses were all over the place, and dishes with peanuts in them. "Excuse the appearance of the place," he said. "We've been entertaining some Buffalo friends of Mrs. Antolini's ... Some buffaloes, as a matter of fact."

I laughed, and Mrs. Antolini yelled something in to me from the kitchen, but I couldn't hear her. "What'd she say?" I asked Mr. Antolini.

"She said not to look at her when she comes in. She just arose from the sack. Have a cigarette. Are you smoking now?"

"Thanks," I said. I took a cigarette from the box he offered me. "Just once in a while. I'm a moderate smoker."

"I'll bet you are," he said. He gave me a light from this big lighter off the table. "So. You and Pencey are no longer one," he said. He always said things that way.

Sometimes it amused me a lot and sometimes it didn't. He sort of did it a little bit *too* much. I don't mean he wasn't witty or anything—he was—but sometimes it gets on your nerves when somebody's *al*ways saying things like "So you and Pencey are no longer one." D.B. does it too much sometimes, too.

"What was the trouble?" Mr. Antolini asked me. "How'd you do in English? I'll show you the door in short order if you flunked English, you little ace composition writer."

"Oh, I passed English all right. It was mostly literature, though. I only wrote about two compositions the whole term," I said. "I flunked Oral Expression, though. They had this course you had to take, Oral Expression. *That* I flunked."

"Why?"

"Oh, I don't know." I didn't feel much like going into It. I was still feeling sort of dizzy or something, and I had a helluva headache all of a sudden. I really did. But you could tell he was interested, so I told him a little bit about it. "It's this course where each boy in class has to get up in class and make a speech. You know. Spontaneous and all. And if the boy digresses at all, you're supposed to yell 'Digression!' at him as fast as you can. It just about drove me crazy. I got an *F* in it."

"Why?"

"Oh, I don't know. That digression business got on my nerves. I don't know. The trouble with me is, I *like* it when somebody digresses. It's more *in*teresting and all."

"You don't care to have somebody stick to the point when he tells you something?"

"Oh, sure! I like somebody to stick to the point and all. But I don't like them to stick *too* much to the point. I don't know. I guess I don't like it when somebody sticks to the point *all* the time. The boys that got the best marks in Oral Expression were the ones that stuck to the point all the time—I admit it. But there was this one boy, Richard Kinsella. He didn't stick to the point too much, and they were always yelling 'Digression!' at him. It was terrible, because in the first place, he was a very nervous guy—I mean he was a very nervous guy—and his lips were always shaking whenever it was his time to make a speech, and you could hardly hear him if you were sitting way in the back of the room. When his lips sort of quit shaking a little bit, though, I liked his speeches better than anybody else's. He practically flunked the course, though, too. He got a *D* plus because they kept yelling 'Digression!' at him all the time. For instance, he made this speech about this farm his father bought in Vermont. They kept yelling 'Digression!' at him the whole time he was making it, and this teacher, Mr. Vinson, gave him an *F* on it because he hadn't told what kind of animals and vegetables and stuff grew on the farm and all. What he did was, Richard Kinsella, he'd *start* telling you all about that stuff—then all of a sudden he'd start telling you about this letter his mother got from his uncle, and how his uncle got polio and all when he was forty-two years old, and how he wouldn't let anybody come to see him in the hospital because he didn't want anybody to see him with a brace on. It didn't have much to do with the farm—I admit it—but it was *nice*. It's nice when somebody tells you about their uncle. Especially when they start out telling you about their father's farm and then all of a sudden get more interested in their uncle. I mean it's dirty to keep yelling 'Digression!' at him when he's all nice and excited ... I don't know. It's hard to explain." I didn't feel too much like trying, either. For one thing, I had this terrific headache all of a sudden. I wished to God old Mrs. Antolini would come in with the coffee. That's something that annoys hell out of me—I mean if somebody says the coffee's all ready and it isn't.

"Holden ... One short, faintly stuffy, pedagogical question. Don't you think there's a time and place for everything? Don't you think if someone starts out to tell you about his father's farm, he should stick to his guns, *then* get around to telling you about his uncle's *brace*? *Or*, if his uncle's brace is such a provocative subject, shouldn't he have selected it in the first place as his subject—not the farm?"

I didn't feel much like thinking and answering and all. I had a headache and I felt lousy. I even had sort of a stomach-ache, if you want to know the truth.

"Yes—I don't know. I guess he should. I mean I guess he should've picked his uncle as a subject, instead of the farm, if that interested him most. But what I mean is, lots of time you don't *know* what interests you most till you start talking about something that *doesn't* interest you most. I mean you can't help it sometimes. What I think is, you're supposed to leave somebody alone if he's at least being interesting and he's getting all excited about something. I like it when somebody gets excited about something. It's nice. You just didn't know this teacher, Mr. Vinson. He could drive you crazy sometimes, him and the goddam class. I mean he'd keep telling you to *un*ify and *simp*lify all the time. Some things you just can't do that to. I mean you can't hardly ever simplify and unify something just because somebody *wants* you to. You didn't know this guy, Mr. Vinson. I mean he was very intelligent and all, but you could tell he didn't have too much brains."

"Coffee, gentlemen, *fin*ally," Mrs. Antolini said. She came in carrying this tray with coffee and cakes and stuff on it. "Holden, don't you even peek at me. I'm a mess."

"Hello, Mrs. Antolini," I said. I started to get up and all, but Mr. Antolini got hold of my jacket and pulled me back down. Old Mrs. Antolini's hair was full of those iron curler jobs, and she didn't have any lipstick or anything on. She didn't look too gorgeous. She looked pretty old and all.

"I'll leave this right here. Just dive in, you two," she said. She put the tray down on the cigarette table, pushing all these glasses out of the way. "How's your mother, Holden?"

"She's fine, thanks. I haven't seen her too recently, but the last I—"

"Darling, if Holden needs anything, everything's in the linen closet. The top shelf. I'm going to bed. I'm exhausted," Mrs. Antolini said. She looked it, too. "Can you boys make up the couch by yourselves?"

"We'll take care of everything. You run along to bed," Mr. Antolini said. He gave Mrs. Antolini a kiss and she said good-by to me and went in the bedroom. They were always kissing each other a lot in public.

I had part of a cup of coffee and about half of some cake that was as hard as a rock. All old Mr. Antolini had was another highball, though. He makes them very strong, too, you could tell. He may get to be an alcoholic if he doesn't watch his step.

"I had lunch with your dad a couple of weeks ago," he said all of a sudden. "Did you know that?"

"No, I didn't."

"You're aware, of course, that he's terribly concerned about you."

"I know it. I know he is," I said.

"Apparently before he phoned me he'd just had a long, rather harrowing letter from your latest headmaster, to the effect that you were making absolutely no effort at all. Cutting classes. Coming unprepared to all your classes. In general, being an all-around—"

"I didn't cut any classes. You weren't allowed to cut any. There were a couple of them I didn't attend once in a while, like that Oral Expression I told you about, but I didn't cut any."

I didn't feel at all like discussing it. The coffee made my stomach feel a little better, but I still had this awful headache.

Mr. Antolini lit another cigarette. He smoked like a fiend. Then he said,

"Frankly, I don't know what the hell to say to you, Holden."

"I know. I'm very hard to talk to. I realize that."

"I have a feeling that you're riding for some kind of a terrible, terrible fall. But I don't honestly know what kind ... Are you listening to me?"

"Yes."

You could tell he was trying to concentrate and all.

"It may be the kind where, at the age of thirty, you sit in some bar hating everybody who comes in looking as if he might have played football in college. Then again, you may pick up just enough education to hate people who say, 'It's a secret between he and I.' Or you may end up in some business office, throwing paper clips at the nearest stenographer. I just don't know. But do you know what I'm driving at, at all?"

"Yes. Sure," I said. I did, too. "But you're wrong about that hating business. I mean about hating football players and all. You really are. I don't hate too many guys. What I may do, I may hate them for a *little* while, like this guy Stradlater I knew at Pencey, and this other boy, Robert Ackley. I hated *them* once in a while—I admit it—but it doesn't last too long, is what I mean. After a while, if I didn't see them, if they didn't come in the room, or if I didn't see them in the dining room for a couple of meals, I sort of missed them. I mean I sort of missed them."

Mr. Antolini didn't say anything for a while. He got up and got another hunk of ice and put it in his drink, then he sat down again. You could tell he was thinking. I kept wishing, though, that he'd continue the conversation in the morning, instead of now, but he was hot. People are mostly hot to have a discussion when you're not.

"All right. Listen to me a minute now ... I may not word this as memorably as I'd like to, but I'll write you a letter about it in a day or two. Then you can get it all straight. But listen now, anyway." He started concentrating again. Then he said,

"This fall I think you're riding for—it's a special kind of fall, a horrible kind. The man falling isn't permitted to feel or hear himself hit bottom. He just keeps falling and falling. The whole arrangement's designed for men who, at some time or other in their lives, were looking for something their own environment couldn't supply them with. Or they thought their own environment couldn't supply them with. So they gave up looking. They gave it up before they ever really even got started. You follow me?"

"Yes, sir."

"Sure?"

"Yes."

He got up and poured some more booze in his glass. Then he sat down again. He didn't say anything for quite a long time.

"I don't want to scare you," he said, "but I can very clearly see you dying nobly, one way or another, for some highly unworthy cause." He gave me a funny look. "If I write something down for you, will you read it carefully? And keep it?"

"Yes. Sure," I said. I did, too. I still have the paper he gave me.

He went over to this desk on the other side of the room, and without sitting down wrote something on a piece of paper. Then he came back and sat down with the paper in his hand. "Oddly enough, this wasn't written by a practicing poet. It was written by a psychoanalyst named Wilhelm Stekel. Here's what he—Are you still with me?"

"Yes, sure I am."

"Here's what he said: 'The mark of the immature man is that he wants to die nobly for a cause, while the mark of the mature man is that he wants to live humbly for one.'"

He leaned over and handed it to me. I read it right when he gave it to me, and then I thanked him and all and put it in my pocket. It was nice of him to go to all that trouble. It really was. The thing was, though, I didn't feel much like concentrating. Boy, I felt so damn *tired* all of a sudden.

You could tell he wasn't tired at all, though. He was pretty oiled up, for one thing. "I think that one of these days," he said, "you're going to have to find out where you want to go. And then you've got to start going there. But immediately. You can't afford to lose a minute. Not you."

I nodded, because he was looking right at me and all, but I wasn't too sure what he was talking about. I was *pretty* sure I knew, but I wasn't too positive at the time. I was too damn tired.

"And I hate to tell you," he said, "but I think that once you have a fair idea where you want to go, your first move will be to apply yourself in school. You'll have to. You're a student—whether the idea appeals to you or not. You're in love with knowledge. And I think you'll find, once you get past all the Mr. Vineses and their Oral Comp—"

"Mr. Vinsons," I said. He meant all the Mr. Vinsons, not all the Mr. Vineses. I shouldn't have interrupted him, though.

"All right—the Mr. Vinsons. Once you get past all the Mr. Vinsons, you're going to start getting closer and closer—that is, if you *want* to, and if you look for it and wait for it—to the kind of information that will be very, very dear to your heart. Among other things, you'll find that you're not the first person who was ever confused and frightened and even sickened by human behavior. You're by no means alone on that score, you'll be excited and *stimulated* to know. Many, many men have been just as troubled morally and spiritually as you are right now. Happily, some of them kept records of their troubles. You'll learn from them—if you want to. Just as someday, if you have something to offer, someone will learn something from you. It's a beautiful reciprocal arrangement. And it isn't education. It's history. It's poetry." He stopped and took a big drink out of his highball. Then he started again. Boy, he was really hot. I was glad I didn't try to stop him or anything. "I'm not trying to tell you," he said, "that only educated and scholarly men are able to contribute something valuable to the world. It's not so. But I do say that educated and scholarly men, if they're brilliant and creative to begin with—which, unfortunately, is rarely the case—tend to leave infinitely more valuable records behind them than men do who are *mere*ly brilliant and creative. They tend to express themselves more clearly, and they usually have a passion for following their thoughts through to the end. And—most important—nine times out of ten they have more humility than the unscholarly thinker. Do you follow me at all?"

"Yes, sir."

He didn't say anything again for quite a while. I don't know if you've ever done it, but it's sort of hard to sit around waiting for somebody to say something when they're thinking and all. It really is. I kept trying not to yawn. It wasn't that I was bored or anything—I wasn't—but I was so damn sleepy all of a sudden.

"Something else an academic education will do for you. If you go along with it any considerable distance, it'll begin to give you an idea what size mind you have. What it'll fit and, maybe, what it won't. After a while, you'll have an idea what kind of thoughts your particular size mind should be wearing. For one thing, it may save you an extraordinary amount of time trying on ideas that don't suit you, aren't becoming to you. You'll begin to know your true measurements and dress your mind accordingly."

Then, all of a sudden, I yawned. What a *rude bastard*, but I couldn't help it!

Mr. Antolini just laughed, though. "C'mon," he said, and got up. "We'll fix up the couch for you."

I followed him and he went over to this closet and tried to take down some sheets and blankets and stuff that was on the top shelf, but he couldn't do it with this highball glass in his hand. So he drank it and then put the glass down on the floor and *then* he took the stuff down. I helped him bring it over to the couch. We both made the bed together. He wasn't too hot at it. He didn't tuck anything in very tight. I didn't care, though. I could've slept standing up I was so tired.

"How're all your women?"

"They're okay." I was being a lousy conversationalist, but I didn't feel like it.

"How's Sally?" He knew old Sally Hayes. I introduced him once.

"She's all right. I had a date with her this afternoon." Boy, it seemed like twenty years ago! "We don't have too much in common any more."

"Helluva pretty girl. What about that other girl? The one you told me about, in Maine?"

"Oh—Jane Gallagher. She's all right. I'm probably gonna give her a buzz tomorrow."

We were all done making up the couch then. "It's all yours," Mr. Antolini said. "I don't know what the hell you're going to do with those legs of yours."

"That's all right. I'm used to short beds," I said. "Thanks a lot, sir. You and Mrs. Antolini really saved my life tonight."

"You know where the bathroom is. If there's anything you want, just holler. I'll be in the kitchen for a while—will the light bother you?"

"No—heck, no. Thanks a lot."

"All right. Good night, handsome."

"G'night, sir. Thanks a lot."

He went out in the kitchen and I went in the bathroom and got undressed and all. I couldn't brush my teeth because I didn't have any toothbrush with me. I didn't have any pajamas either and Mr. Antolini forgot to lend me some. So I just went back in the living room and turned off this little lamp next to the couch, and then I got in bed with just my shorts on. It was way too short for me, the couch, but I really could've slept standing up without batting an eyelash. I laid awake for just a couple of seconds thinking about all that stuff Mr. Antolini'd told me. About finding out the size of your mind and all. He was really a pretty smart guy. But I couldn't keep my goddam eyes open, and I fell asleep.

Then something happened. I don't even like to *talk* about it.

I woke up all of a sudden. I don't know what time it was or anything, but I woke up. I felt something on my head, some guy's hand. Boy, it really scared hell out of me. What it was, it was Mr. Antolini's hand. What he was doing was, he was sitting on the floor right next to the couch, in the dark and all, and he was sort of petting me or patting me on the goddam head. Boy, I'll bet I jumped about a thousand feet.

"What the hellya *do*ing?" I said.

"Nothing! I'm simply sitting here, admiring—"

"What're ya *do*ing, anyway?" I said over again. I didn't know *what* the hell to say—I mean I was embarrassed as hell.

"How'bout keeping your voice down? I'm simply sitting here—"

"I have to go, anyway," I said—boy, was I nervous! I started putting on my damn pants in the dark. I could hardly get them on I was so damn nervous. I know more damn perverts, at schools and all, than anybody you ever met, and they're always being perverty when *I'm* around.

"You have to go *where?*" Mr. Antolini said. He was trying to act very goddam casual and cool and all, but he wasn't any too goddam cool. Take my word.

"I left my bags and all at the station. I think maybe I'd better go down and get them. I have all my stuff in them."

"They'll be there in the morning. Now, go back to bed. I'm going to bed myself. What's the matter with you?"

"Nothing's the matter, it's just that all my money and stuff's in one of my bags. I'll be right back. I'll get a cab and be right back," I said. Boy, I was falling all over myself in the dark. "The thing is, it isn't mine, the money. It's my mother's, and I—"

"Don't be ridiculous, Holden. Get back in that bed. I'm going to bed myself. The money will be there safe and sound in the morn—"

"No, no kidding. I gotta get going. I really do." I was damn near all dressed already, except that I couldn't find my tie. I couldn't remember where I'd put my tie. I put on my jacket and all without it. Old Mr. Antolini was sitting now in the big chair a little ways away from me, watching me. It was dark and all and I couldn't see him so hot, but I knew he was watching me, all right. He was still boozing, too. I could see his trusty highball glass in his hand.

"You're a very, very strange boy."

"I know it," I said. I didn't even look around much for my tie. So I went without it. "Good-by, sir," I said, "Thanks a lot. No kidding."

He kept walking right behind me when I went to the front door, and when I rang the elevator bell he stayed in the damn doorway. All he said was that business about my being a "very, very strange boy" again. Strange, my ass. Then he waited in the doorway and all till the goddam elevator came. I never waited so long for an elevator in my whole goddam life. I swear.

I didn't know what the hell to talk about while I was waiting for the elevator, and he kept standing there, so I said, "I'm gonna start reading some good books. I really am." I mean you had to say *some*thing. It was very embarrassing.

"You grab your bags and scoot right on back here again. I'll leave the door unlatched."

"Thanks a lot," I said. "G'by!" The elevator was finally there. I got in and went down. Boy, I was shaking like a madman. I was sweating, too. When something perverty like that happens, I start sweating like a bastard. That kind of stuff's happened to me about twenty times since I was a kid. I can't stand it.

XXV

When I got outside, it was just getting light out. It was pretty cold, too, but it felt good because I was sweating so much.

I didn't know where the hell to go. I didn't want to go to another hotel and spend all Phoebe's dough. So finally all I did was I walked over to Lexington and took the subway down to Grand Central. My bags were there and all, and I figured I'd sleep in that crazy waiting room where all the benches are. So that's what I did. It wasn't too bad for a while because there weren't many people around and I could stick my feet up. But I don't feel much like discussing it. It wasn't too nice. Don't ever try it. I mean it. It'll depress you.

I only slept till around nine o'clock because a million people started coming in the waiting room and I had to take my feet down. I can't sleep so hot if I have to keep my feet on the floor. So I sat up. I still had that headache. It was even worse. And I think I was more depressed than I ever was in my whole life.

I didn't want to, but I started thinking about old Mr. Antolini and I wondered what he'd tell Mrs. Antolini when she saw I hadn't slept there or anything. That part didn't worry me too much, though, because I knew Mr. Antolini was very smart and that he could make up something to tell her. He could tell her I'd gone home or something. That part didn't worry me much. But what *did* worry me was the part about how I'd woke up and found him patting me on the head and all. I mean I wondered if just maybe I was wrong about thinking he was making a flitty pass at me. I wondered if maybe he just liked to pat guys on the head when they're asleep. I mean how can you tell about that stuff for sure? You can't. I even started wondering if maybe I should've got my bags and gone back to his house, the way I'd said I would. I mean I started thinking that even if he was a flit he certainly'd been very nice to me. I thought how he hadn't minded it when I'd called him up so late, and how he'd told me to come right over if I felt like it. And how he went to all that trouble giving me that advice about finding out the size of your mind and all, and how he was the only guy that'd even gone *near* that boy James Castle I told you about when he was dead. I thought about all that stuff. And the more I thought about it, the more depressed I got. I mean I started thinking maybe I *should've* gone back to his house. Maybe he *was* only patting my head just for the hell of it. The more I thought about it, though, the more depressed and screwed up about it I got. What made it even worse, my eyes were sore as hell. They felt all sore and burny from not getting too much sleep. Besides that, I was getting sort of a cold, and I didn't even have a goddam handkerchief with me. I had some in my suitcase, but I didn't feel like taking it out of that strong box and opening it up right in public and all.

There was this magazine that somebody'd left on the bench next to me, so I started reading it, thinking it'd make me stop thinking about Mr. Antolini and a million other things for at least a little while. But this damn article I started reading made me feel almost worse. It was all about hormones. It described how you should look, your face and eyes and all, if your hormones were in good shape, and I didn't look that way at all. I looked exactly like the guy in the article with lousy hormones. So I started getting worried about my hormones. Then I read this other article about how you can tell if you have cancer or not. It said if you had any sores in your mouth that didn't heal pretty quickly, it was a sign that you probably had cancer. I'd had this sore on the inside of my lip for about *two weeks*. So figured

I was getting cancer. That magazine was some little cheerer upper. I finally quit reading it and went outside for a walk. I figured I'd be dead in a couple of months because I had cancer. I really did. I was even positive I would be. It certainly didn't make me feel too gorgeous.

It sort of looked like it was going to rain, but I went for this walk anyway. For one thing, I figured I ought to get some breakfast. I wasn't at all hungry, but I figured I ought to at least eat something. I mean at least get something with some vitamins in it. So I started walking way over east, where the pretty cheap restaurants are, because I didn't want to spend a lot of dough.

While I was walking, I passed these two guys that were unloading this big Christmas tree off a truck. One guy kept saying to the other guy, "Hold the sonuvabitch *up!* Hold it *up*, for Chrissake!" It certainly was a gorgeous way to talk about a Christmas tree. It was sort of funny, though, in an awful way, and I started to sort of laugh. It was about the *worst* thing I could've done, because the minute I started to laugh I thought I was going to vomit. I really did. I even started to, but it went away. I don't know why. I mean I hadn't eaten anything unsanitary or like that and usually I have quite a strong stomach. Anyway, I got over it, and I figured I'd feel better if I had something to eat. So I went in this very cheap-looking restaurant and had doughnuts and coffee. Only, I didn't eat the doughnuts. I couldn't swallow them too well. The thing is, if you get very depressed about something, it's hard as hell to swallow. The waiter was very nice, though. He took them back without charging me. I just drank the coffee. Then I left and started walking over toward Fifth Avenue.

It was Monday and all, and pretty near Christmas, and all the stores were open. So it wasn't too bad walking on Fifth Avenue. It was fairly Christmasy. All those scraggy-looking Santa Clauses were standing on corners ringing those bells, and the Salvation Army girls, the ones that don't wear any lipstick or anything, were ringing bells too. I sort of kept looking around for those two nuns I'd met at breakfast the day before, but I didn't see them. I knew I wouldn't, because they'd told me they'd come to New York to be schoolteachers, but I kept looking for them anyway. Anyway, it was pretty Christmasy all of a sudden. A million little kids were downtown with their mothers, getting on and off buses and coming in and out of stores. I wished old Phoebe was around. She's not little enough any more to go stark staring mad in the toy department, but she enjoys horsing around and looking at the people. The Christmas before last I took her downtown shopping with me. We had a helluva time. I think it was in Bloomingdale's. We went in the shoe department and we pretended she—old Phoebe—wanted to get a pair of those very high storm shoes, the kind that have about a million holes to lace up. We had the poor salesman guy going crazy. Old Phoebe tried on about twenty pairs, and each time the poor guy had to lace one shoe all the way up. It was a dirty trick, but it killed old Phoebe. We finally bought a pair of moccasins and charged them. The salesman was very nice about it. I think he knew we were horsing around, because old Phoebe always starts giggling.

Anyway, I kept walking and walking up Fifth Avenue, without any tie on or anything. Then all of a sudden, something very spooky started happening. Every time I came to the end of a block and stepped off the goddam curb, I had this feeling that I'd never get to the other side of the street. I thought I'd just go down, down, down, and nobody'd ever see me again. Boy, did it scare me. You can't imagine. I started sweating like a bastard—my whole shirt and underwear and everything. Then I started doing something else. Every time I'd get to the end of a block I'd make believe I was talking to my brother Allie. I'd say to him, "Allie, don't let me disappear. Allie, don't let me disappear. Allie, don't let me disappear. Please, Allie." And then when I'd reach the other side of the street without disappearing, I'd *thank* him. Then it would start all over again as soon as I got to the next corner. But I kept going and all. I was sort of afraid to stop, I think—I don't remember, to tell you the truth. I know I didn't stop till I was way up in the Sixties, past the zoo and all. Then I sat down on this bench. I could hardly get my breath, and I was still sweating like a bastard. I sat there, I guess, for about an hour. Finally, what I decided I'd do, I decided I'd go away. I decided I'd never go home again and I'd never go away to another school again. I decided I'd just see old Phoebe and sort of say good-by to her and all, and give her back her Christmas dough, and then I'd start hitchhiking my way out West. What I'd do, I figured, I'd go down to the Holland Tunnel and bum a ride, and then I'd bum another one, and another one, and another one, and in a few days I'd be somewhere out West where it was very pretty and sunny and where nobody'd know me and I'd get a job. I figured I could get a job at a filling station somewhere, putting gas and oil in people's cars. I didn't care what kind of a job it was, though. Just so people didn't know me and I didn't know anybody. I thought what I'd do was, I'd pretend I was one of those deaf-mutes. That way I wouldn't have to have any goddam stupid useless conversations with anybody. If anybody wanted to tell me something, they'd have to write it on a piece of paper and shove it over to me. They'd get bored as hell doing that after a while, and then I'd be through with having conversations for the rest of my life. Everybody'd think I was just a poor deaf-mute bastard and they'd leave me alone. They'd let me put gas and oil in their stupid cars, and they'd pay me a salary and all for it, and I'd build me a little cabin somewhere with the dough I made and live there for the rest of my life. I'd build it right near the woods, but not right *in* them, because I'd want it to be sunny as hell all the time. I'd cook all my own food, and later on, if I wanted to get married or something, I'd meet this beautiful girl that was also a deaf-mute and we'd get married. She'd come and live in my cabin with me, and if she wanted to say anything to me, she'd have to write it on a goddam piece of paper, like everybody else. If we had any children, we'd hide them somewhere. We could buy them a lot of books and teach them how to read and write by ourselves.

I got excited as hell thinking about it. I really did. I knew the part about pretending I was a deaf-mute was crazy, but I liked thinking about it anyway. But I really decided to go out West and all. All I wanted to do first was say good-by to old Phoebe. So all of a sudden, I ran like a madman across the street—I damn near got killed doing it, if you want to know the truth—and went in this stationery store and bought a pad and pencil. I figured I'd write her a note telling her where to meet me so I could say good-by to her and give her back her Christmas dough, and then I'd take the note up to her school and get somebody in the principal's office to give it to her. But I just put the pad and pencil in my pocket and started walking fast as hell up to her school—I was too excited to write the note right in the stationery store. I walked fast because I wanted her to get the note before she went home for lunch, and I didn't have any too much time.

I knew where her school was, naturally, because I went there myself when I was a kid. When I got there, it felt funny. I wasn't sure I'd remember what it was like inside, but I did. It was exactly the same as it was when I went there. They had that same big yard inside, that was always sort of dark, with those cages around the light bulbs so they wouldn't break if they got hit with a ball. They had those same white circles painted all over the floor, for games and stuff. And those same old basketball rings without any nets—just the backboards and the rings.

Nobody was around at all, probably because it wasn't recess period, and it wasn't lunchtime yet. All I saw was one little kid, a colored kid, on his way to the bathroom. He had one of those wooden passes sticking out of his hip pocket, the same way we used to have, to show he had permission and all to go to the bathroom.

I was still sweating, but not so bad any more. I went over to the stairs and sat down on the first step and took out the pad and pencil I'd bought. The stairs had the same smell they used to have when I went there. Like somebody'd just taken a leak on them. School stairs always smell like that. Anyway, I sat there and wrote this note:

DEAR PHOEBE,
    I can't wait around till Wednesday any more so I will probably hitch hike out west this afternoon. Meet me at the Museum of art near the door at quarter past 12 if you can and I will give you your Christmas dough back. I didn't spend much.

Love,
HOLDEN

Her school was practically right near the museum, and she had to pass it on her way home for lunch anyway, so I knew she could meet me all right.

Then I started walking up the stairs to the principal's office so I could give the note to somebody that would bring it to her in her classroom. I folded it about ten times so nobody'd open it. You can't trust anybody in a goddam school. But I knew they'd give it to her if I was her brother and all.

While I was walking up the stairs, though, all of a sudden I thought I was going to puke again. Only, I didn't. I sat down for a second, and then I felt better. But while I was sitting down, I saw something that drove me crazy. Somebody'd written "Fuck you" on the wall. It drove me damn near crazy. I thought how Phoebe and all the other little kids would see it, and how they'd wonder what the hell it meant, and then finally some dirty kid would tell them—all cockeyed, naturally—what it meant, and how they'd all *think* about it and maybe even *worry* about it for a couple of days. I kept wanting to kill whoever'd written it. I figured it was some perverty bum that'd sneaked in the school late at night to take a leak or something and then wrote it on the wall. I kept picturing myself catching him at it, and how I'd smash his head on the stone steps till he was good and goddam dead and bloody. But I knew, too, I wouldn't have the guts to do it. I knew that. That made me even more depressed. I hardly even had the guts to rub it off the wall with my *hand*, if you want to know the truth. I was afraid some teacher would catch me rubbing it off and would think *I'd* written it. But I rubbed it out anyway, finally. Then I went on up to the principal's office.

The principal didn't seem to be around, but some old lady around a hundred years old was sitting at a typewriter. I told her I was Phoebe Caulfield's brother, in 4B-1, and I asked her to please give Phoebe the note. I said it was very important because my mother was sick and wouldn't have lunch ready for Phoebe and that she'd have to meet me and have lunch in a drugstore. She was very nice about it, the old lady. She took the note off me and called some other lady, from the next office, and the other lady went to give it to Phoebe. Then the old lady that was around a hundred years old and I shot the breeze for a while. She was pretty nice, and I told her how I'd gone there to school, too, and my brothers. She asked me where I went to school now, and I told her Pencey, and she said Pencey was a very good school. Even if I'd wanted to, I wouldn't have had the strength to straighten her out. Besides, if she thought Pencey was a very good school, let her think it. You hate to tell *new* stuff to somebody around a hundred years old. They don't like to hear it. Then, after a while, I left. It was funny. She yelled "Good luck!" at me the same way old Spencer did when I left Pencey. God, how I hate it when somebody yells "Good luck!" at me when I'm leaving somewhere. It's depressing.

I went down by a different staircase, and I saw another "Fuck you" on the wall. I tried to rub it off with my hand again, but this one was scratched on, with a knife or something. It wouldn't come off. It's hopeless, anyway. If you had a million years to do it in, you couldn't rub out even *half* the "Fuck you" signs in the world. It's impossible.

I looked at the clock in the recess yard, and it was only twenty to twelve, so I had quite a lot of time to kill before I met old Phoebe. But I just walked over to the museum anyway. There wasn't anyplace else to go. I thought maybe I might stop in a phone booth and give old Jane Gallagher a buzz before I started bumming my way west, but I wasn't in the mood. For one thing, I wasn't even sure she was home for vacation yet. So I just went over to the museum, and hung around.

While I was waiting around for Phoebe in the museum, right inside the doors and all, these two little kids came up to me and asked me if I knew where the mummies were. The one little kid, the one that asked me, had his pants open. I told him about it. So he buttoned them up right where he was standing talking to me—he didn't even bother to go behind a post or anything. He killed me. I would've laughed, but I was afraid I'd feel like vomiting again, so I didn't. "Where're the mummies, fella?" the kid said again. "Ya know?"

I horsed around with the two of them a little bit. "The mummies? What're they?" I asked the one kid.

"You know. The *mum*mies—them dead guys. That get buried in them toons and all."

Toons. That killed me. He meant tombs.

"How come you two guys aren't in school?" I said.

"No school t'day," the kid that did all the talking said. He was lying, sure as I'm alive, the little bastard. I didn't have anything to do, though, till old Phoebe showed up, so I helped them find the place where the mummies were. Boy, I used to know exactly where they were, but I hadn't been in that museum in years.

"You two guys so interested in mummies?" I said.

"Yeah."

"Can't your friend talk?" I said.

"He ain't my friend. He's my brudda."

"Can't he talk?" I looked at the one that wasn't doing any talking. "Can't you talk at all?" I asked him.

"Yeah," he said. "I don't feel like it."

Finally we found the place where the mummies were, and we went in.

"You know how the Egyptians buried their dead?" I asked the one kid.

"Naa."

"Well, you should. It's very interesting. They wrapped their faces up in these cloths that were treated with some secret chemical. That way they could be buried in their tombs for thousands of years and their faces wouldn't rot or anything. Nobody knows how to do it except the Egyptians. Even modern science."

To get to where the mummies were, you had to go down this very narrow sort of hall with stones on the side that they'd taken right out of this Pharaoh's tomb and all. It was pretty spooky, and you could tell the two hot-shots I was with weren't enjoying it too much. They stuck close as hell to me, and the one that didn't talk at all practically was holding onto my sleeve. "Let's go," he said to his brother. "I seen 'em awreddy. C'mon, hey." He turned around and beat it.

"He's got a yella streak a mile wide," the other one said. "So long!" He beat it too.

I was the only one left in the tomb then. I sort of liked it, in a way. It was so nice and peaceful. Then, all of a sudden, you'd never guess what I saw on the wall. Another "Fuck you." It was written with a red crayon or something, right under the glass part of the wall, under the stones.

That's the whole trouble. You can't ever find a place that's nice and peaceful, because there isn't any. You may *think* there is, but once you get there, when you're not looking, somebody'll sneak up and write "Fuck you" right under your nose. Try it sometime. I think, even, if I ever die, and they stick me in a cemetery, and I have a tombstone and all, it'll say "Holden Caulfield" on it, and then what year I was born and what year I died, and then right under that it'll say "Fuck you." I'm positive, in fact.

After I came out of the place where the mummies were, I had to go to the bathroom. I sort of had diarrhea, if you want to know the truth. I didn't mind the diarrhea part too much, but something else happened. When I was coming out of the can, right before I got to the door, I sort of passed out. I was lucky, though. I mean I could've killed myself when I hit the floor, but all I did was sort of land on my side. it was a funny thing, though. I felt better after I passed out. I really did. My arm sort of hurt, from where I fell, but I didn't feel so damn dizzy any more.

It was about ten after twelve or so then, and so I went back and stood by the door and waited for old Phoebe. I thought how it might be the last time I'd ever see her again. Any of my relatives, I mean. I figured I'd probably see them again, but not for years. I might come home when I was about thirty-five, I figured, in case somebody got sick and wanted to see me before they died, but that would be the only reason I'd leave my cabin and come back. I even started picturing how it would be when I came back. I knew my mother'd get nervous as hell and start to cry and beg me to stay home and not go back to my cabin, but I'd go anyway. I'd be casual as hell. I'd make her calm down, and then I'd go over to the other side of the living room and take out this cigarette case and light a cigarette, cool as all hell. I'd ask them all to visit me sometime if they wanted to, but I wouldn't insist or anything. What I'd do, I'd let old Phoebe come out and visit me in the summertime and on Christmas vacation and Easter vacation. And I'd let D.B. come out and visit me for a while if he wanted a nice, quiet place for his writing, but he couldn't write any movies in my cabin, only stories and books. I'd have this rule that nobody could do anything phony when they visited me. If any body tried to do anything phony, they couldn't stay.

All of a sudden I looked at the clock in the checkroom and it was twenty-five of one. I began to get scared that maybe that old lady in the school had told that other lady not to give old Phoebe my message. I began to get scared that maybe she'd told her to burn it or something. It really scared hell out of me. I really wanted to see old Phoebe before I hit the road. I mean I had her Christmas dough and all.

Finally, I saw her. I saw her through the glass part of the door. The reason I saw her, she had my crazy hunting hat on—you could see that hat about ten miles away.

I went out the doors and started down these stone stairs to meet her. The thing I couldn't understand, she had this big suitcase with her. She was just coming across Fifth Avenue, and she was dragging this goddam big suitcase with her. She could hardly drag it. When I got up closer, I saw it was my old suitcase, the one I used to use when I was at Whooton. I couldn't figure out what the hell she was doing with it. "Hi," she said when she got up close. She was all out of breath from that crazy suitcase.

"I thought maybe you weren't coming," I said. "What the hell's in that bag? I don't need anything. I'm just going the way I am. I'm not even taking the bags I got at the station. What the hellya *got* in there?"

She put the suitcase down. "My clothes," she said. "I'm going with you. Can I? Okay?"

"What?" I said. I almost fell over when she said that. I swear to God I did. I got sort of dizzy and I thought I was going to pass out or something again.

"I took them down the back elevator so Charlene wouldn't see me. It isn't heavy. All I have in it is two dresses and my moccasins and my underwear and socks and some other things. Feel it. It isn't heavy. Feel it once ... Can't I go with you? Holden? Can't I? *Please.*"

"No. Shut up."

I thought I was going to pass out cold. I mean I didn't mean to tell her to shut up and all, but I thought I was going to pass out again.

"Why can't I? *Please*, Holden! I won't do anything—I'll just go with you, that's all! I won't even take my clothes with me if you don't want me to—I'll just take my—"

"You can't take anything. Because you're not going. I'm going alone. So shut up."

"*Please*, Holden. *Please* let me go. I'll be very, very, very—You won't even—"

"You're not *going*. Now, shut up! Gimme that bag," I said. I took the bag off her. I was almost all set to hit her. I thought I was going to smack her for a second. I really did.

She started to cry.

"I thought you were supposed to be in a play at school and all. I thought you were supposed to be Benedict Arnold in that play and all," I said. I said it very nasty. "Wuddaya want to do? Not be in the play, for God's sake?" That made her cry even harder. I was glad. All of a sudden I wanted her to cry till her eyes practically dropped out. I almost hated her. I think I hated her most because she wouldn't be in that play any more if she went away with me.

"Come on," I said. I started up the steps to the museum again. I figured what I'd do was, I'd check the crazy suitcase she'd brought in the checkroom, and then she could get it again at three o'clock, after school. I knew she couldn't take it back to school with her. "Come on, now," I said.

She didn't go up the steps with me, though. She wouldn't come with me. I went up anyway, though, and brought the bag in the checkroom and checked it, and then I came down again. She was still standing there on the sidewalk, but she turned her back on me when I came up to her. She can do that. She can turn her back on you when she feels like it. "I'm not going away anywhere. I changed my mind. So stop crying and shut up," I said. The funny part was, she wasn't even crying when I said that. I said it anyway, though. "C'mon, now. I'll walk you back to school. C'mon, now. You'll be late."

She wouldn't answer me or anything. I sort of tried to get hold of her old hand, but she wouldn't let me. She kept turning around on me.

"Didja have your lunch? Ya had your lunch yet?" I asked her.

She wouldn't answer me. All she did was, she took off my red hunting hat—the one I gave her—and practically chucked it right in my face. Then she turned her back on me again. It nearly killed me, but I didn't say anything. I just picked it up and stuck it in my coat pocket.

"Come on, hey. I'll walk you back to school," I said.

"I'm not going back to school."

I didn't know what to say when she said that. I just stood there for a couple of minutes.

"You *have* to go back to school. You want to be in that play, don't you? You want to be Benedict Arnold, don't you?"

"No."

"Sure you do. Certainly you do. C'mon, now, let's go," I said. "In the first place, I'm not going away anywhere, I told you. I'm going home. I'm going home as soon as you go back to school. First I'm gonna go down to the station and get my bags, and then I'm gonna go straight—"

"I said I'm not going back to school. You can do what *you* want to do, but I'm not going back to school," she said. "So shut up." It was the first time she ever told me to shut up. It sounded terrible. God, it sounded terrible. It sounded worse than swearing. She still wouldn't look at me either, and every time I sort of put my hand on her shoulder or something, she wouldn't let me.

"Listen, do you want to go for a walk?" I asked her. "Do you want to take a walk down to the zoo? If I let you not go back to school this afternoon and go for a walk, will you cut out this crazy stuff?"

She wouldn't answer me, so I said it over again. "If I let you skip school this afternoon and go for a little walk, will you cut out the crazy stuff? Will you go back to school tomorrow like a good girl?"

"I may and I may not," she said. Then she ran right the hell across the street, without even looking to see if any cars were coming. She's a madman sometimes.

I didn't follow her, though. I knew she'd follow *me*, so I started walking downtown toward the zoo, on the park side of the street, and she started walking downtown on the *other* goddam side of the street. She wouldn't look over at me at all, but I could tell she was probably watching me out of the corner of her crazy eye to see where I was going and all. Anyway, we kept walking that way all the way to the zoo. The only thing that bothered me was when a double-decker bus came along because then I couldn't see across the street and I couldn't see where the hell she was. But when we got to the zoo, I yelled over to her, "Phoebe! I'm going in the zoo! C'mon, now!" She wouldn't look at me, but I could tell she heard me, and when I started down the steps to the zoo I turned around and saw she was crossing the street and following me and all.

There weren't too many people in the zoo because it was sort of a lousy day, but there were a few around the sea lions' swimming pool and all. I started to go by it, but old Phoebe stopped and made out she was watching the sea lions getting fed—a guy was throwing fish at them—so I went back. I figured it was a good chance to catch up with her and all. I went up and sort of stood behind her and sort of put my hands on her shoulders, but she bent her knees and slid out from me—

she can certainly be very snotty when she wants to. She kept standing there while the sea lions were getting fed and I stood right behind her. I didn't put my hands on her shoulders again or anything because if I had she *really* would've beat it on me. Kids are funny. You have to watch what you're doing.

She wouldn't walk right next to me when we left the sea lions, but she didn't walk too far away. She sort of walked on one side of the sidewalk and I walked on the other side. It wasn't too gorgeous, but it was better than having her walk about a mile away from me, like before. We went up and watched the bears, on that little hill, for a while, but there wasn't much to watch. Only one of the bears was out, the polar bear. The other one, the brown one, was in his goddam cave and wouldn't come out. All you could see was his rear end. There was a little kid standing next to me, with a cowboy hat on practically over his ears, and he kept telling his father, "Make him come out, Daddy. Make him come *out*." I looked at old Phoebe, but she wouldn't laugh. You know kids when they're sore at you. They won't laugh or anything.

After we left the bears, we left the zoo and crossed over this little street in the park, and then we went through one of those little tunnels that always smell from somebody's taking a leak. It was on the way to the carrousel. Old Phoebe still wouldn't talk to me or anything, but she was sort of walking next to me now. I took a hold of the belt at the back of her coat, just for the hell of it, but she wouldn't let me. She said, "Keep your hands to yourself, if you don't mind." She was still sore at me. But not as sore as she was before. Anyway, we kept getting closer and closer to the carrousel and you could start to hear that nutty music it always plays. It was playing "Oh, Marie!" It played that same song about fifty years ago when *I* was a little kid. That's one nice thing about carrousels, they always play the same songs.

"I thought the carrousel was *closed* in the wintertime," old Phoebe said. It was the first time she practically said anything. She probably forgot she was supposed to be sore at me.

"Maybe because it's around Christmas," I said.

She didn't say anything when I said that. She probably remembered she was supposed to be sore at me.

"Do you want to go for a ride on it?" I said. I knew she probably did. When she was a tiny little kid, and Allie and D.B. and I used to go to the park with her, she was mad about the carrousel. You couldn't get her off the goddam thing.

"I'm too big," she said. I thought she wasn't going to answer me, but she did.

"No, you're not. Go on. I'll wait for ya. Go on," I said. We were right there then. There were a few kids riding on it, mostly very little kids, and a few parents were waiting around outside, sitting on the benches and all. What I did was, I went up to the window where they sell the tickets and bought old Phoebe a ticket. Then I gave it to her. She was standing right next to me. "Here," I said. "Wait a second—take the rest of your dough, too." I started giving her the rest of the dough she'd lent me.

"You keep it. Keep it for me," she said. Then she said right afterward—"Please."

That's depressing, when somebody says "please" to you. I mean if it's Phoebe or somebody. That depressed the hell out of me. But I put the dough back in my pocket.

"Aren't you gonna ride, too?" she asked me. She was looking at me sort of funny. You could tell she wasn't *too* sore at me any more.

"Maybe I will the next time. I'll watch ya," I said. "Got your ticket?"

"Yes."

"Go ahead, then—I'll be on this bench right over here. I'll watch ya." I went over and sat down on this bench, and she went and got on the carrousel. She walked all around it. I mean she walked once all the way around it. Then she sat down on this big, brown, beat-up-looking old horse. Then the carrousel started, and I watched her go around and around. There were only about five or six other kids on the ride, and the song the carrousel was playing was "Smoke Gets in Your Eyes." It was playing it very jazzy and funny. All the kids kept trying to grab for the gold ring, and so was old Phoebe, and I was sort of afraid she'd fall off the goddam horse, but I didn't say anything or do anything. The thing with kids is, if they want to grab for the gold ring, you have to let them do it, and not say anything. If they fall off, they fall off, but it's bad if you say anything to them.

When the ride was over she got off her horse and came over to me. "You ride once, too, this time," she said.

"No, I'll just watch ya. I think I'll just watch," I said. I gave her some more of her dough. "Here. Get some more tickets."

She took the dough off me. "I'm not mad at you any more," she said.

"I know. Hurry up—the thing's gonna start again."

Then all of a sudden she gave me a kiss. Then she held her hand out, and said, "It's raining. It's starting to rain."

"I know."

Then what she did—it damn near killed me—she reached in my coat pocket and took out my red hunting hat and put it on my head.

"Don't *you* want it?" I said.

"You can wear it a while."

"Okay. Hurry up, though, now. You're gonna miss your ride. You won't get your own horse or anything."

She kept hanging around, though.

"Did you mean it what you said? You really aren't going away anywhere? Are you really going home afterwards?" she asked me.

"Yeah," I said. I meant it, too. I wasn't lying to her. I really did go home afterwards. "Hurry *up*, now," I said. "The thing's starting."

She ran and bought her ticket and got back on the goddam carrousel just in time. Then she walked all the way around it till she got her own horse back. Then she got on it. She waved to me and I waved back.

Boy, it began to rain like a bastard. In *buckets*, I swear to God. All the parents and mothers and everybody went over and stood right under the roof of the carrousel, so they wouldn't get soaked to the skin or anything, but I stuck around on the bench for quite a while. I got pretty soaking wet, especially my neck and my pants. My hunting hat really gave me quite a lot of protection, in a way, but I got soaked anyway. I didn't care, though. I felt so damn happy all of a sudden, the way old Phoebe kept going around and around. I was damn near bawling, I felt so damn happy, if you want to know the truth. I don't know why. It was just that she looked so damn *nice*, the way she kept going around and around, in her blue coat and all. God, I wish you could've been there.

XXVI

That's all I'm going to tell about. I could probably tell you what I did after I went home, and how I got sick and all, and what school I'm supposed to go to next fall, after I get out of here, but I don't feel like it. I really don't. That stuff doesn't interest me too much right now.

A lot of people, especially this one psychoanalyst guy they have here, keeps asking me if I'm going apply myself when I go back to school next September. It's such a stupid question, in my opinion. I mean how do you know what you're going to do till you *do* it? The answer is, you don't. I *think* I am, but how do I know? I swear it's a stupid question.

D.B. isn't as bad as the rest of them, but he keeps asking me a lot of questions, too. He drove over last Saturday with this English babe that's in this new picture he's writing. She was pretty affected, but very good-looking. Anyway, one time when she went to the ladies' room way the hell down in the other wing, D.B. asked me what I thought about all this stuff I just finished telling you about. I didn't know what the hell to say. If you want to know the truth, I don't *know* what I think about it. I'm sorry I told so many people about it. About all I know is, I sort of *miss* everybody I told about. Even old Stradlater and Ackley, for instance. I think I even miss that goddam Maurice. It's funny. Don't ever tell anybody anything. If you do, you start missing everybody.